Cervantine Journeys

Publication of this volume has been made possible in part by a grant from the Program for Cultural Cooperation Between Spain's Ministry of Culture and United States' Universities.

Cervantine Journeys

Steven Hutchinson

The University of Wisconsin Press

The University of Wisconsin Press
114 North Murray Street
Madison, Wisconsin 53715

3 Henrietta Street
London WC2E 8LU, England

Library of Congress Cataloging-in-Publication Data
Hutchinson, Steven D., 1952–
      Cervantine journeys / Steven Hutchinson.
      288 pp.   cm.
      Includes bibliographical references (pp. 251–263) and index.
      ISBN 0-299-13480-6 (cloth)   — ISBN 0-299-13484-9 (pbk.)
      1. Cervantes Saavedra, Miguel de, 1547–1616—Criticism and
interpretation.   2. Travel in literature.   I. Title.
PQ6358.T73H87   1992
863′.3 — dc20   92-50253

A Sharon —viajera, compañera

Contents

Preface

As for what motivated me, it is quite simple; I would hope that in the eyes of some people it might be sufficient in itself. It was curiosity—the only kind of curiosity, in any case, that is worth acting upon with a degree of obstinacy: not the curiosity that seeks to assimilate what it is proper for one to know, but that which enables one to get free of oneself. After all, what would be the value of the passion for knowledge if it resulted only in a certain amount of knowledgeableness and not, in one way or another and to the extent possible, in the knower's straying afield of himself.

Foucault, *The History of Sexuality*

On scientific rigor:—"In that Empire, the Art of Cartography reached such Perfection that the map of a single Province occupied a whole City, and the map of the Empire, a whole Province. In time those Enormous Maps no longer sufficed and the Colleges of Cartographers raised a Map of the Empire that was the size of the Empire and coincided with it exactly. Less Addicted to the Study of Cartography, the Following Generations understood that that expanded Map was Useless, and not without Impiety they relinquished it to the Inclemencies of the Sun and of the Winters. Disintegrated Ruins of the Map remain in the Western deserts, inhabited by Animals and Beggars; in the whole Country there endures no other relic of the Geographic Disciplines." Suárez Miranda: *Viajes de varones prudentes,* fourth book, chapter XLV, Lérida, 1658.

Borges, *El Hacedor*

If the mercurial subject of this book could be represented by a single deity, it would be Hermes—not exactly the rarified and impersonalized Hermes presented by Michel Serres, though not excluding this either, but rather Hermes the divine messenger and interpreter, god of travelers (Baltasar Gracián calls him the *numen vial,* "spirit of the way" [121, 634]), the orator and inventor of letters (Vico 98, 118, 181–83).[1] The most mobile of the gods, Hermes the wayfinder displays all the skills that mobility requires. Nearly all of his attributes and functions in fact issue out of his traveling. Hence his protection of roads and boundaries, his connections with stones, his associations with all manner of beasts and fertility, his patronage of shepherds, strangers, merchants, and thieves, his communicative skills and inventions, his charismatic eloquence and social charm at assemblies, his role as the guide of souls to Hades (Psychopompos), his knowledge and inventiveness of arts and sciences, his amorous errancy, his swiftness and cunning, his love of novelty and variety, his transcendance of the limits of place. He is the god of the course, of discourse, intercourse, recourse, and concourse. He connects and communicates geographically, verbally, socially, musically, commercially, technologically, scientifically, eschatologically, hermeneutically. Moreover, he is the great-grandfather of Odysseus, the archetypal traveler, in whose story he intervenes at critical moments to undo the spells of Calypso and Circe and thus allow the journey and its narrative to continue. As Josué Harari and David Bell point out in their introduction to Serres' *Hermes,* the nonthanatocratic Hermes reactivates and revitalizes myth so that procreation and journeys can go on (xxxi–xxxiv). To travel, or to participate in the narrative of travel, is to enter the deterritorialized domain of Hermes—or of Iris, the messenger goddess.

Within Hispanic literature, Cervantes is certainly the most prolific and diverse inventor of journeys. As is the case with a great number of the world's narratives, and especially with the European novel from around the fifteenth to the eighteenth century, his three long novels and twelve novelas set his characters en route, and most coincide from beginning to end with journeys. Without the journey there would scarcely be anything left in his novelistic writings. Louis Combet has asserted that the "erotic theme" gives coherence to Cervantes' oeuvre, which offers about a hundred amorous intrigues (39). While the importance of the erotic is undeniable, there are long stretches of *Don Quixote* and other Cervantine novels where the erotic is secondary if not altogether absent, and in any event, nearly all of Cervantes' lovers in the novels are also travelers. What gets these texts started and keeps them going is primarily the journey. Cervantes' novels are so enlightening about the journey, and so suggestive and varied, that I never felt confined in the writing of this book by my concentration on a single writer. Nor did I feel I had to limit myself to an "author study" given the universal appeal of the journey, or study these fictive journeys exhaustively for that matter (as if that were possible). Without all the material extraneous to Cervantes I couldn't have discussed Cervantine journeys as I thought they called for. I see little value in involuted studies, especially when the theme in question has no boundaries.

Significantly, Cervantes strikes up an intimate relationship with none other than Mercury[2] in his long allegorical narrative poem, *Viaje del Parnaso* (*Journey to Parnassus*). Mercury shows up at the port of Cartagena in a boat composed entirely of verse, carrying with him Apollo's list of possible voyagers to Mount Parnassus. Distinguished by his winged sandals and wand, he is the eloquent speaking god, the messenger of the gods, the bearer of news, the ambassador of Apollo ("el dios parlero," "el dios hablante," "de los fingidos dioses mensajero," "paraninfo," "embajador de Febo" [60–61,

66–67, 82, 90]). As a god, he commands respect, but otherwise his bonhomie and delight mixed with a touch of vulgarity render him as charmingly human as Lucian's deities. He sees in Cervantes a kindred spirit, praising him above all as an inventor, and appoints him to declare which of the poets on the list deserve to make the voyage, so that Mercury in turn can report their merits to Apollo. There's thus a double mediation between the poets and the god of poetry: Cervantes mediates between the poets and the ambassador Mercury, and Mercury between the mediator Cervantes and Apollo. So close is their affiliation that each refers to the other as *paraninfo*—"bearer of news" and by extension "emissary"—and Mercury addresses Cervantes as "exalted superhuman and supermercurial spirit [oh sobrehumano y sobre / cilenio espíritu levantado!]" (60–61). The adjective *cilenio* refers to Mount Cyllene where Mercury himself was raised; throughout the poem, Cilenio is another name for Mercury. Cervantes comes very close to identifying himself with Mercury. The intimacy continues throughout the journey and sojourn at Mount Parnassus, Mercury acting as a personal guide in the fullest sense of the word. And the voyage, I might add, passes from the western Mediterranean so familiar to Cervantes into mythical sea routes past Scylla and Charybdis, the Sirens, and the isle of Calypso, with explicit reference made to Mercury's visit when Ulysses was there (92–95).

Within the allegorical adaptation of myth, there's nothing very remarkable in the fact that Mercury guides the poets to Mount Parnassus. What does stand out, however, is the affinity between Cervantes and the wayfaring god especially in view of the uneasy relations between Cervantes and the god of poetry. Not only in this poem but elsewhere too, Cervantes presents himself as a traveler and also as an inventor of fiction and initiator of new modes of narrative. The primary activity of his novelistic characters is one or another sort of traveling, and the narratives themselves travel their own courses: "In my *Novelas* I have opened a way [*camino*] by which the Castilian language can show folly with due composure," he tells Apollo (103). Along with such qualities as mobility, gaiety, and discretion, Hermes' skills in eloquence, interpretation, and improvisation are shared by many of Cervantes' characters. Cervantes is a nomadic writer. So imbued are his novels in the spirit of Hermes that they could almost be considered a libation to the god.

In a much more modest way, my own (l)iterological exploration has also been conducted in the spirit of Hermes. Whether it appears so or not, the writing of this book has been a very personal endeavor, allowing me to inquire into issues that have always engaged me both as a reader of literature and as one who has lived in three continents and traveled widely in four. Never have I been so sedentary as when writing this book, though the writing itself always had something of a journey about it—entertaining, difficult at times, with plenty of surprises and no clear-cut itinerary. I found that I was left with a vast amount of space to explore the fictive journey and related themes. My critical, discursive mode of travel and chosen landscapes restrict some paths of inquiry and open up others. Since the terrain is varied and irregular, the "traveling" must also be so. I direct and pace myself according to what I see as interesting, sayable, and worth saying. Looking back, I'm amazed at how much I managed not to say, at how many digressions I refrained from taking. Some issues I inquire into at length, others I merely indicate in passing, and yet others undoubtedly pass me by altogether. The subject of the journey allows any number of discursive itineraries through it, any number of partial maps. Throughout the course of the book I've set up many signposts but haven't wanted to overdo this for fear of depriving readers of the experience of not knowing where they're going once in a while. I'd like this to be the kind of book that not only provides interesting and informative passage for readers but also suggests connections to things outside itself through either what it says or what it doesn't say.

Of the five chapters, the first and second form a sequence dealing with movement as concept and metaphor. The third and fourth form another sequence dealing with travelers and their worlds. The fifth brings together virtually all the themes of the book, often quite implicitly, as it reflects on the narration of journeys both as memory and invention.

Chapter 1, "Motion in Language, Language in Motion," begins by affirming the centrality of metaphors of movement in the conceptualization of discourse not only in the works of Cervantes and his contemporaries but also in many other writers both within and outside the West. By deactivating discourse in various ways, especially through spatial analogues, formalizing and structuralizing tendencies in both ancient and modern thought (including much of poststructuralism) have essentially blocked inquiry into this aspect of discourse. Seeking alternatives, this essay draws on writers including Heraclitus, Plato, Longinus, Rabelais, Nietzsche, Frances Yates, Henri Meschonnic, Julia Kristeva, and Gilles Deleuze. The concepts of rhythm and topos are then shown to apply to the "movement" of discourse or of those engaged in discourse. Episodes from Rabelais' works provide two major paradigms for the dynamization and mobilization of discourse, and an analysis of passages primarily from Longinus and Nietzsche illustrates three principal modes of discursive movement: how discourse is thought to move of its own accord, how it conveys those active in it in a vehicular manner, and how it constitutes pathways along which thinkers, speakers, listeners, writers, and readers move.

Chapter 2, "The Language of Movement in Cervantes' Novels," explores how metaphors of movement and the journey, appearing on nearly every page of the texts, dominate the conceptualization of the soul, the self, discourse, desire, love, and life processes. These metaphors multiply the journeys in Cervantes' novels. The first section deals with the specific ways in which "motion" applies to the common terms *discurso* and *discurrir,* and to thinking, speaking, narrating, writing, and reading. The analysis ends with a discussion of the association of silence with immobility and death. The next section, "Desire Mobilized," shows the dynamics of love and desire to be represented by a wide range of metaphors of movement, each defining its own sort of space and interpersonal relationships. It discusses Neoplatonist love theorists of the Renaissance and reexamines both Plato and Lacan with respect to the notion of desire constituted by lack as opposed to movement. The third section, "Life's Movements," considers the life-as-journey metaphor so prevalent in the works of Cervantes and his contemporaries, and shows how time and change are represented as movement.

The central chapter entitled "Travelers" engages directly with journeys as such in Cervantes' novels. An opening section, "Becoming Animal," probes comparatively into the concept of errancy, the initial break from home on the part of errant characters, the nature of "place" and travelers' relationships to it. An essay by Montaigne proves to be exceptionally insightful on these issues. The second section examines the distinct types of errancy practiced by Don Quixote and Sancho Panza in relation to place and placelessness. The third section looks into many other errant characters including: (1) Cervantes' Gypsies, whose entire communities are mobile in relation to sedentary society; (2) traveling women, whose motives and conditions of travel are entirely different from those of men, and who are not "possessed" by anyone while en route; (3) an array of traveling characters who practice different modes of errancy; and (4) two mobile characters who try to settle down in marriage but fail to become sedentary. Finally, "En Route" deals with (1) travel as a composite of concurrent modes of experience with differing content and rhythms, (2) movement as such and its modalities, (3) the shifting identity of mobile characters, (4) experience en route, (5) characters' improvisation and the values attached to it, and (6) adventure in literary travel with respect to ideology, temperament, and personal intervention in the determination of events.

The following chapter, "Cervantine Worlds," reexamines Bakhtin's notion of the "chronotope" in light of Cervantes' novels, where the experiential domains of travel dominate, e.g., roads, inns, seas, the space of imaginary flight. The idea of "world" is redefined as a species of chronotope characterized by enclosed, autonomous sociocultural systems. Cervantes' novelistic enterprise is unique in the Spain of his time in its proliferation of other worlds both within and outside of "this" world. These include the many remote islands in the *Persiles,* various autonomous communities in the *Novelas ejemplares,* the cave of Montesinos and Sancho's *ínsula* in *Don Quixote,* as well as the pastoral idyll and the Muslim "other" in all the major volumes. Unlike typical Renaissance utopias, Cervantine worlds have the principles of becoming and dissolution inscribed in them.

The final chapter, "Narrative Passages," examines the relationships between travel experience and travel narrative with regard to mimetic movement, diversity, openness, temporality, episodic sequences, narratability, memory, empathy, the subordination of experience to narrative, and other topics. In invented journeys, discourse makes rather than remakes the journey's course as writers and narrators "travel" their characters. Prior to genre, the journey allows the narrative to keep going, and vice versa. Parallels between improvisatory music and journey narrative—including their aesthetics, their methods and modes, and the relationships of each to movement—indicate the ways in which Cervantes could be understood as an improvisatory writer who practices relatively "unfettered" writing (*escritura desatada*). The last pages address the problem of the whereabouts of the writer and readers in Cervantes' novels.

I should clarify once and for all that I use the word "journey" as a comprehensive term for all kinds of going from one place to another, whether it be near or far, by land, sea, or air, regardless of motives, methods, means, and goals. The equivalent in Cervantes' texts is *viaje,* with its evocation of the *vía,* the way. The term encompasses travel ranging from a short walk to remote maritime journeys, a knight-errant's wanderings, and the passage from this life to the next (e.g.,*Gal* 100; *PS* 85, 188, 315, 342; *DQ* I.47.566, II.19.180, II.23.220). In actual practice, more specific terms are often used instead of *viaje.* Don Quixote's three journeys, for instance, are *salidas,* "sallies," which stresses their "going out," but they're also *viajes* and *peregrinaciones.* The most frequent term for travels in Cervantes' novels, *peregrinación* in its neutral sense is almost as comprehensive as *viaje* except that it evokes distant journeys, while its less common religious sense denotes pilgrimage. The connotations of these and related terms will become apparent in the course of the book. Their specificity is important, but so are the general concepts of journey and movement, without which this book couldn't have been written.

The editions of Cervantes' works that I've used are indicated in the bibliography together with the abbreviations for the novels. I've consulted Ormsby's and Cohen's translations of *Don Quixote,* Weller and Colahan's translation of *Persiles y Sigismunda,* and Jones's translation of six of the *Novelas ejemplares,*[3] but have usually modified them to bring out textual meanings bearing on my arguments even if this means rendering them into less than idiomatic English. Unless indicated otherwise, all other translations are mine. In general, I've included the original in the notes except when the translation is so literal that it could easily be translated back into something resembling the original.

Thanks to a summer grant from the University of Wisconsin–Madison and a fellowship from the Institute for Research in the Humanities in the spring of 1989, I was able to do a pilot study and make considerable headway into the project itself. A second summer grant in 1990, also from the University of Wisconsin Graduate School, provided further assistance. An earlier (and much shorter) version of the section "Desire mobilized" in Chapter 2 was published as "Desire Mobilized in Cervantes' Novels" in the *Journal of Hispanic Philology* (1990). I appreciate the journal's permission to reedit the text.

For motives and emotions I won't express, I dedicate the book to Sharon Hutchinson—only she knows what went into it, and what didn't go into it. With gratitude and sadness I remember Ricardo Gullón and Paul Riesman. I'm also deeply grateful to Alberto Moreiras, and much indebted to Robert ter Horst, the anonymous readers of the manuscript, and to Barbara Hanrahan of the University of Wisconsin Press. In one way or another, the project has crossed paths with Teresa Vilarós, Guido Podestá, Benito Brancaforte, Catherine Connor (Swietlicki), Jane Tylus, Mary Layoun, Ibrahim Abu-Lughod, Janet Abu-Lughod, Frank Salomon, Kirin Narayan (who gave the manuscript an impromptu blessing), Juan Temprano, Brian Dutton, Biruté Ciplijauskaité, David Hildner, Margarita Zamora, Jill Kuhnheim, David Bethea, Farouk Moustafa, George Haley, Paolo Cherchi, Edward Rosenheim —as well as my parents, brother, sister, and others—to all of whom I express my thanks for their thought and encouragement. My children, Jasmine and Teddy, have been a splendid impediment and diversion throughout the writing process, and promise to obstruct further labors.

Finally, in lieu of a Rabelaisian curse on anyone who might be tempted to do unwarranted harm to this book, let an aphorism of Nietzsche serve as a postscript in the spirit of the *gaya scienza:*

In favor of critics.—Insects sting, not out of malice, but because they too want to live. Likewise our critics: they don't want to hurt us but only to take our blood. (*Human* 250)[4]

Cervantine Journeys

Motion in Language,
Language in Motion

"Whither dost thou wandering go?" . . . I go out of my way, but rather by licence than carelessness. My ideas follow one another, but sometimes it is at a distance, and they look at one another, but with a sidelong glance. I have run my
eyes over a certain dialogue of Plato divided into two parts in a fantastic motley—
the front part about love, and all the lower part about rhetoric. They [the ancient
authors] are not afraid of these changes and have a marvellous grace in letting
themselves roll with the wind, or seem to. The names of my chapters don't always
embrace their matter; often they denote it only by some mark . . . I love the poetic
gait, by leaps and gambols. It is an art, as Plato says, light, winged, and daemonic.
There are works in Plutarch where he forgets his theme, where the purpose of his
argument is only found by chance, all stifled in foreign matter. See his movements
in the *Daemon of Socrates*. Lord! What beauty there is in these spirited sallies and
this variation, and more so as they seem the more carefree and haphazard. It is
the negligent reader who loses sight of my subject, not I . . . I head for change,
undiscerningly and tumultuously. My style and my mind go roving in the same
way. "You must have a dash of madness if you do not want to have still more stupidity," say both the precepts of our masters, and even more their examples.

Michel de Montaigne

Discurso, as Cervantes uses the word throughout his novels, refers variously
to traveling, writing, speaking, thinking, remembering, feeling, flowing, the
passing of time. It delineates the pro-cess of these and many other activities,
or the duration of anything from lives to days and texts, figuring them as irregular routes of movement, as the Latin *discurrere* indicates: to run about
or in different directions. *Discurso* tracks movement in process, even when
process involves no comings or goings as such. Common uses of the word

discurso reflect this range of meanings overtly indicating movement not only in the Spanish of Cervantes' time, but also in equivalents in other Romance languages and English.[1] Some of this movement survives today, as in the verb *discurrir* (to move about, roam), despite the gradual stifling of movement in "discourse" and exclusion of meanings referring to nonlinguistic processes over the last couple of centuries. The new powers that the term has taken on in the work of such thinkers as Foucault and Bakhtin may well compensate for the loss of movement and range. Yet because movement, as I hope to show, has nearly always been invoked in one form or another and in varying degrees to characterize the workings of language, the figures and currents of movement in language and through language are well worth looking into. Perhaps discourse ought to be set in motion again and let loose to a wider range of activity.

From the outset I would like to suggest that *discurso,* far from being an isolated instance evoking a mise-en-mouvement, to a large extent characterizes an attitude toward process, activity, and event manifest throughout Cervantes' novels. Travelers, speakers, speech, writing, thought, emotion: all are in motion. So is the "soul": "As our souls are in continual movement, and cannot stop or rest except in their center, which is God. . . ."[2] This passage from Cervantes' last novel, *Persiles y Sigismunda,* echoes very similar words in his first, *La Galatea,* and owes its general idea to a tradition ascending through Christian theology to Augustine (*Confessions* I.1 and *City of God* X.13) and further yet to Plato, whose "Athenian" defines the soul as "the primal becoming and movement of all that is, has been, or shall be. . . ."[3] Aristotle in fact shows the soul's movement to be a notion shared by every major Greek thinker from Thales to himself (*De anima* 403b–407b, 415b, 427a, 432a–433b; cf. *Physics* VII–VIII). The kind of souls Cervantes envisions are as erratic as his novelistic characters, caught up in many "discursive" movements. The soul rests only when it leaves this life, when it departs from the novel's terrain. Movement runs through every aspect of Cervantes' narrative texts like a varying pulse.

That this might also be true to one degree or another of countless other texts only highlights the need to inquire into how "movement" is manifest and operative in textuality and in discourse in general. Borrowing especially from philosophy and linguistics, mainstream literary theory and criticism have all but barred access to this aspect of textuality—though paradoxically they often incorporate movement without acknowledging the fact. Why is it that among the transient practices including music and dance, only verbal discourse is systematically thought of in such fossilized ways? My approach to movement in discourse will both examine some of the blockages set up by antikinetic and antidynamic thought and follow up on some important leads and breakthroughs by writers who conceive of language in dynamic ways and express this dynamism through kinesis. Plato, Longinus, Rabelais, and Nietzsche are among the names that recur. An exploration of Cervantes' metaphors of motion concerning not only discourse but many other domains of human experience is reserved for the following chapter. My gamble is that a broadly based inquiry into some of the major modalities of movement in this chapter will illuminate the contours of Cervantes' obsession with movements in the next—with a bare minimum of repetition, given the different procedures in each case. Although the two chapters are separate essays, each presupposes the other.

Theoretical Blockages

The principal blockage results from the hold that static concepts both ancient and modern have had on much twentieth-century thinking on language, discourse, and textuality. Form, structure, structurality, unity, totality, parts, wholes, identity, essence, idea, horizon, ground, level, frame, langue, sign, construct, embedding, configuration, plot, and a host of other words have all served as immobilizing metaphors. Not that they always do so, but that they have generally done so. To my knowledge, all major twentieth-century thinkers including poststructuralists have availed themselves widely of such terms.

Structure as applied to discourse has had a singularly icy effect on it. Although the euphoria of high structuralism is long gone, the consequences of structuralism are everywhere in evidence, not least of all in the general faith that the term structure can be applied to almost anything, even to the most transient event, even to "Being" (*Seinsstruktur*). Mental constructions, deconstructions, and reconstructions depend upon similar presuppositions. For all its variety of usage, structure betrays its architectural bias, lending itself easily to physiology, geology, and other disciplines dealing with the makeup of concrete objects or even of society and institutions. Its extension into linguistics, philosophy, and literary criticism, whose objects of study are primarily processive in space-time, has brought about a spatialization and detemporalization of process. Such a space is not the space of processes/events in question—it is not Henri Lefebvre's *espace vécu*, for example (Soja 17)—but rather time projected into a spatial analogue. Time thus tends to be spatialized and space ignored or converted into nonspatial relations. Graphing temporality no doubt implements a visual understanding of its variations in activity according to selected criteria, but the rhythmic and dynamic aspects of change are largely lost by such recontextualization. Regardless of the most elaborate

schemes concocted to supply quasi-generative models of temporal phenomena, the ineptitude of structure-based models in matters of process and change
is proverbial. Structures have a hard time "moving"; sometimes they exhibit
a clumsy articulation like a fleshless skeleton or a tree diagram, but their main
way of accommodating change is to *be* transformed, that is, restructured in
their constituent elements and the relations among these. Structure assumes
a passivity in the face of agencies of change, and should not be confused here
with system, to which some kind of functioning is integral.

The main advantage of the concept of structure as applied to language
and discourse seems to be that it immobilizes or regularizes everything it
touches. In doing so, it enables one to take time out of process so as to fix
the object of study in a pre-Heideggerian being and extract essential meanings from the relationships that appear. Saussure's fateful choice of privileg-
ing *langue* as the prime object of linguistic theory places discourse necessarily
in a derivative position with regard to a structure of signs and a structure
of syntax. The synchrony he opposes to diachrony is less a simultaneity than
a licence to deal with language achronically, ahistorically, nondiscursively,
while diachrony takes on the character of a schematic series of structural shifts
over long periods of time. Discourse means the syntagmatization of signs having their own internal duality, their dictionary structure that happily corresponds to the physical and psychic structure of Saussure's famous talking heads.
Selection and combination are the discursive principles par excellence for this
sort of linguistics, and the largest meaningful units of discourse are of course
sentences as grammatical structures.

Paul Ricoeur has shown at length how the structure-based narrative models
of Vladimir Propp, Claude Bremond, and A.-J. Greimas all logicize and at
the same time detemporalize narrative, however much they try to account for
narrative sequencing (*Time* 2:29–60). Similar examples abound. Gerald
Prince's call for a grammar of narrative promises a core of rule-ridden sequences reminiscent of the early Chomsky's goal of finding all the grammatical sequences of a language (Hopper 19–20). Claude Lévi-Strauss's classic
analysis of the Oedipus saga charts out "bundles" of preselected sorts of relations in several columns (176–82). The meaning of the myth emerges out of
the relations between these bundles of relations, divorced from any sort of
process. The method predicates getting rid of discourse and passing over
chronology in order to understand what the narrative is about. Just as Saussure looks for meaning in a configuration of decontextualized signs deriving
their negative identity from phonetic and semantic differences among them,
Lévi-Strauss finds meaning in a logical, achronic structure spatialized in columns autonomous of any aspect of the eventfulness of narrative. There is no
place for "movement" here. Bakhtin and Wittgenstein, among others, have

amply demonstrated the limited usefulness of locating meaning outside of its discursive context.

Structure in Gérard Genette's *Narrative Discourse,* in contrast, does take on a temporal guise. Of his three temporal categories, however, "duration" is the only one that Genette really deals with in terms of anyone's experience of time; the language of structure curiously disappears here as Genette turns to the language of movement, referring to speed, fluidity, rhythm, continuities and discontinuities, and so forth. The other two categories compare discursive time with that of the narrated events and express these relationships as a linear arrangement ("order") or as a ratio ("frequency"). The relationships between the telling and the events of the story itself thus largely constitute the "temporal structure" of a narrative discourse. Exemplary for its clarity, such a concept of structure is highly applicable to most any narrative text. The only drawback is that it, too, tends to immobilize the text as static and quasi-visual, treating discourse as an edifice, a layered topography or a linear order.

The structure of discourse derives from activity, sequences of events, ongoing process, yet all too often sets itself up as a more or less closed, stable, self-sufficient unity disavowing its origins. Structure treats words as nonevents, as would-be signs collectively yielding some abstract design. Similarly, it maps discourse within some sort of conceptual space with definite coordinates spatializing time and petrifying movement. Map and corresponding territory become confused when the structure of any discourse is thought to inhere in that discourse. Yet the problem is more critical in the case of discourse: whereas maps translate territory in territorial terms, structure translates discourse out of the process appropriate to it into a spatialized abstraction of process.

Many of the same illusions appear in discursive "form"—e.g., textual, poetic, narrative, dramatic—which likewise derives from complex process and tends to reduce such process to a state of suspended animation. "Form" is of course extremely versatile in its uses, pertinent to anything from Plato's immutable "ideas" (i.e., forms, from *idein,* "to see") to fleeting dance movement. Applicable to shape or composition of any kind, and by extension, to any sort of mode, genre, manner, sequential order, etc., "form" is often set up in opposition to materiality, content, event, dynamics, and other such notions from which it is obviously abstracted. "Form" converts discourse into a metaphorically spatialized object divisible into discrete "parts." At the price of deactivating eventful sequence, "form" renders the transience of discourse intelligible.

"Level," another unavoidable term, falsifies discourse to the extent that it spatializes and immobilizes speech and writing. Such is the case with the multiple "levels" of textual exegesis. Similarly, the common view of citation as "levels" set one above another turns citation into verbal "embedding."[4] Thus a complex event in which, say, X quotes Y who in turn quotes Z loses its dynamism as it becomes conceptually graphed as three levels of speech or writing. The lines show some sort of movement but they themselves remain inert. This obscures citation as a discursive activity—as precisely a setting in motion of one discourse by another, as its etymology aptly suggests (cf. other words from the same Indo-European root, *kei,* such as cinema, kinetic, incite, resuscitate, excite, recite . . .).

Let the above examples of supposedly neutral terms suffice for now to illustrate how contemporary thought is still heavily biased against discourse as "movement" or "activity." It would be easy enough to show how other metaphoric concepts bring about similar effects. My purpose here is not to advocate doing away with any of these words, but rather to expose some of the presuppositions of such terminology so as make way for a critical language more suitable to discursive activity. The "movement" of discourse is obviously as metaphorical as the "structure" or "form" of discourse. The issue here is one of adequacy: what these metaphors disclose and what they foreclose about discourse.

The impediments to thinking eventfully are undoubtedly much more fundamental and diffuse than any specific set of concepts. With few exceptions, canonic Western philosophy from Parmenides and Zeno to Kant—or even the present for that matter—offers a series of strategies for subduing or thinking away becoming and movement. Some of the champions of temporality and process may even have unwittingly contributed to antidynamic thought—it's hard to be too circumspect about this. (I myself am often haunted by the fettering of thought when I use the verb "to be," when I say or write some variation of "this is that.") Henri Bergson diagnoses the problem as intrinsic to human thought, which operates "cinematically" to reduce movement and change to a series of illusory states just as film captures movement as a series of still frames (*Creative* 272–370). Nietzsche more uncannily locates the problem in logic and language, which falsify a world of becoming to the point that "knowledge and becoming exclude one another."[5] For him, both the syntax and the vocabulary of language depend on the most naive prejudices concerning the identity of things and their interrelationships, while logic, partly by means of a paralyzing and equalizing Eleatic "is," attempts to fix the workings of the world in stringent formulas.

The ill fortune of the dynamic aspects of discourse should come as no surprise against such a backdrop. Integral to this backdrop are the subtle but pervasive effects of the technology of writing on conceptions of discourse. Specifically, scriptural features infiltrate into discourse, turning it into a visual (or tactile) object with graphed words set out in a definite spatial arrangement. Consequently, words sit where they are, never going anywhere or doing anything. Through the graphics of textuality discourse becomes dormant, an extensive unit of permanent, immobile words. St. Augustine points out as much without confusing the graphics with the figured words: "But because vibrations in the air soon pass away and remain no longer than they sound, signs of words have been constructed by means of letters" (Bloom, *Art* 1:438). Isidore of Seville also emphasizes the permanent and inert character of script technology with the vivid image of letters tying "things" down: "Letters were invented to maintain the memory of things; in order for things not to escape into oblivion, they are bound to letters."[6] Letters serve as fetters to bind fugitive language and thereby supplant faulty memory.

Characterized by spatiality, visibility, permanence, and immobility, the graphics of writing deeply affects the experience of textuality. It couldn't be otherwise. But this also leads, I think, to false assumptions about the nature of written discourse. The very fact that a reader can find a passage laid out exactly where it's supposed to be, skip back or ahead to other ciphered surfaces, scan a text at variable pace, and so on, reinforces the stereotypes by locating discourse on the page. The frequent inseparability of printed discourse from the physical format in which it appears also attests to script's powerful hold over discourse. Yet this carry-over extends to misleading notions of discourse as always "there," static, objectified, endlessly equal to itself, figured into eternity. What graphics does confer on written discourse is rather an immanence that unwritten discourse mostly lacks, not so much an immanence of "being there" as one of linguistically specifiable potentiality always ready to turn kinetic through writing, reading, reflecting, remembering, and so forth.

In a paradigmatic episode of Rabelais's Fourth Book (IV.55–56), Pantagruel and his companions hear strange, disembodied sounds erupting out of nowhere in the open sea—chaotic sounds of men, women, children, horses, trumpets, and cannons. The ship's captain explains that just there at the edge of the glacial sea a battle took place between two (imaginary) peoples at the beginning of the winter. The shouts, cries, and other sounds of din froze in the air, but now with the warm season coming on they've begun to melt explosively back into sound. Pantagruel scoops up whole handfuls of words (*parolles, motz*) resembling crystallized sweets of different colors; some of them are witty words, others sharp and bloody. Like snow they melt in the hand, giving off sound in "barbarous" languages as well as nonverbal battle noise.

Rabelais plays upon the reification of language by treating words as a unique category of objects that can be seen, felt, given (by lovers), sold (by lawyers), and preserved like ice in oil and straw. These objects are neither the graphemes nor the referents of words, but rather sounds congealed (silenced) into things.

The sonar sequence of the battle gets jumbled into a new aleatory discourse as words float around, form heaps, and explode out of turn. Nonetheless, the freezing and subsequent releasing of words into fluid sound parallels textual processes in the sense that script contains the potentialities of language in a state of immanence until human contact releases its energy. By analogy, writing and reading, as they happen together or separately, may both be understood as ephemeral occurrences, repeatable perhaps, but not exactly repeatable. *Graphein,* or scripting, would be that aspect of writing which freezes discourse and thereby materializes, disembodies, autonomizes, displaces, and preserves it for subsequent kinesis in often very different circumstances. (The unfrozen anguish of battle sounds stirs up some fear and wonder in the travelers, but mostly amusement.) I would stretch the analogy further: graphed words are not only once but limitlessly "explosive" whenever minds are engaged with them. They never remain passively frozen when caught up in activity. And they explode in discursive sequence (unlike the frozen words, which are mostly nonsyntactic exclamations anyway), sinking back into immanence whenever they are out of sight and out of mind.

"I remember, too," says Pantagruel, "that Aristotle maintains Homer's words to be bounding, flying, and moving, and consequently alive [*animées*]." This recalls the winged words of Homer's epithet, yet what allows the oral words of the *Iliad* and *Odyssey* an enduring life is recording through memory or script. Pantagruel expounds further (in effect suggesting the genesis of the episode): "Antiphanes, also, said that Plato's teaching was like words that congeal and freeze on the air, when uttered in the depths of winter in some distant country. That is why they are not heard. He said as well that Plato's lessons to young children were hardly understood by them till they were old" (cf. Socrates' image of words as seeds, *Phaedrus* 276b–277a). These autonomous words live on in a sort of hibernation until they actualize themselves as comprehension in minds mature enough for them. Pantagruel also speaks of Orpheus, whose head, torn from his body by the Thracian women, hauntingly drifts in the seas singing laments accompanied by his wind-strummed lyre. These words seem to have inherited Orphic powers to keep them flowing even after the death and dismemberment of their source.

Another example, from a Pythagorean philosopher named Petron (Rabelais IV.55.204), locates the abode of truth, of names and forms altogether outside this world and time although they figure within themselves all things past and future; now and then they fall like dew on humans and thus enter into Time (*le Siecle*). Like Plato's ideas, which Eric Havelock and Walter Ong attribute mainly to an internalization of writing, i.e., script (Ong 79–81), such a vision gives words power, independence, and duration, but in so doing deterritorializes and dehumanizes them, sacrificing their vitality and compromising the courses of history. Petron thus mystifies language by mistaking the characteristics of script (permanence, visibility, autonomy, disembodiment, etc.) for the nature of language, as though human activity such as writing, reading, speaking, listening, and thinking were merely incidental to language as we know it. The analogy of the frozen words, in contrast, brings out the transitions between eventfulness and immanence in all spoken and written discourse.

It would be too simple to read this episode as an allegory of speech and writing. The technology of writing does help to bring about, in Ong's words, "the reduction of dynamic sound to quiescent space" (82), but *writing and reading are not contained by their technology.* Ong perceptively stresses the eventfulness of the spoken word: "The Hebrew *dabar,* which means word, means also event and thus refers directly to the spoken word. The spoken word is always an event, a movement in time, completely lacking in the thing-like repose of the written or printed word" (75). It would be a mistake, however, to deny eventfulness to written discourse, whose oral basis is after all inescapable no matter how its technology and corresponding thought processes may differ from those of spoken discourse. The apparent noneventfulness of the written word corresponds only to its immanence, to its potentialities when inactive. Writing, reading, remembering, and other human activities bound up with the technology of script make discourse eventful upon contact, thereby "dereifying" scripted language to a large extent even if they do leave some exteriorized linguistic residue behind. By the same token, spoken discourse can also be immanent rather than eventful—when, for example, the memory of any given speech isn't being remembered at any given time.[7]

Most kinds of discursive "movement" are openly metaphorical. Event, process, sequence, rhythm, and other transient phenomena all lend themselves easily to characterization as movement, which is "trans-ient" par excellence. Naturally, these metaphors aren't entirely innocent as they predispose how their referent is to be thought of. Unlike static concepts, however, terms of movement and dynamism accentuate rather than neutralize intensities, transitions, and variations integral to the experience of events and processes: they are closer to experience than static spatializations, but may not offer models as intelligible as the latter, which abstract their schemata precisely from activity.

In contrast to the immobilizing ways of thinking about language and textuality, "movement" within other transient practices such as music has always been openly recognized. Long compositions are often performed in movements or acts, in tempos from *andante con moto* to *prestissimo:* the ways of speaking about music summon metaphors of movement at practically every turn. Music, too, is discourse in the wide sense, having its phrasing, articulation, melodic lines, script, traveling chords, transitions, modulations, rhythms, temporal harmonies, returns, slowings, periods, pauses, and so on—when John Coltrane once described his own saxophone playing as like starting in the middle of a sentence and moving in both directions at once, there was nothing incongruous in his simile. A comparative view of discursive practices could reveal much about the workings of linguistic discourse without overlooking its specificity.

Motion in Language

"Movement" of and within language and discourse suggests very diverse phenomena including (1) movement figured within etymologies, (2) mimetic assimilation of sound and rhythm to movement, (3) words thought of as moving autonomously, (4) discursive processes imagined either as the routes of movement or movement along routes, and (5) other processes such as intellectual exploration expressed metaphorically in terms of movement and traveling. What I mean by the first two, both of them categories of "motion in language," will soon be clear. The last three will come up as "language in motion." These five types of verbal "movement" by no means exhaust the possibilities. For example, nearly all models of signification in rhetoric and in language in general depend on movement imagery: some kind of "movement" occurs within the sense-making activities. I leave for other chapters the complex issue of how discourse deals with actual movement and travel.

An inspired Socrates develops (1) and (2) with amazing agility in Plato's *Cratylus*. The overarching question in this dialogue is whether "names" (mostly nouns, but actions too have "names") are conventional or natural, that is, somehow "true" and appropriate to what they mean. Socrates assigns the making of language to one or more ancestral artificers of words—after all, only the most skilled artist of words could be entrusted to their making—and he not surprisingly designates the dialectician as the person most capable of evaluating the work of the word maker. Unsure as to whether he is talking wisdom or nonsense, Socrates soon hits upon a striking hypothesis: that the primeval givers of names—both Greek and barbarian—were thoroughly Heraclitan *avant la lettre* and forged words according to the mistaken principle that all things are in motion and flux like an ever-flowing, ever-changing river. Socrates runs the gamut of key words from divinities and the elements to humans, the body and soul, virtues, vices, the sexes, pleasures and pains, thought and ignorance, and the like, demonstrating almost without exception (till near the end) that everything good or desirable expresses in its derivation the all-pervasive principle of motion, flux, and generation, while everything bad or undesirable expresses stasis or impediments to motion or flux.

The gods, he says, were originally identified with the heavenly bodies, which are always running and moving, and from their running nature were called gods or runners (435). Apollo is the mover-together, Hermes and Iris are messengers of the word, and Pan is the declarer of all things and the perpetual mover (442–44). Good sense (*phronēsis*) means the "perception of motion and flux" or the "blessing of motion," judgment (*gnōmē*) contains the notion of generation or desire for the new, knowledge (*epistēmē*) comes about when the good soul follows the motion of things, understanding (*synesis*) means "going along with," and wisdom (*sophia*) means "touching the motion or stream of things" (448). Whereas virtue (*aretē*) means ever flowing, vice (*kakia*) means going badly, ugly (*aischron*) signifies a prevention of flowing, *aporia* impedes going, and harmful (*blaberon*) is that which harms the stream (450–53). Woman and female stem from the same words as birth and breast—implying generation and growth—while man and male both allude to the principle of "upward flux" (449). Thinking is moving (of the mind), eros is influx, truth (*alētheia*) is divine wandering, falsehood (*pseudos*) derives its "stagnation" from the idea of sleep, name (*onoma*) is the contraction of a phrase meaning "being for which there is a search," being (*on*) is going (*ion*) and not being is not going (455–56).

As instances of what I've referred to as "movement figured within etymologies" (category 1), these and many other words that fall to Socrates' etymological speculations point to motion and generation, or their opposites. But they're derivative. Only a few words belong to the "primitive" class of source words, among them *roē* (stream) and *ienai* (to go) (459). These, too, indicate movement, but do so mimetically by imitating their meanings through sound and rhythm (category 2). The letters *r* and *i,* for example, imitate motion in their sound; by the same token, all the letters and their sounds evoke qualities. The qualities of a thing may be evoked in the sounds of the word for that thing. Thus far the Heraclitan language makers seem to have applied their principles systematically.

The system breaks down, however. Socrates goes on to assert that mimetic resemblance is a "shabby thing" without the supplementary principle of convention. What's more, he points out several instances indicating contradictions in the Heraclitan language principle: some words denoting bad things are allied with motion, and others denoting good things including knowledge are allied with stasis. His conclusion: if you want to know things you can't trust words, not only because they may contradict the major principles of word making, but more importantly because the Heraclitan word makers themselves were in all likelihood deceived. As he puts it earlier on: "I believe that the primeval givers of names were undoubtedly like too many of our modern philosophers, who, in their search after the nature of things, are always getting dizzy from constantly going round and round, and then they imagine that the world is going round and round and moving in all directions. And this appearance, which arises out of their own internal condition, they suppose to be a reality of nature; they think that there is nothing stable or permanent, but only flux and motion" (447). Socrates takes refuge in permanent absolutes and Parmenidean logic denying change and motion. The most troubling aspect of Heraclitan thought for him is that it implies that knowledge also undergoes change and therefore is ultimately unreal. Either there's a transcendent order to which a transcendent beauty and knowledge belong, or there's no such thing as knowledge. The dialogue ends on an open question with Socrates inclined toward Parmenides, and Cratylus towards Heraclitus.

The question of natural versus conventional language thus gives way to the logically subordinate but more intensely engaging thesis positing the original Heraclitanism of both "primitive" and "derivative" words. It would of course be easy to dismiss Socrates' arguments altogether as a misguided quest for origins in language. I suspect that few of his etymologies are valid, and that his conjectures about the mimesis of sound are no more promising than other efforts of this sort have proved to be. Moreover, dividing words according to whether they mean something good or bad is a dubious procedure, and making primeval word artists responsible for language is at best an imaginative error.

Despite all this, the thesis of linguistic Heraclitanism may well show some bold insight into language and could be supported by a few remarks following different lines of reasoning. To begin with, the verb/noun distinction is universal, and as one might expect, verbs are especially charged with activity: "most verbs, in all languages, are inherently dynamic, in that they normally denote either events (including acts) or processes (including activities), rather than states" (Lyons 706; see also 485, 429, 435). Even "stative" verbs—like the "standing" of the Latin *stare* from which so many words of stasis derive— often convey some kind of activity,[8] if often sluggish, as Heidegger did his best to show in the special instance of *sein* and its homologues in other European languages. Furthermore, except in such instances as copulative utterances in languages in which verbs are not always necessary, the pivotal role of verbs in syntax also appears to be universal (Lyons 437)—as is obvious in case systems where nouns are inflected largely with respect to their relationship with verbs.

This would imply a preponderance of dynamism in discourse owing to the syntactic functions and semantics of verbs, which of course differs somewhat from Socrates' thesis that "names" derive etymologically from principles of motion and becoming, or imitate these principles in sound (except for "names" with disagreeable meanings, which negate or retard the positive principles of motion and change). Nonetheless, within the Western European languages at least, any study of what linguists call second- and third-order nouns[9] will show, I think, the overwhelming majority of them derived from verbal root notions indicating action. These nouns contain the dynamism of verbs even if such dynamism is often not readily apparent in the actual meanings of the words. I would surmise, too, that nearly all verbal roots somehow involve movement and change, the Heraclitan principles par excellence. Consider, for example, the extraordinary proliferation of words, including a great many nouns, in the Romance languages and English from Latin verbs of motion such as *ire, venire, ducere, movere, agere, trahere, sentire, quaerere, cedere, sequi,* and *egredi,* not to mention verbs of generation. Deriving from *ire,* to go, is an array of words from initiation to exit, coitus to obituary, and including transition, issue, circuit, ambience, itinerary, errant, perish, and many others with their equivalents in other languages. Indo-European etymological dictionaries plot out much larger families of words derived from single roots. The system of radicals in Semitic languages, where each combination of radicals allows for numerous verb forms along with derivative nouns, adjectives, and adverbs, reveals much more clearly the dynamism inherent in "names"—had Socrates spoken a Semitic language he might never have had to resort to farfetched etymologies to demonstrate the Heraclitanism of language. Indeed, he might never have had any Eleatic hangups about motion and stasis had he thought of them with the same root as in the Arabic *rāḥa,* "to go," and *istarāḥa,* "to rest"—both as activities associated with nouns from the same root including *rīḥ,* "wind," and *rūḥ,* "soul."[10]

Language in Motion

A traveling paradigm

I turn now from the semantics of movement in etymology to movement as metaphor for discourse and discursive processes. Words move, or people move along or with words: the metaphor has countless variations and, as far as I am aware, finds its way not only into everyday language but also into texts of practically every kind. This includes not only openly metaphorical recourse to movement but also philosophical and critical language that often employs the metaphor as though it were a concept free of tropical overtones. The metaphor spatializes discourse in such a way as to accentuate the experiential dimensions of discourse in all its temporality.

But what moves here? Is anything really moving besides human bodies engaged in discursive activity? The metaphor sometimes designates moving words, sometimes moving people, sometimes both people and words moving. Given the temporal nature of discourse, it is no coincidence that metaphors of movement relating to time closely resemble those relating to discourse: time moves with respect to us, we move with respect to it, or we move together with it.[11] Metaphors of this sort are extremely widespread. The beautiful opening of Basho's travelogue, which echoes a text by Li Po from a thousand years earlier, provides an exceptional instance: "The months and days are the wayfarers of the centuries, and as yet another year comes round, it, too, turns traveler" (157).

Questions as to who or what moves, and in relation to what, rarely arise in connection with conventional representations of space or conventional uses of language having clear subjects and predicates. But when discourse is supposed to move somehow, or when its practitioners are supposed to move, the space and image of movement are often nebulous, to say the least. In so undefined a context for movement, the agency of movement varies.

Here again a Rabelaisian episode provides a paradigm of sorts. In the Fifth Book (V.25)[12] the Pantagrueline voyagers arrive at the isle of Odes (from the Greek *hodos*, meaning road, path, way, journey), "en laquelle les chemins cheminent." The island is inhabited by animated roads that wander, pass, cross, and go wherever they go like animals. In fact they are animals, for animals, as the narrator informs us on the authority of Plato and Aristotle, move of their own doing (cf. Rabelais III.32.540). The narrator recognizes many of the roads as ones he has traveled elsewhere; all of them are present in animalized form with attributes of their landscapes. The germ of the episode is contained in an equivocation of the stock phrase "Où va ce chemin?" (Where does this road go?), understood literally as though the road were capable of going somewhere. In a deliberate confusion, roads do what they are instead of being what or where they are. The phrase "les chemins cheminent," without an equivalent in English, yokes a noun and its correlative verb in a subject-verb relation that eludes total redundancy in that the noun *chemin* (way, road) is semantically only incidental to the action *cheminer* (to walk) and thus appropriates for itself the habitual movements of animated beings (people, animals) that normally are subjects for the verb *cheminer*. Since the roads do the traveling, people merely have to get onto a convenient one to get to their destination without the least sweat or bother. Such traveling is compared to the way people go by boat on the Rhone; roads become vehicles, active means of conveyance, while human riders are simply taken along once they get on. Pantagruel recalls the remarkable hypothesis of Philolaus (fifth century B.C.) according to which it is the earth that moves, not the sky, despite all appearances. The initial pleasantry has led to reflections on what really moves with regard to what in the cosmos.

Paths in space have become despatialized and animated as moving agents. They've become the experience of people who travel them. They've become the traveling itself. They do so in the fictive space of a nowhere island, where by their movement they recreate the space that corresponds to them.

Like Rebelais' *chemins,* discourse in "motion" behaves variously as path, as "animal" (self-moving), and as vehicle, and sometimes as all three simultaneously: "el discurso discurre," we might say, with all the implications of "les chemins cheminent" (*discurrir* is to roam). The "course" in discourse suggests a route in space, but as past participle of the verb *currere* it also brings to mind the movement that makes it a route. In discourse the route is made by the "going," and the space of this route opens up as a shifting landscape and horizon, so to speak. Discourse itself moves, appropriating for itself the human activities that animate it. As such it appears "animated" (souled) and "auto-matic" (self-willed), words that Rabelais defines as self-moving (I.24.100, V.25.373). (It should be remembered that for Aristotle, who regarded motion as essential to the understanding of nature, all things that move are moved by something else—except animate beings.) Moreover, moving discourse is often vehicular, taking the discursive participants with it along its own sequences.

If metaphors expressing discursive "movement" can be found practically everywhere one looks for them except where immobilizing modes of thought have managed to suppress them, their particular manifestations naturally vary widely in different times, places, discursive circumstances, etc. When words "move," they may fly, walk, flow, dance, drag, leap, pass along conduits or lines of transmission, and so on ad infinitum. I doubt there is any movement words are incapable of simulating. My aim here is to give some indication of the range of these metaphors and their implications with regard to various modes of discourse. I'm interested in how people imagine discourse in terms of motion, and how motion both sensitizes thought to workings of discourse that otherwise might pass unnoticed and provides means of representing these workings—or misrepresenting them, as the case may be. I make no attempt at present to deal historically with the metaphors in question.

Of exceptional interest for the study of discursive movements is the unknown author of *On the Sublime* (ca. first century A.D.) known as "Longinus" because of an erroneous attribution of his work to a certain Cassius Longinus of the third century. The treatise deals with how the noble emotions find ways to infuse discourse (especially the text) with "a kind of madness and divine spirit," and how discourse in turn stirs up such emotions in readers and listeners. For Longinus, discourse is charged with vitality that expresses itself primarily as movement. "Strong and appropriate emotions and genuine sublimity," he writes, "are a specific palliative for multiplied or daring metaphors, because their nature is to sweep and drive all these other things along with the surging tide of their movement" (346). Always alive to how discourse moves or how people and their emotions move with it or on it, Longinus draws attention to the actual experience of discourse as it occurs. Every thought, emotion, technique, turn of phrase and trope affects the experience somehow. Longinus' project is more radical than it has been made out to be: he is not merely interested in what a text signifies, nor in how techniques and devices produce this or that effect, nor in how discourse may be formalized (experience as ongoing process is prior to form). The sense of discourse is inextricable from the full experience of discourse. There is no intellect/emotion split in his dealings with literature, nor is there any static moment, but only momentum throughout.

True to his emphasis on the dynamism of reception, Longinus characterizes discourse more as vehicle and traversable route (examples of these will appear in due time) than as self-mover. But he does refer here and there to language as flowing in an open sea, or as displaying rapidity and force, or as taking leaps, and so on. Most of these remarks in fact have a bearing on discursive rhythm—a very elusive topic that has nearly always been treated with metaphors of movement.

The etymology of rhythm—allegedly from the Greek *rhein,* "to flow" (Meschonnic 149)[13]—carries through even to recent analyses of rhythm in language. By rhythm I mean the temporal organization or enactment of discourse, including the velocities, the slowings and accelerations, the runs and pauses, the durations and transitions of language in action. But it is much more than the temporal behavior of discourse. Rhythm shares in all the intensities and energies of discourse, in the accentuations, in the intonations, in innuendos and expectations, in the vibrations of speaking voices and the motion of reading eyes, in the impulses and momentums of discursive activities, in the ever-shifting referentiality, and above all, in the largely unknowable workings of emotion and sense as experienced in discourse. Impetus affects rhythm greatly, including, say, the kind of long-range impetus that drives people to keep reading or speaking or that flags into boredom. From a pedestrian point of view, most of these features of rhythm involve little or no apparent movement from one place to another. The measurable aspects of rhythm could be dealt with clinically as timing, or formally as groupings of elements in sequence. Yet metaphors of movement have nearly always dominated notions of rhythm, not only because the analogue of musical rhythm brings with it strong associations with dance, but more fundamentally, it seems to me, because rhythm is so often experienced as movement and because rhythm can be expressed verbally by means of the language of movement more easily than by other sorts of language.

Movement metaphors for the rhythm of language seem inescapable, even in critical studies. Julia Kristeva speaks of the rhythmic movements of discourse in relation to the *chora* (*Revolution* 26, 29). In a very different key, D. W. Harding resorts constantly to metaphors of movement in his *Words into Rhythm*. He concludes: "The literary significance of rhythm and rhythms can best be understood by regarding language movement (created by the muscles at work in speech or imagined in silent reading) as comparable to such systems of bodily movement as walking, gesture, and patterns of changing posture. Like these it can be described in terms of broad characteristics — flowing, jerky, patterned, disjointed, and so on" (153; cf. 150).

Henri Meschonnic, in his wide-ranging *Critique du rythme,* cites dozens of writers who define discursive rhythm in terms of movement while he himself manages by and large to avoid the metaphor. Nonetheless, in one of his culminating definitions of rhythm he does admit the notion of movement, if partly in quotation marks: "Le rythme est continu-discontinu. Il est un passage, le passage du sujet dans le langage, le passage du sens, et plutôt de la significance, du faire sens, dans chaque élément du discours, jusqu'à chaque consonne, chaque voyelle. Aussi le rythme n'est-il pas une 'fluidité,' l'écoulement,' comme dit Bergson . . . ?" (225). The reference to Bergson comes some time after a critique of how Bergson estranges language, which he regards as discontinuous, from the supposedly continuous rhythms of the rest of life (176–82). But the key word in the above quote is *passage,* which is movement: this *passage* reveals the limitations of a linguistics of the sign and the possibilities of a linguistics of discourse. Rhythm, he writes, "montre que le poème n'est pas fait de signes, bien que linguistiquement il ne soit composé que de signes. *Le poème passe à travers les signes.* C'est pourquoi la critique du rhythme est une anti-sémiotique" (72; my emphasis). In the last analysis, movement is the principal way of thinking rhythm. The successive nature of discursive activity translates into going. The moving agents of this general *passage* seem to be almost interchangeable. The experience of discourse passes through the visual or auditory materiality of language.

Different modes of discourse predispose the ways their words "move." Words in thought move as thought does. Oral words take shape in the mouth and move through the air with multiple directionality, already fading before they've fully materialized. Such discourse tends to move evanescently in lived space and time except when it works on memory: words fly, escape, hit their mark, pass by, disappear, etc. Written words, if they move at all, do so either according to the conditions of script in all its technologies or according to the conditions of the discursive activities engaged with script. In the cited passage of St. Isidore, writing ties down fugitive words, it immobilizes and preserves them. But even script is often thought of as flowing, or running along, as the word *cursive* indicates. Chinese calligraphy offers an extreme example of this, especially the "cursive" and "grass" scripts that "allow the hand, prompted by the momentary intuition or inner spirit of the writer, to execute a vivid dance across the paper. . . . Each linked group of strokes becomes an expressive kinetic trace which has never been written like that before, and never will be again" (Rawson 19).

In general, written words tend to move much more readily as active discourse (exploding words) than as script (frozen words). Words flow into each other, styles wander or move directly, narrative progresses or digresses or regresses. When Walter Benjamin speaks of Proust's "syntax of endless sentences (the Nile of language, which here overflows and fructifies the regions of truth)" (201), he is elaborating a metaphor of this kind. Hélène Cixous says that woman's writing "can only keep going, without ever inscribing or discerning contours, daring to make these vertiginous crossings of the other(s) ephemeral and passionate sojourns in him, her, them . . . and then further, impregnated through and through with these brief, identificatory embraces, she goes and passes into infinity" (Moi 113).

The language of movement infiltrates critical terminology nearly always when processes and events need to be characterized. Erasmus draws attention to one instance of this when discussing proverbs as popular currency: "for this is the origin of the word *paroimia* in Greek (from *oimos,* a road, as though well polished in use and circulating), that which travels everywhere on the lips of men" (4–5).

This is also true of some major critical categories, at least in origin. Etymologically, both "verse" and "prose" (like "trope") denote discursive movements. As is common knowledge, "verse" (from the past participle of *vertere,* "to turn") describes periodic turnings and obviously implies a linear movement between turnings. "Prose" comes from the same root. In their lengthy discussion of the etymology of "prose," Jeffrey Kittay and Wlad Godzich oddly seem to miss the directionality and mobility implicit in the Greek *pros* (near, toward, to, before, ahead) and in the Latin *prosa* (ultimately from *provertere,* "turning forward") though they do pick up on the instability implied in these turning practices (193). Kittay and Godzich mention other instances of mobile language, however, including a term the Greeks often opposed to verse and used distinctly from the more ordered *logos*—"*ton koine,* vernacular, speech, 'what is poured forth promiscuously: in flowing, unfettered language'" (192).

I might mention in passing the odd case of the metrical "foot" that from

Greco-Roman antiquity to the present has suggested a pedestrian movement of verse. Some feet are slow, others fast and nimble, some move haltingly, but always the idea seems to be that "just as we walk on our feet, so verse advances as though by means of feet" (Isidore 300).[14]

As already noted, citation understood as a "setting in motion" of one discourse by (or within) another focuses attention on the dynamics of interdiscursive relations as they occur rather than on merely formal characteristics yielded by a static picture showing levels of discourse (who says or writes what to whom, where, when, and for how long?). Citation activates two or more discourses simultaneously, making every word and utterance multidiscursive and thus polyrhythmic. All the modes of discursive interaction that actually come into play in citation realize themselves when citation is not denied its complex "motion," that is, simultaneous discursive activity.

All of this metaphorical language pertains strictly to questions of rhythm as they focus on how discourse "happens." Very few writers in fact pursue these questions. Longinus is one. Another is Nietzsche, who shows uncommon attentiveness to matters of rhythm both within and outside of discourse. His exemplary analysis of vengeance, for instance, captures the importance of timing in the functioning of vengeance (*Human,* 316–18). Though no authority on relations between the sexes, he interestingly attributes mutual incomprehension to differences not of affects but of "tempo" (*Beyond* 272). Here and there throughout his writings he refers to discursive rhythms, too. "Paying attention to pace" is the title of one aphorism in *Human, All Too Human:* "The pace [the German *Gang* is more expressive] of his sentences shows whether the author is tired; the individual phrase can still be good and strong notwithstanding, because it was discovered earlier and independently when the idea first dawned on the author. This is frequently so in the case of Goethe, who too often dictated when he was tired" (333). Elsewhere Nietzsche devotes a lengthy passage to tempo with a lament on the stylistic clumsiness and viscosity of German writers, unlike such masters of tempo as Machiavelli and especially Petronius, who has "the feet of a wind" that "makes everything healthy by making everything *run*" (*Beyond* 230–31). Nietzsche's own prose not only moves with agility but often catches its subject matter by surprise.

The idea of sending and receiving discourse has obviously been around since time immemorial, ever since messengers and letters (missives) started to transport words, ever since there were trans-scribers, trans-lators, interpreters, and the like. The many related metaphors of this sort constitute a major subcategory of the words-in-movement metaphor, one that has served oral tra-dition, enjoyed scientific authority since before Saussure, and has dominated thinking about all the modern technologies of "transmission" and "reception" (telegraph, telephone, radio, television, computers, etc.). Everyday speech, too, makes use of these metaphors (Lakoff and Johnson classify them as "conduit" metaphors [10–12]). "Reception theory" adopts this metaphor while much of semiotics has incorporated it into some of its major models of communication. Jakobson's model of addresser, message, and addressee together with the other paraphernalia (code, context, contact) and their corresponding "functions" not only develops a transmission/reception metaphor but also is largely contained by the implications of the metaphor. (It should be borne in mind that this metaphor, despite its prestige as concept, is no more than a subsubcategory of discursive movement.) Transmitted words (or meanings, information, ideas) move, but usually in a very controlled way, not exactly of their own doing.

Like any activity, the happening of discourse is, I think, inconceivable without some mental representation of movement; conversely, to imagine discourse as either movement or as a way or locus of movement is to think discourse as an ongoing occurrence. It is by no means coincidental that in so many languages "happening" can be expressed as "coming" or "going"—even in the most common greetings. To pay attention to discursive "movement" is to look into how discourse happens in experience: there is a "coming" in discourse's "becoming," a *venir* in its *devenir*.

Traveling discursive routes

Thus far I've discussed discourse as "moving," either of its own doing or through some other agency. A second major mode of discursive movement exposes the language of discourse as some kind of pathway, mainly stationary in relation to discursive movement taking place through it or on it. Though immobile, language as path always "leads" elsewhere along its own itineraries. The alleged linearity of both spoken and written discourse on account of temporal and sometimes spatial sequentiality corresponds to this sort of discursive "movement," because the lines of discourse are traveled when discourse is active. This is especially obvious in the case of script with its visual routes along sequences of letters, ideograms, or hieroglyphs. Isidore of Seville supposes curiously that *litterae,* "letters," and by extension, "literature," are so called because they literally show the *way* to readers ("quod iter legentibus praestent" [278]). If the etymology lacks rigor, his observation has merit nonetheless, since it picks up on the nature of reading as moving along lines materialized outside the mind. Whether reading is assumed to be visual, or vocal and auditory but set in motion by sight, is of little concern here. (An alternate etymology, equally false but likewise processive, surmises that *litterae* are so called because letters are repeated in the course of reading—"quod in legendo iterentur.") Elsewhere Isidore assigns mobility to the reader, who does the traveling, for the verb *legere*, "to read," also means to pass through or travel as Virgil's voyagers do through straits (828). Augustine refers to reading in comparable terms: "we were forced to go wandering ourselves in the tracks of these poetic fictions" (I.17).

Saussure similarly conceptualizes the "signifier" in speech as linear: "The signifier, being auditory, is unfolded solely in time from which it gets the following characteristics: (a) it represents a span, and (b) the span is measurable in a single dimension; it is a line" (70). The flat linearity of the "signifier" is thus a spatial abstraction of auditory duration which links up in succession to form a "chain." Not surprisingly, Saussure resorts to the visual linearity of script to illustrate the auditory linearity of speech. Even Saussure's linearity, despite its dullness, implicitly traces the course of "movement," allowing the duration of speech to be rethought processively as linear movement.

Moving along routes of language or thought: from the ancients to the postmoderns — and of course outside the West too — this has been one of the dominant metaphors of discourse. Though I have no intention of documenting all the interesting uses of it that I've "come across" from Socrates' running and getting lost and quickening his pace along lines of inquiry in the *Cratylus* to Edmond Jabès' white page full of pathways, a few instances might once again be helpful to show some of its range.

The first difficulty here is to define what kinds of "routes" discourse has. Isidore's road of letters refers partly to the visual routes of script where discursive sequence in the most "literal" sense is plotted, but this *iter* is also, and much more importantly, the full sequential experience of reading. One should bear in mind, too, that reading was hardly a silent matter in Isidore's time. By the same token, the linearity of Saussure's signifiers derives from the temporal sequence of sound in speech, but the sequence of sound images also implies a sequential transmission of sense. In both cases, then, process (temporal sequence of discourse) translates into linear movement; the visual sequence of script, in contrast, seems largely incidental because the "space" of written discourse is by no means limited to or determined by the space of script.

The always proliferating language of discourse provides the ever-shifting "way." Normally happening one word at a time with a changing locus of signification, discourse marks out the thinness of a "pathway" within the semantic and affective environment manifest at any moment. This is not to deny that there are means of multiplying meanings or playing with verbal sequence in one way or another or even transcending the limits of linear sequence, but simply to affirm that sequentiality with all its implications of linear movement is intrinsic to discourse. Language already enacted in discourse constitutes the routes already traveled; what has yet to be said, written, heard, read, or thought is still ahead. This provides some directionality to discourse, but the primary directionality seems to be determined by the sense of any particular discourse as it "leads" from one thing to another, as the associative surroundings of thought and mood change with each utterance and turn of phrase, as it passes through the rhythms of its language. As though there were an invisible cursor of awareness running along the course of discourse.

Like Rabelais' *chemins,* discursive paths are hard to hold still under discussion: they seem to want to move this way and that and lead somewhere. They do so by appropriating the experience of those who travel them. Nonetheless, what actually moves in the discourse-as-pathway metaphor are people engaged in discourse, and language is the way. To be active in discourse is to move along the language of discourse. The routes may already be mapped out, as in reading, or somewhat familiar, or uncharted; regardless of degrees of predeterminacy, the route is realized in the traveling, and the experience of traveling is often unpredictable even when the routes are charted. According to this metaphor, "being there" in discourse becomes kinetic as "going along," because the "there" doesn't stay in one place but rather moves along the sequence of language. It is mainly this metaphor that, in relation to discourse in the wide sense encompassing thought and memory, allows one to progress, digress, regress, have a point of departure, get somewhere, jump ahead or backloop, get sidetracked, speed up or slow down, stop or go on, follow a method or story or argument or line of thought, get lost, go back to an earlier point, find a way, approach an issue, distance oneself, retrace steps, reach a cul-de-sac or impasse, choose one course rather than another, have a short or long way to go, and so on. This is a metaphor we live by and think by, one that inhabits both colloquial and theoretical language. For Heidegger it is a supreme metaphor: "Alles ist Weg" (All is way), he declares, echoing countless path-oriented passages in his work. A corollary to this would be that value resides in the traveling.

Longinus' *On the Sublime* draws considerable attention to the discourse-as-pathway metaphor. "If you tie a runner's arms to his side, you take away his speed; likewise, emotion frets at being impeded by conjunctions and other additions, because it loses the free abandon of its movement and the sense of being, as it were, catapulted out" (341). Emotion runs freely or encounters impediments along the language of discourse. Whose emotion? Presumably that of "readers" (a category that may include writers, speakers, and listeners), though Longinus treats emotion here as almost self-moving and disengaged from human beings. Compare this with the following statement: "Disconnected and yet hurried phrases convey the impression of an agitation which both obstructs the reader and drives him on. Such is the effect of

Homer's asyndeta" (340). "Reader" and "emotion" in these two statements would appear to be interchangeable terms, although emotion is somehow more mobile than the rest of us: "emotion carries us away," and is itself "a disturbance and movement of the mind" (340). Writers travel the language of discourse, as Longinus points out in the case of one author: "Then, to save the sentence from monotony and a stationary effect—for this goes with inertia, whereas disorder goes with emotion, which is a disturbance and movement of the mind—he leaps immediately to fresh instances of asyndeton and epanaphora . . ." (340). Longinus reads Sappho as a coming together of simultaneous emotions analogous to mobile pathways: "The result is that we see in her not a single emotion but a *synodos* of emotions" (quoted in Arac 354); as Jonathan Arac points out, "*Synodos* is combined from *syn-* (together) and *hodos* (road)." As motion, emotions thrive on discursive disorder and discontinuity; their pathways are no simple lines here, but instead irregular routes whose traveling involves leaps and unexpected moves of the mind choreographed so as to let emotions exert themselves. As Longinus makes clear, there is a strong correlation between emotion and rhythmic aspects of discourse: "People who in real life feel anger, fear, or indignation, or are distracted by jealousy or some other emotion . . . often put one thing forward and then rush off to another, irrationally inserting some remark . . . They seem to be blown this way and that by their excitement, as if by a veering wind. They inflict innumerable variations on the expression, the thought, and the natural sequence" (341). These people in real life are speakers whose emotion affects rhythm, altering ordinary discourse to make its own passionate routes. For Longinus, whoever is engaged in discourse—speakers, writers, listeners, readers, etc.—travels the routes of discourse, which often are charged with currents of emotion. This is not identical to "traveling the roads of positionality," as Kittay and Godzich phrase it (124, 137), because in the reading of narrative prose, for example, there may be no positions to be had if this traveling means moving. Defining positionality along a trajectory of motion resembles Zeno's project of dividing up motion into static frames charted along an infinitely divisible time line. Zeno's intention, after all, was to deny the reality of motion.

The paths of discourse are rarely ones that can be plotted on a piece of paper. Neither continuous nor direct, the discourse that interests Longinus in the above passages traces no simple line, but rather a *via rupta*. This linearity is also such that the whole line of a discourse is rarely called to mind, is rarely "visible" or "present" all at once. When readers, for example, move along a discursive path, their awareness of the route itself depends on the peculiar interplay of memory, perspective (from "where" they happen to be moving, with all the effects of nearness and distance), and anticipation. Furthermore, the *via* should not be confused with the experience of the discursive journey. Just as the experience of a journey is by no means limited to the narrowness of the road traveled or to the physical locomotion of traveling—these are often merely the conditions or premises of traveling—so the experience of traveling a discursive route as Longinus characterizes it isn't limited to the actual linearity of the path or the mental locomotion along it.

John Berger's notion of linearity in narrative discourse merits close attention in this regard. Edward Soja, in *Postmodern Geographies,* lauds Berger's call for a spatialization of critical thought, as opposed to what Soja sees as an unfortunate temporal bias in modern thought. Berger asserts that the modern novel has radically shifted its mode of narration, and that critical thinking ought to follow suit: "It is scarcely any longer possible to tell a straight story sequentially unfolding in time. And this is because we are too aware of what is continually traversing the story *laterally.* That is to say, instead of being aware of a point as an infinitely small part of a straight line, we are aware of it as an infinitely small part of an infinite number of lines, as the centre of a star of lines. Such awareness is the result of our constantly having to take into account the simultaneity and extension of events and possibilities" (Soja 21). A "straight story" probably can't be found in any long narrative new or old, though modern narrative does tend to problematize the tensions between the linear and "lateral" (or sequential and simultaneous) dimensions of discourse. The "lateral" dimension is integral to the discourse-as-path metaphor as the surrounding "space" of awareness along discursive routes—awareness of the kind that Berger indicates. It should be noted that Berger's scheme retains the linearity of temporal sequence as a route to be traveled, even though the resultant line to some extent detemporalizes the very sequence that it represents by being entirely present and visible at any given moment. The lateral lines represent the awareness of much else that is going on while one proceeds along the narrative sequence. These lines are thus of a quite different sort from the tracing of a discursive route.

What Soja hails as a "spatialization" of critical thinking appears instead to be a despatialization: the substitution of a representational scheme for the lived "space" of discourse—a "space" which may not correspond to objective space but which nonetheless is experienced as space. We actually lose space rather than recover it by Berger's schematization of narrative: the map encroaches on the territory. The discourse-as-pathway metaphor, in contrast, doesn't need to invent a supplementary scheme since it functions within the sense of space that opens up in discourse, and is itself one mode by which the temporality of discourse and the spatialization of thought are realized in their togetherness. There is no need to sacrifice time to space or vice versa:

movement, including discursive movement, is inconceivable without either one, and each is essential to the other.

As pathway, the language of discourse assumes the character of place: it is the locus where movement literally takes place. Everywhere along discursive routes the particularities of place are manifest. A conversation or narrative, for example, has its "places" you can start out from or get to or go through or return to. This is perhaps even more obvious in the case of texts, whose passages are in definite places you can point a finger to and focus your eyes on — even if the visual script doesn't contain the discursive space it opens up. Latin expresses this extension of place into discourse in the word *locus,* whose meaning ("place," in every sense of locality) stretches to textual "passage" as well as topic, theme, argument, and commonplace.[15] The Greek *topos* likewise makes a topography out of topics. Whereas the place of a textual passage is within discourse, however, the "true" place of *topoi* or *loci communes* would appear to be in artificial categories outside discourse: *topoi,* says Quintilian, are *argumentorum sedes* (the sites of arguments or "storehouses of trains of thought," as Curtius has it [70]). Just as Rabelais' *chemins* belong ambiguously to their geographical context in the known world and to an imaginary isle of Odes where they are brought together as a category, so *topoi* belong to two places at once: in discourse, and outside it in the categorized topography of memory (similar *topoi* are kept in the same storehouse of memory, as it were).

Yet the word *topoi,* like *loci communes,* indicates that they are out of place in discourse, that they have lost their placeness to become "things" that come from places, from "storehouses." As Frances Yates observes in her exploratory study *The Art of Memory,* "Topics are the 'things' or subject matter of dialectic which came to be known as *topoi* through the places in which they were stored" (31). She is referring here to an art of memory practiced at least from Greek antiquity to the European Renaissance by which people would remember discursive sequences such as speeches by visualizing places (*topoi, loci*) on a route and assigning images (*imagines*) to these places. The route usually led from one memorable spot to another through a large building with numerous chambers; this would give a definite order to memory, since the imagination could proceed (or go backward) from one place to another along this route, and each place would call to mind some vivid image which in turn would trigger the memory of some part of the discourse associated with the image. This association could operate through any number of principles, including symbol, metaphor, analogy, synecdoche, metonym, and wordplay.

The places are mnemonic only because they punctuate a mnemonic itinerary traveled by the imagination—and the ancient texts are explicit about the mental "running" that goes on along these routes. Before any images are placed at *loci,* one has to think out a route "in order that thought may be able to run through all the parts without let or hindrance." The traveling may take place, says Quintilian, not only in a house, but "in public buildings, or on a long journey, or in going through a city, or with pictures. Or we can imagine such places for ourselves" (Yates 22). Metrodorus used his knowledge of astronomy to make a route with 360 places along the zodiac, while others many centuries later would route their memory through the celestial spheres, Dante's hell, or any other zoned space real or imaginary. These routes could be used again and again with different images deposited at the *loci* for different discursive sequences.

The same route with its *loci,* then, supplements any number of different discursive routes. Its efficacy comes from the fact that it is mimetic of discursive pathways and that the two sorts of routes are quite distinct, that of *loci* being much more tangible, visual, solid, and definite than that of discourse, and thus useful as a course parallel and "other" to discourse. "We have to think of the ancient orator," says Yates, "as moving in imagination through his memory building *whilst* he is making his speech, drawing from the memorised places the images he has placed on them" (3). It is quite uncanny to think that while you are supposed to be addressing a law court about the witnesses to a crime, you are simultaneously—as the anonymous *Ad Herennium* advises (Yates 11)—visiting a *locus* with the active image of a man who, among other things, has a ram's testicles (*testes,* "witnesses") on his fourth finger. You move along a double route, one having all the hidden signposts indicating the mnemonically more elusive thought sequence of the other. By way of a planned itinerary, the art of memory to some degree systematizes the normal haphazard movements of memory and association in and around the actual language of discourse.

According to all three of the important Latin texts on memory, the *loci* of memory resemble the *loci* of script. As the author of *Ad Herennium* puts it, "the places are very much like wax tablets or papyrus, the images like letters, the arrangement and disposition of the images like the script, and the delivery is like the reading" (Yates 7). Quintilian, however, objects to the art of memory in that, unlike writing, it merely serves as a series of cues without being able to "grasp a whole series of connected words" (Yates 24). There is no image for words like conjunctions, and even if there were, the art of memory would prove too cumbrous since memory would be required to perform a double task that would actually impede the flow of words. His solution is to abandon the artificial mnemonic system and learn a passage by heart from another sort of visual route with *loci,* that of script. The lines of (chirographic) writing will provide the student with "certain tracks to guide him in pursuit of memory" (Yates 25). Quintilian correctly observes that the two mnemonic techniques resemble each other. Memorizing a passage involves "committing" its sequence to the sparse linearity of writing and inscribing the routes of writing in the mind; remembering involves traveling/reading the language of discourse according to the prompts of a hidden script.

The art of memory provides one example among many of the complex interrelationships between verbal discourse and other "mobile" activities such as thinking, feeling, remembering, and imagining, all of which overlapped with the term "discourse" in several languages until at least the seventeenth century, thus keeping intact their kinship with irregular movement, but which currently tend to fall outside "discourse" except when verbally articulated. One corollary of this exclusion may well be the subordination of all psychic processes to language. By deeming language in one way or another synonymous, coterminous, or equiprimordial with the unconscious, with Being, and ultimately with thought and meaning, the various sects that have made a cult of language (e.g., Heideggerianism, Lacanianism)[16] present a major obstacle to thinking about how "thinking" takes place. Reflections on preverbal babies or jazz musicians could dispel such naïveté in no time.

Movement (as Freud was well aware) opens up a world of analogues for conceptualizing psychic processes, enabling us to differentiate the various agencies that seem to be at work (or at play) and gauge the interactions "going on" in the mind. Whereas thought-as-language paradigms grossly yoke together disparate activities of the psyche and summarily exclude from thought all that isn't somehow "language," freer metaphors of movement tend to differentiate and dynamize psychic factors with a minimum of preestablished conditions. Augustine talks about flight in the vast space of his memory: "Through all this I range; I fly here and I fly there; I dive down deep as I can, and I can find no end" (X.17). Similarly, Lu Chi of the third century resorts to the language of movement to account for how writers experience emotion in response to the changes in the world:

> At the beginning,
> They all stop their seeing and hold in their hearing,
> To think deeply and search widely;
> Their quintessential spirits [*ching*] gallop to the eight
> extremities of the earth,
> Their minds wander to the region thousands of feet above.
> (Liu 33)

This diverse movement, remarks Liu Hsieh of the sixth century in a similar passage, is "brought about by the natural order of thought" (Liu 34)—an order more akin to spiritual "roaming" than to logical sequence. The agents of psychic movement are various (thought, emotion, spirits, desires, imagination, the mind, etc.), and their movement differs with every kinetic formulation of their activity. Metaphors of movement allow such agents to move in and around language without being chained to it at every step; more generally, they provide a field of representation for psychic activities without reducing them to bare schemata. Consider, for example, how Nietzsche represents thinking by resorting to a metaphor of movement:

> "Causality" eludes us; to suppose a direct causal link between thoughts, as logic does—that is the consequence of the crudest and clumsiest observation. Between two thoughts all kinds of affects play their game: but their motions are too fast, therefore we fail to recognize them, we deny them—
>
> "Thinking," as epistemologists conceive it, simply does not occur: it is a quite arbitrary fiction, arrived at by selecting one element from the process and eliminating all the rest, an artificial arrangement for the purpose of intelligibility. (*Will to Power* 264)[17]

The thoughts he refers to are obviously ones that can be identified by language and probably are formulated in language. In retrospect they appear as more or less stationary *loci* along a not only sequential but also consequential route, each formulated thought premising the next. But this is illusory: multiple motion runs through thought, constituting the ways of thought in and around language. Imperceptible though they may be, mobile affects are the main discursive travelers and route makers in this version of the pathway metaphor.

Unlike immobilizing conceptual metaphors, route metaphors rarely allow discourse to be cut off from the subjectivities and circumstances involved in its making. Far from being abstracted out of critical representation, discursive activity is transformed by this metaphor into movement along routes. The discourse of ways is never simply out there somewhere: at the very least, something or someone travels routes that may be known or unknown, and normally the movement is quite complex, even multiple. This metaphor cautions against reducing discourse to extant language because such language is inextricable from the movements of thought that made it extant. Thinking, remembering, feeling, musing, expecting, speaking, writing, reading, listening: the multiple activity that these and other such words distinguish are bound to interact (to "move" with respect to each other) in different ways in any instance of discourse. To resort to the obvious analogy, a person's travel obviously can't be reduced to the physical route traveled, nor the locomotion along the route. The traveling is the full experience of going along a route, even if much of this experience may have little or nothing to do with the route as such or its passage. Thoughts, conversations, observations, encounters, etc., all accompany the physical movement and combine with it to constitute the evanescent experience of travel. Likewise, discursive traveling involves much more than moving along words. From one word or phrase or other verbal sequence to another, any number of intraverbal, paraverbal, or extraverbal agents may move, as it were. To limit discourse to extant uses of language is to sever it artificially from the processes that go into its making and from processes that obviously behave similarly (thinking, emotive experience, the nonverbal transient arts, etc.) but that don't always express themselves in audible or visible language.

Nietzsche brings out this wider sense of discourse when he refers to writing, thinking, speaking, etc., as movement of one sort or another. Sometimes even "great spirits," he says, reveal their uncouthness: "it is above all the gait and stride of their thoughts that betrays them; they cannot *walk*." And later in the same aphorism: "There is something laughable about the sight of authors who enjoy the rustling folds of long and involved sentences: they are trying to cover up their *feet*" (*Gay* no. 282). Thinking and writing thus translate into a rhythmic process as complex and habitual—and as revelatory of personal style—as walking. In a similar vein he says one ought "to be able to dance with one's feet, with concepts, with words: need I still add that one must be able to do it with the pen too—that one must learn to *write?*" (*Twilight* 513).

Passages like this appear to have led Derrida into *errance* in *Writing and Difference* (29–30). He cites an aphorism by Nietzsche on Flaubert: "On ne peut penser et écrire qu'assis (G. Flaubert). There I have caught you, nihilist! The sedentary life is the very sin against the Holy Spirit. Only thoughts reached by walking have value" (*Twilight* 471). Derrida endorses Flaubert by affirming that writing is in fact a matter of sitting and bending over rather than "dancing." He goes on to say that Nietzsche despite himself was convinced of this too: Zarathustra speaks of old and new tablets around him, and of descending to the valleys (*Zarathustra* 308–27). Yet contrary to Derrida's contention, there is no hint anywhere in this long section that the descent as such (*Niedergang, Untergang*) has anything to do with writing (engraving) or reading or with bending down to pick up tablets: the obsessive ups and downs and overs and unders throughout these pages refer to hierarchies, power, values, and struggles, not to hunching over a piece of script (the best of the new tablets are to be placed *over* people). But even if bodies do bend over when writing, there is nothing to prevent nonalienated pens from "dancing" at the same time. The movements and intensities of discursive thought canalize themselves kinesthetically (and perhaps even mimetically) into manual movements and flowing strokes and loops of the pen. By synecdoche, too, the movement of the pen comes to represent the movement of discourse.

Furthermore, although Flaubert's statement refers to both thinking and writing, Nietzsche's commentary refers only to thinking, not writing, as valuable when ambulatory rather than sedentary. Nowhere does Nietzsche deny that writers find it convenient to sit down once in a while. What he dislikes is writing engendered by the enclosure, staleness, and stagnation of sedentary existence, as he makes quite clear in another passage:

> It is our habit to think outdoors—walking, leaping, climbing, dancing, preferably on lonely mountains or near the sea where even the trails become thoughtful. Our first questions about the value of a book, of a human being, or a musical composition are: Can they walk? Even more, can they dance?
> . . . How quickly we guess how someone has come by his ideas; whether it was while sitting in front of his inkwell, with a pinched belly, his head bowed low over the paper—in which case we are quickly finished with his book, too! Cramped intestines betray themselves—you can bet on that—no less than closet air, closet ceilings, closet narrowness. (*Gay* no. 366)

For Nietzsche, thoughts arising from movement outdoors are qualitatively different from those arising from sitting. Though external to thought, the paths of mountains and shores themselves "become thoughtful," providing the wherewithal for thought to find its own routes and *loci:* thinking interacts with its changing surroundings by traveling them, and moves also to the rhythms, moods, and energies of the body. The qualitative difference is hard to define: thought can obviously "move" as much when one sits still as when one moves; one might even think about the same sorts of "things" in either case. Nonetheless, besides the ways that bodily movement might affect thought, the mode of experience in which one is engaged is likely to affect the ways of thinking about things even extrinsic to that experience: the experience of traveling would subtly lend to concurrent thinking both the particulars and general aspects of its modality. Among much else, this might include a sense of directional movement, of going somewhere along marked routes, of rhythm and velocity, of accompaniment, of mood, of passing through "terrain," of leaving and arriving. Thinking as discursive movement is bound to move in ways analogous and responsive to those of concurrent traveling rather than entirely disparate from them.

Before turning to discourse-as-vehicle metaphors, I'd like to remark in passing that discourse as a traveling of routes belongs to a much larger category of metaphors whereby any process, any event or series of them, any undertaking whatsoever may be thought of as some kind of journey. I need hardly stress how important metaphors of the Way are in all the major religions of the world, from Taoism (*tao,* "way") to one of the names of Christ. Notions of procedure and method in many sorts of mysticism as well as devotional practices and doctrines translate into the traveling of ways, and ecstasy too is often experienced as movement or transport ("trance" is transit). Life-as-a-journey is also one of the most insistent, diverse, and universal of secular metaphors, one that breaks down into many shorter journeys (like *journées*) within it. Nations, too, run their course (*corso*) and run it again (*ricorso*), says Vico. Such notions generate an inexhaustible number of traveling metaphors.

Of special interest here owing to its kinship with discourse as journey is the intellectual undertaking as journey. Bernd Jager shows how the word *theoria* in ancient Greece includes the idea of the journey—initially to the dwelling of a god or goddess—and how the meaning evolved from "the experience of travel" to "the experience and knowledge one acquires while traveling" and later, in Plato's *Laws,* to "a voyage of enquiry by land and by sea" (236–38).[18] Parmenides represents his discovery of the Ways of Truth and Opinion as a breathtaking journey with mares and chariot driven by daughters of the sun. Parmenides' traveling the "road of inquiry" in a poem in which he denies the reality of movement and change creates a major paradox in his famous work, one that attests to the power of the journey metaphor and possibly undermines his denial of movement.[19] Montaigne has no such problems, and perhaps no goals either in an endless wandering: "Who does not see that I have taken a road along which I shall go without cease and without effort, so long as there is ink and paper in the world?" (922).

As far as I am aware, most of the well-known Western intellectuals since Marx use variants of the journey metaphor to characterize their own enterprises. In one way or another, journey metaphors enable them to express notions of orientation, search, struggle, fatigue, perseverance, aloneness or companionship, uncertainty, chance, risk, method, means, choice, goals, attempts, novelty, excitement, encounters, otherness, discovery, and so on. Such metaphors pervade the work of Nietzsche, Freud, and Heidegger in particular. The personal uses of these metaphors read almost like a Rorschach test, raising the question of whether writers with radically different journey metaphors are really capable of understanding one another. For Marx, science is a "fatiguing climb" up the paths of a mountain to the "luminous summits" (298–99), while for Max Weber science "follows those stars which alone give meaning and direction to its labours" (112). Freud sails uncharted waters and explores dark caverns. Foucault portrays the bleakest of landscapes in his earlier writings, and throughout his work refers to his own endeavors as testing and venturing from boundaries of knowledge. Deleuze and Guattari are interested in underground burrows, thresholds, avenues and lines of escape. Nietzsche has a marked predilection for the vastness and wildness of mountains, seas, and shores. Heidegger prefers paths through woods and fields close to the homestead, the darkly lit forest ways (*Holzwege*) that lead to the clearing (*Lichtung*), or the paths that lead circuitously homeward through language to language, the "house of Being." For Heidegger, philosophy is a pilgrimage, every inquiry is a seeking, every question has its paths, all learning is traveling, all thinking is being on the way, and being on the way is all that matters.

Discursive conveyance

As with Rabelais' *chemins,* people take discursive ways or those ways take people "somewhere": the relative motion can be conceived both ways, but with different implications, because people either move *along* (the routes of language, for example) or move *with* (the language of discourse, or other people involved in discourse). In the same way, in the metaphor of discourse as self-moving, discourse may seem to move on its own, but its animation or flux depends on its being set in motion by discursive activity: its rhythms induce movement in people, but people also rhythmize discourse by setting the pace and actualizing the runs and pauses and accentuations, thus influencing the resultant rhythm by the performance of movement according to the inducive rhythm. Metaphors of discursive conveyance constitute by no means a hard and fast category but rather a group of variants of the other two categories discussed (discourse as self-mover and as route). What is more or less special to them is their sense of moving *with* someone or something. Whereas self-moving discourse often behaves as though the presence of humans were unnecessary, and discursive routes are very often traveled alone, metaphors of discursive conveyance allow for more communication, interaction, and a sense of involvement and immediacy.

When a story transports you to another time and place, when the locus of attention in discourse keeps shifting and taking you along, when the rhythms of discourse impel you onward or hold you back (as reader, writer, speaker, listener, etc.), when the narrator of *Tom Jones* talks to you as a companion in a horse-drawn carriage, when Socrates or anyone else gets lost or carried away in discourse and then asks: "And now let me see, where are we?"—in all these instances someone or something is taking (or carrying, or guiding) someone along with her/him/it in discursive travel.

There's something very cinematic about most metaphors of this sort: the sense that you're there or at least within eyeshot or earshot and moving along with the panning and tracking and changes of view as they largely dictate the rhythm. Roland Barthes' designation of the almost subliminal features of sight and sound in film as "fellow travelers" of the story characterizes the activity of spectators as traveling (Bordwell 53). The movement of the camera in a particular shot is aptly referred to as "traveling" (e.g., by Godard, who uses the English word): such traveling functions as the guide and vehicle for traveling viewers. Verbal discourse no doubt has some rough equivalents for such cinematic experience.

Had Longinus had the notion of cinematization at his disposal he might have used it in connection with what he calls "visualization" (*phantasia*), and what he says others call "image production": a means by which "enthusiasm and emotion make the speaker *see* what he is saying and bring it *visually* before his audience" (326). Longinus wants what's being told to come alive, to be felt as "urgent" and present despite its remoteness and invisibility. No matter what techniques are employed (e.g., visualization, shifts to the present tense and to first- and second-person pronouns), a sense of motion is necessary to reduce distance to immediacy: people travel with respect to the story, or vice versa, or they travel with it. After quoting a dramatic passage in which Helios hands the reins to Phaethon, Longinus comments: "May one not say that the writer's soul has mounted the chariot, has taken wing with the horses and shares the danger? Had it not been up among those heavenly bodies and moved in their courses, he could never have visualized such things" (337).

Being there means moving there, because "there" is always shifting in discourse. The flaming chariot and winged horses help a great deal, of course, in evoking a vivid image of motion and in carrying the "soul" along with them. Yet even if no action or movement were taking place in the story, if the story were engaged instead, say, in describing a motionless scene, there would still be discursive "motion," and it is ultimately this motion rather than that of a chariot and steeds that bears "souls" along with it. Longinus' reference to the writer's "soul" tacitly acknowledges the schizoid character of all discursive experience: *the sense of being "there" in the mobile whereabouts of discourse*—a "there" that is always a mobile "here"—and of being elsewhere in another "here" at the same time. The writer's "soul" accompanies Phaethon and shares in the danger, while the "rest" of the writer remains more earthbound: a normal case of divided stream of con-sciousness.

If the writer's journey were a solo journey it would be of scant interest to Longinus, who sees the primary purpose of literary art to be a communication through motion of certain types of thought and emotion. If there were nothing to convey, or no one to take along, there would be little point in undertaking the journey. Unwritten but understood in the commentary on Phaethon is a sense that the vivid narrative of the writer or teller takes the reader's or listener's "soul" with it through the same exhilarating experience. Even more than the *aulos* (oboe) and lyre, which move listeners to their rhythms and cast a spell over them with their harmony, words ("man's natural instrument") "convey the speaker's emotions to the minds of those around him and make the hearers share them" (350).

The sense of traveling together emerges strongly in a cited passage of Herodotus—who switches to the second person—and Longinus' commentary: "'You will sail upstream from Elephantine, and then you will come to a smooth plain. After crossing this, you will embark on another boat and sail for two days. Then you will come to a great city called Meroe' (Herodotus [2.29]). Do you see, my friend, how he grips your mind and takes it on tour through all these places, making hearing as good as seeing? All such forms of expression, being directed to an actual person, bring the hearer into the presence of real events" (343). Various sorts of traveling are going on here. Herodotus is recounting his own journey as far as Elephantine; for knowledge of what lies beyond this city he has to rely on what was told to him in answer to his questions. Interestingly, the answer comes not as a general description but as an itinerary, as though his journey were to continue. Presumably, unnamed and perhaps generalized speakers address Herodotus as hypothetical traveler beyond Elephantine. If this is so, they are the ones who take Herodotus the listener on a discursive journey. Herodotus' text functions as a kind of citation of the initial discursive journey; here it is Herodotus the writer (or narrator, or writing subject, or what you will) who takes readers/ hearers along on a discursive journey. This is the journey that Longinus refers to. Once again, although the geographical itinerary helps convey a sense of traveling, the actual "traveling" is discursive, not geographical, and its togetherness derives from communicativeness. Writers and speakers take their counterparts along with them (in one example, Demosthenes "drags his hearers with him into the hazards of his long hyperbata" [342]), and their discourse serves variously as medium, route, vehicle, etc. What goes on tour, of course, is the "mind," or at least part of it: the travel is schizoid. Here, consciousness may be doubly divided due to double movement of cited and citing discourses.

Commenting on this very passage of Longinus in an essay on historically changing notions of "the reader," Jane Tompkins argues that Longinus is interested in effect rather than meaning, whereas modern critics instead focus on meaning since they "equate language not with action but with signification" (203–4). Speech-act theory and its derivatives would obviously constitute an exception (though Longinus' movement corresponds to none of the categories of act defined by this theory), as would Peirce and Dewey as well as Habermas with their insistence on language as communicative action. Nonetheless, Tompkins' statement revealingly signals the obsessive search over the last several decades for signification, as though there were nothing more to discourse than ciphering and deciphering, articulating and interpreting, cuing and inferring. Longinus is not merely interested in effect here. Rather, his approach leads him to define some of the essential *conditions* of discourse, those sorts of con-ditions that make "saying-together" and moving together almost synonymous and enable meaning to be sensed.

Of all the metaphors of discursive movement, those of discourse as conveyance (a means of taking others along) come closest to the spirit of what Bakhtin calls "utterance"—a recognition that speaking (and writing) can't be understood as discrete acts in isolation from listening (and reading), as opposed to the Saussurian model, for example, which has people doing one or the other but not both simultaneously (Clark/Holquist 216–17). These metaphors tend to be the most communicative and communal, the most social, because they involve moving together in the pro-cess of discourse. Common parlance in many languages has equivalents for expressions such as "Are you with me?" "Do you follow me?" "Where are you leading us?" In each case the locative reference is to the moving whereabouts of discourse, and at least two people move along together: *discurrunt.*

Every metaphor of discursive movement expresses discursive activity somehow, translating the active "being-there" (the becoming) of discourse into a "moving-there." Undoubtedly, many of these metaphors are commonplace, many distort or even falsify discursive activity, and many are insights; as a group, they characterize the principal ways that people across the spectrum think of discourse. Because their movement is open, rhythmic, flowing, animated, transient, and transgressive, these metaphors are overwhelmingly opposed to static conceptualism of all sorts.

Bearing in mind the frozen words, the animated roads, and much else, we move on now to Cervantes' ubiquitous metaphors of movement.

The Language of Movement in
Cervantes' Novels

To appreciate Cervantes' figural language of movement one has to read his novels rather as Borges reads Pierre Menard's *Don Quixote* (*Prosa* 1:425–33): not as exercises in conventional rhetoric but as strange, surprising formulations of textual worlds. Instances of figurative movement appear on nearly every page, most often as evanescently as shooting stars but sometimes insistently through long passages. A considerable proportion of these are integral to the Castilian of Cervantes' time. They are the "natural" way of saying things, independent of rhetorical codes; if this takes away from their value as personal metaphors, it adds value to the rhetoric of natural language in its narrative or descriptive modes. But many such expressions belong to specific discourses (in Foucault's sense), revealing particular ways of representing and evaluating.

The amazing frequency of figural expressions of movement would seem to be offset by their inconsequentiality when considered in isolation. What does it really matter if a character says, "Fear entered my soul" rather than "I got frightened"? or "The words left her lips" rather than "She spoke"? or "Madness often came to him" rather than "He often acted out of madness"? Yet when considered in relation to hundreds of analogous expressions, such statements take on a resonance that can hardly be ignored. Metaphors of movement more than any other sort of language in Cervantes' texts have the prime role of expressing the workings of discourse, of time, of life's "journey," of mental, emotional, and spiritual processes, of love and desire, and much else. Taken together, they have a significant bearing on the notions of person, language, interpersonal relationships, and "world." While patterns of such metaphorical behavior are quite discernible, some metaphors are contradictory and others entirely anomalous. What they do have in common is movement in some sort of space—a movement and space that interact in countless ways with those of actual journeys undertaken, and create many journeys of their own. The figural language of movement multiplies the journeys of Cervantes' novels.

I have no interest in classifying the thousands of such metaphors I've come across. The task would get dull and, what's more, I doubt that any scheme of classification would be of much use. The vast majority of them nonetheless seem to cluster around (1) discourse (in the wide sense), (2) love and desire, and (3) a range of life processes somehow relating to the life-as-journey metaphor. These are the rubrics under which I'll discuss Cervantes' metaphors of movement, aware that their domains overlap a great deal, and that other headings might serve as well as these. Although these metaphors are by no means evenly distributed throughout the novels, I'm less concerned here with novelistic chronotopes and subgenres than with recurrent images of movement.

Discourse and Movement

Discurso, discurrir

Scarcely more than a rarity in Spanish before the 1530s, when Juan de Valdés called for its introduction into Spanish, the word *discurso* burst into a multiple trajectory over the next century. The generating spark in this case was obviously Italian—Machiavelli's *Discorsi*, to name one example, appeared in 1517. By the 1580s, when Cervantes wrote *La Galatea, discurso* and its verbal counterpart, *discurrir,* were not only very common but much more intense and varied in meaning than dictionaries then or now credit them with being. Sebastián de Covarrubias, in his *Tesoro de la lengua castellana o española* (1611), defines *discurso* as "la corrida que se haze a una parte y a otra; tómase por el modo de proceder en tratar algún punto y materia, por propósitos y varios conceptos" (the running that is done [or course made] to one place and another; also understood as the means of procedure when treating some point or matter, through purposes and diverse concepts). The *Diccionario de autoridades* (1726) elaborates a little more along the same lines, beginning with "La carrera, el camino que se hace a una parte y a otra, siguiendo algún rumbo" (The course, the way that is made to one place and another, following some direction).[1] Consistent with the etymology, this definition and the first of those of Covarrubias suggest the common denominator of perhaps all instances of *discurso* in Cervantes' writings: movement along routes. What differs from one instance to another is the nature of the movement, routes, and space of *discurso.*

Out of curiosity I randomly checked about a dozen instances of *discurso* and *discurrir* in a standard English translation of *Don Quixote,* and found that a different equivalent was used every time.[2] Although certain words and phrases would no doubt have started to reappear had I looked any further, the readiness of *discurso* to adapt its meaning to context is quite remarkable.

One of the basic meanings of *discurso* is simply *curso,* "course": most often the course of time, life, travel, and narrative. Time not only functions as a category in its own right—e.g., "con el discurso del tiempo" is a standard expression for "in the course of time"—but also enables many other terms to delineate their *discurso* through durative process and sequentiality. So it is that a battle, a dinner, a friendship, a conversation, someone's absence—in short, anything that lasts—has its *discurso.* Duration translates into a passage of some sort often articulated by a sequence of activities and/or events. Specific happenings within experienced time thus determine the pace, directional shifts, mood, and many other characteristics of what would otherwise be either the regular movement of natural time or the shapeless duration of uneventful time.

The temporality of experience likewise allows a course to be traced in people's lives, as is obvious in common Cervantine expressions like "el discurso de mi vida" (the course of my life). Various presuppositions are operant here: (1) that the journey marks an individual destiny (unlike, say, the collective destiny of the course that nations run in Vico's work); (2) that duration and experience can be cast into a topographical analogue; (3) that the sequence of experience marks out a route with a clear sense of backward and forward representing before and after, and a definite line of access from one state or event to the next; (4) that even in the most sedentary of cases, to live is to "move" in ever-changing circumstances, companionship, spaces, and so on; (5) that there is some component of self-determination on the part of the "traveler"; and (6) that the "traveler" maintains some kind of identity from beginning to end, even if this amounts to little more than a wandering name with a locomotive self attached to it.

In Gracián's *Criticón* (1651–57), where the notion of life as journey is perhaps more developed than in any other European text, the *discurso* of human life designates "course" (e.g., 535), just as it does for Don Quixote, Berganza, and numerous other Cervantine characters. Yet Gracián also deftly plays off course with discourse, as in the opening lines of the prologue to the reader: "This courtly philosophy, the course of your life in a discourse, I present to you today, judicious reader. . . ."[3] With this statement, Gracián approaches the semantic domains of modern usage, where life has its course and language its discourse.

Cervantes prefers *discurso* to *curso* with regard to eventful human lives. *Curso,* as Cervantes uses the word, nearly always evokes a sense of order:

the heavenly bodies have their regular movements, their *curso,* as do rivers; when human life proceeds according to natural rhythms or flows, it too has its *curso.* Nature gets off course ("sale de su curso") when the aging king Policarpo hankers for possession of the beautiful, untouchable Auristela: "the course of my good life has been disturbed," he says, "and consequently I've fallen from the heights of my presumed good sense to the deep abysm of I know not what desires."[4] Don Quixote comments that enchanted flights such as the one he and Sancho are undertaking on the wooden horse Clavileño "are out of the ordinary course of things [van fuera de los cursos ordinarios]" (II.41.349): much more often than not, the *curso* is the linear pattern of the "ordinary," allied to the normative, the perpetual, the harmonious. When life has none of these qualities, it adopts the disruptive, unruly prefix *dis-* to destabilize *curso.*

Just as Rabelais' narrator in the Fourth Book refers to "tout le discours de nostre naviguaige" (IV.4.45), Cervantes' characters, including Don Quixote and Sancho Panza, speak about the *discurso* (rather than *curso*) of their journeys and peregrinations. The *discurso* of the journey is much like that of time and life — derivative of successive experience — but is reinforced by the image of actual movement along spatial routes. Hence the journey metaphor of *discurso,* elsewhere autonomous of journeys in space/time, combines inseparably with journey movement to produce a sort of mental outline or itinerary of ways traveled.

Similarly, the *discurso* of a book (or story, or "true" history, or work) derives from the processive nature of written and spoken discourse, but owes its special efficacy to the "movements" and "courses" of language and accompanying thought processes. This usage of *discurso* implicates writing, reading, speaking, and listening as processes of movement on or along the language of discourse.

Discurso as a special sense of "course" is always a course *of* something else. It calls up the image of movement this way and that, or of a shifting route, but how it really behaves depends largely on the behavior of that something else. The *discursos* of a battle, of a tale, of a dog's travels, and of an amorous afternoon may have little in common with one another. But *discurso* also has a domain of its own. Most instances of the word refer to the very *movement of thought* itself, or the sequence of thought. As such, it often works in alliance with speaking, writing, listening, reading, imagining, reasoning, understanding, deliberating, pondering, intending, remembering, and many other sorts of thought processes, but seems to be autonomous of all of them.

Consider reason, for example, which is sometimes synonymous with *discurso.* The *Coloquio de los perros* begins as the dogs Berganza and Cipión marvel at suddenly finding themselves empowered with speech. Cipión observes: "the miracle is even greater in that we not only speak, but we speak with *discurso,* as if we were capable of reason, whereas we are so much without it that the difference between man and beast lies in man's being a rational animal, and the beast, irrational."[5] Berganza, too, is amazed at possessing some sort of "understanding capable of *discurso*" (300). *Discurso* differs from speech, since one can speak with *discurso* or without it. One can also write without *discurso,* as Don Quixote, hearing that the history of his first two journeys has been written, suspects the Moorish author of doing: "Now I believe that the author of my story was no sage but an ignorant blabberer, who blindly and without *discurso* set about writing it with no thought as to how it might turn out. . . ."[6] Within writing or speech, *discurso* is the movement of thought, or the alignment of language according to the purposes of thought. Reasoning (*razones*) and understanding (*entendimiento*) obviously participate in the discursive process here. Purpose and method (in the sense of *meta-hodos*) are also implied, especially in the cited words of Don Quixote above.

It is by no means unusual to find *discurso* somehow paired with *razones* (thoughts, reasoning). In fact, the very common expression *encaminar razones* (literally, to put speech or thoughts en route, i.e., to guide or direct them) could be taken as a synonym of some senses of *discurrir.* But even so, *razones* are more substantive, more "reifiable" than *discurso* because *discurso* passes through *razones* or somehow arranges them along its route or carries them with its current, as is evident in the following passage from the *Persiles* comparing a lover's thoughts to water constricted at the narrow mouth of a bottle: "The same thing happens with the thoughts [*razones*] conceived in the mind of a wounded lover. Sometimes all of them rush together toward the tongue and block each other's way, so that the *discurso* doesn't know which ones the imagination should give itself to understand first."[7] Moreover, contrary to accepted notions of the word, *discurso* often leads to illusion and self-deception rather than understanding, and frequently proceeds along the paths of irrationality: *discurso* can move in the absence of understanding and reason, particularly when it gets mixed up with or driven by jealousy, anger, fear, desire, and the like. And when passions and errors enter into thought, *discurso* tends to proliferate into many *discursos,* an erratic confusion of thought-movements.[8]

In short, if *discurso* is associated more with the rational than with the irrational, the insightful than the obtuse, the agile than the clumsy, and so on, it is nonetheless an autonomous term that in Cervantes' works is coupled with adjectives as diverse as good, bad, feeble, superhuman, human (as opposed to canine), true, impoverished, immature, blind, prudent, rapid, concerted, confused, etc. *Discurso* is the passage of thought through "thoughts," the move-ment of sense through and around language, the path or multiple paths in and around every specifiable mental process (imagining, speaking, writing, reasoning, etc.) from which it can nonetheless disengage itself. It turns all modalities of thinking into movement—reasoning into methodic procedure, remembering into returning, imagining into exploring, erring into errancy, wondering into wandering, and so forth, thereby tracking the mind's versatile activity through analogues of mobility.[9]

Let me remark in passing that such discursive activity has its limits, par-ticularly when it yields to impulsive action. On several occasions, *discurso* explicitly gives way to different resolves including escape, attack, pursuit, and suicidal desperation.[10] It seems that extreme mental states locked into an im-perative for immediate action impede the movement of thought.

Less common than the noun, the verb *discurrir* corresponds closely in mean-ing to *discurso,* yet tends to evoke movement much more vividly, as might be expected from such an expressive verb of motion.[11] Whereas the *discurso* of a journey, narrative, dialogue, or thought process tends to call to mind the residue of traveling, telling, conversing, or thinking, and only secondarily the movement of such action, *discurrir* directly calls to mind the action itself in all its mobility. Lights flit about in the forest, ships travel in between islands or veer this way and that in the open sea, Don Quixote gallops here and there in combat, the Knight of the Mirrors travels about the provinces of Spain: *discurrir* serves to convey these and many other movements.[12] *Discurrir,* like its nominal counterpart, tends to operate more often within the space of thought than within conventional external space, and likewise adapts its ki-netic behavior to diverse situations. It can refer to reflecting, meditating, fren-zied racing of the mind, farfetched imagining, wondering, discussing, pro-pounding, and many other modes of thinking, speaking, and writing.[13]

The uses of *discurso* and *discurrir* in Cervantes' works suggest that although thought very often moves along or by means of language, it is in no way restricted to language (not even in the loosest sense of the word). It moves around and in between language and unworded images in a space charged with value and affect. The more silent Lotario is (*DQ* I.33.417), the more his thought runs on (*discurría*) as he contemplates the forbidden beauty of Camila. A character like Periandro can conjure up a "thousand" *discursos* in an instant, and yet he also finds himself groping at times for language ade-quate to the expressive purposes of his multiple thought-movements. By way of contrast, the suppleness, versatility, and autonomy of discursive activity in Cervantes' texts expose as inept various twentieth-century notions of the relations between thought and language (beginning with Saussure's concept of the sign as it operates in the talking heads). For Cervantes and his contemporaries both in Spain and elsewhere, the predominant medium for portraying such mental activity is the language of mobility.

Traveling narratives

One of the passages that do much to add wit, warmth, and depth to an initially rather nondescript Sancho Panza is the sparkling story he tells Don Quixote in the dead of night while warding off fear (I.20.241–45). The story is exemplary for the ways it fuses and confuses telling with traveling. The tale gets sidetracked immediately by the opening formulas whose purpose is normally to lead into the story, not out of it: to Sancho, however, the phrase "may evil come to those who seek it out" seems applicable to Don Quixote's stubborn bent for seeking out danger, and prompts him to suggest they take another route, to which the knight replies: "Follow your story, Sancho, and leave the road we are to follow to me."[14] Sancho's discourse has transgressed from his narrative track to the spatial route of his journey with Don Quixote.

Back on course, Sancho tells of a goatherd who falls in love with a mannish shepherdess and later comes to hate her so much that he decides to migrate to Portugal, whereupon she becomes duly infatuated with him and follows in pursuit. Sancho introduces the characters with a string of dependent clauses in which a name generates a clause starting in the same name and ending in another, and so on without any relative pronouns until Don Quixote again interrupts to ask Sancho to tell his story successively (*seguidamente*) without saying everything twice. Repetition involves needlessly "going over" the same words, retracing the same narrative steps rather than going ahead "followingly."

Don Quixote soon interrupts again to comment on the story, and tells Sancho to "go ahead" with it ("Pasa adelante"). Sancho's narrative traces the flight and hot pursuit of the characters until the goatherd is faced with getting his three hundred goats across the river Guadiana, which can be done only one by one in a tiny fisherman's boat. Sancho's story follows the back-and-forth motions of the boat and requires Don Quixote to keep track of the number of goats that have passed to the other side. "Take it that he got them all across," says Don Quixote, "and don't go coming and going like that, or you won't get them all over in a year." When Don Quixote fails to keep count, the rest of the story automatically deserts Sancho's memory (or so he says), and the narrative comes to an abrupt standstill: "no hay pasar adelante" (there's no going ahead with it).

In this passage, as in nearly all passages where Cervantine characters, narrators, or authors speak or write about narration, the language of commentary represents narration primarily as a kind of journey, i.e, as a process, a going from somewhere to somewhere else. All the typical verbs describing the narrative process, such as *pasar, seguir, proseguir, volver, ir, venir, andar,* and *llegar,* are the prime verbs of motion with regard to the narrative of journeys. One factor strongly favoring the language of motion here—as opposed to static formalist language, for example—is that most commentary on narrative in Cervantes' works occurs in response to stories still in process. Don Quixote's interruptive commentary uses the language of motion to characterize the ongoing narration, but assumes that the telling moves somewhat autonomously with respect to the journey narrated. For him, the story ought to move lightly with regard to detail and advance according to its own criteria as to what should and shouldn't be said; things that happened aren't necessarily worth telling, and monotonous repetitions of events can be passed over in a few words.

Sancho's joke, however, consists in making the movement of narrative so mimetic of the journey narrated that it actually gets caught up in the characters' (or goats') movements and takes over the job of traveling. The story ends up mired in the back-and-forth action of transporting goats: by repeating verbs of going and returning, each applied to a unique event of transportation, the narrator mimes the fisherman's job of getting the goats across so that the story and its journey can go on. The listener (Don Quixote) is given the unwanted task of keeping track of the goats, like the goatherd: thus the listener turns traveler in the narrated as well as the narrative process, but botches the job assigned to him and is denied any further progress in the dual journey.

Much the same language of movement surrounds the telling of another of Sancho's anecdotes (II.31.278–81), this time in the house of the duke and duchess. Both Don Quixote and the stern cleric enjoin Sancho to go ahead ("pasar adelante") with his story, because at the rate he's going on the narrative route ("que llevas camino"), he won't be done in days or even in this lifetime. The irrelevant detail of Sancho's going harvesting somewhere exasperates the cleric, who says: "On your life, son, come back quickly from Tembleque without burying the gentleman and finish your story if you don't want any more funerals."[15] Here again the narrative goes wherever the movement in the tale takes it; the cleric would have Sancho keep to the proper path of the narrative, which ought to move to the crux of the matter without getting sidetracked by digressive movements. As Don Quixote tells the child who narrates the story of Maese Pedro's puppet show, "follow your story in a straight line, and don't get into its curves or transversals."[16] This was to become one of Sterne's favorite topics in *Tristram Shandy.*[17]

Berganza's life story in the *Coloquio de los perros*—a dog's errant adventures and adversities through Andalusia and Castile—elicits similar commentary from Cipión, except that here the routes Berganza travels as wanderer lend their topography to those he travels as narrator, as is evident in the following passages commenting on digression:

> Enough, Berganza; go back to your path and walk.

> Follow your story and don't deviate from the main road with impertinent digressions; in this way, no matter how long it is, you'll finish it quickly.

> I see very well, Berganza, the wide field that opened itself up for you to stretch out your tale, and it seems to me you should leave it as a story of its own. . . .[18]

By way of narrative, Berganza retravels his life's paths and revives the experiences en route, while Cipión, lying next to him, monitors the movement of the peregrine tale. Because the narrative is bound to the journey it recounts, and because the journey traveling keeps shifting ground, the telling is also bound somewhere with the traveling.

If the language of motion tends to characterize discourse in general,[19] it pervades characterizations of narrative even more. As we'll see in the final chapter, this is as much the case with the narrative of invention as it is with the narrative of memory, and hence movement has as much a making as a remaking role with respect to the world and narratable experience. When movement is sustained and varied, as in a journey, narrative more than follows the movements it narrates, it accompanies them, in some sense moves with them. How? One way to answer this is to look into commentary on narrative at critical moments when stories start to stop or switch their attention from one subject to another.

Throughout his novels, Cervantes plays ironically with narrative formulas as immemorial as "Let's leave character X and go back to character Y." Let one example suffice for many. Amidst all the intrigues going on at the inn toward the end of *Don Quixote* I, the innkeeper is attacked by two men he has discovered trying to escape without paying. In the heat of the action, the narrator decides to switch over to another unrelated scene nearby: "But let us leave him there, for someone is bound to help him, or, if not, let him suffer in silence for his rashness in taking on more than his strength warrants; and let us go back fifty paces and see how Don Luis answered the judge, whom we left asking him privately the reason for his traveling on foot in such wretched clothes."[20] Faced with the problem of simultaneous occurrences some distance apart, the narrator opts for alternating between them, that is, for simulating a going from one to the other in the company of whomever he is addressing (e.g., "us"). Since he is able to recover what happened while he was elsewhere, his absence is as relative as his presence: while he feigns being more in one place than another at any given moment, his being there doesn't preclude his later presenting simultaneous action having taken place elsewhere as though he were there too. The formulaic *dejemos/volvamos a* (or *dejemos/vamos a*) turns out to be a device by which the narration can place itself as though within earshot and eyeshot of simultaneously occurring action that has long since happened in different places. In this particular example, the narrator and his audience "move" in the space of the characters but not with them, because it moves back and forth between scenes of action, keeping track of various occurrences at the same time.

Just as Sterne's Tristram Shandy (a self-consciously Cervantine writer) seizes the chance to write the prologue when he finds all his characters occupied in their own concerns (III.20), Cervantes' narrators and their companionship usually "leave" characters when there's nothing more to say about them for the time being—especially when the characters are occupied in some activity such as sleeping, waiting, pining, trying to write, or going off somewhere. By the same token, we "return" to them or "go" to others only when there's something deemed worth saying about them. Thus the temporary abandonment of the innkeeper is rather unusual in this regard, comparable to the moment in Part I when the narrative breaks down at the climax of a duel between Don Quixote and a Basque squire because the "first author" finds nothing more written on the subject; there too "we left" the unresolved action in high suspense (I.9.139). In both cases the comic effect calls attention to the playful artifice of the narration—specifically to the presentation of *ficta* according to the pedestrian norms of knowledge concerning *facta*.

The illusion of "being there" on the fringes of the characters' space implies accompaniment when the locus of "there" moves. Quasi-cinematically, yet brought about by verbs of motion rather than cuts, our simulated movement not only takes us in the blinking of an eye from one scene to another, but keeps pace with characters who are themselves in motion. So it happens, for instance, that the narrator has us leave Don Quixote and "accompany Sancho," who is riding his ass away from the *insula*—and the ensuing narrative certainly conveys a sense of going along with him (II.54.447). Cervantes' narrators nearly always seem to know where they're going, and have no qualms about bringing their "audience" with them at will. Diderot, an innovative inheritor of this sort of narrative play, takes the game further in *Jacques le fataliste,* where the temporary separation of Jacques from his master places the narrator in a predicament as to which of the two characters to accompany. The problem is put to the reader (*lecteur, vous*) as though the latter had any choice in the matter: if you want to follow Jacques in search of the master's purse and watch, the trip may be long and involved and will take you away from the narration of the master's *amours;* if you want to accom-

pany the master, "you will be polite, but very bored." As it turns out, the narrator talks about the master until he thinks we've had enough, then has us
catch up to where Jacques is moving along (59–60).

Although narrative, owing to its intangibility, frequently imitates the space
and movement of what it narrates, it has its own metaphorical space and movement independent in principle from those it represents. To narrate all that
happened in the house of Monipodio, says Berganza, "would be to get into
a labyrinth I wouldn't be able to get out of when I wanted."[21] The image of
the labyrinth is extremely evocative here: the labyrinth would materialize
only in the telling; the narrator would become the traveler of a maze of sequences without any known order or way out. As always in Cervantes' texts,
however, the dominant metaphor for ongoing narrative activity is movement
along terrestrial routes. This normally implies more or less preestablished suc-
cessions of "things" to say, which make up the linear routes of stories; tellers
and their receptive companions pass along them as discursive travelers. Again
and again, characters and unnamed narrators "get to" (by the verb *llegar*) certain "points" in their stories (or other forms of discourse) where they stop
for one reason or another. The arriving is nearly always "here," "at this point,"
implying that "we" too are now "here" together with the commentator of the
narrative. The notion of "point" in conjunction with movement reinforces
the linearity of narrative travel. The verbs *seguir, proseguir,* and *pasar,* often
used with the adverb *adelante,* give a sense of forward motion as people then
go on with their stories.[22] Especially in narratives recounting series of events
that supposedly happened, relevant sequences mark out itineraries which narrators follow or deviate from. Logical discourse also travels paths, as when
Don Quixote tells the priest and barber to accompany him in his reasoning:
"Listen carefully, and come along with me."[23]

Since metaphors of telling as traveling occur as particular instances of speaking and writing as moving, an understanding of narrative's movement depends
on an awareness of verbal discourse's mobility. In Cervantes' novels there is
no end to the variations on speaking as moving along pathways, or of speech
as directed along pathways. The verb *encaminar* and the noun *camino* figure
in a wide range of these, since people habitually put their thoughts, words,
razones, tongues, nonsense (*disparates*), speech (*plática*), prayers, songs, praise,
flattery, and so on en route to somewhere. To where? Toward other people,
God, the devil, etc., or specifically to someone's ears or heart; or toward a
stated purpose such as cursing fate, praying for someone's soul, dishonoring,
advising, giving false hopes, instilling fear, obtaining pleasure, and so forth.
The full formula, though rarely given, would normally have someone put discourse on its way to some addressee (singular or plural, mortal or divine)
toward some intended end. But this is just one formula among many. Speak-

ers and their speech are constantly coming and going in one direction or another, beating around the bush in *rodeos,* losing their way, forgetting where they are, and so on. The word *camino* itself appears with extraordinary frequency and variety of context, even in phrases judging the sense of discourse: when something does or doesn't make sense, it's either on track or goes off track according to common expressions like "(no) llevar camino" and "(no) ir fuera de camino."

In Cervantes' novels, the maps of verbal discourse are graphed largely by analogy to the space of terrestrial travel. Verbal discourse moves in a field of constraints, of sequential choices, of easier and harder ways, of more or less direct routes. Characters and narrators keep to — or go off — the pathways of truth or reason or a virtue such as *honestidad,* or, alternately, move within the confines (*términos*) of such terms. In prescriptive cases like these, pathways are akin to boundaries and interchangeable with them, not only marking out passages of movement but also differentiating zones of space according to their qualitative effects on discursive movement. This bears primarily on what kinds of "things" should or shouldn't be said, and on the corresponding series of choices to be made at every turn. Some of these limits point, albeit very naively, to a couple of Foucault's main groupings of discursive constraints: the prohibited, and the true/false opposition (*Archaeology* 216–19). But on the less naive side, Cervantes' narrators and characters are occasionally astounded at what they don't say, at how much they leave unsaid or refrain from saying. For them, speaking and writing resemble traveling a wilderness of forking paths. Given such an openness, Cide Hamete feels irked at having to confine himself to a definite narrative path (*DQ* II.44.366; cf. *CP* 310). If discourse travels routes, the desired paths may not be apparent, let alone existent.[24]

Narrative movement not only appropriates the sorts of movement articulated by most other forms of verbal discourse but also tends to develop them further. Land travel, especially walking, dominates Cervantes' imagery of narrative movement, as already shown with regard to verbs of motion. Not uncommonly, listeners ask speakers where they're going, where they'll end up, or what they're aiming at.[25] As governor, Sancho tells a tiresome fellow to "get to the point without circumlocutions or sidestreets."[26] To speak frankly or tell a story straight is to speak without *rodeos.*

Stories have steps (*pasos*) with their own measure and rhythm. Cardenio retells his tale "almost in the same words and *pasos*" as before till he "gets to the *paso* of the letter that Don Fernando had found" (*DQ* I.27.332; cf. *DQ* II.20.187; *AL* 164), which is where he broke off the story before. *Pasos* may correspond to words or points or narrative turns or places, but aren't identifiable as any of these: they are an undefined measure of the going.

Even more than retelling stories, reading presupposes the traveling of already existent *caminos* (e.g., *DQ* I.6.119) within books or texts. Don Quixote uses the verb *pasar* (to pass, go over, study) as a reinforcing near synonym of *leer* (to read) in a passage that also refers to the steps (*pasos*) of reading: "Had he read and gone over [the books of chivalry] as carefully as I read and went over them, he would have found at every step . . ." (I.37.459; cf. I.16.202, II.17.163). The word *paso* appears quite commonly with regard to reading and writing. So do expressions referring to writing as going along or deviating from paths of truth, propriety, etc. (e.g., *DQ* I.1.71, I.9.144–45, II.12.123), because, after all, writing plots out the routes that reading will follow. Hence much of the language of movement pertaining to oral narrative applies also to written narrative; and like speakers and listeners, readers and writers are "carried" (*llevados*)—or we might say "driven"—in their respective activities by certain kinds of thoughts, inclinations, and pleasures.

Yet some metaphors of discursive movement belong, if not exclusively to writing, at least more to writing than to speaking. One of these is the recurrent image of the broken thread of a story that is knotted together after an interruption so that the narration or its author can go on (*pasar adelante, proseguir* [*DQ* I.28.344, II.17.164; *CP* 359; cf. *DQ* I.27.334]). Although threads in principle evoke associations with spinning, weaving, and so forth, what these passages emphasize is the pathlike nature of threads—their sinuous linearity and the motion that explicitly takes place along them when the line isn't broken. Threads and narrative paths may well coincide in other ways too: the entwining of fibers in thread and the entanglements of thread suggest equivalents in textile/textual narrative, while lines of cursive handwriting reveal a certain threadlike quality.

Another group of metaphors brings out the openness of writing when its routes aren't predetermined. These include images of large fields in which writers can run freely (e.g., *Gal* 58; *DQ* I.47.566), or of writing as navigating in the open sea (e.g., *Gal* 55, 452; *PS* 162). Unlike the historian Cide Hamete, who complains of having to follow Don Quixote and Sancho around without being allowed to digress into "episodes" of his own (*DQ* II.44.366), writers of certain fictive and poetic genres have a wide range to move about in or to steer their course through.

The sailing metaphor is richly suggestive with its vast horizons, unmarked routes, shifting orientation, companionship, symbolism of flags and mascots, its struggle between human control and natural forces, its pleasures and dangers, and so on. Dante, Ariosto, and Rabelais all use the metaphor very effectively with regard to their own narratives, in ways ranging from the sublime to the parodic.[27] Discourse has its equivalents for all of these aspects of maritime travel. At times discourse even collapses into the terms of the journey it narrates, as when we are told that "it seems that the overturning of the ship overturned, or rather, disturbed the judgment of the author of this history," who loses his bearings, not knowing how to begin a chapter or where it's going to end up (*PS* 162). Just as the dog Berganza mimetically retravels his land routes in narrative, the mind of this historian navigates its own perilous course, being susceptible to the same kinds of mishaps as those it narrates.

These, then, are some metaphors of motion relating to writing.[28] It should be noted that imaginative or inventive writing moves primarily as discursive activity. In contrast, writing as a setting down of things already said or thought "fixes" discourse, immobilizing and preserving it. In this latter sense, writing functions like memory.[29] The associations between memory and writing (or the press) are in fact very pervasive in Cervantes' novels.

As already indicated, a good share of what is considered *discurso* is neither spoken nor written, neither heard nor read. Motion takes place with respect to thoughts, imagination, memory, the soul, and so on. An exhaustive treatment of discourse in motion would focus on all of these types of kinesis. My intention here has been to develop an awareness of discursive movement in view of the fact that, with few exceptions, mainstream literary criticism from Aristotle to the present has dulled our senses with regard to motion and its correlates including process, change, intensity, and dynamism. One way to bring discursive motion into further relief is to see how it functions in relation to the stasis of silence.

Silence

In a climactic scene early in *Persiles y Sigismunda,* the barbarian Bradamiro rashly claims possession of Periandro, whom he believes to be a woman, and declares that Auristela, disguised as a man, is to go free. His arrogance is answered by the barbarian governor, who draws his bowstring to his right ear and lets an arrow fly "with such good aim and such fury that in an instant it reached Bradamiro's mouth and closed it for him, taking the tongue's movement from it and the soul out of it; all those present were amazed, astonished, and dumbfounded."[30] Shooting from the governor's ear to the loudmouth's tongue, the lethal arrow thus travels the same route as the haughty words, but in reverse, and silences Bradamiro by piercing none other than his speech organs. Curiously, of all the things the narrator might have said at this point, he mentions three results which bring together three phenomena so often associated in Cervantes' novels: silence (the mouth closes), immobility (the tongue stops moving), and death (the soul departs). For the briefest moment the only movement seems to be the exit of Bradamiro's soul as all the onlookers are themselves stunned (a volley of three near synonyms nuances their awe) into inaction and speechlessness. A strikingly similar event takes place much later when the young Antonio draws his bow on the lusting enchantress Cenotia; she manages to dodge, but happily the slanderer Clodio happens to enter the room just in time to have the arrow pass through his mouth and tongue and impose "perpetual silence" on him (203).

While silence, immobility, and death often coincide in multiple negativity, their association obviously varies. Whereas death is always shrouded in silence in Cervantes' novels, silence has no definite relation to death as it shifts in essence and meaning according to context: *silencio* and *callarse* (to be silent) are in fact among the richest words in the novels, usually occurring at moments of emotional intensity. There is the silence of *admiratio,* of enchantment, of idyllic stillness, of suspense, of estrangement, of oblivion, of sleep, of death. And there is a wide range of silences having to do with "not saying": the silence of being interrupted by some other intrusive event, of not being allowed to speak, of not wanting or not being able to speak, of not knowing what to say, and so forth. What concerns me here, however, is not silence as such, but its static and sometimes deathly qualities.

Just as narrators speak of death in terms of silence, they also use the imagery of death to speak of silence in common expressions like "sepultado en silencio" (buried in silence) and in the notion held by lovers that silence kills: not only does it kill words ("My passionate lady, don't let your words die in your mouth," says Auristela to the pent-up Sinforosa [*PS* 170]) but also those afflicted by uncommunicated love, as it constricts the lifeline of desire. The lady Altisidora, returning from a feigned death, tells the professed object of her love, Don Quixote, that her soul burst because of her silence and she lost her life as a result (II.70.565). Her tomb, says the narrator, was a place where "silence itself kept itself silent" (II.69.558). Time and again in the novels, the imagery of silence and death converges with the domains of imprisonment, sleep, and oblivion, all of which suppress motion.

Auristela's words to Sinforosa are worth looking at more closely for the underlying conceptual alliances they reveal:

> don't let your words die in your mouth . . . for when misfortunes are told to others, they may at least find some relief, if not a cure. If your passion comes from love, as I have good reason to believe, then there's no doubt in my mind that you're made of flesh—though you seem to be of alabaster—just as I also know our souls are always in continual motion. . . . I too am a woman; I have my desires, which for my soul's honor haven't yet left my mouth, though they might well do so as signs of fever; but in the end they'll surely break through no matter how opportune or impossible they may be, and, if only in my last will and testament, I'll make known the cause of my death.[31]

This is one of several passages in the *Persiles* referring expressly to the continual motion of the soul—a motion concurrent with being alive. As long as the soul is in motion, there is desire, and there is *discurso*. The image of alabaster, as opposed to the mobile vitality of flesh and blood, is one of many stone and statue metaphors in Cervantes' prose, all of which evoke physical immobility together with either an absence or a paralysis of desire, thought, speech, passion, and the like. Although *discurso* is in the first instance the movement of thought, whether uttered or not, it acts here in conjunction with desire to force silence to give way to verbal expression. Desire and *discurso* produce an inner turmoil or *turbación* that strives for a communicative outlet. When silence prevails in containing these forces, it holds the discourse of desire to a deep interiority or kills it in the very site of its expressive formation, the mouth; and here as elsewhere, repressive silence can even be fatal to those who suffer it, putting an end to life, spiritual motion, desire, and *discurso*.

Silence quells all the sorts of motion that speech activates. Channeled from some interior chasm or organ, words often go only as far as the throat, which forms a knot, or the voice, which suddenly fails, gets lost, or gets stuck in the throat, or the tongue, which gets bitten, stuck, paralyzed, tied, or reined in, or the mouth itself, which closes off access to the public world outside it. The imagery of immobile statues often coincides with moments of speechlessness. There is thus a double stoppage here since the paralysis of one or another of the speech organs blocks the passage of words physically "moving" toward enunciation. More significantly, the *discursive* movement of speech never even gets under way if blocked by silence; or when silence intervenes at some point, this movement is literally brought to a standstill, inter-rupted. If to speak is to go somewhere, to be silent is not to go anywhere, and to stop speaking is to stop moving along the routes of discourse.[32]

Even silence, which immobilizes so much else, sometimes moves in a singular way: it spreads among people, or in a space. The typical verb here is *extenderse*. The negativity of silence at once becomes apparent, however, since it implies the spreading of nonspeaking, or the immobilizing of everything that might make sound, even the air: "A mute silence then spread among all the people, so quiet that the air scarcely moved" (*PS* 214). Like debts, utopias, and other negativities, silence takes on a chimeric presence, substance, and agency, but its movement is no more than a nonmovement of everything else. In other ways, however, silence as agent takes on more substance in its own right. To say that silence kills is to refer to an entire psychology of inner turmoil and repression. To say that silence speaks, as sometimes happens in Cervantes' writings, is to point beyond the apparent paradox to the reality that silence can reveal thoughts and intentions as well as if not better than words—

silence is negative gesture allowing one to sense what won't or can't be rendered into language.

Desire Mobilized

> y si quiero subir a la alta cumbre,
> a cada paso espántanme en la vía
> exemplos tristes de los que han caído;
> sobre todo, me falta ya la lumbre
> de la esperança, con que andar solía
> por la oscura región de vuestro olvido.
> Garcilaso de la Vega, Sonnet 38

What desire "is"

From Plato to Lacan, the Western philosophical tradition has defined desire primarily in terms of lack. In several of Plato's dialogues, Socrates examines the peculiarities of desire, which is most often for something or someone that is not in one's presence or possession. Desire is inhabited and motivated by absence, by incompleteness; the presence or possession of what is desired nullifies desire. With some textual justification,[33] this is usually assumed to be Plato's last word on the question of desire. It is also a dominant mode of desire in much of Western literature.[34] Yet in Plato there are variant portrayals of desire — e.g., as horses that impel the charioteer (the governing part of the soul) forward, or as a flowing medium, or a powerful attraction even in the presence of what is desired, or a motion that varies in pace and force.

The orthodox concept of desire in terms of lack, governed as it is by the "here/not here" and "have/not have" oppositions, has suppressed desire's dynamism and heterogeneity and removed it from its vital processes. This is not to say that such terms as lack, absence, gap, and difference are irrelevant, but rather that there is nothing fixed about them, that by themselves they deactivate and detemporalize desire, and most important, that they offer no definition of desire as experience. Lack indicates little if anything about the qualities and intensities, let alone the means and processes, of such experience. My aim here is to reconsider the general problematic of "desire" in light of the actual language of desire in Cervantes' novels, where images of movement articulate the dynamics of desiring.

No doubt deriving in large part from received notions of what desire is and how it functions, discourse about desires constitutes a central leitmotiv in all of Cervantes' novels. My concern is not with influence or originality, but with how the question of desire might be opened up by delving into Cervantes' language of desire. In many instances, of course, the workings of desire may diverge from the language in which such desire is expressed. There may be little difference, for example, between the imagery of desire used by male as opposed to female characters in the novels, yet their experience of desire diverges considerably.[35] Though the specific language of desire by no means accounts for all the workings of desire, it does to a large extent give a profile of the modalities in which desire is thought. To ignore this language, as René Girard does in *Deceit, Desire, and the Novel,* is in large part to miss the peculiar ways in which writers and characters configure desire. More on this later.

Tirsi, a shepherd in *La Galatea,* speaks of love in the following way: "Love is truly the father of desire, and among other definitions that are given of love, here is one. Love is that first alteration we feel in the mind owing to the appetite that moves us and draws us to itself, and delights and pleases us. This pleasure engenders movement in the soul, a movement called desire. In sum, desire is movement of the appetite with respect to what is loved, and a wanting of what is possessed; its object is goodness. . . ."[36] He is referring here not to desire in general but to amorous desire—desire engendered by love (hence the paternal metaphor, in accordance with the masculine *amor*). The prime mover is love, characterized as the initial *mutación*. The locus of this stirring or alteration is the mind. The feeling works through "appetite," a word that evokes hunger and thirst and their demands for gratification if not indulgence. Amorous appetite moves us (*nos conmueve*) and draws us to itself, as thought it were situated both within us and outside us in the object of desire, thus impelling and attracting us at the same time, while "we" acquiesce as passive but delighted subjects. The resultant pleasure in turn engenders a movement of desire in the soul. Thus, rather than initiating this process, desire issues from it as movement; it is the movement of appetite in relation to what is loved.

This "definition" of desire undoubtedly idealizes the amorous process in its own ways (distinguishing various agents, situating them in the mind and soul, casting their supposed causes and effects in terms of engendering, valorizing it all positively, and so on), and could be accused of putting the cart (love) before the horse (desire). Yet the notion of (falling in) love as alteration, and desire as movement, is critical to the conceptualization of desire.[37]

First, desire is an activation of the "soul," an activity expressed metaphorically as movement and felt in certain ways by the lover as movement. No matter how the relationship between mind, soul, and body might be conceived here, the motion of desire obviously affects all three.[38] Desire acts as it were of its own accord, moving through the multiple agencies of the self and orienting them toward the desired: it sets up currents of motion both *within* the self and *between* the self and the desired. It acts on the emotions, on the faculties (*potencias*) of the soul, on the imagination, and mobilizes them in the direction of the desired.

Second, if desire is "movement," then absence and lack define desire no more than difference (or any of its permutations) defines language and discourse. Just as difference is a condition of language, absence and lack often set the stage for desire's activity. As Tirsi puts it, "desire *presupposes* the lack of what is desired . . ." (*Gal* 313; my emphasis). But difference says nothing about what *happens* in discourse, and lack says nothing about what *happens* in desire. Words like *apetito* and *objeto* certainly indicate a wanting and a distance between desire and its "object." Yet appetite too is thought of as movement, and the object is the goal of movement.

This is entirely consonant with Renaissance erotology. In *Dello appetito* (ca. 1454), Marsilio Ficino defines appetite, widely conceived to include the natural elements, as "an impulse and inclination moving the nature to unite itself with that thing which corresponds to it"; the "thing" toward which movement takes place is the "object." Paul Kristeller notes that appetite and movement are interchangeable terms for Ficino (178–80). Judging by their terms and topics, Cervantes' shepherds would seem to have taken their language of love and desire straight out of treatises resembling those of Ficino, León Hebreo, Pietro Bembo, and Giovanni Pico della Mirandola, or out of literary works drawing from such treatises. The pastoralists, however, regard movement differently from the way Ficino does. For the Neoplatonist Ficino, all movement, and consequently all desire, ultimately yields to a blissful state of rest: "For rest is more perfect than movement, and for the sake of rest the individual things are moved. Moreover, the body of the world will be most beautiful in that most perfect state" (quoted in Kristeller 189). The raison d'être of movement and desire turns out to be their annulment in rest and fulfillment. Even if, as Edgar Paiewonsky-Conde infers with regard to Ficino (78), repose and satisfaction have to give way again to a new movement of desire, rest is the value-laden term, the be-all and end-all of existence.

This mode of thinking echoes faintly in some of Cervantes' passages referring to God as the ultimate locus of rest for souls in continual motion, as well as in passages praising peaceful ways of life—a sixteenth-century commonplace. Yet the ultimate repose in divinity lies outside the scope of Cervantes' novels, which deal with the perpetual wanting and striving of this life and, apart from a few passages in the *Persiles,* show little direct interest in the life beyond desire, or in life without desire. (Even in the opening chapter of Augustine's *Confessions,* the heart's future repose in God signals the afterlife, while its restlessness is a condition of this life.) In Cervantes' novels, the question as to whether rest is preferable to motion simply doesn't arise because it's a nonissue: the soul's continual motion propelled by desire is a condition, perhaps *the* condition, of being in the world; perfect repose has no place here. Often fascinated and delighted with the manifestations of motion, Cervantes' characters and narrators, given the choice, might show themselves less inclined toward Ficino than toward the mercurial Tristram Shandy when he says in a very different context "that so much of motion, is so much of life, and so much of joy—and that to stand still, or get on but slowly, is death and the devil—" (Sterne VII.13.471).

Tirsi's enigmatic reference to desire as "a wanting of what is possessed" touches on the topical question that introduces León Hebreo's influential *Dialoghi d'amore* (written ca. 1502): how desire relates to love, and how each of them relates to possession and lack. Tirsi's statement suggests that desire can be active even in the presence and possession of the desired, implying in turn that absence and lack are not necessary conditions of desire. Other statements by Tirsi contradict this by affirming that desire and possession are mutually exclusive, though love and possession may coincide (308, 313). Besides the changeable love/desire relationship, various factors complicate the issue here: (1) presence and absence aren't stable categories any more than "here" and "elsewhere" are, admitting instead both a relative shifting and an infinite gradation between them; (2) possession and nonpossession admit similar shifts and gradations; (3) presence and absence don't necessarily correspond to possession and nonpossession, respectively; (4) each of these oppositions may be experienced as an infiltration of one term into the other whereby both are perceived simultaneously; and (5) these oppositions have practically no meaning at all until the object and field of desire are specified. Given these fluid conditions, "desire" may behave, or move, in many ways.

In *Cratylus* (419e–420a), Socrates hits upon a partial solution to the problem by distinguishing two kinds of desire: *himeros* (etymologized as desire flowing like a stream) is active as "violent attraction of the soul" in the presence of the desired, while *pothos* (etymologized as desire for what is in another place) is felt in the absence of the desired. This is common usage, he says. Both terms figure movement within them, as do hundreds of others including *eros* (etymologized as flowing in from without), thus exemplifying the "misguided" Heraclitan principles of movement and change held by the primeval word maker. Nearly homogenized in translation, *himeros* and *pothos* reappear in a key passage of *Phaedrus* (253c–256e), where the desiring soul is compared to a trinity composed of a charioteer and two powerful steeds, one of them dark, unruly, and id-like. *Pothos* is desire felt in the absence of the loved one, while *himeros* is desire felt as a flowing stream leading to an erotic crescendo. This distinction within "desire" conveniently accommodates the reality of presence and absence, of possession and lack, within the experience of desire without forcing us to make idle choices concerning what desire "is." Furthermore, even in the case of *pothos,* desire isn't lack or absence, but rather a spiritual motion experienced under the conditions of lack and/or absence. The forceful image of the horses and charioteer with their disproportionate impulsions and harnessed energies applies to both *pothos* and *himeros.* I might add that these aren't the only words translated indiscriminately as desire in Plato's writings: *epithumia,* for one, pertains to diverse domains within "desiring."[39] Perhaps "desire" (or *deseo, desejo, desiderio, désir,* etc.) deceptively labels incompatible phenomena with a single word.

Having studied at famous academies, the self-made shepherd Tirsi is conversant with the "ancient philosophers" and their theories of love and desire. Although he begins his long speech by differentiating love from desire in the manner of the *Dialoghi d'amore* (you can love what you have but not desire it, and you can desire what you don't love, e.g., your enemy's death), he most often treats love and desire as interchangeable, referring to them as primary movement—"this first movement—love or desire, call it as you will—."[40] In the tradition of the *cuestión de amor* (Lowe, M. G. Randel), the speech forms part of a debate with the loveless Lenio, who vilifies the same kind of love and desire that Tirsi celebrates. Though they espouse antithetical views of love, they agree in so far as their language of desire shares an obsession with metaphors of movement throughout. This is also the case in *La Galatea* as a whole, and in all of Cervantes' novels for that matter: rarely is there a mention of desire that doesn't implicate movement in one way or another.

In all the passages in *La Galatea* and the *Persiles* which refer to the continual movement of the soul, whose center is God, this movement is one of desire.[41] In *La Galatea,* the topos emerges precisely in Tirsi's discourse on love and desire: "But our Creator, seeing that it is the very nature of our soul to be always in perpetual *movement and desire,*" willed that certain reins such as marriage be placed on our desiring of transitory things such as human beauty.[42] Book III of the *Persiles* opens with similar words, already cited, for which the stated pretext is Arnaldo's changeable desires (275). Arnaldo echoes the formula to Auristela, but puts her instead of God in the center of his soul's errant desire (422). Finally, Auristela herself expresses the idea twice, once with regard to amorous desires in particular, and the other time with regard to the infinite desires of all kinds that form a chain leading ultimately to heaven or hell (170, 458). Desire's movement is of an originary nature: as one character says in *La Galatea,* "desire" (which for him is synonymous with love) "is the beginning and origin from which all of our passions proceed, like any stream from its spring."[43]

Desires in Cervantes' novels are usually impulsive, quasi-autonomous agents with wills of their own. Highly responsive to changing realities, but also inventive of realities and nonrealities, they are born or awakened, they grow or diminish, they can die and even be revived. Some are capricious and short-lived, others resolute and enduring. Some kill or hinder each other, others proliferate, and yet others change. Frequently they are identified in the singular, but they also form loose collectivities. Both between and within people, desires enter into conflict but also accumulate and collude, as the case may be. Though they sometimes feel like ice, their natural element is fire. They have varying force, weight, impetus, and heat. Adjectives qualify them typically as good, pure, chaste, enamored, curious; or as foolish, lightweight, impertinent; or as bad, impure, libidinous, lascivious, lewd (Turks and barbarians have more than their fair share of this last group). Desires affect the experience of time to the extent that there is no such thing as an atemporal desire, or desireless time. If desires seem to have their objects in people or things, their real object is obviously an activity or relationship involving people or things. Most often they are amorous (in the novels), but they operate in every other domain of wanting as well, including the commonly stated desire to *know*—to know who strangers are, or to know what happens in stories, and so forth. Desires to *see* something or someone and to *go* somewhere also animate the pages of these novels. Desires can be located in the desiring subject or in the desired object, or between them. Characters live by desire and sometimes die because of it too. All of these are among the attributes and vicissitudes of desire, along with others discussed in relation to *discurso*.

How desire "moves"

Above all, desires *move* and *motivate* in Cervantes' novels. So do other closely related terms, such as (erotic) love, which tends to converge with desire or complement it. How then do desires move? We've already seen various instances of desire's movement as inner agitation (e.g., *turbación*) and as the undefined movement of the soul. What this sort of movement emphasizes in fact is the continual activity and changeability of desire. The moving of desire doesn't always imply the going of desire.

But desire most often does go places, and it does so by various means. At times it soars away on its own wings, flying as far and as fast as the imagination lets it, and not without danger (*Gal* 289, 69; *DQ* I.33.406). This of course is a familiar image that goes back to Greek antiquity, especially in connection with *eros.* In *Don Quixote,* the servant Leonela says that love "sometimes flies and sometimes walks. With one person it runs, with another creeps; . . . in a single instant it starts on the race of desires, and in the same instant concludes and ends it. . . ."[44] Movement offers representational analogues for the experience of love and desire in terms of pace, intensity, relationship, and so on.

The space in which desire moves tends to be as autonomously allegorical as desire itself—a space populated with other animated abstractions such as love, disdain, hope, fear, jealousy, intention, will, pleasure, beauty, deception, etc., all of which move about, and define their relationship to desire in terms of movement. Proximity and distance, togetherness and separation are all spatial conditions that movement can alter or maintain. An example from the shepherdess Marcela in *Don Quixote:* "But supposing that both beauties should run equally, desires need not necessarily run equally; . . . for if all beauties were to enamor and make conquests, people's wills would wander confused and astray, not knowing which one they would end up with; because as beauties are infinite, desires must also be infinite."[45] Here, beauties, desires, and wills all move—like species of animals responsive to the movements of other species. Quite obviously, parallel motion expresses sameness or compatibility, unequal motion expresses difference, and deviation expresses disarray and confusion.

Elsewhere, the companionship of two different sorts of things expresses their concurrence or association: "desires and deceit [*engaños*] usually walk together," the movements of Arnaldo's desires "were in stride with those of reason," "unrestrained lust carries ardor and desires with it," "love and fear go about in a pair, for wherever you turn your head you'll see them together," "love and finery walk the same road" (*PS* 252, 137, 124, 194; *DQ* I.11.159).[46] In this all-too-human landscape there are scarcely any people to be seen apart from sufferers or observers of their own affects. More than anything else, the subjectivity of usually one or two people constitutes the vulnerable space in which this movement takes place. Movement characterizes relationships between affective agents and at the same time adumbrates, if ever so sketchily, the kind of topography in which they are supposed to occur.

Perhaps the most common image with respect to mobile desires is that of their being en route toward some end ("se encaminan a un fin," and variations)—where the verb *encaminarse* contains within it the noun *camino* and the verb *caminar*. Since a similar formula applies to discourse, it's not surprising that desires and discourse can combine their movements, as in the case of an enamored character in *Don Quixote* (Lotario), whose "desires and writings were directed to her" ("a ella se encaminaban" (I.34.422; cf. *DD* 228; *CEx* 114]). But the movements of desires tend to be more tortuous than those of limited discourse channeled to someone in particular, and their goals out of immediate reach. Desires wend their way toward their objects, ends, intents, etc. By this metaphor, the fulfillment of desire is the destination, and desire is the "thing" that moves, or the impulse to move, or the movement itself. The route is the method (*meta-hodos*), the "way" by which desire sets about getting to the intended goal. Traveling desires can actually go astray,[47] losing track of their original intentions or erring in their approach. The route itself is typically beset with obstacles (*estorbos*) and dangers that offer resistance to wayfaring desires, which don't always get to where they're going. A shepherd in *La Galatea* warns his own amorous thought—his desire—that it may die a glorious death along the way (70).

Because desires are inclined to get out of hand, they need to be kept within limits and boundaries. Here again, the kinds of expressions that refer to the restraints of discourse also apply to the limits of desire: "tener a raya," "tener por término," "contenerse en los límites de," "sin salir de," etc. The limits are likely to be allegorized moral terms. It seems to me significant, however, that in the case of several important female characters (Marcela, Camila, and Leonora), the boundaries of their living space are also said to be the boundaries of their thought and desire: a valley, and a house (*DQ* I.14.188, I.33.416; *CEx* 106).

These are among the primary ways in which quasi-autonomous desire moves. Other sorts of movement in its repertoire could be singled out, of course, not least of all the more regulated movements of constant desires. The flow of a river expresses this, as does heavenly motion. Auristela rightly "imagined herself to be the peg of [Periandro's] wheel of fortune and the sphere of his desires' movement" (*PS* 473). Transcendent love and desire either move in such rhythmic patterns, or they don't move at all, as when Periandro, in a passage reminiscent of Shakespeare's sonnet 116, speaks of destined love—as opposed to the inferior elective love—as being always in its place, an ever-fixèd mark (*PS* 185; also *EI* 270). Not surprisingly, an absence of love or desire likewise produces images of stasis, such as that of the rock unmoved by waves or winds symbolizing the will of characters unmoved by the desires of others (*EI* 275; *LV* 52).

Another major mode of desire's movement is transitive: desires move people to do their dictates. One of the main verbs for this setting-in-motion is none other than *mover*, "to move"; another is *incitar*, "to incite." The loveless Lenio uses both in this interesting passage: "every time the desire for something flares up in our hearts, it moves us immediately to go after that thing and look for it; and as we go and look, desire leads us to a thousand chaotic ends. It is this desire that incites a brother to solicit the abominable embraces of the sister he loves. . . ."[48] Everywhere in the novels, desires or other reified motives "move" people to action. People then put desires into effect ("poner en efeto"), as though they were in control as the movers of desire, but this reversal turns out to be illusory: in one way or another, their desires drive them to put desires into effect. Don Quixote, for instance, finds himself both transported and directive in this circuit of motivation: "carried away by the strange pleasure he derived from these agreeable thoughts, he hastened to translate his desires into action."[49]

As in the case of Don Quixote here, motivation is habitually expressed in terms of the conveyance of desire: by means of the verbs *llevar* and *traer,* specific desires lead, guide, take, bring, or carry people to certain situations or actions. At times desires become explicitly vehicular, having sails, currents, wheels, or reins. Whoever experiences such desires becomes a passenger on desires' journeys to their ends. Hence the active part of desiring is embodied in some reified force which takes you along with it in a temporal space defined by changing relationships and activities. These propelling desires recognize no bounds of selfhood, coming as though from without and yet from within, intimate and alien at the same time. Without them you might not get where you want to go, because this "where" is their destination, and they are your wanting.

As hinted at above, the transitive causality is often reversed; people move desires rather than the other way around. Especially prominent is the verb *llevar,* which has people carry their desires with them. The main interest of this expression is perhaps that, unlike verbs that might express having or possessing desires, *llevar* implies that the bearers of desire are mobile. Otherwise it seems to matter little whether desires motivate or are moved.[50]

Desire motivates in compelling ways. Its "force" is strange and at times irresistible. Its "impetus" combines force and movement, carrying people along with it. Its autonomous will subtly guides thoughts on their way and dictates the movements of those who desire. The heat of its fire drives people on to action. How? The narrator of *Las dos doncellas* strikingly compares beauty's effect on the desiring soul to the lighting of gunpowder; and gunpowder's purpose, of course, is to propel (221–22; cf. *FS* 94). A loss of heat implies a loss of mobility, as occurs in the *Persiles* when a pair of lovers become hermits on an island, burying "the fire in ice" and living for ten years "in peace and love, like two movable statues" (*PS* 264).

To say that desire is the lifeblood of every one of Cervantes' novels—that desire sets them going and keeps them going in their macro- and micro-movements until it resolves much of its disruptiveness in marriage, death, disease, knowledge, etc.—may seem all too obvious if not entirely meaningless. After all, what novels aren't somehow motivated by desire? And yet some novels are more charged with desire than others, and those of Cervantes tend to be very highly charged. If you were to ask who has desires, for what or whom, in what circumstances, how these desires manifest themselves, how they're pursued, whether they're fulfilled, and so on, you could sketch a fairly distinctive profile of any novel, or of the loose agglomeration of Cervantes' novels (not to mention the plays or poems), showing evident individual and generic variations among them. Desire appears explicitly at crucial moments at the beginning of Don Quixote, precisely when both the knight and his squire, with different desires, initiate their errant quest. Often "the desire came" to Don Quixote to take up the pen and finish—or perhaps prolong—the books of unending adventure, but he resolves to take up arms instead, for analogous purposes (I.1.72–74). Before Sancho Panza even opens his mouth in the novel, we are told of Don Quixote's promise to him of an *insula*, and without farewell he abandons his family and village "with great desire to see himself soon governor of the *insula*" (I.7.127). In all its protean guises, desire reappears countless times thereafter to keep the characters and the novel in motion. All fifteen novels—the three long and twelve short ones—delineate their own sorts of motivating desires.

Thus far we've seen some of the ways in which desire agitates, goes from place to place, accompanies, transports, and motivates. One further modality of desire is its spatialization—as territory, or route, or destination. At first glance such metaphors would appear to fix desire in some kind of figured space and deprive it of movement. What they actually do, however, is transfer movement mainly back onto the desirers themselves, who then move with reference to the rather shifty space of desire.

Territorialized desire amounts to little more than a small and anomalous set of metaphors whose recurrent image is the abyss or labyrinth of desires (*Gal* 247; *PS* 170, 175; *DQ* II.7.89; cf. *DQ* I.33.403; *AL* 143). Drawing from a mass of associations relating to infernal worlds, this suggestive image magnifies desiring into a vast space inhabited by a host of desires, which seem to haunt the place and thereby constitute its locality; these are, after all, abysses and labyrinths *of* desires, and wouldn't be anything without desires. People somehow find themselves in abysses and try to get out of them. Hence it's not desires but people (e.g., I, you, she, he) who travel about in this territory that is theirs and not theirs, a confusing space zoned with different desires not necessarily reconciled to each other. The "I" that identifies itself with the moving locus of thinking, feeling, doing, and wanting acts as an animate wanderer in a seductive labyrinthine expanse made to accommodate all the desirous alterity that the "I" has to contend with. Metaphors like these, then, bring about the simultaneous mobilization and spatialization of a dual self, as occurs also in other writers of the period, most notably Teresa de Jesús (the personified soul moves about within the spatialized chambers of the soul) and Juan de la Cruz. By emphasizing motion within inner topographies, they also bear some resemblance to certain twentieth-century models of the psyche, most notably Freud's.

Desire as destination or as route likewise involves the movement of desirers or their surrogates (their words, their hopes, their hearts, etc.), but this movement tends to be much less confused or aimless: its goals are known, and there are usually ways to get to them. The desirer here doesn't try helplessly to escape a world of anonymous desires, but to "move" along paths leading to the realization of specific desires. Whether desires are means or ends, paths or goals, is largely a matter of emphasis. Paths, after all, have ends. One common expression with many variants, "llegar al fin de su(s) deseo(s)" (to arrive at the end of one's desires), presupposes a pathway *of* desire conducive to some kind of fulfillment. Rarely is there any indication as to whether the implied *camino* is a pathway "of desire" only because it leads there, or because the pathway and the traveling along it also participate already in the benefits of desire.

As destination, desire inheres in a "place" or in its own "object" located in such a "place." Besides *llegar,* "to arrive," several verbs express transitively the enjoyment or possession of desire, including *conseguir, cumplir, alcanzar, lograr* (to obtain, fulfill, reach, achieve), of which only *alcanzar* necessarily implies motion—a motion as varied as the English "reach." It's not at all unusual, however, to find these verbs used in conjunction with motion, particularly along routes:[51] in order to do whatever you're going to do with your desires, you first have to get to where they are. This may mean knowing how to fly or navigate or get to places by land, depending on whether the desired place is heaven, a seaport, or some terrestrial haven (*PS* 191; *Gal* 381, 204, 248). In the case of pathways, some lead you there, others don't (*AL* 159): the terrain is crisscrossed with potential courses of action.

The transitive verbs mentioned above all treat desires as their "objects," as though desires were things existing outside of the desiring subject. This could no doubt be explained in more modern terms as the work of cathexis, whereby desire becomes embodied, objectified, in other people and in things, taking on the contours and properties of what they embody. Something like this seems to happen to desires in Cervantes' novels. The desired thing ("la cosa deseada") becomes the desire itself, which can as such be reached, attained, obtained, possessed, etc. The verb *alcanzar* plays an especially important role in the attainment of desires in various senses: characters reach for desires (as though for fruit or some other coveted object), they overtake or catch up to evasive desires, and they arrive at desires dwelling in places. In amorous relations in particular, the objectification of desire means that desire comes to inhabit the loved one and even become the loved one. But no matter how exteriorized desires may be, possessive adjectives still lay claim to desires: they are your/my/his/her/their/our desires. Desiring then involves imagining some sort of conjugation of the desiring subject and the desired object in which desires in their differential aspects occupy both places at once.

This is not so farfetched when one considers how a lover's soul—or, as is just as common in Cervantes' texts, *half* a lover's soul—is said to reside in the beloved. Souls and desires seem to follow the same logic, and could at times be alternate names for the same phenomenon, or at least companions in movement. The language of love, in which souls and desires tend to be protagonists, often expresses being in love as moving outside of oneself, where the "I" and "myself" are disjunctive and alienated from each other. Desires and souls are much more likely to go with the mobile "I" than stay behind with the abandoned "myself." The shepherd Elicio sings, "I am far from and near myself . . . I go up to the heavens and down to the abyss."[52] In a similar vein, the shepherdess Theolinda recounts: "I don't know how in so short a time I changed into another being from the one I had, because I no longer lived in myself but in Artidoro—for this is the name of the half of my soul I'm looking for—wherever I turned my eyes I thought I saw his figure. . . ."[53] There is nothing unusual in such formulations. In these and various other ways, love and desire confuse the boundaries between subject and object, and between self and other, often dividing the soul into two in a movement that seeks to incorporate part of the self into the object of its desire, and then bring the parts together somehow in a more inclusive alliance.

What happens where some kind of desiring is clearly going on but where the term "desire" (or "love" or any other equivalent) is either absent or has no autonomous role? Several of the kinds of motion I've discussed so far can take place without the agency or spatialization of reified desires. In the absence of the auxiliary term "desire," lovers may be motivated directly, as it were, by their beloveds. Auristela says she lives and moves for or because of Periandro (*PS* 461); similarly, a character in *La ilustre fregona* sings of Costanza as the "primer moble," or *primum mobile,* who carries the fate of many behind her (171). In both cases, people's amorous motives are embodied in the loved one, who then becomes the lover's mover.

In the absence of desires moving autonomously in an allegorized space of selfhood and interpersonal relations, the desiring subject and desired object move in relation to each other: one or the other moves, or both do. They do so in a space that may simulate lived space but which is essentially the psychic space of human relationships, where close and far, coming and going, flying and walking, fast and slow, and so on, are gauged in terms of the kinds and intensities of people's affects with regard to what they desire. One person may flee from, pursue, lose sight of, catch up to, enter into, withdraw from, or approach another (e.g., *Gal* 89; *PS* 141; *Git* 86, 103; *DD* 217) according to how they perceive their changing relations. In the same vein, the countess Trifaldi in *Don Quixote* says that "my great ignorance and little caution opened the way [*camino*] and cleared the path [*senda*] for the steps of Don Clavijo" (II.38.334).

In many poems especially, novelistic characters express their amorous experience in terms of lone journeys through difficult waters or terrain toward destinations such as harbors and shelters that somehow symbolize togetherness with the loved one. They often lose their bearings, their way, their control, and even their hope; they "err" (*errar* [*Gal* 366]) from the way. Some don't know where they're coming from or where they're going. The goal is usually to get "there," but at times it seems that being on the way and following a guiding light is good enough (*Gal* 338, 366; *DQ* I.34.423–24, I.43.521–23).

Finally, eroticism too converts its activities into journeys and traveled topographies, even when desire isn't reified as such.[54] In a moment of indelicacy, the lascivious Rosamunda speaks of sexual union in terms of two sorts of traveling: horse riding and navigating. On the grounds that knowledge and experience (like those of a rider or pilot) are better for the bride than is ignorance, she defends the custom whereby the groom's male kin have sexual rights to the bride before he does. Her words are to be viewed as scandalous, of course, revealing from the outset what sort of person she is (*PS* 117). But it should be noted that her analogies aren't out of line with images in erotic poetry in Cervantes' time, where coitus (consider the etymology) is repeatedly referred to as traveling *caminos,* riding horses, and sailing ships (Alzieu 31, 40, 79, 184, 198, 213, 214, 236, 296). In one burlesque poem, in fact, characters with erotic names undertake an impossible quest in an equally eroticized geography (Alzieu 296–98).

As an ensemble of means by which desire is represented, the language of movement has its limitations, too, primarily in the fact that it doesn't account directly for the social complexity of desire. It largely suppresses the roles that others play—as intermediaries, rivals, obstructors, sanctioners, distractors, advisers, participants, paradigms, and so forth—both in giving value to objects and hence making them desirable and in affecting the processes of desiring. René Girard's influential thesis on the "triangularity" of desire, on the contrary, does attempt to explain the role of others. His point of departure is none other than a quotation in which Don Quixote speaks of Amadís as the supreme model of knight-errantry. Having established Amadís as the one who "mediates" Don Quixote's desire by functioning as a model and thereby "choosing" his objects of desire for him, Girard tries to show that Don Quixote, by initially putting the idea of the *ínsula* into Sancho's head, mediates Sancho's desire in exactly the same way. The figure which describes this, he says, is the isosceles triangle. He goes on to discuss love triangles in similar terms, referring to the rival as the mediator. The novelistic truth ("vérité romanesque") of mediated desire supersedes the romantic lie ("mensonge romantique") of the straight line between desiring subject and desired object (1–52).

Yet in the language of movement, to which Girard pays no attention, there are no such straight lines of desire. Although this language does suppress the roles of others by representing desire in a field in which relations between subject and object predominate, it figures the social context into the landscape and into the process of movement: hence the indirect routes, the difficulties, obstructions, deviations, favorable and contrary forces, and so on. Instead of bringing out the social complexity of desire, Girard's model oversimplifies desire beyond recognition, forcing the roles of others, which are far more diverse than he acknowledges, into a Procrustean triangle which in fact fits only the classic "love triangle." As Deleuze and Guattari put it, "Desire is not a form, but a procedure, a process" (*Kafka* 8): desire moves.

According to the language of movement, the dynamism of desiring sets desires or desirers in motion and charges the surrounding space as a field of psychic energy. It does so whether or not "desires" as such are reified into moving agents or into the space in which such motion takes place. Nowhere is desiring a static image of lack, a mere difference.

It often does presuppose lack, however. This, as noted, is the basis of León Hebreo's initial distinction between desire and love: Philo defines desire as "an affect of the will aimed at the coming to be or coming to be ours of a thing we judge good and have not," and love as "an affect of the will to enjoy through union the thing judged good" (12). Yet in the third dialogue, Philo emphatically annuls the distinction by arguing that love, too, uncannily involves lack: "Not the present possession, but its continuation, is lacking" (Hebreo 241–46; Nelson 86–87). Again and again, the interlocutors of the *Dialoghi* refer to both love and desire as motion—the very same motion, as it turns out: "And although desire is motion, it is the motion of the soul towards the object of desire as love is the motion of the soul towards the beloved, and pleasure is the origin of this motion we call love and desire" (Hebreo 245). Both are motion, and both presuppose lack, a lack which means present or future nonpossession and which may be felt even more in the presence than in the absence of the desired.

Cervantes' narrators and characters are of several minds when it comes to comparing love and desire, but mostly agree that lack generates desire. Preciosa cautions Andrés in *La gitanilla:* "when [the will] comes up against obstacles, it senselessly hurls itself after what it desires, and thinking it will come upon the bliss it imagines, it lands instead in the hell of disappointment. If it attains what it desires, the desire diminishes with the possession of the desired object. . . ."[55] Although God created human nature perfect, says the narrator of the *Persiles,* we find in it a lack which will always be there as long as we desire (176; cf. *Gal* 313; *DQ* I.33.403, I.42.519; *CEx* 125; *SJ* 2:30). A person enjoying the good life in the country, however, lives "without any other appetite or desire than for what is at hand," according to Selanio in *Las semanas del jardín* (11:24–25). In Socrates' terms, the kind of amorous desiring that Cervantes' narrators and characters *talk* about most is closer to *pothos* than *himeros* because of this sense of lack, absence, nonpossession. Yet nearly all of the passages which acknowledge lack as a condition of desire—quite different from thinking desire exclusively in terms of lack—represent desire vividly in terms of mobility.

Nonetheless it seems to me a mistake to conceptualize *all* desire as necessarily constituted in lack, regardless of historical period. Desiring can issue out of anything whatsoever, including itself or plenitude or satiety or a will to continuity. It would of course be easy to counter this by positing lack—or absence, void, difference, gaps, etc.—in any desiring experience whatsoever such that you're never satisfied or never for long, or satisfied by mere substitutes for the "real" object of desire. What I mean, however, is that (1) defining desire in terms of lack involves structuralizing it and suppressing its rhythmic, improvisatory character; (2) lack acquires (negative) value only with reference to what it is supposed to be a lack of, and how intensely it is so, and thus there's no such thing as lack-as-such; (3) it would be absurd to exclude the possession and togetherness of types of desire such as *himeros* from the heterogeneous category called amorous desire; (4) desire's immediate goal sometimes turns out to be a landmark on a longer itinerary of desiring.[56]

In the wake of so many writers dealing with desire, then, Cervantes draws continually on the language of movement to articulate the essentially non-kinetic dynamics of desire. Except in passages of the *Novelas ejemplares* where economic metaphors sometimes dominate (e.g., desire as wanting to possess something of value), the language of movement provides the primary metaphors with regard to desire and desiring in the novels.[57] However naively Cervantes' characters may speak about the mobility of desire, they always link desire to the experience of it, thus recognizing its dynamic, processive nature. The same is true for Freud, whose *Triebe* (drives, not instincts) simulate movement and operate, in principle at least, in accordance with their thrust, source, object, and aim (*Drang, Quelle, Objekt, Ziel*).

Brilliant as always, Lacan draws on Freud's own arguments to "deconstruct" (the word is his in 1964) the Freudian drive. He asserts, among other things, that drives may be satisfied by sublimation rather than reaching their object, that drives are constant forces having nothing to do with kinetic energy, that no "object" ever satisfies a drive, and that the cause of desire (primordial loss) is much more important than the "object" it attaches itself to. This is not to say that Lacan abandons the language of motion (Lacan, *Four* 161–86). His *pulsion* more or less reproduces the motion of Freud's *Trieb*. Some of his diagrams with their arrows also trace motion within a field of desire, and his explanation of the dynamics of various impulses relating to desire often resorts to the language of motion. Moreover, desire as a negative field of energy occupies a central place in Lacan's theory: desire is a charged void that sets other things in motion. Largely independent of specific experience, *désir* becomes by and large a premise, an empty space in a paradigm of human motivation.

What interests me here are the implications of a theory of desire in which *désir* itself is largely immobilized—and let me add that the following remarks will scarcely do more than allude to the complexity and development of this theory. Maintaining that the primary energy of the *pulsion* eludes consciousness, Lacan shifts attention to secondary energy, desire. The mobile *pulsions* come to be replaced by a less mobile desire flanked by need and demand. Desire, he says, "is neither the appetite for satisfaction, nor the demand for love, but the difference resulting from the subtraction of the first from the second, the very phenomenon of their splitting (*Spaltung*)" (Ragland-Sullivan 75). Empty, subtracted *space* seems to open up everywhere there is desire: desire is the void between need and demand, it is the place of the lack, the hollowing out of being, the space between the *moi* and the Other(A). Again and again, Lacan defines desire, as he does the subject and the unconscious, in terms of lack, absence, rupture, gap, incompleteness, the Other, irretrievable loss, metonymy, difference, and so on.[58] I have no quarrel with any of these terms as such. To think desire as lack—or as constituted in and by lack —however, is to confuse desiring with what is often but not always a condition of its articulation. Lacan's insistence on the constancy of drives and desire also draws attention away from articulation. What this abyss model of desire lacks is a sense of how desire deploys its energies, how it's felt and how strongly, how it interacts with the desired other and redefines human relationships, how it improvises, fluctuates, emerges, and submerges. The language of desire in Cervantes' novels, in contrast, is mobilized in these sorts of ways.

One further remark: given the classification of Cervantes as "Baroque," one might argue that his notion of desire, while indebted to "Renaissance" thought, was anti-"Renaissance" in its dissociation from memory or lack or primary plenitude and its rethinking in terms of errant movement. One might even be tempted to relate desire to changing concepts of the cosmos and to the irregularity of planetary motion. The "Baroque" is obviously a convenient designation for *some* of the works of writers such as Góngora, Quevedo, Gracián, Calderón, and Sor Juana—and by extension, for the entire epoch in which they wrote in Spain or Spanish America, as Bruce Wardropper and many others have argued.[59] The problem is that many writers including Cervantes share little with such authors regarding the kinds of characteristics commonly identified as "Baroque." What's more, many features thought to be quintessentially "Baroque" can be found in abundance in the pre-"Baroque." Severo Sarduy's very suggestive but (in my opinion) ill-founded book *Barroco* unintentionally calls into question whether the "Baroque" he so takes for granted is anything more than a critical-metaphysical analogue of the emperor's new clothes. It seems to me that the profusion of styles at the time of Cervantes (in Spain and elsewhere) was far more interesting and diverse than what "Baroque" denotes, and that the term moreover can't hold together the range of artistic practices called "Baroque" which emerged in a number of countries over several centuries. Yet it *is* possible, I think, to oppose the general Cervantine notion of wayward desire to the Neoplatonic philosophy out of which it arises, and from which it turns away in multiple movements. Writing with an awareness of anteriority and contemporaneity, and with an articulated ideology of literary invention that impels him to diverge from both, Cervantes sets desire in motion just as he mobilizes discourse, life processes, his characters, and his own novelizing. Who knows, it may be precisely the move from *imitatio* to *inventio* that makes him—"Baroque."

Life's Movements

"Oh! Caminho de vida nunca certo!"

Camoens, Os Lusíadas

Topamos un muchacho medio rapado, que por andar no tanto como las cabalgaduras, en alcanzándole preguntóle el oidor: "¿Adónde vas, mozo?" El respondió: "A la Vejez." Oidor: "No digo sino ¿qué camino llevas?" Muchacho: "El camino me lleva a mí, que yo no llevo a él." Oidor: "¿De qué tierra eres?" Muchacho: "De Santa María de todo el mundo."

Vicente Espinel, Vida del escudero Marcos de Obregón

Grades of traveler. —We can distinguish five grades of traveler: those of the first and lowest grade are those who travel and, instead of seeing, are themselves seen—they actually become traveled [sie werden eigentlich gereist] and are as though blind; next come those who actually see the world; the third experience something as a consequence of what they have seen; the fourth absorb into themselves what they have experienced and bear it away with them; lastly there are a few men of the highest energy who, after they have experienced and absorbed all they have seen, necessarily have to body it forth again out of themselves in works and actions as soon as they have returned home.—It is like these five species of traveler that all men travel through the whole journey of life, the lowest purely passive, the highest those who transform into action and exhaust everything they experience.

Nietzsche, *Human, All Too Human*

Borges remarks with characteristic outlandishness in one of his essays: "Perhaps universal history is the history of the diverse intonation of a few metaphors" (*Prosa* 2:137). There's no question of taking this notion of history at face value, of course. What Borges calls "a few metaphors" could be modified to something like "systemic nexes of metaphoric thought," each generated from a different "domain" of human experience or knowledge. I have in mind such categories as the organic (the countless metaphors derived from planting, growing, flowering, bearing fruit, reaping, decaying, etc.), the economic (metaphors derived from evaluating, exchanging, buying, redeeming, selling, giving, stealing, etc.), the anatomic (metaphors derived from the human body in all its aspects)—and to these I would add metaphors derived from kinship, food, buildings, machines, landscapes, the elements, the heavenly bodies, books, visibility, and so on. Though by no means self-contained, each of these rough categories employs its own sense of logic (admitting endless variation) regarding how things are related to each other and how processes/events happen. I consider movement—especially going, traveling—to be one such metaphor-generating nexus, obviously interrelated with many of the others but retaining its own sorts of logic. As far as I am aware (and if there are exceptions I doubt it matters much), people everywhere have always resorted to metaphors of movement and traveling to express important aspects of human experience; in this sense Borges' word "universal" could be salvaged from the wreckage of "universal history." Especially felicitous in Borges' statement is the expression "diverse intonation," which I take to mean the specific ways in which metaphors are articulated.

In effect, what I've been saying with reference to Cervantes' novels is (1) that the language referring to discourse and desire is highly metaphorical, (2) that metaphors of movement predominate over every other sort of metaphor in the way discourse and desire are thought about (with far-ranging implications), (3) that discourse and desire pervade through practically all domains of human experience, and (4) that the "diverse intonation" of these metaphors is of prime importance. As I see it, mobilized discourse and desire represent special developments of the mobilization of human experience in general. Any event or state whatsoever, any process, any endeavor or behavior, any thought or discourse may be thought of in terms of movement within some space appropriate to it. Many examples already cited will bear this out.

What concerns me now is the totalizing metaphor of life as a journey, and the dynamics by which life at every turn is said to be motivated.

Life's "journey" appears to be one of those universal metaphors whose "diverse intonation" reveals a great deal about how people in different places, times, and persuasions characterize and valorize their own being in the world. Empedocles, for example, sees himself as "a fugitive from the gods and a wanderer" and generalizes this status to all human beings; birth, for him, is "a journey abroad," and metempsychosis means "changing the painful paths of life" (*Early* 193–94). The faithful of the Old Testament "confessed themselves no more than strangers or passing travellers on earth," writes the author of *Hebrews* (11:13).[60] Owing to a tradition passing through Augustine and spanning over a millennium and a half, the notion of the soul as *peregrinus* or pilgrim condemned to a wandering life of exile from God was a pervasive theme in Spanish writings of the sixteenth and seventeenth centuries, as Juergen Hahn has amply demonstrated (86, 114–80). Dante begins his *Divine Comedy* with a version of this metaphor ("Nel mezzo del cammin di nostra vita"), while works like Bunyan's *Pilgrim's Progress* and Gracián's *Criticón* elaborate it to the extent that all of human experience forms part of life's journey. Nietzsche radically alters it with about three different twists: "*The Wanderer.* — He who has attained to only some degree of freedom of mind cannot feel other than a wanderer on the earth — though not as a traveler *to* a final destination: for this destination does not exist. . . . within him too there must be something wandering that takes pleasure in change and transience" (*Human* 203).

In the *Criticón* in particular, *viandante* (wayfarer) is made synonymous with *viviente* (one who lives). "Tell me, don't you travel every hour and every instant on the thread of your life?" asks one character along the way.[61] The protagonists Critilo and Andrenio are "passengers of life," "pilgrims of living," and their life is nothing but a "pilgrimage," a "tiring journey of life."[62] Their arduous route through some eight hundred pages is lined with allegorized monstrosities in a world of diverging and converging paths where allegorical and geographical space are made to coincide, and the different stages of life are marked by true rites of "passage" between contrasting landscapes. Every aspect of the book reaffirms the metaphor, which is not limited to life *in* the world since there is also a journey *into* the world from the island of St. Helena where Andrenio has been raised by beasts (a premature birth, perhaps, but necessary for the allegory), and a journey *out* of the world from Rome down to the domain of Death and beyond through an ink-colored sea to the isle of Immortality.

Cervantes' varied handling of this metaphor is very different from Gracián's. The *Persiles* itself, written about forty years before the *Criticón,* opens on the Barbarous Island and likewise makes its way to the earth's celestial city,

Rome, but the allegory of life's journey in the *Persiles* is much less explicit than in the *Criticón*.[63] In the prologue, Cervantes uses the metaphor on himself in his powerfully moving *adiós* just days before his death; he also uses the metaphor in the prologues to *La Galatea,* the *Novelas ejemplares,* and both parts of *Don Quixote,* albeit very transiently. In the novels themselves, the metaphor emerges here and there only to disappear and reemerge in another guise. But when narrators and characters do talk about their own "life" or someone else's, they are likely to do so in terms of movement, especially traveling. Let me recall the common expression "discurso de mi vida," discourse of my life, in the sense of an erratic course already traveled to the present; sometimes life's journey is nuanced differently with the words *curso* and *carrera* instead of *discurso.*

Reflecting on the sudden disintegration of Sancho's government, Cide Hamete contrasts the circularity of diurnal and seasonal time with the unrepeatability of human time: "only human life runs to its end more swiftly than time, without hope of renewal unless it be in the other life . . ." (II.53.440). If all journeys are temporal, life's journey is essentially so: lived experience marks out an itinerant movement determined by temporal succession rather than spatio-temporal succession; consequently, the space of such movement, no matter how much it may resemble lived space, is opened up by the experience of time. Don Quixote brings this out eloquently when speaking of marriage in terms of a journey of two: "The man who wants to take a long journey will, if he is wise, seek some trusty and pleasant companion to go with him before setting out on the road. Why then should a man not do likewise when he has to travel all his life, right to the final halting place of death; more especially since his companion must be with him in bed and at the table and everywhere, as the wife is with her husband."[64] Life at its most sedentary is as much a "journey" as errant life because its traveling is done by living and its end is determined not by a place but by death, which takes on the character of place, as do all moments of experience. Lying in bed and sitting at the table, in Don Quixote's analogy, are "traveling." To live in a certain way is to go a corresponding way. Every *vita,* individual and collective, has its *curriculum* strongly accentuated by what is deemed memorable or significant. As will be discussed in the last chapter, discrete experiences (*Erlebnisse,* from *leben,* "to live") mark out an itinerary comprising cumulative experience (*Erfahrung,* related to *fahren,* "to travel").

If people can "travel" life's journey without going anywhere, they travel in (at least) two ways at once when they do actually go on a journey. The full experience of traveling pertains to both journeys but derives its significance according to rather different criteria. A strenuous journey may serve the important purpose of getting someone somewhere, but may have little importance in life's more psychic/spiritual journey; conversely, an event of enormous significance for the metaphorical journey may figure as little more than one of a series of happenings on a journey from one place to another. If to some extent the route makes the traveling in the spatial journey, the traveling makes the route in the "meta-journey." Nonetheless, the co-incidence of these two sorts of journey enables discourse to modulate quite easily from one to the other, as happens here and there in the novels. Asked how his trip to Valladolid went, the licenciado Vidriera replies: "No road is bad as long as it ends, except for the one that leads to the gallows" (*LV* 58; cf. *LV* 63; *PS* 246, 342, 456; *DD* 207). For some, life really is a journey, a continuous series of displacements in the most literal sense, such that the two sorts of journeys become coextensive, con-fused to the extent of inseparability. This is implicit in Cipión's suggestion to Berganza "that tonight you tell your life story and the steps [*trances*] by which you came to the point where you now find yourself" (301). We've already seen how life's double journey becomes further confused with yet another sort of journey, the discursive one that narrates the life.

Because life's journey is essentially temporal, the experience of time has everything to do with traveling life's routes. Like many of his contemporaries both in Spain and elsewhere, Cervantes treats the movement of time as something forever worth mentioning and contemplating. The motion of heavenly bodies, which actually determines natural time and makes time itself move, largely transcends human experience. But many representations of time are more immediate to human life, which in turn often affects the way time moves or is perceived to move. Time—or any substitute such as hours, days, years, the dawn, the night, the day, etc.—typically flies, runs, walks, comes, goes, approaches, takes us with it (examples are countless); or we move along routes marked by the units of time. Consider how desire's anticipation affects the movement of time: "And although the night flew lightly with its dark wings, to Rodolfo it seemed to make its way not with wings but with crutches: so great was his desire to be alone with his beloved wife."[65] Or again, how moods and amorous situations affect time, as when Silerio in *La Galatea* addresses the coming hours:

> No os pido que vengáis dulces, sabrosas,
> pues no hallaréis camino, senda o passo
> de reduzirme al ser que yo he perdido.
>   ¡Horas a cualquier otro venturosas!
> ¡Aquella dulce del mortal traspasso,
> aquélla de mi muerte sola os pido.[66]

The first of these tercets highlights the movement of time and its irreversibility with reference to the journey of life; the second brings out the simultaneous approach of time and the passage from life to death. Here time and life seem to meet head-on. At times life is stationary as time passes by, or time is the route of life, or time takes life with it. In one way or another, the movements of life and time are synchronized and coordinated because in fact they have to happen together.

Deathly imagery overshadows many of Cervantes' life-as-journey metaphors. Again and again, characters speak of the mortal "step," the way to the grave, the approach of Death, or the road to heaven. Rarely if ever do these metaphors refer to the beginnings of the journey (unlike, say, those in *El Criticón* or *Tristram Shandy*); even Dante's midpoint of life is of little concern. Hence the metaphor functions by no means as a simple image mapping life from beginning to end. In Cervantes' novels, life's journey is laden with futurity, especially the sense of an end and continuation beyond the end, which implies that the metaphor serves in part to come to terms with death by representing death in terms of the journey. Its focus is often the passage over the boundary between life and death, or between this life and the next. What it assures is the continuity of the "traveler" and ultimately of the society of "travelers" despite the radical discontinuity of death; death itself becomes a destination, boundary, or gateway, not a state of being (or nonbeing). The journey *to* the other world comes out above all in the *Persiles*, beginning with Cervantes' own anticipated journey from this life to the next in the prologue, and culminating in Auristela's intense desire to take the straight road to heaven rather than bother with the rest of the journey to Rome or the byways of married life with Periandro (48–49, 342, 397, 459, 461).

On the less eschatological side of the metaphor, all action and behavior, all modes of being, all "ways" of life translate into the traveling of routes. The professions, standardized as routes traveled by their practitioners, are all ways of traveling life's journey. Don Quixote is particularly fond of this metaphor whenever he compares the arduous road of knight-errantry with the ways of other professions (e.g., *DQ* I.37.466, II.6.83, II.8.98, II.18.176). There is no end to the kinds of *caminos:* there are those of heaven and hell, of virtue(s) and vice(s), of good and bad fortune, of remedies of all kinds, of love, of political favor . . . Some exist in advance as well-trodden routes while others are made in the traveling. Some have yet to be discovered, as in the case of Teodosia (*Las dos doncellas*), who, like many characters, thinks of herself as traveling within a chaotic labyrinth: "Where is the irresistible force of my fate leading me? What path [*camino*] is mine or what way [*salida*] can I hope to find out of this intricate labyrinth where I find myself? What end will this unknown journey of mine have? . . . woe is me a thousand times, I who let myself be taken by my unbridled desires."[67] While the journey (*peregrinación*) she mentions refers primarily to the actual journey she has undertaken, the rest of the traveling she talks about is a metaphorical rendering of her present difficulties and confusion which offer no apparent way out. The logic of traveling paths converts lived situations into territorial equivalents, and living into traveling.

What are these *caminos*? They are representations of identifiable sequences of human activity according to a kinetic/territorial analogue. Common to all sequences is their "linearity" (single, multiple, parallel, intertwined, etc.), i.e, the sense that this follows from that in one way or another, that anyone involved in a sequence is in one "place" at a time and always moving to trace an itinerary, that other possible sequences exist, and that constraints and viabilities affect the course of any sequence. The common denominator of all such sequences is temporal duration: the successiveness of experience translates as (spatio-temporal) movement along a spatialized time-route. One thing follows another on the route simply because one moment leads to another, regardless of the qualitative relationship between them. Thus some sequences are scarcely anything but duration, especially when they give little sense of qualitative difference between the way behind and the way ahead. Other sequences reveal method, means, strategy, logical process, objectives, a will to "arrive" at desired situations, and so on. Sequences are of course determined by the nature of the activity or process in question, by who is engaged in it, and in what circumstances. The corresponding routes and landscapes exteriorize these characteristics.

Whereas the person who does or undergoes certain things translates easily into the traveler along such routes, and the doing or undergoing turns into going, there seems to be no simple counterpart in experience to the route itself. The route appears to be a supplementary third term deriving from a splitting of experience into going and the "whereness" required by going; the route is that "whereness."

People move along routes, along *caminos*. Hence whatever gets people "going" and keeps them "going" is highly significant for this sort of traveling. It should come as no surprise by now that the language of motivation in Cervantes' novels is dominated by movement imagery. To begin with, as already noted with regard to motivating desire, the verbs *mover* and *incitar* (to set in motion) are frequently invoked to explain why people do things. The formula "something/someone moves someone to do something" appears with countless variations, as when Periandro refers to "the causes that moved us to leave our country" (*PS* 413), or when the captive in *Don Quixote* says, "All this moved [*incitó y conmovió*] me to take part in the expected campaign"

(*DQ* I.39.476). This is quite different from saying, for instance, "For this reason I decided to do such-and-such," because (1) the *mover* formula expresses motivation in terms of mobilization and hence projects the situation into a corresponding space of mobility, (2) the motive is nearly always external to the person or is externalized (e.g., thoughts, desires, etc.), (3) what is set in motion is people, who are not exactly self-movers in this regard, and (4) the action or passion into which someone moves somehow has within it its own viability, its own pathlike possibilities.

When narrators and characters assign motives to their feelings and actions, they have an enormous range to choose from. To complicate matters, the value of these attributions varies greatly. By the time the word *fortuna,* for example, finds its way into the discourse of Cervantes' characters, its evocation of a transcendent motivating and determining force is all but lost, and yet for all its emptiness it still serves the function of identifying some external motivation. Similarly, the attribution of motivating force to the stars, God, heaven, the devil, someone else, someone else's discourse, magic spells, fate, luck, *ventura,* love, desire, the circumstances of a situation, and so on ad infinitum, varies from sincerity to facetiousness and depends heavily on context for meaning. The attribution of motives can of course be extremely tricky. How do people know what moves them? And when Auristela says that "Periandro" moves her, what does this really mean? She's obviously referring to her love for him. But this only begs the question as to what "love" consists of for her, and what that in turn consists of, and so on in regressive masks of motivation. Then there is the problem of multiple attribution, as when one character says that "fortune, love, or my insufficient forewarning" precipitated her downfall, or when another character says she was "taken by my star, or rather, by my weak nature . . ." (*DD* 217; *PS* 362). These supposed motives illustrate how slippery if not misleading the attribution of motives can be, since characters always have any number of possible explanations available to them drawn from different orders of the world.

What matters here, however, is not the explanatory efficacy of motivational statements so much as the fact that the vast majority of these statements materialize as variants of the formula "something/someone moves someone to do something." Instead of *mover* or *incitar,* the verb might be *llevar, guiar, encaminar, abrir camino, inclinar, impeler,* etc., all of them somehow inducive to movement. Such thinking has considerable consequences for the notions of person and world. The boundaries of person are sufficiently undefined and traversible to allow all kinds of traffic in and out of oneself. God and the devil, for example, can find their way in without any trouble provided the way is open to them, while thoughts and desires also come inside or move outside the self to act as quasi-external agents motivating the self. People are dividuals rather than individuals, and their divisibility itself generates motion. Expressed in terms of movement, the highly dynamic relationship between person and world renders all stable concepts of person and world irrelevant. Characters learn how to let themselves be taken along, or they struggle against the currents of destiny in an effort to determine their own course.

The metaphors of discourse, love and desire, life processes, and so on discussed in this chapter coincide largely with what linguists call "localism," that is, the thesis that in many and perhaps all languages, "first-order" entities (people and things located or moving in perceptual space) provide the "templates" according to which many "second-order" (events, states, processes that actually occur in space and time) and "third-order" (the objects of propositions, judgments, beliefs) entities are thought and expressed (Lyons 442–46, 718; Anderson 12–13). Central to localist theory is the so-called spatialization of time evident, for instance, in the common derivation of temporal prepositions from spatial ones, or in the recognition that verb tense is a deictic category (Miller and Johnson-Laird 417–23). "The human spirit," wrote Gustav Guillaume a half century ago, "is made in such a way that it has the experience of time, but has no representation of it"; in order to represent it, according to him, one needs to resort to the language of spatial relations (Traugott 207).

The observation holds, although it should be understood that time is not necessarily converted into space as some linguists would have us believe. Formal/structural thinking (by no means limited to formalism and structuralism since we all engage in it to some extent) does in fact reduce time to space. In the metaphors that concern us here, however, the experience of time relative to "second-order" phenomena is represented as *movement* within a conjugated space/time. Time traverses its own space without losing its temporality. Otherwise expressed, movement channels dynamism without suppressing it. Even "first-order" phenomena are often dynamized by implied movement, as John Lyons remarks with regard to locative expressions and visual perception: "the asymmetrical and dynamic construction 'How far is it from X to Y?' can be seen as more basic than the more symmetrical and static construction 'What is the distance between X and Y?' Distance is always measured from a point-of-reference. . . . Furthermore, visual perception can be seen in terms of the metaphor of travel: one looks into the distance at, or towards, an object; one's gaze travels to and reaches, or grasps, the object" (700). This raises the question as to whether anything can be conceived as entirely static or inert. The issue, it seems, is not whether something is thought to be static or dynamic, but rather in what ways and to what degree it is thought to be dynamic, and how this dynamism comes to be expressed or suppressed. Much of what is called localism could more aptly be called mobilism.

Apart from what Vico calls the "corso che fanno le nazioni" and the "ricorso delle cose umane nel risurgere che fanno le nazioni" (281, 349), the life-as-journey metaphor is perhaps the most comprehensive mobilization of human experience. It is the macrojourney made up of innumerable passages and *jornadas,* or microjourneys, all with their motives, routes, and modes of travel. Regardless of how the metaphor is nuanced, it brings out the essential transitoriness of life, the disquieting sense that you never really stay in the same place but are always "moving" on a finite route. "To live is to travel for a short day [Vivir es caminar breve jornada]," begins a well-known sonnet of Quevedo which ends with sudden "arrival." The metaphor admits companionship and allows generalization in terms of common routes of human life, but its points of departure and arrival ultimately refer solely to the individual life. Companionship breaks down into distinct journeys undertaken together. In the words of a priest in Tayeb Salih's *Season of Migration to the North,* "All of us, my son, are in the last resort traveling alone" (28, 24).

Universal as the metaphor may be, it reveals a peculiar view of human life. Unlike, say, the world-as-stage metaphor, it deemphasizes society (except in so far as lives travel together), tracing instead, as it were, the wandering strands of social fabric as they pass through different relations; every strand makes its own way somewhere, pursues its own journey. As the life-as-journey metaphor measures its units according to the individual *bios,* it posits identity in the traveler from beginning to end and yet its motion implies continual change. The traveler is the "same" person throughout but never quite the same from one step to the next. Change is manifested most obviously in the shifting whereabouts of the traveler, but these whereabouts are understood to represent the traveler's change of being and circumstance. Whether this means authentic change beyond mere aging or the moving of wooden characters along a temporal itinerary depends on how dynamically the metaphor is made to function. To a greater or lesser extent, the metaphor transforms the dynamism of being-in-the-world into motion such that incessant transition is expressed as irreversible transit.

As with the life-as-dream metaphor, the life-as-journey metaphor in the first instance issues from a synecdochic relationship — the so-called "part for the whole." Life figured as a dream derives from the experience of dream as opposed to waking consciousness, and the subsequent diffusion of the characteristics of dream (whatever they may be) throughout the experience of life as a whole. Similarly, the life-as-journey metaphor extends the experience of traveling to characterize all of life, including experience which has little to do with going places. This is made possible by the "natural" representation of becoming (including duration conceived in terms of Heraclitus' *ta onta*) by movement. The journey is to life as movement is to change.

Because of its comprehensiveness, life's journey implicitly coincides with and interconnects all the diverse mobilizations of experience, including discourse and desire and various other sorts of movement metaphors I've barely alluded to here. There's nothing monolithic about these metaphors as they appear in Cervantes' novels. Yet despite the transitory nature of most of them, their cumulative effect obliges us, I think, to reconsider the notions of language, person, society, and world precisely *as transitory,* as highly *dynamic,* in Cervantes' novels. The fact that many of these metaphors are conventional in one way or another, and that Cervantes is by no means unique in his obsessive use of them, only adds to their import and calls for an understanding of their "diverse intonation."

Travelers

Becoming Animal

. . . si mouvement propre est indice certain de chose animée, comme escript Aristoteles, et tout ce qui de soy se meut est dict animal . . .

Rabelais

La vie est un mouvement materiel et corporel, action imparfaicte de sa propre essence, et desreglée; je m'emploie à la servir selon elle.

Montaigne

A vida é o que fazemos dela. As viagens são os viajantes. O que vemos, não é o que vemos, senão o que somos.

Fernando Pessoa

No matter what else Cervantes' novels deal with, they recount journeys of one sort or another, and without journeys none of them would hold together as such. This is perhaps all they have in common with regard to what they're about. Cervantes' wandering, searching, or fleeing characters go on quixotic quests, amorous journeys, pastoral ambulations, pilgrimages, journeys of war and enslavement, imaginary flights, utopian voyages, touristic trips, mercantile ventures, picaresque adventures, canine wanderings, journeys of sorcery and witchcraft, and various other sorts of travel. Rare are the moments that someone isn't in some sense en route. Journeys are vital to every one of the novels, and are often coextensive with the novels.

This is most obvious in the cases of *Don Quixote, Persiles y Sigismunda, El amante liberal, Rinconete y Cortadillo, La ilustre fregona, Las dos doncellas,* and *El coloquio de los perros,* whose *fabulae* begin with departure from home and end either with the return home or with some indeterminate continuation of the journey. But it's also true of the other novels. The char-

acters of *La Galatea,* even if they sometimes sleep at home, are forever following their nomadic sheep and amorous inclinations in the circuits of a more
or less bounded terrain. *La gitanilla* tracks the movements of a young woman
stolen as a baby by a group of Gypsies, as well as the integration of her suitor
into the wandering group, until events bring about their reinstatement in sedentary society. *La española inglesa* also begins with the theft of a girl and traces
several journeys back and forth between Spain and England, likewise ending
in marriage. *La fuerza de la sangre* begins with an abduction en route and
subsequent rape, and ultimately brings the offender Rodolfo back from Italy
to marry his one-time victim, who suffers several displacements herself. *La
señora Cornelia* focuses on two transient Spanish *caballeros* as highly mobile
mediators in a crisis of love and honor among Italy's high nobility, and likewise follows the movements of the lovers. *El licenciado Vidriera* tells of one
the most errant characters of all the novels, not only in his initial and final
trips but also in his primary role as itinerant *loco.* Centered on a single house,
El celoso extremeño might seem to be an exception. The opening pages,
however, characterize Carrizales as a lifelong traveler around Europe and America; his settling down with a young wife and enclosing her from the outside
world ends in the failure of his attempt at sedentary life. What's more, the
bulk of the tale follows the itinerary of a young would-be seducer from outside the doubly fortified house through various thresholds (architectural and
human) to the inner sanctuary, the wife's body, though she doesn't allow him
inside.[1] *El casamiento engañoso* also shows the failure of sedentary life, this
time due to mutual deception, and ends with the characters more homeless
than before they met.

One could no doubt cite the importance of journeys in a few of Cervantes'
plays as well, not to mention the long poem *Viaje del Parnaso,* but I'm concerned with the novels mainly because the journey appears to be the major
vehicle of Cervantes' novelizing, whereas this is not the case with the plays
and poems as a whole. The same might be said of countless narratives ranging from the *Odyssey* to *Ulysses,* from the *Cantar de mío Cid* to Cortázar's
Rayuela (*Hopscotch*), from picaresque novels to mystic discourse, from "Man-
deville's" *Travels* to Calvino's *If on a Winter's Night a Traveler,* from the
Sumerian *Gilgamesh* to the Chinese *Journey to the West.* With few exceptions, I would argue that from early medieval times till the late eighteenth
century in Europe the journey provides the primary means of sustaining long
narratives. That so many of the world's narratives tell about journeys makes
it all the more necessary to treat journeys as an object of inquiry in relation
to literature, on the one hand, and human experience on the other. I need
hardly point out how seldom this has been done with any seriousness (or
humor), and how most attempts to do so have narrowed the scope to some
subgenre such as the quest, the pilgrimage, the picaresque novel, or the trav-

elogue.[2] As we know all too well, dynamism, movement, and becoming are rarely put on the agenda of literary criticism. In this chapter I leave aside questions of narrative so as to focus on the experiential aspect of Cervantes' novelistic journeys; I do so by regarding characters *as* travelers.

But how do you keep your hold on such a protean phenomenon as the "journey," which in the abstract denotes little more than someone going somewhere without giving any sense of who goes where, or of how, why, when, and with whom this happens, and in the concrete assumes an enormous diversity with few common strains? This difficulty has undoubtedly contributed to the marginalization or exclusion of the journey even in criticism on works that primarily recount journeys. The uncontainably mobile phenomena of the journey in Cervantes' novels resist a logically sequential treatment. Perhaps a discursive errancy through an endless series of di-gressions on digressions is the mode of commentary most appropriate to it, because most mimetic of it. But this would obviously be pointless. Somewhat against the currents of the material itself, then, I make my own discursive way into Cervantine journeys by in-quiring into certain aspects of them—and resisting most of the digressions they seem to invite.

Some of the most telling aspects of the journey for both real and fictional travelers could be summed up in the following questions: What are they escaping or leaving behind? What is their relationship to place? What are they seeking? Whom do they travel with? How do they meet, and how do they part? How do they determine their route? What is their mode of travel? How do they value the traveling itself? How do they deal with the time-space in which they find themselves, and to what extent does this time-space generate their experience for them? How do they construe encounters, and how do other characters construe them? In what ways do travelers exert control over what happens? What do adventures consist of for them? In what ways do travelers change? What images of self do they project en route? How do they incorporate their experience, and how do they recount it? Most of these questions will be dealt with or touched upon with regard to Cervantes' novelistic travelers in this and subsequent chapters.

I begin with *place*. The bare notion of travel as someone going somewhere has profound implications, since it involves changing relationships with regard to *place*—or more precisely, to a plurality of *places*. Although there are cases of traveling at "home," such as Maistre's *Voyage autour de ma chambre,* traveling generally means moving in some space where neither the locality lays claim on the person nor vice versa. More simply, traveling means moving in a space that's not one's own, it means having simultaneous but shifting relationships with more than one place, continually dis-placing oneself. This mutual nonpossessiveness between travelers and places affects the kinds of movement and relations that occur in traveling.

It goes without saying that places aren't inert physical shells, but localities of experience or of being where interaction not only "takes place" but also "makes place." The people of a place constitute an essential part of that place (in fact, sometimes place—"home," for example—consists of nothing but people, regardless of where they are). Quite obviously, much of what we do and think relates specifically to place. I suspect that the stress on location and movement in Melanesian and some North American Indian languages, in which "everybody and everything spoken of are viewed as coming or going, or in some relation to place" (quoted in Tuan 46–47), codifies a feature of human thought latent in other languages. Scholars as diverse as Jonathan Z. Smith, Yi-Fu Tuan, and Edward Soja have emphasized how symbolic systems, social behavior, and the wider endeavors of whole societies are generated out of people's attitudes toward and relations with place. Crucial to an understanding of these attitudes is the kind of zoning that people impose on space, and particularly the character of the "center" in relation to an individual or collective "self"—or more rarely the decentered character of space.

My interest in such questions here springs from the fact that travel and travelers come into relief only against a backdrop of many unspoken assumptions about what it means to belong to a place. To anticipate what I'll be discussing further on, many of Cervantes' characters including Don Quixote and Sancho Panza undergo the most radical turnabout from extreme sedentariness to extreme errancy, while a few of them, most notably Carrizales in *El celoso extremeño,* go the other way. These transformations largely determine the fate of the characters and the narratability of their experience.

To be of a place implies being bound to that place and appropriating it for oneself not necessarily as property but certainly as one's own. It implies, inter alia, participating as a member in a social, cultural, and economic system, being subject to a network of power, authority, and obligation, maintaining strong family ties and primary relationships with people nearby *because* they're nearby, placing value in autochthony and sacralizing or fetishizing the characteristics of one's place and of one's "roots" in it, living among the familiar in highly repetitive ways, and perpetuating the permanence of place. Leaving such a place for an indefinite period of time doesn't necessarily mean abandoning all of this, although it does impose some limits since many aspects of local experience aren't transportable. Hence the errant/lococentric distinction I am proposing admits a range of hybrid variants. Among the more important of these are (1) exile and diaspora, where no matter how settled people may be there is always a sense of the center being elsewhere and of life as trans-ient; (2) transhumance, which involves seasonal migration, a sense of back-and-forth, a dual or multiple centricity; (3) nomadism, which usually involves well-established circuits of movement and surprisingly strong attachments to place (Tuan 156–58), though less routinized forms of nomadism do approximate wandering; and (4) itinerancy in types such as merchants, sailors, muleteers, pirates, and performers of all sorts, many of whom, no matter how far and wide they travel, orient themselves toward the distant center of home.

Places attach themselves to people and possess them, and vice versa. Hence people's lococentrism depends a great deal on the nature and degree of such attachment and possession. Hugo of St. Victor, in a rich passage quoted for similar reasons by both Erich Auerbach and Edward Said, writes in the 1120s of ties of place chiefly in affective terms: "The man who finds his homeland sweet is still a tender beginner; he to whom every soil is as his native one is already strong; but he is perfect to whom the entire world is as a foreign land [*exilium*]. The tender soul has fixed his love on one spot in the world; the strong man has extended his love to all places; the perfect man has extinguished his. From boyhood I have dwelt on foreign soil, and I know with what grief sometimes the mind takes leave of the narrow hearth of a peasant's hut, and I know, too, how frankly it afterwards disdains marble firesides and panelled halls" (Said 7). Though Hugo's assignation of different values (tender, strong, perfect) to the three categories probably reveals more about his own willed homelessness than about the categories themselves, what concerns us here is the way he maps out the stages of emancipation from place: (1) love for one place, (2) love for all places, (3) no love for any place. Whereas the territorial object of love is generalized from somewhere to everywhere as one passes out of lococentrism from (1) to (2), the love itself is negated from (2) to (3), both of which correspond to errant attitudes. Thus love is associated with a sense of familiarity with respect to place, whether this be a central somewhere or a decentralized anywhere, and full emancipation comes about only through an attitude of estrangement toward everywhere, including one's own homeland.

Despite Hugo's personal testimony with regard to these stages, his categories are open to question. After all, if space is perceived as heterogeneous, it would seem that the place-oriented affects of even the most indifferent or estranged person are likely to be heterogeneous as well. Furthermore, the examples of some of the archetypal travelers of Western literature both within and outside of fiction betray strong attachments to "home." Odysseus feigns madness so as not to leave home, departs with great reluctance, and spends a decade after the war trying to get back—even if he does take off again, as the Ulysses of both Dante and Tennyson so movingly narrates. Aeneas' attachment to a forever lost home expresses itself partly in his taking his *penates* or household deities with him in his travels, eventually to establish a new abode for them. The will to return home or to compensate for an irretrievable loss by trying to transport home, respectively, guides the movements of these two travelers to some extent. But at the same time their traveling takes on its own impetus quite at odds with their sedentary yearnings. Thus even in the case of paradigmatic travelers, these opposing attitudes coexist—sometimes symbiotically, sometimes conflictively. Within the range of "emancipated" attitudes regarding place, moreover, love and estrangement are often hard to tell apart; they, too, may coexist in such travelers as Odysseus and Aeneas, or Marco Polo and Ibn Battuta.

In the sixteenth century, the nonattachment with regard to place which emerges so strongly in both More's *Utopia* and Montaigne's writings owes itself largely to the universalist tendencies of humanistic praxis. Societal comparativism—the sense that things have been, are, or could be otherwise—disengages both of them from at least some of the dominant ideology of place. To Raphael Hythlodaeus, the archtraveler of *Utopia,* the place where he eventually dies is a matter of indifference: "for he had two favourite quotations, 'The unburied dead are covered by the sky' and 'You can get to heaven from anywhere'—an attitude which, but for the grace of God, might have led to serious trouble" (More 39). By adapting Cicero's quotation of the dying Anaxagoras, "You can get to the Underworld from anywhere"—all the more remarkable considering the localistic nature of Greek and Roman religion, the importance of burial rites and grave sites—Raphael denies the eschatological relevance of locality and implies that ritual is dispensable as a passport to the beyond. Having been adrift ever since he divided out his property at an early age among relatives in Portugal, the enlightened discoverer of Noplace and other nonexistent isles is bound only *for* places, not *by* them.

Montaigne echoes Raphael's attitude in his own way: "If I feared dying in another place than that of my birth, if I thought that I should die less at ease far from my family and friends, I should hardly go out of France; I should not without terror go out of my parish. I feel death continually clutching me by the throat or by the loins. But I am of another temper: death is the same to me everywhere. Yet if I had to choose, it would be, I think, rather on horseback than in bed, away from home and far from my people."[3] Unlike the fictional Raphael (and more like Thomas More), Montaigne has a place and social web and necessities he unwillingly returns to from his travels. Yet his attitude is equally remarkable for its nonattachment bordering on aversion in relation to the values, institutions, and ritual rooted in place. He mimics those who warn him that at his age he may never return from a long journey, and responds: "What do I care! I undertake it neither to return from it nor to complete it. I undertake it solely to keep in motion while motion pleases me, and I travel for the sake of traveling. They who run after a benefice or a hare do not run; they only run who run at prisoner's base and to practice running."[4] Montaigne comes close here to defining the essence of errancy — a will to mobility, or to what Basho calls "random travel" (175). Reasons for travel extraneous to the actual process of traveling override the traveling as traveling. Montaigne isn't so naïve as to exclude motives, of course, as a good part of his long essay "On Vanity" (III.9) probes into the grounds of his own wanderlust. Most striking about his formulation of traveling is that he takes it as an activity to be practiced and valued in its own right (even if there is *vanité* in it — "Mais où non?") and understood in its own terms, rather than as a means to other ends or as a subsidiary category. Destination and the return home are deemphasized, as are all concerns with property and authority, giving way to sensations of simply moving along, exerting oneself, and experiencing things en route. Indefiniteness and uncertainty pervade nearly every aspect of the traveling process in its ongoing incompleteness. Nonchalance regarding one's whereabouts and direction of movement by no means implies that places are equalized in value, as the examples of Montaigne and Raphael, two of the keenest observers of life's diversity, readily show. Perhaps never actualized in its rarest form, errancy is a tendency toward unrestrained movement attaching itself to no place in particular.

Montaigne's essay, the most insightful piece I know of on travel, in effect reflects on the ideology and praxis of sedentary life versus those of travel. As usual, Montaigne's main object of study is himself, but his observations are so resonant that they touch off questions as applicable to fictional travelers as to historical ones. He writes at length about his domestic and local life — his interaction with people, his obligations, his work, his incompetent managing of affairs, and all the cares accompanying these activities which both hold him in place and make him want to be out of place. These cares even detract from the visits of friends at his house, which he would like to enjoy. "Away from home, I cast off all thoughts of such things, and would feel less the ruin of a tower than I feel, when on the spot, the fall of a tile" (II.9.931); en route, he only has to think about *himself* and how he uses his money. His temperament, he says, is quite unsuited to a life bound by property and alliance, and he gladly gives it up when he can: "I have taken a mortal hatred to being held either to someone or by someone other than myself" (III.9.947). He is also fed up and at odds with French *moeurs*. One gets the sense that he's always having to explain his travel motives to people who are slow to understand the value of abandonment, especially when they're the ones he abandons. He recognizes the wisdom of being content with one's lot — and his lot is far better than most — but realizing this is about as meaningless as trying to follow the maxim "Be wise." Undermining such repose are all sorts of desires, disaffections, and anxieties. To leave is to escape from an undesirable state to an uncertain one: "I know well what I flee from, but not what I seek" (III.9.949). Montaigne himself points out the dominant "qualities" that goad his travel urges: idleness and independence, but also restlessness and indecisiveness. Each of these terms serves as shorthand for a nexus of conditions and attitudes.

The benefits and charms of travel attract Montaigne as much as domestic existence repels him. Not least of all is the sheer pleasure of coming into contact with things new and unknown. Traveling continually exercises the soul in salubrious ways and e-ducates better than any other method by offering a great diversity of human life for the soul to reflect on. Furthermore, Montaigne advocates universality over and above nationality and locality: "not without some excess, I regard all men as my compatriots, and embrace a Pole as a Frenchman, subordinating this national bond to the universal one common to all. . . . New acquaintances of my own making seem to me to be worth as much as these other everyday and fortuitous acquaintances issuing out of vicinity" (III.9.950). En route, he loves foul weather as much as fair weather, always following his whims and inclinations to the extent that there's no such thing as getting lost or getting off the track, because wherever he happens to go *is* his route. His *allégresse,* natural curiosity, playful malice, affability, and capricious style of travel overflow in the *Journal de voyage en Italie.*

Montaigne's essay calls attention to many issues relevant to the problematic of the journey and errancy, including the following: What binds people to place? How does it do so, and with what intensity? What, if anything, estranges or alienates people from their own place? What prompts people to leave? What is there in temperament, in ideology, or social/economic situation that persuades or compels breaking away? Is the journey more an escape or a search (or neither), and from or for what? How variable is identity en route? How does nonattachment express itself? What are the general mood and style of travel? What are the modes of interaction? Here the questions widen into a span of travel issues. Of prime importance is the contrast of two radically different praxes and outlooks, and the transition between them. "A journey of a thousand miles," says the *Tao te Ching,* "starts from beneath one's feet" (125). How does the ground one lives on change from property to a point of departure, and what happens to its character in this dizzying change of orientation?

A pair of vivid anecdotes about Alexander's dealings with naked sages of India illustrates sharply contrasting relationships between people and place.[5] Plutarch recounts that Alexander met with a philosopher who threw down a dry and shriveled hide and set his foot on different parts of the edge, whereupon the other side would rise up, until he put his foot on the middle and flattened it firmly. This demonstrated the efficacy of governing from the middle of the empire rather than wandering far away from it (Plutarch 409;

chap. LXV). The other anecdote, recounted by Arrian, tells of Alexander's coming upon a group of sages stamping the earth with their feet. They explain: "every man can possess only so much of this earth's surface as this we are standing on. You are but human like the rest of us, save that you are always busy . . . traveling so many miles from your home, a nuisance to yourself and to others" (J. Z. Smith 102). Whereas the first anecdote stresses possession as territorial control, the second undercuts the notion of possession altogether: there is no possession of the changing ground under your feet apart from the mere fact of transient occupation. The first contrasts a mobile and marginal (or even alienated) style of governing with a central one. In the second anecdote, the sages would dispossess the ruler of territory entirely, ownership being illusory, and thereby challenge the legitimacy of governing, especially when this means governing somewhere other than where one "belongs." The message of both anecdotes is "Go home!" What we have here, then, are two lococentric perspectives with very different views of property and governance, both opposed to the foreign conquests, the expansionism, the intrepid boundlessness and errant transgression of limits that Alexander exemplifies.

Of special relevance to Cervantes' Spain in this regard is the gamut of sedentary and errant rule practiced ever since the late fifteenth century. Cervantes himself was drawn by the shifting magnet of the court to Valladolid and then to Madrid. Over a century earlier, Isabella and Ferdinand practiced the most itinerant and personal style of rule throughout their reign, literally governing on the move as they spent several weeks in every single town of both kingdoms. Their peripatetic grandson, the emperor Charles V, after spending one of every four days in his forty-year reign on the road throughout his unwieldy territories, could rightly say, "my life has been one long journey." His son, Philip II, who had his massive live-in imperial center built for him at El Escorial, traveled extremely little in his four decades of rule despite insurmountable difficulties in governing lands so distant; true to his sedentary temperament, he declared in the year he died that "traveling about one's kingdom is neither useful nor decent" (Kamen 16, 25–27, 64–65, 147, 158, 200, 282). It would hence be a mistake to assume sedentary rule as the norm, since these examples show competing ideologies and practices of monarchic rule. Mutatis mutandis, such ideologies repeatedly come into open conflict in *Don Quixote,* where the protagonists' knightly and squirely errantry is opposed to "governing" what's theirs.

With rare exceptions, the history of social life strongly favors lococentrism over errancy, and there are of course compelling reasons why this should be so. A truly errant and independent society is almost inconceivable. At the same time, nearly every society seems to have its marginal or errant types to whom literature and lore tend to accord a disproportionate importance, an obsessive but often ambivalent interest. For even in fictive works of travel, reasons for staying at home abound as centrifugal and centripetal forces gravitate in opposite directions. Don Quixote's peculiar madness motivates him to leave home while efforts to bring him back to sanity by and large direct him homeward. In *Gargantua,* hostile conquests and superstitious pilgrimages are criticized as harmful and senseless and as contrary to an ethic of managing one's own (bk. 1, chaps. 45–46). A group of pilgrims, who earlier had the misfortune of being eaten as part of Gargantua's salad, are advised by Frère Jean of the hazard of cuckoldry in their absence — even the shadow of an abbey tower is fecund, he tells them. Voltaire's Scarmentado, in contrast, settles down after a grim tour of the world to enjoy the sweetness of marriage and cuckoldry (167), anticipating Candide's famous resolution (one of the most succinct expressions ever of lococentrism): "il faut cultiver notre jardin" (259). The tension in literature between place-centeredness and a will to else-whereness, or their odd forms of coexistence, are as old and as new as narrative itself.

Both Antonio Vilanova and Juergen Hahn provide a wealth of documentation on attitudes for and against travel in medieval Europe and especially in sixteenth- and seventeenth-century Spain. A few examples will indicate something of the range. Thomas à Kempis writes in his *De imitatione Christi* (ca. 1433): "What can you see elsewhere that you cannot see here? Behold the sky, the earth, and all the elements, for of these are all things made. What can you see anywhere else, which can endure for long?" He not only denies the educational value of the journey but sees travel as downright harmful to the soul because of its sensory contagion with the world, its incitement of sensuality: "The desire of the senses compels you to roam about, but when their hour is spent, what do you bring back but a burdened conscience and a distracted heart?" (Hahn 27).[6] In sixteenth-century Spain the widespread practice of (male) travel generated its own cult glorifying travel as a school of experience and virtue (as would later be the case in England). Fray Luis de León remarks in his *Exposición del Libro de Job* that the Spaniards are the "traveling people" (*pueblo peregrino)* par excellence, "who among all nations excel in foreign travel [*peregrinar*], voyaging very far from their lands and homes, to such an extent that in their voyages they circled the world" (2:442). Lope de Vega in *Peregrino en su patria* exalts the knowledge, glory, and merits attained by traveling: "he who has not traveled [*peregrinado*], what has he seen? He who has not seen, what has he attained? He who has not attained, what has he come to know? And he who has not undergone tempests [*fortunas*] at sea or on land, what can he call respite?" (Vilanova 139). The practices and ideologies of travel permeate the narrative literature of the times, not only in Spain but also in many other European countries, to the degree that such literature is incomprehensible without the notion of journey.

So basic are errant and lococentric dispositions as representing mutually antagonistic perspectives, impulses, and temperaments—no matter how these may vary within each category—that they provide significant criteria whereby not only people but also social groupings, ideologies, and so on may be differentiated and to some degree understood. The same applies to literary works and characters. It is literally a matter of *what* values are placed *where*.

Don Quixote and Sancho Panza: Transportable Worlds

Don Quixote opens by *locating* the *hidalgo* Alonso Quijano in an unnamed but namable place in La Mancha, and describing his habitual existence in and around the property which belongs to him and to which he belongs. Autochthony, repetition, local economy, and local society characterize his uneventful life. Only a few aspects of his past ever become known, and they do so almost incidentally; otherwise his present is understood as an almost organic outgrowth of his past. Like his neighbor Sancho Panza, he is one of the most sedentary characters imaginable, in fact hardly a character at all since there is as yet nothing novelistic about him—until his obsessive reading and disregard for body and property whirl him into the most extravagant madness. So it appears in the novel, although a convincing case can be made for a reversal whereby Don Quixote's readings are a symptom rather than a cause of his madness (Brancaforte 337). His madness informed by reading, at any rate, is what initiates the novel and sustains it till Don Quixote's definitive renunciation of knight-errantry and reintegration into the identity of his person and place at the hour of his death. Especially in recent years, there has been much critical insight into Don Quixote's obsessive reading, madness, and departure: Gonzalo Torrente Ballester, for instance, posits boredom as a remote cause (46–48); Carroll B. Johnson sees Don Quixote as attempting to escape from a repressed desire for the two women of his household (*Lust*); while for Ruth El Saffar, Don Quixote reveals the characteristics of "the archetypal hero-son of the Virgin Mother" caught in his devotion to the "mother principle" ("Sex" 85–87).[7] What I would like to stress here from the outset is that his is an errant madness, one that dislodges him from the attachments of his sedentary life and propels him unbound into a decentered world of adventure.

Even before the bizarre idea of knight-errantry dawns on him, however, his sedentariness is open to question because of the hybrid sedentary/errant nature of reading. On the one hand, reading tends to rank among the most *sedentary* (i.e., characterized by sitting) of activities along with writing. So it is for Don Quixote, who reads only at home until his library is purged and walled off into an inaccessible space; he takes no books on his travels, though mentally he may take all his readings with him. On the other hand, to read is in some measure to be elsewhere, to be "absentminded" through radical displacement and to move along with the mobile locus of extraneous discourse. If the place in which a text is read is usually irrelevant, there nonetheless tends to be some experiential link between the whereabouts of reading and the whereabouts of discourse, by contagion if not by association. Yet indications are that Don Quixote reads with such intense engagement as to be entirely oblivious to his surroundings, thus allowing the here and now of his elsewhere-mindedness to eclipse the here and now of his sedentary existence. He literally wanders outside himself. This alienation from "himself" brought about by reading is compounded by madness, which is consistently referred to in the novel in terms of loss and exteriority with respect to oneself: Cardenio's madness "so often took him out of himself," Don Quixote "loses" his mind and eventually regains it or comes back into it, he is "out of his mind," "he is breaking out through the door of his madness" ("And where is he breaking out, lady?" asked Sansón. "Has he ruptured any part of his body?") (I.27.331, I.1.73, I.44.532, I.7.85). One is reminded here of Astolfo's journey to the moon to recover Orlando's wits in *Orlando Furioso,* for everything that is lost on earth, such as reputations, prayers, and wits, can be found in reified form in a valley on the moon (canto 34).

As an avid reader, Don Quixote is already a traveler who transcends some of the limitations of place. His kind of traveling may be surmised from numerous speeches inspired by his readings in chivalric literature. He envisions, for example, a Knight of the Lake who, at the behest of a lady, throws himself into boiling, reptile-infested waters, and before he knows it finds himself in the environs of idyllic nature and a castle out of which come beautiful enchanted maidens to tend to him. Don Quixote's geography is as immense and often as imaginary as that of his readings, which give constant examples of extra-ordinary movement traversing such space. His sense of being there is all the more acute because he believes what he reads and identifies with the knightly protagonists. The literature which most enthuses him, it should be kept in mind, is largely that of (chivalric) travel and adventure, which brings on a sensation of sympathetic movement and accompaniment.

The question of the sedentary/mobile nature of reading comes up in a dispute in Fielding's *Joseph Andrews* as to whether real traveling is geographical or discursive. The eccentric Abraham Adams, whose literary ancestry can be traced in part to Don Quixote, argues in the face of his alehouse host, a former seaman, that reading is a more efficacious means of traveling than journeys by land and sea: "Master of mine, perhaps I have travelled a great deal farther than you without the assistance of a ship. Do you imagine sailing by different cities or countries is travelling? No. . . . I can go farther in an afternoon, than you in a twelve-month. What, I suppose you have seen the Pillars of Hercules, and perhaps the Walls of Carthage. Nay, you may have heard Scylla, and seen Charybdis . . ." (180). Adams' traveling is in books, "the only way of travelling by which any knowledge is to be acquired" (181). His host hotly contests this, and the quarrel degenerates. Adams thus tries to wrest the title of traveler from travelers themselves, identify it only with textual sources of "knowledge," and apply it exclusively to the reader, whose psychic mobility is unrivaled by travelers' geographical mobility. Don Quixote, in contrast, doesn't take sides as such but rather turns from a reader into a knight-errant, i.e., from one sort of "traveler" into another. Both forms of travel take him away from home. The switch-over modulates through a passing urge to pursue the ever-unfinished travels of the knights he reads about by *writing,* but this gives way to a different sequel to the books he reads: actually becoming a knight-errant and *traveling.* This, he believes, would best promote his honor and benefit the world at large (I.1.75). Recreative traveling thus yields first to a frustrated and then to an enacted form of creative traveling, all in the chivalric mode. It is no surprise that he continues to associate reading and traveling as alternate modes of acquiring knowledge—albeit delusory, as when he discovers that monkeys can divine: "Now I declare that he who reads much and travels much, sees much and learns much" (II.25.236).

Don Quixote's errant madness, already active before he assumes knight-errantry, generates its own utopia (no place) within which the goal of action is an eutopia (good place), even if the undesirability of fully achieving this may be integral to his scheme. Don Quixote lives in a two-world condition. The notion of *world* here uniquely comprehends all the oppositions by which Don Quixote's thought and behavior are usually explained: appearance (or fiction, imagination) versus reality, the extra-ordinary versus the ordinary, archaic chivalric language versus modern sorts of language, chivalric modes of behavior versus currently practiced ones, etc.[8] As the novel's readers are well aware, anything whatsoever relating to Don Quixote's reading of chivalric romances may touch off his madness: "For at every hour and every minute his imagination was full of those battles, enchantments, happenings, absurdities, loves, and challenges which are told in books of chivalry; and everything he said, thought, or did was directed to such things" (I.18.218). Yet this is only partly true. The text reminds us time and again that Don Quixote's madness, like Cardenio's, flares up erratically according to when and how he himself associates experience with the leitmotiv of his *locura;* his "lucid intervals" are quite as astonishing as his madness.

The books of chivalry, diverse as they are, present an identifiably unique order of personages, landscapes, forces, values, modes of interaction, perception, symbolism, causality, explanation, and so on, in short, a world, one quite different from the more mundane world as perceived by other characters in the novel. Although he rarely defines the difference between the two worlds except by terms such as *vía ordinaria* and *vía extraordinaria,* Don Quixote himself suscribes to the notion of chivalric world when, for instance, he advises Sancho not to go against written precedents established for knights-errant: "Do not seek to make a *new world,* nor wrench knight-errantry from its hinges" (I.10.152). For the other characters in the novel, the legends of chivalry nonetheless make up a considerable stock of verbal tradition—written, read, told, sung—and are thus not only familiar but also somehow latent in the experience of "this world." For the less credulous characters, such legends and the books that recount many of them are patently false in their elaboration if not entirely unauthorized in their sources, and this of course is a basic premise of the novel, which reverberates in a mistrust of texts in general and playfully undermines its own pretense of being a *historia.* Nevertheless, the familiarity of the peasantry, the artisan/entrepreneurial and urban classes, nobility, and clergy even with textual examples of this body of lore is remarkable. There are exceptions, of course: Sancho Panza for one seems to be rather ignorant until his apprenticeship with Don Quixote enables him to manipulate the conventions of chivalry as well as any of the other characters who do so (the first innkeeper, Dorotea, the barber and priest, Sansón Carrasco, the entire household of the duke and duchess, the hosts in Barcelona, etc.). Such manipulation reveals a profound awareness of the essentials of a chivalric world.

Three examples merit attention for their peculiar relationship to Don Quixote's own madness. To begin with, the first innkeeper (or "castle warden"), who humors Don Quixote by knighting him in a mock ceremony, tells him (in the words of the narrator) that in his youth he, too, "had devoted himself to that honorable profession, traveling through divers parts of the world in search of adventures [in various places] where he had exercised the agility of his heels and lightness of his fingers, doing many wrongs, wooing many widows, ruining sundry maidens, and cheating a few minors—in fact, making himself well known in almost all the police courts and law courts in Spain."[9] The picaresque subversion of Don Quixote's agenda, phrase by phrase, shows an intimate knowledge of the norms of chivalry by this anti-Quixote, who even instructs the new knight on some key matters concerning knight-errantry.

Second, the next innkeeper (Juan Palomeque el Zurdo) staunchly defends books of chivalry, owns a few of them himself, and says that at harvest time there are always some who read aloud with more than thirty people eagerly gathered around. The books put life into him and many others, he says: "At least I can say for myself that when I hear about those furious, terrible blows the knights deal one another, I get the fancy to strike a few myself. And I can go on listening night and day" (I.32.393). He gets so carried away describing some of the knightly feats that Dorotea and Cardenio suspect he is little short of becoming a second Don Quixote. The priest finds no way to convince him that such books authorized by the Royal Council might be a pack of lies and nonsense, but when he suggests that the innkeeper might be ailing from the same malady as Don Quixote, the host insists that he would never become a knight-errant because the world has changed. The innkeeper thus shares the impulses and beliefs of Don Quixote, but recognizes at least the anachronism of knight-errantry. Maritornes, who works at the inn in several capacities, also loves to hear narratives of knights-errant, identifying with the enamored ladies. The innkeeper's daughter, too, is sentimentally attached to these stories, sometimes crying out of compassion when she hears the lamentations of enamored knights. All of these characters demonstrate the endemic presence of the chivalric world within or beneath or alongside "this world," a shadow world inhabiting their own world. Only in Don Quixote does the latency of tradition become manifest as recognizable madness.

Third, it turns out that the canon, who is every bit in his right mind, knows more about books of chivalry than about theological works and confesses to having written over a hundred pages of a chivalric romance, that is, to having succumbed to the same temptation that Don Quixote was about to fall into before becoming a knight-errant (I.47–48). His motives differ, but the coincidence is striking nonetheless, and points to the possibilities of pursuing fantasy in a genre having a powerful hold over people's imagination.

Don Quixote's self-appointed eutopian task of reviving an obsolete and, in any case, essentially imaginary order of knighthood so as to right the world's wrongs results in his resuscitating at least in his own mind a whole never-as-such-existing utopian world to which that order supposedly belonged; or more accurately perhaps, the utopian world gives rise to an eutopian task within it. Throughout the novel, *imitation* of such figures as Amadís de Gaula provides compelling precedents for his thought and behavior. He thus superimposes a fictitious version of the world's past onto much of the present so that "this world" becomes another, namely, a falsified and anachronistic rendering of itself. The chivalric world is no longer "this world" even if the geography of the former coincides largely with the latter: somewhere has become a kind of nowhere. But just as his madness fluctuates in intensity from one moment to the next and at times seems absent altogether, so does his participation in the chivalric world. Nearly every adventure and speech of his juxtaposes the two worlds, exposing his schizo-phrenia. Without realizing it as such he moves in two worlds, one mundane and the other chivalric, whose relationship is perhaps analogous to that of the profane and the sacred in the sense that although there is plenty of ground common to both, there tends to be a radical disjuncture between them. The more his madness prevails, the more otherworldly he becomes. He himself appropriates religious terminology when defending his resuscitated order of knight-errantry, whose creed needs to be confessed and affirmed against the "blasphemies" of those who refuse to believe in "a thing so accepted in the world" (I.4.100, I.20.238, I.49.579).

In the sense that Don Quixote mimetically makes and remakes the chivalric world, he takes it with him—his is a transportable world. Surrounded by diabolic visions which Sancho judges as not altogether "Catholic," Don Quixote remarks that devils *carry hell with them, and can receive no kind of relief from their torments*" (I.47.558; my emphasis). This enormously suggestive phrase could be adapted to him and the world that accompanies him, and even to Sancho and his *insula* for that matter. Teresa Panza writes to her husband: "Sansón says that he is going to look for you, and knock the governorship out of your head and the madness out of Don Quixote's skull" (II.52.438). Both of them carry their worlds around with them in their heads, even if Sancho's world is no more than a desire for one until it actually materializes. Their respective worlds are integral to their character, and guide their actions including the initial resolution to leave home. Heraclitus expressed it in a more general way: "a man's character is his fate" (*Early* 124).

Sancho's sudden switchover to errancy is perhaps more surprising than Don Quixote's since the only ostensive motive for his abandonment of home is the *insula* which Don Quixote vaguely promises him when proposing the job as squire. His oft-mentioned "simplicity" comes into play here as well as his naive sympathy with Don Quixote's enthusiasm. Considering his workable relationship with his wife and aspirations for his children as well as his integration in village social life and economy, he otherwise seems to have much less reason to fly the coop than Don Quixote, whose idle existence and nonbinding relations with his household pose no need for him to stay—unless his kinship duties oblige him to see his niece not only into maturity but also into marriage or the convent. In any event there are various hints that the attempts of Don Quixote's niece and housekeeper to control his thoughts and movements are irksome to him. In fundamental ways, Sancho's errancy is quite different from Don Quixote's. First, he is a follower, not an initiator, dependent on his master for the realization of his governorship (even though the *insula* eventually comes from another source). The play on words, "tal caballero andante y tal escudero andado" (II.30.273), using the active and passive participles of *andar* with reference to Don Quixote and Sancho, evinces this relationship. Second, the condition of Sancho's tenure is one of servitude, though this is combined with genuine companionship, an ambiguity which reflects his relationship with Alonso Quijano as neighbor but also as member of a lower class. In fact his errancy is rooted in sedentary ties: his being of the same place as Don Quixote and his having known him all his life emerge as motives not only at the beginning but also at times when his other motives for travel are exhausted. Sedentary bonds form the nucleus of errant companionship in a mode of travel that becomes a destiny without destination. What's more, many of his attitudes and actions en route can be seen as oriented by sedentary concerns (his fear of danger, acquisition of money, etc.). Third, while the nebulous idea of the *insula* sets him off on a quest marked by an unwitting utopianism, Sancho's attraction to it (goaded by various ostensive motives) betrays a sedentary desire to govern a place. His actual governorship strongly confirms his lococentrism at every step. Indeed his concept of government resembles that of the Indian sages mentioned above: "a good governor and a broken leg are best at home."[10] More on this elsewhere. The fact is that Sancho, like Don Quixote, abandons home with great illusions without so much as saying goodbye.

But Sancho, unlike his master, vacillates between errancy and his desire to return, and on occasion postpones the moment of a decision which in any event he appears incapable of making (I.18.225, I.32.398, II.13.133–34, II.30.268). Understandably, his longing for home prevails at the worst of times when the pains and meaninglessness of traveling bring family and domestic responsibility to mind: "these adventures which we are always seeking will lead us in the long run to such misadventures that we shan't know our right foot from our left. It would be a good deal better and more sensible . . . for us to go home, now that it's harvest time, and look after our own affairs, and stop wandering from Cecca to Mecca . . ." (I.18.216). Sancho echoes this passage much later in the novel, but with more emphasis on family: "I should do much better . . . to go back to my house, and to my wife, and to my children, to support her and bring them up with what God was pleased to give me, than to wander behind you along ways without ways and along paths and roads where there aren't any, drinking poorly and eating worse" (II.28. 258). Whereas "home" for Don Quixote becomes chiefly a place to get away from, a place to be left in his own past, for Sancho it always remains a point of reference to which he intends to return. These divergent attitudes emerge, among other places, in their final return where they come over a rise and see their village. Sancho falls on his knees and cries: "Open your eyes, my beloved country, and see your son Sancho Panza returning—if not rich yet well beaten. Open your arms and receive your son Don Quixote too, who, though conquered by another, has conquered himself . . ." (II.72.580). Sancho's reunion with the earth where he was born is both physical and filial: nowhere

else in the novel is there such a clear expression of autochthony. Don Quixote, however, rejects the implications: "Stop these fooleries, and let us enter
our village right foot foremost. Once there, we will give play to our imagina-
tions and devise the scheme of the pastoral life we mean to follow." The possessive adjective ("*nuestro* lugar") is significant but unavoidable; otherwise
his village is not so much a place he lays claim to as a launching ground for
new ambulations, this time pastoral ones since chivalric ones are proscribed
for the time being.

This difference of attitude between knight and squire doesn't prevent Sancho from being the one to urge a renewal of their travels at the end of both
parts of the novel, and at the beginning of the second. Teresa Panza in fact
approves of his second departure, confident that Sancho is ultimately oriented
toward familial interests. With some justification the niece and housekeeper
accuse him of corrupting Don Quixote, of literally leading him astray, while
Sancho insists that it was his master who led him "por esos mundos," and
Don Quixote more accurately insists on their inseparability, on their being
one hierarchical body (II.2.55). This last notion obviously stems from their
being of one place, which Sancho expresses to the duchess as the main reason
why he keeps company with Don Quixote despite his recognition of the lunacy
of it all: "if I were wise, I would have left my master days ago. But this is
my lot and my ill luck; I can do no more; I have to follow him: we're from
the same place, I've eaten his bread, I love him well, he's grateful, he gave
me his ass colts, and above all, I'm faithful; and so it's impossible for anything
to part us other than the pick and shovel" (II.33.298). Once again, his errancy issues from the bonds of *locus.* Perhaps his most unequivocal errancy
emerges when he leaves his *insula,* because with it he all but abandons part
of the lococentrism which has motivated his traveling up to this point. Sepa-
rated from Don Quixote, he is more alone than ever, having only his cher-
ished ass as a companion. It is here that he speaks of returning to his former
"freedom" (II.53.444), the touchstone of errant ideology, and contrasts a carefree, mobile life with the burden and anxiety of governing a place. When Sancho later asks the enchanted head whether he'll govern again, the head replies, "You will govern in your own house" (II.62.516). This is no news to
him. The dream of governing elsewhere is now reduced to his original "government," that of his own domus. [11]

Sancho's mixed tendencies find expression in an occasional proverb (*re-
frán*), too. On the more errant side are the sayings "Dime con quién andas,
decirte he quién eres" (Tell me whom you go with and I'll tell you who you
are" [II.10.106]), which follows upon reflections on his likeness to his companion with respect to lunacy, and "Cuando a Roma fueres, haz como vieres"
(When in Rome, do as the Romans do [II.54.449]). On the sedentary side—

reflecting the locative bias of most traditional parlance, including the view that honorable women stay at home — are proverbs such as "Quien busca el peligro perece en él" (He who seeks danger perishes in it [I.20.239]), which Sancho learned from the village priest; "A idos de mi casa y qué queréis con mi mujer, no hay responder" ("'Get out of my house, what do you want with my wife?' admits no answer" [II.43.364]); "La doncella honrada, la pierna quebrada, y en casa; y la mujer y la gallina, por andar se pierden aína; y la que es deseosa de ver, también tiene deseo de ser vista" (An honest maid and a broken leg are best at home, a woman and a hen are soon lost by roaming about, and a girl who's anxious to see also longs to be seen [II.49.414]); and "Más sabe el necio en su casa que el cuerdo en la ajena" (The fool knows more in his own house than the wise man in another's" [II.43.365]). Local ethos is self-evident here where "knowledge" and family honor (deriving largely from the women's behavior) are concentrated at home, and can't be transported without loss or danger. Significantly, Don Quixote objects to the last of these *refranes* as it goes much against the grain of his logically consistent errancy.

Errancy being integral to Don Quixote's madness, there's never any question of willingly returning to his previous sedentary existence while the madness lasts. It should be noted in passing here that Louis Combet's reduction of the journeys undertaken by Don Quixote and other male characters to the notion of "escape" (429–33) misses most of what these journeys are about: a passage from the undesirable to the indefinite but desirable, to echo Montaigne. Whenever Don Quixote explains his strange calling and the tasks incumbent on him, incessant wandering in search of adventure always figures integrally. The ideology of errancy so unquestioned by him is made the object of debate by numerous other characters including a sour clergyman who reprimands him severely for roaming about so foolishly and not tending his own estate. Don Quixote's response not only defends his own errancy on personal and professional grounds but also counterattacks the cleric's narrow and blameworthy lococentrism:

> for what follies that you have seen in me do you condemn and reproach me, and tell me to go home and attend to my household [*gobierno*], and to my wife and children, though you do not know if I have any or not? Is it right to enter other men's houses by hook or by crook and rule [*gobernar*] their owners, and — after a narrow upbringing, without having seen more of the world than the district sixty or seventy miles around — roundly to lay down the law to chivalry and judge of knights-errant? Is it, perchance, idleness and waste of time to wander through the world, seeking no pleasures but the austerities by which the virtuous ascend to the seat of immortality? (II.32.283; cf. a similar confrontation in Barcelona, II.62.512)

With its emphasis on "governing" households of different rank and category, this key passage gives a decidedly political turn to the ethics of errancy versus those of sedentary life. Traveling and governing are here viewed as mutually exclusive activities. The cleric, who practices lococentrism to a fault by trying to dominate the sovereign household of the duke and duchess, assumes that people are essentially domestic and ought to stay at home in order to carry out the duties that fall within their lot; errant travel is consequently evidence of grave irresponsibility. For his part Don Quixote, well mounted on his hobbyhorse, implies he's dispensable as a governor at home and says his wandering is undertaken for purposes of gaining honor by exerting his innate power in beneficent ways away from home; the cleric, who may never have traveled out of the vicinity, is no more entitled to judge over him and his errant order than the ignorant would be over the experienced. Here as elsewhere dialogue between the two radically different standpoints proves useless.

This doesn't mean, of course, that from one errant person or character to another there's much in the way of shared principles apart from the denial of lococentrism, as the comparison of any two sorts of travelers will readily show. Far from Montaigne's admission of vanity in traveling and from his desire to live a merely excusable life on the move, Don Quixote's errant ideology is one of personal potency (in all likelihood intended to compensate for his idleness and impotence), of *being more* than others by *doing more* than others (see I.18.225).

Those most instrumental in bringing Don Quixote's two main journeys to an end—first by caging him and later by defeating him in single combat—are none other than neighbors of his for whom a sedentary life at home divorced from all thought and practice of chivalry is the key to the recovery of Don Quixote's sanity. For them, he is one of theirs and can never be otherwise: his errancy in a sense *is* his madness. The fact is, however, that enviable models of sedentary life are scarce. Though the novel carries Don Quixote's follies to the extreme, it offers little reason for him not to be a mad traveler. Even in his right mind, there's no reason why he should emulate any of the sedentary characters who appear except perhaps Diego de Miranda (the so-called Knight of the Green *gabán*), the exemplary country *hidalgo* who lives at peace with himself and in harmony with his family and community, and who has managed to create an eutopia of sorts around himself (II.16.153). But Don Quixote's restless temperament and the emptiness of his home life preclude such a possibility from the start. His final renunciation of madness and reintegration into sedentary life, though it has its logic, is less than convincing as a life decision, taking place as it does in the shadow of his imminent death and of the novel's closure.

Other (Ab)errant Characters

Don Quixote is populated by a wide variety of traveling types, including performers, pilgrims, students, muleteers, galley slaves, soldiers, bandits, marginalized lovers, a returning captive with his fugitive Moorish wife, and so on, all of whom meet the wandering protagonists on the road, at inns, or in the wilds. These are the places where errant types meet other errant types in a dynamic quite different from errant-sedentary interaction. Other novels especially rich in errant types include the *Persiles*—where itineraries converge and diverge in seas and on islands, and later the mainland—and the *Coloquio de los perros,* although all the novels develop errancy in one aspect or another. Here I'd like to discuss briefly a few of the more salient examples.

A mobile community

The first of the *Novelas ejemplares, La gitanilla,* opens by characterizing Gypsies as innate thieves, a view increasingly shared by much of the host society including the dog Berganza in his own tale (347–49) and the contemporary lexicographer Covarrubias, who refers to "this awful rabble whose profession is to steal in town and rob in the country" (under *Conde;* see Leblon, *Les Gitans d'Espagne* 17–53, *Les Gitans dans la littérature espagnole* 108–13). For readily apparent reasons, travel and deception—particularly stealing—are highly compatible occupations, and in any case are likely to be conflated by sedentary folk. In an anti-Gypsy discourse directed to Philip III in 1619, Sancho de Moncada wrote that "it is a doctrine entertained by theologians, that the mere act of wandering, without any thing else, carries with it a vehement suspicion of capital crime."[12] It should be recalled that the Greek deity of travel and inventor of letters, Hermes, was a thief no less, and an honorable one, and that the ancient "heroes" found honor in the title of robber (Vico 194, citing Plutarch). Vico goes on to cite Thucydides as remarking "that down to his time when travelers met on land or sea they would ask one another if they were robbers, meaning foreigners" (195). Cervantes' Gypsies are naturalized aliens who travel and steal, albeit without honor. In *La gitanilla,* however, the initial portrayal soon becomes complex as Gypsies both interact with the host society, offering their wares, songs, dances, and occult expertise, and reveal their insiders' view of themselves as well as their outsiders' view of sedentary society.

The Gypsies of the novel appropriate for themselves the lands of their travels—"we are lords of the fields and the crops, of the forests, of the woods, of the springs, and of the rivers" (101)—and yet proudly maintain their cultural differences and fleetness of foot, traveling about in what they call confraternities (*cofradía, confraternidad*) and living by their skills and wits. An old Gypsy gives an eloquent profile of their way of life, laying stress on their freedom of movement: "We prize these carriages and movable ranches like gilded ceilings and sumptuous palaces" (102). Although subject to the powers of political and legal institutions as well as dependent on exchange with sedentary society for their livelihood, their social autonomy asserts itself in their endogamy, code of ethics and justice, communal property, organization of labor, and their self-determination (more on the eutopian aspects of this elsewhere). Moreover, each group moves about with an awareness of the activities and whereabouts of other groups. Unlike nomads such as pastoralists, who normally have set routes coordinated according to the seasons, and unlike other kinds of exiles who normally settle in places, these nomadic Gypsies exercise wide options with regard to their directions of movement. Each group is a moving center, continually reorienting itself parasitically but also symbiotically with regard to sedentary communities. The word *aduar,* referring to the actual village-like camp of each group, presupposes communal mobility. It derives from the Arabic *dawwār,* meaning a circle of tents around livestock, which in turn stems from the verb *dāra,* "to go around," "encircle." Significantly, the noun *dār,* from the same root, means "house," "dwelling." The *aduar,* then, is a collective mobile home whose enclosure symbolizes both internal cohesion and external detachment. The novel in general, I might add — and especially those novels that value improvisation — seems predisposed to a fascination with the unique phenomenon of the Gypsies, sharing some of their exoticism, aesthetics, (alleged) skills of deception, autonomy, and homelessness.

The primary interest of *La gitanilla* is not the group as such, but the Gypsyness of Preciosa, stolen as a child, and the becoming Gypsy of her *amante,* who assumes the name Andrés Caballero. Both are from noble families. Preciosa, while dissociating herself from thievery and claiming exemption from an ideology of male ownership of women, excels in all the Gypsy arts and thereby becomes more Gypsy than the Gypsies, to the amazement of Gypsies and non-Gypsies alike; this seems to be possible only because she's not a Gypsy in the first place.[13] For his part, Andrés accepts the condition of two years' training in Gypsy "schools," undergoes a ceremonial entry into the group, and is accepted with full rights. But he becomes Gypsy only to the extent that he becomes errant, since the rest of his Gypsyness is no more than an act. Since he is at the age of youth's breakaway, and has love as the prime mover, the change of life suits him well. A crisis at the end of the novel precipitates a disbanding of the *aduar* and, more important, the return of Preciosa and Andrés to their families and sedentary life, with the certain prospect of their marriage.

Wandering women

The mobility of women is particularly problematic in Cervantes' novels, reflecting a social reality everywhere in evidence of domineering males concerned with family honor and advantage.[14] Courtesans, prostitutes, and *pícaras* both within and outside Cervantes' works show the seamy side of this reality, of course. But Cervantes' female protagonists for the most part internalize honor as personal honor based on chastity (understood within the context of marriage or promises of marriage) while at the same time asserting their free will with regard to choosing prospective husbands. Whereas male mobility very often has nothing to do with making or breaking potential marriage bonds, female mobility normally can't be understood without reference to love and marriage. Apart from a few remarkable cases of adultery where marriage itself is problematized, Cervantes' nubile female protagonists move about until their marriage or impending marriage converts them and their male counterparts into sedentary beings beyond novelistic interest. An exception might be made for those pastoral characters who, like the resilient Marcela in *Don Quixote,* guard their independence from love and marriage, a stance facilitated by the mitigation of male authority in the literary pastoral world; but even Galatea, who moves about by and large free of love within the terrain which contains her thoughts and desires (as she puts it), initially consents out of filial obedience to a marriage her father has arranged for her. Otherwise, desired and undesired marriages figure strongly in the departures and subsequent travels of these women, defining their movements in terms of flight, search, and accompaniment in relation to fathers, brothers, and/or potential husbands.

Their period of travel — coextensive with the novel's interest in them — tends to be a kind of hiatus between the family's and the husband's control over them. This is the time when *no one possesses them* as such, the time they have no place. In conjunction with the common metaphors of a woman's value expressed in terms of jewelry and other objects of wealth, the rhetoric of possession is in fact extremely pronounced in many of the novels including *La gitanilla, El amante liberal, La española inglesa* and *La ilustre fregona.* The relationship between "possession" and control, both of which correspond to sedentary life before and after the period of movement (except in the case of Preciosa), needs to be nuanced, however. *El amante liberal,* for example, tells of the fortunes and misfortunes of an amorous hexagon[15] ("sexagon" might be more appropriate, with emphasis on *agon*), five men vying for the possession of Leonisa in an ambience of piracy, war, slavery, and anarchy. The rhetoric of possession asserts itself from the very beginning of the action as the eventual victor Ricardo accuses his chief rival Cornelio of aiming to take away the "prize" which is due to the former's good desires rather than to the latter's idle ones. Having won her favor by his proven love and generosity, Ricardo "gives" her to Cornelio when they return home to Nicosia: "I hand over to you the jewel [*prenda*] which you must value over all other things worth valuing . . ." (186). But he awkwardly stops short, realizing he can't give what's not his to give. Leonisa intervenes, saying she always belonged to herself, being subject to none but her parents; then, with her parents' consent to dispose matters as she will, she gives herself over to Ricardo: "I am yours, Ricardo, and will be yours till death" (187). She, like Preciosa and various others, has gained the freedom to "give" herself, a freedom that at the very inception of marriage assures her some degree of autonomy and respect, despite the language of possession. What has enabled her to realize this freedom is the journey, one which begins with her actual enslavement and issues into her fullest emancipation. She and many other female characters manage not only to liberate themselves but also to free their male counterparts from one or another form of bondage.

If travel is no easy matter in sixteenth- and seventeenth-century Spain, hampered by hardship and danger, it is especially formidable for women, a fact reflected throughout Cervantes' novels. As highly coveted and defenseless (unless accompanied) objects of desire moving in lawless zones, they primarily run the dangers of rape and family vengeance. Some women actually fall victim to rape, including Leocadia in *La fuerza de la sangre,* while others manage to escape masculine coercion, whether this be enacted or intended. The frequent transvestism of female characters is at least partly accounted for by the downright dangerous conditions of women's travel. Leocadia in *Las dos doncellas* says as much when she begs Teodosia not to let her disguise be known, "since she saw how many dangers she would be exposed to if she were recognized as a woman" (220). There is of course much more to the transvestism of Cervantine characters than this. For both men and women, travel at times involves an alteration of identity as radical as that of crossing sexual boundaries by disguise. If there is always a sexually oriented strategy based on some form of necessity (e.g., to escape Turkish homosexual bondage in the case of Don Gaspar Gregorio [*DQ* II.73] or to escape human sacrifice meted to foreign males and carry out amorous designs in the case of Periandro [*PS* 60]), the fact is that these cross-dressing travelers assume a dual sexuality whose recurrence in Cervantes' texts signals a leitmotiv that transcends the practical considerations of each case.[16] Authorial sympathy rests entirely with young female travelers. At the same time, though women such as Auristela constantly prove their fortitude, various characters express the notion that "woman is an imperfect animal" likely to trip and fall where there are obstacles on her path (*DQ* I.33.408; cf. *PS* 186, 462)—a view which only heightens their vulnerability. Besides being subject to unique external dangers and intrinsic weaknesses, women are also easily stigmatized as travelers. The adjective *vagamundo/a* (vagabond, wandering), hardly complimentary in the best of cases, takes on a decidedly pejorative tone when applied to women including Auristela, the epitome of feminine virtue (*PS* 168). As we've seen, several of Sancho's proverbs look upon women's movements away from home with the utmost suspicion, always bearing their sexuality in mind.

Sancho utters these *refranes* as a gubernatorial admonition to a young girl caught wandering about in her brother's clothes. It turns out that she, unlike her brother, has been confined within her house ever since her mother died ten years back, and has seen nothing of the world but the sun, moon, and stars, "nor do I know what streets or plazas or temples or even men are, apart from my father and a brother of mine and Pedro Pérez the landlord" (II.49.412). Burning with curiosity, she steals away at night with her brother to take a look at the village, only to run into the night watch. All are amazed that her desire to see the world ("ver mundo") extends only as far as seeing her own village by night. Given her domestic enclosure, the excursion around the village represents a boundary-breaking adventure into the world she's been deprived of. Although many characters express their desire to see the world, nowhere is this travel motive so singleminded or so clearly imperative as here. Governor Sancho, anxious to clean the republic of vagabonds and maintain the social order that has enclosed her, has her escorted back home. The ideology of errant freedom which he espouses before and after being governor thus finds no place in his state, least of all in relation to his female subjects.

Preciosa may well be Cervantes' supreme example of a free feminine spirit, even if her reintegration into family and prospect of marriage do compromise her movements at the end. This is due to the fact that her community is a mobile one, that she asserts an extraordinary female independence within it, and that her remarkable talent as improvisatory artist extends itself to open possibilities of action unattainable by other characters. Having been offered as a chattel to Andrés by the males of the group, she brushes their dealings aside and, without promising anything in the long run, lays down stiff terms of a trial period. She thus exerts control over her own destiny by prescribing the terms of her relationship to the surrounding male-controlled world, an arrangement which by and large prevails despite the odd twists of fate toward the end of the story. Auristela and Constanza in *Persiles y Sigismunda* as well as shepherdesses such as Galatea and Marcela exercise a similar autonomy of will. Others such as Dorotea and Luscinda in *Don Quixote* undertake their journeys under much greater constraints but through self-assertion contribute decisively to the resolution of their desires. Their moments of self-determination, like those of the more sedentary Leocadia in *La fuerza de la sangre,* are culminating points in many of Cervantes' novels, moments which celebrate uncoerced femininity. The same is true of Leocadia and Teodosia in *Las dos doncellas,* who come to embody a proud feminine militancy precisely when they fight at the side of the young man they both love: evoking feminine warriors in *Orlando furioso* and a pair of Amazon queens, the narrator refers to them as the "new Bradamante and Marfisa, and Hyppolita and Pantalisea" (224).

When a female character leaves home she usually takes her destiny, if not exactly into her own hands, at least out of the hands of those who would otherwise control it, throwing herself into the utmost uncertainty. By doing so she usually gives up more than her male counterparts do, including family honor, personal reputation, and security; she has more at stake and has to play for broke. Unlike men, who usually have the option of going back and regaining what they had, there tends to be no going back for her except under a very different arrangement such as honorable marriage. Not uncommonly, she flees from her own family. Dorotea, for example, speaks of hiding and fleeing from her father (*DQ* I.28.358)—motives almost unthinkable in male characters. Feliciana de la Voz in the *Persiles* (288–309) and the señora Cornelia in the novel bearing her name also depart in mortal fear of their immediate male kin, having already given birth. Transila in the *Persiles* likewise runs great risk in her spectacular escape (111–14), although in her case her husband and father accompany her and support her, if only timidly, in the face of affinal kin who insist on practicing the custom of the *jus primae noctis.* Sigismunda/Auristela herself leaves home to escape an undesired marriage with Persiles/Periandro's brother, whose feared vengeance forces both protagonists into the wanderings of exile and pilgrimage (*PS* 437).

Sometimes there is no going back at all. So it is with the Mooress Zoraida/María, who definitively abandons her affectionate father, her language, her luxurious life, her high social status, and literally all she has ever known except for some portable wealth in order to risk escaping to Spain with her betrothed about whom she knows next to nothing (*DQ* 385–440). Clandestine religious affiliation decides her desperate break from parental and cultural filiation according to an ideological pattern in Cervantes' works whereby beautiful daughters of prominent Muslims defect to the Christian world or somehow, as though by natural predisposition, betray the paternalistic community of their upbringing in favor of young victimized Christians.

The liberating and salubrious effects of feminine journeys are also evident in negative examples where women are deprived of such self-realization. Despite the very different circumstances of Camila (in the novel of the *Curioso impertinente, DQ* I.33–35) and Leonora (*El celoso extremeño*), their life trajectory appears to trace the shortest of passages from their parents' house to their husband's house to the convent, each place in effect imposing its own mode of domination. Camila is especially happy in her marriage: as the narrator says in an apostrophe to her husband Lotario, "her thoughts keep with the walls of her house; you are her heaven and her earth, the end of her desires" (*DQ* I.33.416). There is no question here of forced enclosure as such, nor of a tyrannical relationship in marriage. Nonetheless Lotario's strangely motivated testing of her fidelity through his best friend destabilizes her domesticity and ultimately brings about the sinister results he nominally fears and may well desire. Whereas many other female protagonists prove their fidelity en route before marriage to the satisfaction of their husbands-to-be, Camila's "trial" takes place later within marriage itself, and within her own home. Once ruin has set in, her only way out is the road to the convent.

Leonora is much more of a possession than Camila, having been acquired by the wealth of her aging husband Carrizales in an agreement with her parents. His strategy is to hoard her by shutting her off entirely from the external world in a feminine world of his own making where he is the only uncastrated male. Her ignorance of the world facilitates her acquiescence and blinds her to her own enclosure: "Her thoughts did not stray beyond the walls of her house, nor did she desire anything but what her husband wanted" (106). The successive advances of the aspiring seducer Loaysa destabilize her domestic world. Significantly, Loaysa doesn't get what he wants, and furthermore Carrizales doesn't find out that this is the case. The convent is a place Leonora chooses to go against both the testamentary dictates of the dying Carrizales and the designs of Loaysa alike. She thus asserts her autonomy from men in two crucial moments: denying herself to Loaysa despite the erotic inclinations she might have, and deciding her future (as a bride of Christ) in the feminine world of the convent. Such autonomy could be seen as illusory since by freeing herself from one sort of subjection she submits to another authoritarian order in each case. Nevertheless, these two acts of hers transform her from a possessed object into a volitional being who has somewhere she can choose to go rather than stay where she is. The final paragraph pits physical enclosure against free will, with obvious reference to the feminine.

In a world where women are possessed as objects, transferred, kept, robbed, seized, bought, and constantly referred to in terms of things of value, Cervantes' female protagonists for the most part realize their emancipation to one degree or another. The journey tends to be very instrumental in this process because it removes them from where they are controlled into a temporary limbo where they attain the self-determination necessary to give themselves over on their own terms. Unlike many male travelers with respect to the opposite sex, and regardless of whether their amorous motives are primary or secondary to other concerns, they travel only in relation to men: away from them, toward them, or with them, or any combination of these. Men constitute their partly fixed and partly shifting points of reference, although how women orient themselves comes to be a matter for them to decide.

Errant types

Errancy in the fullest sense — often involving homelessness, an abandonment of possession, an absence of specific goals either as objects of desire or as places to get to, an indefinite movement en route, and a professionalization of travel where actual journeys shade into life's metaphorical journey — is primarily a masculine prerogative. Cervantes' novels offer an array of errant figures in addition to Don Quixote and Sancho Panza. Here I shall briefly deal in turn with Ginés de Pasamonte and Roque Guinart (both in *Don Quixote*), Periandro (*Persiles y Sigismunda*), Berganza (*Coloquio de los perros*), Tomás Rodaja/Rueda (*El licenciado Vidriera*), Rincón and Cortado (*Rinconete y Cortadillo*), and Carriazo and Avendaño (*La ilustre fregona*).

Outstanding among these is Ginés de Pasamonte, the only minor character not from Don Quixote's village to appear in both parts of the novel, first as galley slave with a brilliant picaresque career behind him and later as traveling performer with a divining monkey and a puppet show (I.22–23, II.25–27). An archetypal trickster (El Saffar, "Tracking the Trickster" 154–60), he transcends by far the limited textual space devoted to him. His crossing of paths with Don Quixote sets in motion a fascinating dynamic due in part to their widely divergent styles of errancy. Associated with crime, deception, the occult, art, and masks, he plays on the social order to subvert it to his own ends and makes an art of improvising in the midst of instability. We never really find out "who" he is because he appears more as a mobile concentration of wily resources than as a definite personality, and also because he is a man without a place, a protean fugitive forever escaping the authority of place.

The bandit captain Roque Guinart in *Don Quixote* (II.60), also a fugitive and subverter of social order, enacts a very different sort of errancy. Modeled with considerable admiration on the historical figure named Perot Roca Guinarda, who was the son of well-to-do laborers, he is less marginal than marginalized. Everything about him except for his lawless practice (which after all is an economic imperative for a lord of thieves) bespeaks a noble bearing guided by magnanimity, rigor, sense, and compassion, in marked contrast to his base but respectful subordinates. While his function as leader of several groups of bandits disrupts the movements of travelers and the order of the state, his demeanor affirms the social order. This is evident in his humane treatment of travelers including Don Quixote and Sancho Panza according to a code of ethics lacking in his men, his role as protector of the star-crossed Claudia Jerónima and his approval of her resolution to enter the convent, his confessed aversion to his lawless way of life, his maintenance of ties with sectors of the nobility, and his establishment of order among thieves on the outer fringes of the society. Nietzsche's insight into the equilibrium and similarity between the brigand and the man of power is worth recalling here: "The brigand and the man of power who promises to defend a community against the brigand are probably at bottom very similar beings, except that the latter obtains what he wants in a different way from the former: namely through regular tributes paid to him by the community and not by imposts levied by force" (*Human* 311). The historical Roca Guinarda's eventual reinstatement as an army commander attests to this.

Roque's lawlessness is in fact the product of a contradiction in the social order, since his "thirst to revenge an injury" (he was motivated by sanctioned honor to an illegitimate use of force, we might surmise) marginalized him and led to an endless chain of feuding. With a price on his head he is continually on the move to dodge both the law and the potential treachery of his own men. He rules over a highly mobile male community which sleeps on its feet and feels the incessant danger of being undone by capture and group hangings. He even comments on his mobile way of life in terms that Don Quixote can identify with: "This life of ours must seem novel to Don Quixote: new adventures, new incidents, and all of them perilous" (II.60.501). Yet his unstable dominion is nonetheless territorial: nearing Barcelona, Don Quixote doesn't even need to be introduced to Roque to recognize him by name as the chief of a lawless terrain.

The *Persiles* is populated with many far-ranging wayfarers, foremost of whom are Sigismunda/Auristela and Persiles/Periandro. Tracing the evolution of the *peregrino* (traveler/pilgrim) in a series of Spanish narratives of the Counter-Reformation, Antonio Vilanova finds in Periandro and Auristela the fullest expression of the exemplary *peregrino/a andante* characterized above all by strong will, stoic resignation, and chastity (147). Their ever-present goal of reaching the holy city of Rome limits their errancy considerably, guiding them with transcendent purposes to which their traveling is subordinated. Nearly everything that "happens" disturbs their progress, particularly in the remote North where the "movable will of the winds" (278) and inconstancy of the seas, barbarity of the peoples and unpredictability of other travelers bring about countless travails and reverses of fortune testing the temper of the characters. Once on land in pilgrims' habit, "peregrinamente peregrinos" (279), they proceed in such a hurry that they forego visiting cities as renowned as Toledo and Valencia, though they do spend time at religious shrines along the way. As I've said earlier, their pilgrimage of love and faith becomes increasingly spiritual, Rome being the gateway to heaven. Other characters, notably the younger Antonio and his sister Constanza, accompany them in their devout enterprise. Their style of pilgrimage contrasts with that of an old woman they meet whose pilgrimage is motivated by idleness and an inclination toward the marvelous, and even more with the "bad pilgrims" she speaks about who make a profit out of sanctity. Throughout the novel, the most diverse sorts of journeys work their way into the principal one, each with its story of how characters become placeless.

Whereas errancy in the *Persiles,* essential as it is to the story, hinders and distracts the pilgrims in their journey, errancy in many of the *Novelas ejemplares* (as in *Don Quixote*) characterizes the journey, *is* the journey par excellence. The dog Berganza tells his life tale without being sure who he is or where he's from, and his companion Cipión seems to be in the same quandary—one which their new-found faculty of speech is unable to solve. These two issues are related. Put baldly, place implies identity and vice versa, while placelessness implies nonidentity and vice versa. As long as there's no significant maladjustment, place positions people in their concept of self and orientation to the world, not only conferring identity on them but also providing the wherewithal whereby identity is internalized. Identity is by and large a concept which makes sense only in relation to place. Is it possible to have an identity but no place? Don Quixote would seem to exemplify precisely this granted at least that he thinks he knows who he is. He certainly displaces himself in relation to home, but does so as a result of placing himself in relation to a whole genre of writing mistaken as history, a genre which provides imitable heroes and an ideology. Ideology is not place as such, of course, but assumes some of the prime functions of place by orienting people to the world and giving them a "place," i.e., a role and identity, within it. Despite occasional self-doubt, Persiles and Sigismunda also know who they are. This knowledge is rooted as much in their transcendent ideology as in their geographical origins. Several of the protagonists of the *Novelas ejemplares,* in contrast, have no such goals or ideological orientation.

For the dogs of the *Coloquio,* the question of who they are is most troubling of all. Berganza begins his life narrative with a tenuous statement on his origins: "As far as I know I first saw the light of day in Seville, in the slaughterhouse, which is outside the Puerta de la Carne. This makes me think—were it not for what I shall say later on—that my parents must have been mastiffs, reared by the practitioners of that wretched trade, the people they call slaughterers" (302). As readers of the novel know, the parenthetical phrase here refers to the central episode in the *Coloquio,* where the witch Cañizares believes Berganza to be one of the puppies her fellow witch la Montiela gave birth to.

Cañizares tells him how it happened, then undertakes a spiritual journey to ask her diabolical *cabrón*—whose answers are equivocal at best—when the dogs will regain their "first form." By dragging the entranced Cañizares into the patio and thereby exposing her witchcraft to the community at large, Berganza never does find out whatever dubious self-knowledge might be gained from her inquiry. Implicated as the other dog from the litter, Cipión is equally repulsed at the idea and rejects it as untenable. The fact is, however, that these miraculously talking dogs are left with more uncertainty than ever.

Berganza's tale reveals him to be a truly homeless being who, like picaresque characters, repeatedly places himself in temporary relations of servitude until inevitable dissolution brings about further displacement. Although a certain amount of design is evident in Cervantes' sequencing of events, Berganza's life journey is without much direction or purpose. His "ongoing" education is more a spin-off than a directive of his movements. He simply happens to run into people, and at one point or another escapes from them into new wandering, new searches for place. Place fails him because the people of places fail him, exposing the beastly side of their nature and compromising his movements. But aside from his present stability at the hospital, Berganza is in any event too errant for place to satisfy him. Errancy runs in his blood and justifies itself in his discourse. After attaching himself to a contingent of soldiers with whom he's willing to go anywhere, he echoes various errant characters in Cervantes' novels by observing: "although the proverb says, 'A fool at home is a fool the whole world over' ['Quien necio es en su villa, necio es en Castilla'], traveling in different lands and communicating with diverse peoples makes men wise" (322)—to which Cipión readily agrees with a reference to Ulysses. Restless and curious, Berganza refuses to endure chains (317) and thrives on both observing and performing novelties. The various names by which people call him fulfill only a passing function as he proceeds in his anonymous going and becoming.

In various respects, the *licenciado* Vidriera represents a rough human equivalent of Berganza, though with some added complications. Asked where he's from, the young boy Tomás at first claims to have forgotten the name of the place, but then withholds it: "no one shall know the name of my country or my parents until I can bring honor to them both" (43). This is the last we hear of his home: from now until his death he is a homeless creature of the road and of urban streets who makes himself in the going. His "forgetting" dissociates him from any definite place of origin and denies him identifying marks. All we're left with is an account of what he says and does told by a narrator likewise excluded from his past. Like Berganza, Tomás comes out of a low social stratum in search of a master to serve and depend on. Like him, he is an outsider endowed with exceptional talents that ought to enable him to survive on his own, and yet (like Kafka's hunger artist) he remains dependent on others for survival.

As a brilliant student at Salamanca he does have a sedentary period in his life, but these eight years occupy only a few lines of text, serving as prologue to the rest of the story. On his return to Salamanca after a brief sojourn in Málaga, his chance encounter with a captain seduces him into a prolonged journey to Italy and Flanders, which he undertakes on condition that he go as a free agent rather than as a soldier under obligation. Like Berganza and so many within and outside fiction (e.g., Montaigne, Descartes), he justifies his journey as profoundly educational: "long journeys make men wise" (46). Travel doesn't seem to make him wise, however, as critics have observed (e.g., El Saffar, *Novel* 50–61; Forcione, *Humanist* 226–316; Dümchen 109–17). It certainly makes him knowledgeable as he moves from one city to another like a traveling eye observing monuments and customs. The narrative proceeds from verb to verb indicating where he goes and what he sees there. His acute observation not only picks up surface detail but also penetrates into human behavior and past histories: "just as one realizes the greatness and ferocity of the lion by its claws, so he came to realize the greatness of Rome by its marble ruins, its statues, damaged or intact . . ." (49). Yet very little "happens" on his journey. Apart from wonder and delight produced by sight and observation, he seems to experience next to nothing. In view of his later traumas, his travels are an escape from himself into novel exteriorities to the point that he almost loses sight of his initial intent (51). Measured against Nietzsche's five grades of travelers (*Human* 272), Tomás remains on the second level in the company of those who actually see the world but don't experience anything as a result of what they've seen, let alone assimilate such experience and body it forth.

Both Rodaja and Rueda, Tomás' surnames before and after the madness, denote wheels, little and big. Tomás is a freewheeling character who, as Paul Julian Smith observes, goes "spinning uncontrollably over Europe before coming to rest at an arbitrary point" (191). Smith also points insightfully to the events instigating Tomás' endless displacement as "strangely, even scandalously, unmotivated" (189). Apart from his will to mobility and independence, he is restless and irresolute. His illness, set on by the miscarried designs of an infamous woman ("de todo rumbo y manejo" [52]) eager to surmount his resistance to her, leads to his strange madness and subsequent confinement by well-meaning friends, but he insists on being let loose to a life as itinerant as before, this time in the streets of Salamanca and Valladolid. The bulk of the novel shows him continually on the move, surrounded by people avid to hear the ingenious answers of a learned *loco*. Not only does he respond with

quick-witted improvisation to every question put to him, but he also extem-
porizes about things and people he sees en route. As noted elsewhere, asked
by a great personage of the court how his trip was, he deliberately confuses
travel with life's journey: "No road is bad as long as it ends, except for the
one that leads to the gallows" (58). For him, in fact, life is one long journey,
one that leads into disillusionment when he recovers his sanity and briefly
attempts sedentary life as a lawyer, and ends abroad with his death as a soldier. The novel offers a bitter example of what it means to have talent but
no place except when one is most alienated from the self. The mad wanderer
has a place or rather a socially sanctioned zone of movement only because
of his estrangement with respect to everyone including himself.

Rinconete y Cortadillo presents two more homeless characters likewise of
low social standing and gifted with quick wits. The question so often asked
in Cervantes' novels, "Where are you from and where are you going?" opens
the novel at the inception of a lasting friendship, and receives an evasive answer from Diego Cortado: "I don't know where I come from, noble sir, or
where I'm going either" (193). Challenged to explain himself, he insists this
is true: "because the place I come from isn't mine, as all I have in it is a father who won't have me as a son and a stepmother who treats me as a step-
son; my way leads wherever chance directs [*a la ventura*], and I shall end it
wherever I find someone to give me the wherewithal to get through this
wretched life." He later goes on to say that the narrow village life and his
stepmother's antipathy toward him made his existence there unbearable,
prompting his departure. His denial of what used to be his own place, then,
results from that place's dispossession of him—a place which in any event
constrains him and offers him very little. He travels with no destination.
Though he says he would willingly settle down somewhere given the means,
his "trade" keeps him on the move, since he has turned his father's trade of
tailoring into the itinerant art of cutting purses. Out of humility, he says, he
shunned an interview with a magistrate in Toledo and took to his heels. His
new companion, Pedro de Rincón, has a similar history. Accompanying his
father, a seller of papal bulls, he took a fancy for a bag of money and ran
off with it. He was later caught and banished from Madrid and now lives
off the proceeds of a stacked deck of cards. The most unstable mobility, then,
is integral to the modus vivendi of these kindred spirits.

Once they begin to exercise their talents in Seville, they discover to their
astonishment that there *is* a place for them, an organized guild of thievery
they're obliged to belong to. Stealing is no longer "a free trade, exempt from
tax or tribute" (206). As of this point, their movements and activities become
regulated according to the needs of an institution which peculiarly replicates
the social order in that it has its own division of labor, revenue collection,

social hierarchy, unique dialect, documentation, code of justice, relations with the outside world, religious devotion, forms of courtesy and ceremony, festivities, and concubinage. Intending to locate them socially and geographically, the potentate Monipodio inquires about their trade, place of origin, and parentage, to which Rincón replies: "The trade speaks for itself, since we have come to you; where we come from doesn't seem to matter much, nor who our parents are, because you don't have to provide this sort of information even to enter an order of nobility" (212). Monipodio heartily approves of their concealment of identity, "for if luck doesn't run as it ought to, it is not a good thing that there should be an entry in the register with the notary's signature over it, with the words, 'So-and-so, son of so-and-so, native of such-and-such a place, was hanged, or whipped on such-and-such a day . . .' And so I repeat that it is a useful document [*es provechoso documento*] to keep quiet about where you come from, to conceal your parentage, and to change your own name, although in our company nothing must be concealed" (212). Whereas documents have the function of fixing people and events with regard to time, place, and attributes, the negative "document" he refers to has the opposite function of not saying, of concealing who they are and thereby unmarking them. For obvious reasons, the trade of thievery demands anonymity in the eyes of society. Yet the two protagonists require a name within the confraternity, and are initiated with alterations of their real names. From the moment they enter the order of thieves, when the focus of narrative marginalizes them into superior observers and commentators, it is apparent that this is not their place but only a temporary stopping point in their more general initiation into the workings of the world. The novel ends with a reference to their future departure, a movement *away* from Monipodio's house toward nowhere in particular, in the guise of nobody in particular.

La ilustre fregona presents another pair of travelers, this time young nobles with picaresque inclinations. The prime mover is a lad named Carriazo only thirteen years old:

> borne by a picaresque inclination, without being forced into it by any bad treatment on the part of his parents, but only out of pleasure and whim, he broke away . . . from the house of his parents and went into the world so happy with his free life that in the midst of its discomforts and miseries he didn't miss the abundance of his father's house, nor did walking on foot tire him, nor the cold bother him, nor the heat gall him. For him all seasons of the year were sweet, temperate spring; . . . with great pleasure he would burrow into the straw at an inn as if he were going to bed between sheets of fine cloth. All in all, he so excelled in the art of the *pícaro* that he could have professed it to the famous Guzmán de Alfarache at the university. (139)

I quote this passage at length because every phrase of it illustrates a particular brand of (literary) errancy, that of adventure-seeking young men of noble birth who exercise the luxury of penury in a spirit of playfulness and who, indifferent to hardship, revel in a free and carefree life of travel and anonymity. Whereas life circumstances normally force picaresque characters into making an errant profession out of survival, Carriazo is attracted to the picaresque life as a calling. His willed homelessness is provisional, predicated on his inevitable return. The difference between the two types is somewhat analogous to that between, on the one hand, Huck Finn and Jim, whose life circumstances force them into errancy, and Tom Sawyer, on the other, who indulges his adventurous inclinations — Mark Twain, after all, was a great admirer of Cervantes and *Lazarillo de Tormes.*

Carriazo's return home to the life of a country *caballero* after three years away submerges him into boredom and melancholy, always bringing to mind his past adventures. His friend Avendaño finds his wanderlust contagious, and soon, under the pretense of going to study in Salamanca, they head for Andalusia in disguise. But they get no further than Toledo, where a maiden at an inn enamors Avendaño. Until now the leading figure, Carriazo becomes secondary to his friend as the focus shifts from travel to love. Like Andrés Caballero in *La gitanilla,* Avendaño falls in love with a woman who appears to be of low birth but who unwittingly transcends her place. It turns out that only by "lowering" himself to her social level is he able to set in motion the events which lead to the revelation of her true identity, marriage arrangement, and subsequent return. Hence the journey is once again an essential part of young men's coming of age, a de facto initiation into the world at large, although here it is cut short by love and marriage.

Marriage and travel are largely incompatible not only in Cervantes' works but elsewhere too. Sancho may well be the only major character in the novels to reconcile them. One need only recall the case of Ibn Battuta, one of the great travelers of all time, who, when his wife started feeling homesick en route, divorced her on the spot and sent her back home. Panurge's exhaustive inquiry into whether or not he should get married, the theme of Rabelais' Third Book, occasions the quest for the oracle of the Divine Bottle in the Fourth and Fifth, thus putting off the decision indefinitely by means of a journey whose ostensive purpose is to solve his quandary about marriage. While the journey manifests irresolution and displacement, marriage is predisposed toward resolution and stability, at least in principle. Travel serves to break up marriages or, more frequently, to establish new bonds of marriage, but rarely to keep marriage intact or foster its growth — except when one of the journey's objectives is to reunite a marriage, as in the case of

Odysseus. Unless there's something unresolved and interesting about marital relations, marriage in literature tends to stifle the journey, tying people to each other and to place. As is reflected in words such as "*hus*band" and "*casa*miento," marriage houses its participants, centering their life in and around a dwelling, a *vivienda*. Marriage sets up one more invisible nexus of attachments where people both possess and are possessed, in varying ways and degrees, in relation to place and other people within place. And while differentials of power and authority—who "possesses" whom or what—are crucial, to possess also means to be possessed, if not by the object of possession, then at least by one's own possessiveness. To cite a line from Yehuda Ha-Levi (b. 1075): "The slaves of the world are slaves of other slaves." Whether it means possessing or being possessed, then, the possessiveness of marriage reinforces mutual dependence, a definite grounding in place, and therefore a limiting of the kinds of events that are likely to happen. It is by no means accidental that in so much of the world's folklore, including the kinds of sources Shakespeare used for his comedies and romances, journeys open up the story into a realm of uncertainty and wider possibilities, while marriage seals the resolution in permanence.

No fewer than seven of the *Novelas ejemplares* follow this pattern of journeys ending in marriage. From near the beginning of *La española inglesa,* marriage, expressed in an overwhelming rhetoric of possession, threatens to put an end to a good story, but one impediment or another always separates the lovers until Ricaredo's final journey ends just as Isabela puts one foot over the convent threshold. *La gitanilla, El amante liberal, La fuerza de la sangre, Las dos doncellas, La ilustre fregona* and *La señora Cornelia* all offer significant variants on the passage from journeys to marriage. The last of these, which begins with the desire on the part of Don Antonio and Don Juan to see the world and show their worth, focuses on these two characters as intermediaries in a dangerous tangle in Italy until they help resolve matters and return to Spain, where they get married to illustrious women and thus turn sedentary. It is perhaps no coincidence that these seven novels are thought to have been written after the other five (El Saffar, *Novel*), just as the *Persiles,* which likewise routes the journey toward a long-anticipated marriage, postdates at least in its final stages the composition of *Don Quixote*. More and more, the way out leads back home, losses are restored, wrongs are righted, the youth lost to society find themselves in others and return transformed and ready to renew the social order. The journey serves all of these ends, but exhausts it raisons d'être in the achievement of its purposes. The journey in these novels circumvents and escapes social institutions only to reaffirm them in new forms adjusted to the shape of legitimate desire. Hence, in terms of the novels' chronology, Cervantes' traveling protagonists become less errant, less anonymous, more directed to specific goals and redirected homeward.

Whereas even in the case of Don Quixote, Auristela, and Periandro, the journey dislocates names from places and either renames or unnames characters, marriage serves to reinscribe characters' names within toponyms, assigning places to people and vice versa. What Cervantes shows again and again in his novelistic journeys is the outgrowing and/or disguising of names and identities. Quite often characters slough names like snakeskins and leave them behind in time and place. Roque Guinart, in contrast, keeps his name perhaps because he is a territorial counterinstitution with respect to the social order. Otherwise, the majority of these traveling characters shake off the attributes of place and erase many of their identifying marks. They become indefinite characters with much more latitude of action, discourse, and movement than before; rather than fixed personalities, they become moving ensembles of potentiality never "equal to themselves," to paraphrase Bakhtin (*Speech Genres* 165). The break from place, especially home, in conjunction with movement elsewhere, enables these potentialities to emerge and dominate in the absence of permanence. The journey thus dynamizes the protagonists as well as the novels in which they move.

Going sedentary

On several occasions in *Don Quixote,* most notably perhaps in the country house of the duke and duchess and the homestead of Diego de Miranda, the narrative provides glimpses into the interiority of domestic life. These intimations serve various purposes, among them that of diversifying the subject matter of the novel and showing different ways of life against the backdrop out of which the protagonists' errancies come into relief. These domestic spheres offer little intrinsic interest for the narrative. What makes them novelistic is the destabilizing presence of Don Quixote and Sancho Panza, who intervene in the workings of the local community and offer occasions for mirth. Don Quixote conveniently gets restless for adventure just when the narrative seems to tire of sitting in one place. Elsewhere, too, including the kingdom of Policarpo in the *Persiles* and the houses of Hazán Bajá and Halima in *El amante liberal,* domestic life becomes novelizable only to the extent that travelers come through to disrupt the norms and routines, giving occasion for festivity, desire, jealousy, exotic tales, and the like. One has the impression that the families and communities of these novels would become stagnant and involuted without the passing through of strangers, or without the departure and return of their people. At the same time intruding travelers are a potential threat to sedentary order; quite often they leave permanent marks, and sometimes even destroy communities (as we'll see in this and the following chapter).

Whatever weaknesses and vulnerabilities a community might have, and whatever subdued desires its members might have, are likely to be exposed and played out according to the dynamics set in motion by the invasive presence of outsiders. Communities depend on travelers, but also can be transformed or broken by them in ways neither they nor the travelers could ever have predicted.

Besides the case of the novela *El curioso impertinente* included in *Don Quixote,* already discussed, only in *El celoso extremeño* and *El casamiento engañoso* is domestic life really developed as such. In both cases an almost rootless protagonist desires to get married and settled down. Sedentary life, it seems, is novelistic only in its failure.

El celoso extremeño begins with Felipo de Carrizales' departure from his native territory, followed by some fifty years on the move. First he wastes his youth and inheritance in Spain, Italy, and Flanders (at least partly as a soldier) and finishes off the little he has in Seville. He then embarks for America to amass a fortune and returns to settle down not in his place of origin, where the poor would pester him, but in a rich neighborhood in Seville. Told in a couple of pages (99–101), all this is prefatory to the main action of the story. The account of his travels is hardly a necessity of "plot," since, as Cervantes' own interlude *El viejo celoso* and analogous tales show, the triad of an aged newlywed husband, a budding wife, and a young seducer forms a sufficient nucleus to generate the story. Rather, it provides a half century of background to render Carrizales' sedentariness understandable as an overcompensated remedy for pathological errancy. Upon leaving Spain for the open sea he takes stock of his past and becomes aware as never before of the lack of direction ("mal gobierno") he has had in the "discourse" of his life. Despite the apparent sea change, the malady persists to manifest its symptoms in a radically different stage (see El Saffar, *Novel* 41–43). Carrizales' restless life of squandering and womanizing turns into an equally restless life of hoarding and wife-keeping as he converts his mansion into a world apart from the worlds he has known, a place meant to contain his wife's thoughts and movements together with his other possessions including black and white female slaves. How much of a "world" his abode becomes will be explored in the next chapter.

Presented as the refuge of European riffraff and as the hope of the desperate, America (*las Indias*), for Carrizales, is less a place to settle than a place to acquire wealth and then abandon. After his twenty years there, his roots are still shallow enough for him to follow the "natural desire" to return to the homeland, *su patria.* Neither in America nor before has he made any permanent human attachments deemed worth mentioning. Never has he lost his sense of center, of belonging to an elsewhere to which he can transfer his riches.

If economic straits dictate his passage to America, he resolves to change his way of life ("mudar su manera de vida" [100]) only when land is out of sight. In calm weather a mental storm (*tormenta*) disrupts Carrizales' journey as the prodigality of his whole life comes to mind, leading to his desire to change himself. When the wind picks up, his storm abates and he lets himself be carried by the cares of the journey itself. Hence two journeys are going on at the same time, one manifest and the other metaphorical, borrowing its terms from the actual voyage in relation to which it diverges and converges. The mental storm represents a crisis in his life journey leading to a change of course. Socrates, when told that someone had in no way changed after a long journey, is supposed to have remarked: "It seems that he took himself with him" (Montaigne I.29.234). In Carrizales' case, the dual journey brings about a dual change—of place, and of modus vivendi—such that present industriousness in America in no way resembles his former wastefulness in Europe. Carrizales seems, then, to have surmounted the limits of Horace's dictum, "Caelum, non animum, mutant, qui trans mare currunt" (Those who rush across the sea change their climate, not their mind" [*Epistles* I.11.27]). He exemplifies the benefits of changing modus vivendi together with place as expressed, for example, in the last sentence of Quevedo's *Buscón* where Pablos reflects on his own hapless journey to America: "nunca mejora su estado quien muda solamente de lugar, y no de vida y costumbres" (whoever changes place only, and not his life and ways, never improves his lot [284]).

Authentic as the change in Carrizales may be, it is mainly restricted to his management of money and sexual desire: in a wide sense, he changes his economy, his *gobierno*. Furthermore, as is evident upon his return, his new attitudes toward money and women reveal less a liberation from his former habits than a mentality of anxious overguarding. Hence he fortifies his house to protect the imbalanced marriage against the kind of person he was, the kind of person who obsesses him with unfounded fits of jealousy. Indications are that he overcomes none of his solipsism. Much as he seeks a break with his past, the ghost of his youth continues to haunt him. In effect, he can't help taking himself—his former self—with him wherever he goes.

Whereas a lack of control over his destiny characterized his pre-American life, a will to control his wealth, both human and nonhuman, characterizes his post-American life, manifesting itself primarily as a desire to control the feminine. Upon his arrival back in Spain, he discovers that his family and friends have all died. After some meditation, he directs his efforts toward the containment and investment of what he has. The precondition for achieving his goals is for him to become sedentary, since he needs a place and people to govern over. Although the pleasure principle allows him to distinguish between wealth and a wife (100), he and his narrator most often speak or think of them in similar terms. It would be easy to show not only that his wife *is* an acquired possession as far as he is concerned, but also that his jealousy and his anxiety about wealth issue from the same psychic disposition. Contemplating his bars of gold and silver, for example, he concludes that "to keep them as they were was *unfruitful* [tenerlas en ser era cosa infrutuosa] and to keep them at home was an incentive to the covetous and a stimulus to thieves" (101, my emphasis). His language of bearing fruit, a metaphor unthinkable during his errant years when he sowed wild oats, applies specifically to wealth here. He is likewise preoccupied with passing on his wealth to possible heirs, and marries Leonora in part for this very reason. One might surmise that she represents both a "fruitful" use of his wealth, since he believes the pleasure she gives him will prolong his life, and the potential bearer of heirs to his wealth. Thus Leonora not only constitutes wealth but also incarnates the "fertility" of his wealth.

For Carrizales, *casa* implies *casamiento* and vice versa, and both epitomize sedentary life. The order in which he goes about setting up house is quite telling: he first gets married, then finds a house and closes it off from the world, then buys household goods and slaves, and finally brings Leonora inside and consummates the marriage. Apart from his maneuvers to keep her from contact with tailors, this significant delay reveals his first psychic manipulation of Leonora: not only is her sexuality an exclusive domain of the husband, but it's also exclusive to the semisacred space of the domus he provides for her. While he brands the slaves on the face, he also premeditates a strategy to brand Leonora as his own: "I'll shut her up and form her in my ways, and so she won't have any way of being other than what I'll show her" (102). Leonora, he thinks, is the girl "that heaven wants me to *have*" (my emphasis). The presence of so many slaves in the house draws attention to the possession of women (and a eunuch) by a man. Although Leonora, like her hired mistress and unlike the slaves, is bound by contract, Carrizales' treatment of her is that of a would-be benign despot who asserts absolute authority over her, treating her as a possession within an enclosed place over which he exercises territorial dominion. The entire domestic setup results from the acquisition, isolation, and regulation of "property," not from the interplay of shared wills.

Carrizales' domestic project in effect bars communication between the outside and the inside, not only the illicit sorts of communication he so fears but also legitimate movement and access within the bounds of marriage. A passage in the *Coloquio* sheds some oblique light on this question of desir-

able movement when Berganza criticizes how the Moriscos confine their economy to the house, the *oikos:* "Their whole object is to make and keep money,
and in order to get it they work and eat nothing. Once a coin gets into their
hands, if it's worth anything at all, they condemn it to perpetual captivity
and eternal darkness; so that by always earning and never spending they col-
lect and amass most of the money of Spain. Where money is concerned, they
are treasure chest, moth, magpie, and weasel; they get hold of it, hide it, and
swallow it up" (349–50). As usual, Berganza's representation of the "other"
peoples of Spain exudes canine xenophobia. In this case, the ever-multiplying
Moriscos — an infection in the body politic (350) — are taking possession of
the limited supply of money and unjustly hoarding it. Of special interest here
is the imagery of money: no sooner does a coin enter into the possession of
a Morisco than it is condemned to life imprisonment. Coins have a life of
their own and are entitled to movement even though they are by definition
possessed. When these innocent beings fall into the hands of Moriscos,
however, they never again see the light of day. Personification quickly gives
way to the reification of money as precious object and as food, but the confinement of coins persists from the dungeon to the treasure chest to the body,
all of which in one way or another stand for the enclosing space of the house.
Money's only way out of the house is to be spent, of course. By the suppression of its legitimate movement, money loses its "currency" and hence its func-
tional value.

Although Carrizales strives to create a tiny, infantile paradise for Leonora,
his treatment of her as a possession is comparable to the way Berganza's
Moriscos treat their money in the sense that he in essence imprisons her within
the house and thereby bars her from the kind of movement and access necessary for her to realize her potential "value" autonomous of her owner. The
once errant Carrizales thus imposes on Leonora an extreme, perverse form
of sedentary life equivalent to house arrest; restrictions are lifted only to allow
her to go to mass at dawn on festive days. Leonora, knowing no other life,
accepts these limits, and so the couple "made a profession in that way of life,
resolving to continue in it to the end of their days" (106). By the same token,
her inaccessibility presents an irresistible challenge to the adventure-seeking
Loaysa, whose entire strategy consists in penetrating Carrizales' system of walls
and locks by exploiting the inmates' sense of sexual deprivation. Carrizales'
notion that wealth should bear "fruit" distances him from the sterile sort of
hoarding allegedly practiced by the Moriscos, yet his enclosure of possessions
within the domestic space amounts to nothing less than hoarding.

Carrizales' sedentary life is doomed from the start not only because he picks
a wife young enough to be his granddaughter, but also because he hasn't over-
come the lingering effects of his former errancy. The young man within him

chooses Leonora, and the old man subsequently governs the marriage in defense against such young men only to witness the apparent disaster he seems to have unconsciously sought. Not until his final hour is he able to conceive of woman apart from an economy of squandering or hoarding. More generally, his restless imagination and temperament preclude any real settling down on his part even when he adopts a supersedentary way of life. It is this restlessness which makes him a novelistic character in the first place. Sedentary life becomes novelistic in Cervantes' writings only when it's unstable, preceded and followed by movement—or when it turns problematic by the suppression of movement.

El casamiento engañoso presents another homeless character in search of a wife and house. His story, told to his friend Peralta, takes him from his first encounter with Doña Estefanía in the dining room of the inn where he's staying through a mutually deceptive courtship to marriage and finally a breakup which lands him in the sweatbaths with syphilis and leads her away with her longtime lover. The deception is possible only because neither character has a place or an identity: staying in temporary lodgings in an urban setting, each is socially unattached with a loose network of friends but no intervening family or community, and can present himself or herself in anonymity to the other. Various studies have dealt with the dynamics of deceit and related topics in this novel. What I'd like to bring out here is the interplay of place and mobility in the actions and discourse of the main characters.

Campuzano's attraction to the seductive Estefanía is intensified by her offer of a house filled with quality goods and her vaunted talents as lady of the house. Wielding the rhetoric of possession, she proposes all of this, herself included, as a package deal: "With this property I am looking for a husband to whom I can give myself over [*entregarme*] and whom I can obey. . . . If you are pleased to accept the prize [*prenda*] you are being offered, here I am all ready to submit to any arrangement you choose, without offering myself for sale, which is the same as moving on the tongues of matchmakers [andar en lenguas de casamenteros]" (285). Overwhelmed at the prospects of an advantageous union, Campuzano declares the great worth of his gold chain and jewels (which turn out to be counterfeit) and proposes marriage to her, calculating that their combined possessions were "enough to enable us to live in retirement in the village where I was born, and where I still had some roots. This property, added to the cash, and by selling our produce [*frutos*] at the right season, could allow us to live happily and at ease" (286). Notwithstanding his deception and his bad intentions to which he twice refers without specifying (286–87), his desire to return to his lost center to recreate a little rural eutopia for himself and Estefanía may be sincere. Campuzano has no hangups about virginity or honor. Stressing her value within the household as cook, manager of servants, economizer, and the like, Estefanía offers him a fully "economic" deal in the root sense, a solution to his homelessness and wife-lessness that would begin with his installation in her house and ultimately modulate to the good life in a fertile place—if indeed such a place exists.

Once married, Campuzano revels in the luxury of his new house. Marriage offers him an orgiastic honeymoon in what turns out to be someone else's house, for the real owner, Doña Clementa, unexpectedly returns with a gentleman. As it happens, no *casa* comes with the *casamiento*. Duplicating her own deception, Estefanía adroitly persuades Campuzano that this is all a staged act necessitating their temporary move to the house of another friend of hers. The marriage is now ambulant and homeless under the pretense of being merely dislodged for a short time. Soon enough he discovers the truth and goes out with vengeful intentions in search of Estefanía only to find on his return that she has taken off with his counterfeit jewelry in the company of her lover. In his empty trunk he contemplates his own grave. Hence the mobile trunk becomes a place symbolically opposed to his dreamed-of eutopia.

For his part, Campuzano becomes even more mobile than he was prior to the marriage. In an interesting antanaclasis on the word *mudar,* meaning to move from one place to another and to change from one state into another, he changes his lodgings and loses his hair ("Mudé posada y mudé el pelo" [292]); the ensuing illness leads to his further displacement to the Hospital de la Resurrección in Valladolid. Used repeatedly in the novel, the verb *mudar* (cognate with a host of Indo-European words relating to motion and muta-tion) fuses movement and change such that each implies the other in the vital trajectory of Campuzano. In the opening scene of the novel he comes totter-ing out of the hospital using his sword as a cane, reduced to a wobbling figure so altered that Peralta sees him as a ghost of what he was. His future spells out a renewed errancy as a soldier subject to the forces of a higher power: "I have a sword, and as for the rest, may God help me" (292). For her part, Estefanía has turned into a fugitive on the run from her own husband, able to shake herself loose of his counterfeit chain that perhaps symbolizes his illusory hold on her (291), but subject nonetheless to the unstable conditions of fear and anonymity.

Campuzano is still married, of course, and therefore still in possession of a wife even if she has run off: "whether I like it or not," he says, "she's mine [es prenda mía]" (291). When Peralta tells him he should be thankful that this thing (*prenda*) of his has feet and has gone off, he replies that without looking for her he always finds her in his imagination. The marriage has split into two errancies, each haunted by the other. Freed from each other, Cam-puzano and Estefanía remain bound to each other by law and by the effects of mutual deceit. The *casamiento* turns into *cansamiento* (fatigue [282]); rather than gaining a house and wife and reaping the fruits of marriage, Campuzano loses his hair, bodily fluid, and vitality. But a renewal of body and spirit is in the making—as the name of the hospital indicates and as Campuzano's manuscript of the *Coloquio de los perros* may well illustrate.

The unstable elements which form the nucleus of the union thus precipitate the breakup into intensified errancies. This is a marriage with two wayward pairs of feet, without dominion, domain, or tangible possessions. The mates are stalemated, fugitives from their own recent past heading into an unknown and unplaced future. The novel is predicated on the instability of the ground beneath their feet and on the imperative of movement. More generally, all of Cervantes' novels graph the dictum "Our souls are always in continual motion," primarily in the form of characters' mobility.

En Route

If you travel every path you will not find the limits of the soul, so deep is its account [*logos*].

Heraclitus

Comme on voit ces routes d'Espagne qui ne sont nulle part décrites!

Flaubert

Cross-rhythms

The common failure to understand movement—or just as common, the tendency to think it away or ignore it—often issues from the kind of logic Zeno used when he denied the reality of motion by abstracting moments out of their momentum and freezing movement in instants or segments of time, thus rendering both time and movement static. At the root of the misconception are, among other errors, a spatialization of time and a neutralization of movement's dynamism and impetus in space. In its prelogical modes, experience also contradicts such reasoning, as Diogenes knew well when he exposed the Eleatic denial of movement to public ridicule by simply walking. Similar experiential demonstrations or probes, if not proofs, could undermine any spatialization of activities, events, or processes. Decades after the decline of structuralism, critics still refer to certain works as being "structured as a journey," as though journeys, or works of literature, or even experience or being for that matter, were structurable. The admirable attempt to find the eternal in the instant likewise replicates the fallacy of the divisibility of time and motion by ignoring the blurring carry-through of motion in time-space. "Momentum" makes "moments" implausible in time and motion.

Momentum takes on more varied properties in relation to traveling, apply-
ing not only to actual physical movement but also to all those motives identifiable as "driving forces" away from or toward somewhere. By extension,
it applies to all the "discursive" activities con-current with travel such as thinking and speaking, not to mention narrative that recounts real or imaginary
journeys. Travel is never simply going but rather a composite of multiple goings-
on, all of which bear momentum and relate to each other in varying counter-
points and rhythms—even when things seem to be at a standstill. All of us
as travelers are aware that conversing or listening to music while en route,
for example, may be integral to the rest of the experience of traveling or may
even nullify or radically alter the sense of space and time of the physical traveling, but no matter what their intrinsic relationship may be, their co-incidence
necessarily brings them into association in a complex process whereby every
experiential mode is somehow affected by every other one. In their own time—
though subject to interventions and influences of other concurrent processes—
conversations begin and end, become enlivened and die down, pause and start
up again—as do sequences of thought and passages of movement and everything else for that matter. Hence the experience of traveling thickens and thins
out according to the timing and association of its experiential movements.
What I am proposing here is the notion of rhythmic overlay, or more precisely, *cross-rhythms*[17] between different goings-on in their distinct "what-
ness" as perceived by travelers—or by readers.

Countless passages in Cervantes' novels stress the simultaneity of processes
and events, suggesting movement as the principle par excellence of all such
happenings. A few passages from a brief stretch of *La Galatea* illustrate how
multiple movement occurs simultaneously:

And seeing that the sun was hastening on its course toward the western gates,
they wanted to tarry there no longer, mindful of getting to the village before
the shadows of the night.[18]

Those who were listening to Elicio and Erastro wished the way were longer
so as to keep enjoying the song of the enamored shepherds. But the closing of
the night, and the arrival at the village made them stop. . . .[19]

The enamored Timbrio and the two beautiful sisters Nísida and Blanca bore
such a longing to arrive at the hermitage of Silerio that the swiftness of their
steps, great as it was, could not keep pace with their desire.[20]

The hurried Timbrio neither could nor would wait for the shepherd Lauso to
go ahead with his song, for . . . he made signs of taking the lead, and all followed him. . . .[21]

While Lauso paused to recite these verses and to praise the singular beauty . . . of his shepherdess, the burdensomeness of the road was lightened for him and Damón, and time passed without their being aware of it until they arrived at the hermitage. . . .[22]

In the first of these quotes, the sun's movement and the imminent approach of night set the shepherds in motion toward the village. In the second, the day's and journey's end puts an end to the concurrent song and the listeners' enjoyment of it. In the third, motivating desire outpaces the steps of the shepherds. In the fourth, Timbrio's impatience drives him on ahead and cuts off the ongoing process of Lauso's song. In the fifth, Lauso interrupts the conversation with a song so absorbing that it alleviates the traveling and makes time pass without their noticing it. Hence traveling, ongoing feelings and desires, different forms of discourse (singing, speaking, listening, and so on), the movement of the celestial bodies, and the passage of time are all characterized as simultaneous processes. After all that has been said about discourse and movement, I scarcely need to insist on how the language referring to "discourse" in such passages as these depends on metaphors of going. One process, then, may set another in motion, put an end to it, interrupt it, accompany it, stimulate it, retard it, diminish or heighten awareness of it, or affect it in any number of other ways. Like any activity, traveling is made up of multiple simultaneities. More than other activities, however, traveling tends to lend its motion to the nonkinetic processes integral to its experience. By no means immune to this movement, the writing and reading of travels add to the simultaneities and hence to the multiple "movement," which in turn implies a coexistence of different orders of "space."[23]

No reader can fail to notice the overwhelming importance of dialogue in *Don Quixote*. It should be borne in mind that these dialogues for the most part occur on the move, and more generally, that nearly all dialogues in the novel refer in one way or another to the journey of the protagonists. Many of them take their cue from something that has happened on the way or might conceivably happen; in many, even those which take place before or after one or another of the journeys, the ultimate reference is to the protagonists as travelers. Speaking and moving along tend to be concurrent activities. Once again it should be recalled that the prime verbs describing both dialogue and narrative coincide with those used to narrate journeys (*pasar, seguir, proseguir, volver, ir, venir, andar, llegar,* etc.).

Moreover, speaking also constitutes an important part of the traveling both as experience of the journey and as discourse recounting it: dialogue reflects on the journey, speculates about it, enriches and entertains it. Sometimes conversation even eclipses physical movement such that the dialogue *is* the journey not only for travelers engrossed in it but also for the novel's narrators and readers, for whom dialogues often "get" the protagonists from one place to another, from one event to another, in the absence of any other indicators concerning what happens during some interval of the way. Common statements such as, "Don Quixote and his squire were talking as they rode along, when Don Quixote perceived approaching on the road they were following . . ." (I.18.217–18), or "As they were talking of these and other matters, night over-took them on the road . . ." (I.19.229), tacitly acknowledge the role of dia-logue in overriding journey narrative to mark out the in-between progress of traveling.

In the reading process, dialogue fosters the textually mediated sensation of "being there," which means "moving there" when one is at all aware of simultaneous movement on the part of the travelers. Citation creates the illu-sion of mimesis in Plato's sense of the term (and so well practiced by him despite his censure of it)—the sense that characters author the text's words with a minimum of intervention. By aligning spoken words with written words of the text, citation sets parallel verbal processes in motion as though the one were a reproduction rather than a representation of the other. In so doing it is bound to be affected somehow by processes simultaneous with the char-acters' dialogue, including motion.

Consider, for example, the multiple processes set in motion at the outset of Don Quixote's first journey just after the departure has been narrated in a spirit of parody very different from the knight's own perception of it:

> As our new-fledged adventurer paced along, he kept talking to himself: "Who can doubt that in times to come, when the true story of my famous deeds comes to light, the sage who writes of them will say, when he comes to tell of my first sally so early in the morning: 'Scarce had the rubicund Apollo spread o'er the face of the broad spacious earth the golden threads of his bright hair, scarce had the little birds of painted plumage attuned their notes to hail with dulcet and mellifluous harmony the coming of the rosy Aurora, who, deserting the soft couch of her jealous spouse, was appearing to mortals at the gates and balconies of the Manchegan horizon, when the renowned knight Don Quixote de la Mancha, quitting the idle feathers, mounted his famous steed Rocinante and began to journey across the ancient and celebrated plain of Montiel.'"[24]

This is a retelling of what has just been told, a reflection on the part of the protagonist of what he perceives to have just happened and to be still happen-ing. He talks to himself *while* he rides along. His thought here is presented as a quotation which in turn generates a quotation from a hypothetical nar-rative of his journey written in the future (note the conventional image of traveling time). The author and style of that narrative, differing markedly from those of the text we read, are here inscribed in the history/novel of *Don Quixote,* and are hence concurrent with it for a few moments. Metaphors of movement characterize both the publication of the hypothetical text ("cuando salga a luz") and more important the writing process ("cuando llegue a contar"), which follows the sequence of events as they occur to Don Quixote in his travels. The inner quote from a future text telling of his present movement evokes the dawn in several images of action in process, mainly the coming of Aurora, while Don Quixote likewise abandons his bed to sally forth. (Let me note in passing that the language of his quote — the jealous husband, the lushness of Aurora, her rising from the soft bed and revealing herself at the same time as Don Quixote leaves his idle bed and goes out to meet her as it were — more than hints at an eroticization of the journey from its very inception.) Thus all of the processes mentioned above are brought together in a complex simultaneity to which may be added all those narrative processes of which Don Quixote is unaware: the novel we read written centuries ago, posing as an edited history based on other histories and perhaps oral accounts, and so on.

As this passage shows, thought and mood are obviously integral to the fuller experience of traveling. Time and again, Don Quixote and Sancho Panza (like Carrizales in *El celoso extremeño,* as we've seen) are said to move along while their thought moves: "these thoughts so carried him away [le llevaban tan fuera de sí] that, without being aware of it, he loosened the reins of Rocinante . . ." (II.11.113); "As he rode on, then, with this thought in mind, he saw . . ." (I.23.284). Don Quixote's "thought" mentioned here is none other than his perpetual expectancy regarding adventures. This "thought," then, is inseparable from his motives for travel, from the creation of the world in which he believes himself to move, from his style of travel, from a sustained mood of expectation in which he travels, and from the ways he deals with what he encounters en route. Characters' thought, shift as it will, may always be assumed to be going on, moving in its own space which sometimes coincides with the space of travel, sometimes not. Integral with thought are moods and e-motions, whether they be prevailing or short-lived, which are of inestimable importance throughout all the novels despite scant critical attention paid to them. The *admiratio,* happiness, melancholy, anxieties, mirth, jealousies, and passions of all sorts on the part of characters carry the travelers along, so to speak, and have a bearing on the reading of their travels as well. Sancho's infectious pleasure in eating and drinking as he follows behind Don Quixote, to take one transient example, makes him oblivious to the hardship and potential danger of seeking quixotic adventures: "And as he went along like this, taking repeated gulps, he entirely forgot the promise his master had made him, and reckoned that going in search of adventures, however dangerous, was more like recreation than hard work."[25]

Both traveling and reading, then, involve a greater or lesser awareness of concurrent processes as they interact in time. How such processes "move" together with respect to what is more static, how they converge and diverge, how they set one another in motion or cut one another off, how their rhythms and attributes mesh or function out of sync, how they vie for more or less attention on the part of those who perceive them — these are among the significant variables of interprocessive relationships. The obsessive language of movement infiltrates into nearly all of these goings-on, as may be appreciated not only from the examples cited here but also from what we've seen regarding discourse, desire, and life processes. A fuller discussion of the simultaneous movement of journeys and life's journey (e.g., *Gal* 95; *DQ* I.44.533; *PS* 177, 188, 246, 253, 282, 394), of life's journey and narrative (e.g., *DQ* I.35.445, I.47.557, II.63.526; *PS* 79, 98, 285; *CEx* 104), or of other simultaneous processes would serve little purpose other than confirming what has already been said. However, the treatment of actual physical movement, considered either apart from or in conjunction with metaphorical movement, figures as the object of inexhaustible fascination in innumerable passages in the novels, and merits further exploration.

Movement and stasis

Given their indeterminacy, the words *movimiento* and *mover(se)* characterize actions strikingly often in lieu of other more telling expressions of motion. While even the vast number of nouns and verbs denoting movement may be poor instruments for defining how movement actually happens — as is evident in the clumsiness of language attempting to convey intricate dances, for instance — *movimiento* and *mover(se)* would seem to impoverish the specificity of movement much further. Their only precision lies in their annulment, since there's no doubt as to what immobility designates. Otherwise, Cervantes' insistent use of these words suggests that movement as a category often outweighs the advantages of more specific terms, as though the fact of movement as opposed to stasis were more significant than internal differentiations concerning how someone or something actually moves.

Besides metaphorical movement, Cervantes and his narrators never tire of telling about physical movement as such. Movement lends its sequences easily if not very precisely to narrative sequencing and provides a continual source of amazement. The fact that someone or something moves seems to be worth telling, like the movements of the protean dog on the beach in the Telemachus episode of Joyce's *Ulysses* — an instance of the "ineluctable modality of the visible." The fascination in Cervantes' novels with movement betrays an attitude comparable to the way Deborah Hay envisages her dancing as Susan

Leigh Foster characterizes it: "Her choreography is informed by her willingness to see the world as motion, to see that movement is everywhere. . . .
Dancing is the activity of being present in and consciously aware of one's
own movement as part of this flux" (Foster 6–7).

Though I'm mainly concerned with movement as going, *movimiento* applies to a broader range of activity including emotive alterations in the body
and soul, gestures, as well as agitations in the surrounding natural world.
Instructing Sancho on how to observe Dulcinea's actions, Don Quixote says
that among lovers, "the outward actions and movements they show . . . are
most certain messengers, bearing news of what is going on in their innermost
souls" (II.10.104). Here, as so often, *movimientos* carry within them the expression of internal affects; they are a sort of natural language to be inter-
preted by other characters. When qualified with adjectives such as *honesto*
or *descortés,* they reveal character.

Furthermore, numerous passages already cited attest to the close attention
paid to movements of the most varied sorts throughout the novels. Many of
the comic effects in *Don Quixote* come about by visualizing movements or
arrested movement: Sancho's flying up and down as he's tossed on the blanket
or his hanging from a tree in unwarranted fear, the moving of the great arms
of the windmills, the many battle charges of Don Quixote, the tying of Don
Quixote's hand, Dulcinea's flying leap onto the ass, the lion's turning about
in the cave and revealing its hind parts, governor Sancho's immobility like
that of an overturned turtle or boat, and so on ad infinitum. Whole chapters
including chapter 20 of Part I could be instructively read in terms of what
moves and what doesn't: e.g., the narrative of Sancho's story, the characters
and goats within the story, Rocinante with his hind legs tied, the wind, the
batanes, Sancho's bowels, the vapors from his excrement as they travel to Don
Quixote's nose, laughter, emotions, etc. Values and expectations are always
attached to these movements. Equally important throughout the novels are
the values attached to immobility, whose various associations with silence,
death, fear, rest, and *admiratio* have been pointed out.

Regardless of what else it may be, Cervantine narration is a choreographic
art, constantly moving its characters about and indicating their relative posi-
tioning and actions as well as the motion taking place around them, not to
mention motions of a metaphorical nature. Let one example suffice for many.
In the first book of the *Persiles,* Periandro takes part in a running race, as
told by a ship captain:

> A trumpet sounded, the cord was released, and the five of them leaped forward
> in flight; but they hadn't gone twenty steps when the newcomer was ahead by
> more than six, and at thirty he was already ahead by more than fifteen. He fi-.
> nally left them little more than half way, as though they were immobile statues,

to the amazement of all present, especially Sinforosa, who followed him with her eyes, both when he was running and standing still, because the youth's beauty and agility were enough to draw behind them not only the eyes but also the wills of all who watched him. I noticed this, because my own eyes were attentively watching Policarpa, the sweet object of my desires, and in passing [*de camino*], I watched the movements of Sinforosa.[26]

There is something of an inversion here of Zeno's paradox of Achilles and the tortoise, where instead of the faster runner becoming essentially immobilized as he approaches the slower, he pulls away from the slower ones with such speed in roughly proportional distances that they rather than the surrounding space become the principal frame of reference: the disparity between the two velocities of movement nullifies the slower velocity into stasis, as it were. Meanwhile, the amazement (*admiración*) of the spectators, mentioned in the same breath as the immobile statues, likewise renders them inactive and presumably speechless—the typical reactions of characters who are *admirados* or *suspensos,* "suspended." But their eyes follow along, both when Periandro is running and when he is standing, as do their affects which are so attracted to the newcomer. The verb *seguir* (to follow) not only refers to spatial movement but also presupposes a more purely temporal sequence, since its object needn't be going anywhere. At the same time, the captain's enamored eyes closely observe Policarpa and shift their gaze to the "movements" of Sinforosa. Hence diverse sorts of movement and nonmovement, which isn't so much the opposite of movement as its zero-degree, interrelate in a quasi-choreographic setting.[27]

A brief look at some of the language dealing with boats in the *Persiles* illustrates how movement and stasis are valued as narrative objects. Just prior to the running race, Periandro's arrival is described in lush detail as the rowboat furiously breaks the water and comes to shore just as the rowers jump out (151). Elsewhere a boat race is described in detail, each boat representing some agency of love and marriage and striving to "conquer" the others by winning (216). At times the language of other domains is transferred to the movement of vessels, such that a boat may "fly" where the sea and wind choose to carry it or slide smoothly kissing the lips of a sea as it breaks the blue water (140, 276). In the Glacial Sea Periandro's ship becomes immobilized in its own medium, "petrified" among mobile boulders and hills of ice (246). The ships in Lisbon's harbor are "mobile forests," while the boats on the river of a remote island are similarly described as moving trees (277, 208). One could find analogous examples with respect to other "vehicles" including carriages, horses, mules, asses, and feet, all of which, as agents of movement and bearers of travelers, receive close attention.

But in Cervantes' novels, as in so many travel fictions from the *Odyssey* onwards—works of Lucian, Dante, Ariosto, Rabelais, Cyrano de Bergerac, and Voltaire, for instance—traveling is by no means bound to the realm of the ordinary. In particular, quixotic madness, dream, and witchcraft bring about extraordinary journeys in what may be the three most important novels: *Don Quixote, El coloquio de los perros,* and *Persiles y Sigismunda.* Corresponding to Don Quixote's two-world condition, the distinction between ordinary and extraordinary ways (*vías*) along which events and processes including travel take place is a leitmotiv in the novel.

One of the festive jokes in the chivalric vein played on Don Quixote and Sancho during their stay with the duke and duchess consists of having them "ride" the giant Malambruno's wooden horse some 3,227 leagues to the imaginary realm of Candaya in order to do battle with the giant and thereby disenchant princess Antonomasia and her husband Don Clavijo as well as unbeard the ladies of the palace (*dueñas*) thought to be accomplices in the unauthorized marriage. The horse, named "Clavileño el Alígero" (formed from wood and peg, and nicknamed the Light-winged), surpasses all the real and mythological horses of yore to compete with none other than Rocinante; it neither eats nor sleeps, and can fly from one part of the world to another in no time. Prompted by cues from the bystanders, knight and squire soar up mounted and blindfolded from the garden through the regions of the air to the zone of fire, whereupon fireworks inside the horse explode and throw the riders to the ground. To their astonishment they find themselves in the garden where they started out; an inscription on parchment informs Don Quixote that the adventure has been completed by his merely attempting it. Malambruno is satisfied and the enchantment undone. Part of the joke derives, of course, from watching the protagonists go on an imaginary journey through space without their going anywhere at all. Absolute immobility and fabulous mobility coincide in a single event. Don Quixote notes as much, but for him the scale of appearance and reality is tipped toward the extra-ordinary: "I could swear that in all the days of my life I've never ridden an easier-paced horse: we seem not to be moving from one spot" (II.41.350). He accounts for the incongruency by affirming that this journey, like so many others in books of chivalry, isn't subject to the natural order of things: "For as these matters of flights go beyond the ordinary courses of things, from a thousand leagues away you can see and hear what you will" (II.41.349).

Consistent with the extra-ordinary travels of knights-errant, this journey turns into psychic travel owing to its antithetical duality. The indeterminate character of the enchantment gives Sancho scope to fabricate what he pleases about the journey—how he saw the world and men below and came within reach of the sky, and how as a former goatherd he got off Clavileño to entertain himself with the seven *cabrillas* (kids) forming the Pleiades—because if the equestrian flight was the work of enchantment so was the experience of the journey including everything he saw and did (II.41.354). For Sancho as for Don Quixote (e.g., II.10.110–11), enchantment transforms not only what one sees, but also the ways in which one sees and understands, working uncannily inside the psyche and senses. All Don Quixote needs is a series of cues for him to give free rein to the overriding logic of the extraordinary in general and enchantment in particular.

In an earlier episode the mere sight of a boat on the bank of the river Ebro prompts Don Quixote to suppose that the boat itself is inviting him to an adventure: "because this is the style of the books of chivalry and of the enchanters who intervene and speak in them: when a knight is placed in some peril from which he can be freed only by the hand of another knight, though the one is three thousand leagues from the other, or even more, they either snatch him up in a cloud or provide a boat for him to board, and in less than a twinkling of an eye they take him through the air or the sea where they want and to where his help is needed."[28] Scarcely have the two travelers drifted a few yards from shore when Don Quixote estimates their having traversed hundreds of leagues and wonders whether they've crossed the equinoctial line. This gives rise to a series of cosmological misunderstandings on the part of Sancho (cf. *PS* 351). Here an enormous disparity between real and imagined velocities corresponding to concurrent but unequal modes of experience, ordinary and extraordinary, produces a dual journey, each mode of which is constituted not only in its own terms but in its contrast with those of the other.[29] Each presupposes different principles of movement: a river current taking a boat carrying passengers, on the one hand, and enchanters transporting people according to laws of movement which cosmically transcend the quotidian.

By no means confined to these episodes, extraordinary travel is an ever-present potentiality for Don Quixote and other characters, having countless precedents both in literature and life, especially the occult. The adventure of the cave of Montesinos also involves extraordinary travel as of the moment Don Quixote falls asleep and thinks he awakens to continue the journey in the dreamlike space of a lush meadow and a crystal palace; here too the logic of enchantment is in full force, affecting what Don Quixote sees and how he sees it. This logic is one of conscious rationalization, however; more profound but unrecognized by any of the characters, least of all by Don Quixote, is a dream sequence releasing the dreamer from his whereabouts and leading him within the space and time of the imaginary (cf. *DQ* I.16.199 and Rabelais III.13.453). Much earlier, before and after Sancho supposedly goes on his mission to El Toboso from the Sierra Morena, the protagonists discuss his journey in terms of the extra-ordinary flights of witches or of people transported by enchanters or a legion of devils—terms which call shamanistic travel to mind (I.25.310, I.31.385; cf. I.47.557, I.49.577, and also Helms 62, 81). Interestingly, while "traveling" on Clavileño, Don Quixote recalls the case of a certain Eugenio Torralba, judged by the Inquisition in 1531, who was said to have ridden a cane through the air with the help of devils, witnessed part of the sacking of Rome, and returned to Madrid the following morning (II.41.350).

Important episodes in the *Persiles* and the *Coloquio de los perros* develop further the transcendence of ordinary time-space via extraordinary movement. In the *Persiles,* a sorceress enables Rutilio to escape a death sentence in Italy once he has given her his promise of marriage. He finds his feet free of chains and the prison doors wide open, and a magic mantle borne by demons lifts them up to the accompaniment of diabolic murmurings and lands them at dawn in the wilds of Norway, whereupon the woman turns into a wolf (89–92). Sources and analogues for this episode abound. What I'd like to stress here is that, given the sequence, extraordinary movement partakes of a process of disengagement from materiality, a release from the ordinary principles and limits of space and time, while at the same time it imposes its own conditions; desire, will, necessity, and discourse govern it over and above physics. Various "explanations" reduce Rutilio's flight to demonic illusion (90, 92, 134–35) in line with official doctrine about flight in sorcery and witchcraft (e.g., Kamen 186), but fail to account for the fact that Rutilio escapes from an Italian prison to find himself stranded in a remote part of the world. Despite the orthodox coverup backed by "science," the novel tacitly substantiates a view of this as actual geographic rather than only psychic displacement.

Journeys contrived by witchcraft lose some of their diabolical aspect in the *Coloquio de los perros* through a more humane, psychological treatment (335–45). La Cañizares, a consciously hypocritical witch capable of pious theological discussion, tells the dog protagonist Berganza about the witches' Sabbaths she often attends. Whether in fantasy or reality, she explains, she and other witches change into cocks, owls, and crows and migrate to a far-off field where the devil as a goat awaits them (cf. Flores Arroyuelo 85–138; Caro Baroja 123–48, 211–61; Henningsen 69–94); there they regain their true form and indulge in feasts and other orgiastic pleasures she refrains from naming. She herself doesn't know whether she actually goes in body and soul or whether, as some people think, the devil fills the fantasy with images that only appear to be real, but she's inclined to believe both of these to be true— sometimes it's one way and sometimes the other. The intensity of the experience makes it impossible to distinguish between the two while the journey is in process. She goes so far as to say that imagined delights are much greater than those physically enjoyed, at least with regard to such false pleasures as the devil has to offer, though the contrary might be true concerning real pleasures. Convinced that Berganza is one of the dogs her friend la Montiela gave birth to, she resolves to go and ask the devil about the dog's future. While smearing herself all over with chilling unguents that deprive her of her senses, she tells Berganza not to be alarmed if her body stays behind or happens to disappear on him. Once she has lain down as though dead on the floor without so much as breathing, Berganza drags her out to the open patio and waits till morning when people come and witness the scandal. Not even pinpricks from head to heel can make her come to until she does so on her own.

Physically motionless but for a continuous pulse, she has been psychically absent on a mission whose outcome is never revealed. This is how Berganza sees it too as he refers to her travel (*ida y vuelta*) despite her physical presence. Once those who congregate around realize she's alive, they at first surmise she's in some saintly ecstasy (*éxtasis*). Though the "ecstasy" is diabolically inspired, the term applies not only to the intensity of her psychic experience but also, in its etymological sense, to her "extra-vagance"—her being and moving out of place, outside herself. As we've seen, Don Quixote practices bilocation[30] in his own way, transporting himself ecstatically from where he "is" into the space of his fantasy. Whether or not they result in bilocation (Rutilio, for example, is never two places at once), all such instances of extraordinary movement involve a radical release from the normal constraints of movement in time-space and a simultaneous streamlining of desire. In most cases, this presupposes not so much an essential alteration in time-space as such (a day is still a day, and distances remain distances) as an annulment of the limitations of movement by way of fantastic velocity, especially through flight. Like Rutilio, other extra-ordinary travelers find themselves willingly but uncontrollably unbound and swept away from a here to an exotic elsewhere.

Identities in movement

> . . . siendo español en lo fanfarrón, y romano en calabaza, y gallego con los gallegos, e italiano con los italianos, tomando de cada nación algo, y de entrambas no nada. Pues te certifico que con el alemán soy alemán; con el flamenco, flamenco; y con el armenio, armenio; y con quien voy voy, y con quien vengo vengo.
>
> Estebanillo González

Thus far under the banner of "En route" I've concentrated on issues concerning relationships between movement and travel, movement and experience; I now move on to discuss issues more focused on travel experience as such. What concerns me at present is how traveling affects the "identities" of characters—and I'd like to deal with this issue lightly. Let me clarify that for me

the term "identity" is a convenient shorthand either for how characters construe themselves or how others do, and always to be understood as within
quotation marks.

Think of a photographic image of human figures blurred in motion, or
better yet, a blurred sequence as in a motion picture conveying the movements
of its human subjects. Behind merges into ahead, before into after, past into
future. Characters en route carry some of their past with them and an open
futurity, the possibility of different futures. Who they were, are, and might
become coincides with where they were, are, and might go. The governor
of Lisbon never tires of asking the travelers in the *Persiles* "who they were,
where they came from, and where they were going"; the viceroy provides them
with documents stating "who they were and where they were going" (279,
282).[31] This "who" is a composite of various factors—their names, their social status, their reasons for being there, and so forth—but is inseparable from
where these pilgrims (*peregrinos*) come from and *where they are going*. The
inclusion of destination in identity may be seen in the way Dante, following
popular usage, differentiates between *pellegrini, romei,* and *palmieri,* pilgrims
to Santiago, Rome, and Jerusalem, respectively (Hahn 18):[32] hence distinctions according to destination override the generic category of pilgrim. For
Periandro, this principle applies to the very being of the protagonists: "Led
by destiny and choice, my sister and I are going to the holy city of Rome,
and until we see ourselves there it seems that we have no being at all [no
tenemos ser alguno] nor any liberty to use our free will" (125). When characters are set on no destination in particular, the indeterminacy of their journey
likewise enters into who they are; their lives are in motion toward who knows
where. Even Periandro and Auristela share in this indeterminacy while en route
because they are always uncertain as to what their fate will be—as is the poet
who wants to write a play about them but doesn't know what genre to use,
"because if he knew the beginning, he didn't know the middle or the end,
for Periandro and Auristela's lives were still running their courses [todavía
iban corriendo las vidas], and the ends to which they came would determine
what their story would be called" (285).

Because characters travel in anonymity, the opportunities for self-misrepre-
sentation are enormous, most obviously in changes of name and appearance.
Numerous instances of this have already been mentioned. Berganza undergoes many name changes according to who he meets up with, a common
fate of stray dogs unable to bark their identities. Don Quixote's initial name
change, along with those of Rocinante and Dulcinea, has everything to do
with his new coming-to-be as an errant traveler, and he also dons a couple
of telling epithets along the way. The *Novelas ejemplares* and the *Persiles*
overflow with cases of changes of name and attire—women dressed as men,

men as women, nobles as commoners or Gypsies, the civilized as barbarians, barbarians as pilgrims, and so on—not to mention other means of concealing identities and assuming new ones, such as Periandro and Auristela's perpetual pose as brother and sister. The narrator of *La ilustre fregona* refers to the disguise of the two young men as "transformations" rivaling those of Ovid's metamorphoses (159). This suggests that the various transformations of beasts into humans and vice versa belong to the same category of *movements* (cf. *transformaciones, mudar forma*) into and out of identities.

But do such name changes, disguises, and other deceptions imply qualitative change? And more generally, does traveling involve qualitative change? The unhelpful short answer would have to be "not necessarily," and the long answer, which could fill a volume and perhaps be carried out along the lines of Bakhtin's penetrating analysis of characters in different chronotopes (*Dialogic* 84–258; *Speech Genres* 10–59), would have to inquire into who travels in what sort of time-space, and whether the journey in question really affects characters subsequent to experienced events and processes.[33] If we take Leibniz's "first truth" whereby "A is A . . . everything is what it is; everything is similar or equal to itself; nothing is greater or less than itself" to define identity as he does, then Cervantes' major characters are by and large "not equal to themselves" either in the ways they exceed the generic roles cut out for them or in the ways they incorporate experience into their subsequent thought and behavior. This is the case even in the *Persiles,* modeled on one of the most static genres from the point of view of character change (the Greek novel), where Periandro and Auristela insist that they are the very same people they were despite all the trials (*trabajos*) they've been through (156, 185, 414, 454). There are all kinds of evidence that their experiences are indeed cumulative, and that "being the same" refers more to their steadfastness than to an immunity to the transforming effects of experience (cf. Ramaiah 4, 16). This *Prüfungsroman* is also a *Bildungsroman*. The one point at which the journey necessarily involves a change in characters' mode of being is in their *becoming travelers,* since they are dis-placed into a very different time-space in which things happen differently and "place" is no longer there to keep conferring its identity on them: characters move into the blur. Whether this leaves lasting marks on them after the journey is another matter.

Ways and wayfarers

Caminos are not only roads or pathways already in place but also the ways travelers take, whether on land or at sea, and in this sense they are made by the traveling. The voyagers in the *Persiles* "continued on their way, uncertain as to which way to take it [siguieron su *camino,* sin llevar parte cierta adonde *encaminalle*]" (105; my emphasis; cf. 148). Theirs is an unrouted route, uncharted but successively defined as they go along. Wayfarers (*caminantes, viandantes*) can likewise go astray (*descaminados*) and still make their way somewhere (e.g., *DQ* I.23.281; *Git* 108, 112).

Don Quixote is, of course, the foremost (I was tempted to say the most pathological) waymaker in Cervantes' novels, as one would expect from a knight-*errant,* the *caballero andante* "who went erring on Rocinante [aquel que en Rocinante *errando anduvo*]," as his epitaph puts it (I.52.605). A goatherd aptly addresses him as Sir Errant (*señor andante* [I.12.165]), and Sancho refers to him as the "*asendereado* caballero don Quijote de la Mancha" (the past participle of the verb formed from the noun *sendero,* "path" [II.10.109; cf. I.25.307; *Git* 122]): the paths he has traveled are integral to who he is. Time and again, especially early in the novel, he lets his *horse* decide the way, in imitation of other knights-errant, since random travel heightens the chances of adventures and gives them their potency (I.2.80, I.4.99, I.21.257, I.23.284). Accordingly he has only disdain for courtly knights, who "travel throughout the whole world looking at a map" (II.6.80) without suffering hunger or foul weather, unlike true knights-errant. Nothing could be more antithetical to Don Quixote's style of travel than reading a map. Yet he does respect people who follow the way of letters rather than arms and come to "govern the world from a chair" (I.37.467).

The squire-errant shares in Don Quixote's openness to the roads of the future, even if he should be taken to the ends of the earth. Referring to his being tossed in the blanket, he says that "such misfortunes are hard to prevent, and if they come there's nothing to do but hunch your shoulders, hold your breath, close your eyes, and let yourself go where luck and the blanket send you [dejarse ir por donde la suerte y la manta nos llevare]" (I.21.256). The traveling mood of both protagonists is actively oriented within the future subjunctive best expressed perhaps in the expression "venga lo que viniere" (come what may). The un-fore-seen allows them to im-pro-vise, and they are willing to accept the outcome, the e-vent, whether favorable or not.

Many other characters in the novels hold a similar attitude, but with different nuances. In quasi-picaresque fashion, Berganza traces lines of escape, running from one master to the next, but if he's not a true wanderer he too welcomes the future, satisfies his curiosity, and follows paths without any destination in particular. This is how he expresses his first escape: "I kicked up dust [puse pies en polvorosa] and taking the road in my hands and feet . . . I went through those fields of God to wherever fortune wished to take me" (305). In another escape he decides to "put land in between [poner tierra en medio]" so as not to have to see his enemies anymore (323). Rincón and Cortado are likewise homeless types whose road is "a la ventura" (193) *away* from where they've been. Tomás Rodaja lets himself be so carried away by his curiosity and pleasures in Italy that he almost forgets why he went there (*LV* 51).[34] Periandro and Auristela never forget their goal, but have no choice but to let themselves be taken by the will of the winds and be confronted by a long series of unexpected and mostly unwished-for trials (*trabajos*). Because their purposes are attached to destinations, as are those of other travelers in the novel, the parting or divergence of ways on sea and land is a frequent image. In one such parting, the narrator remarks: "Now the ships were under way, with the same wind but on different routes [*caminos*], which is one of those things that seem so mysterious about the art of navigation" (*PS* 276).

Agencies at work in the setting out, the choice of ways, and the determination of events in the journey are multiple. If psychic factors and interpersonal relations may be seen as prime movers of much that happens in this regard, characters and narrators identify a much wider range of causes and determinants. The worlds in which these characters move must thus be understood as infused with many types of forces which act on everything that happens, even on the ways characters think. Everything said about the movements of "desire" so far illustrates a gamut of such agencies. Desires move travelers, spur them on, carry them, decide their course, are their course or destination. The will (*la voluntad*) often works in conjunction with desire. Opportunity (*la ocasión*) isn't mere circumstance but an active accomplice of desire. In countless instances unevenly distributed through the novels—and with varying degrees of credibility—God, heaven or the heavens, providence, the devil, enchanters, and the stars all intervene to direct the journey and its events, as do the wills of natural elements. Even more insistent are the agencies of chance and necessity (*la suerte, la ventura, la desventura, la fortuna, los hados, el destino*), all of which act willfully or capriciously on the travelers and their journeys from some locus beyond their control. When Don Quixote in the Sierra Morena says his fate hangs on a throwing of dice and on Sancho's diligence in his mission to Dulcinea, he captures something of the relationship between chance and effective action (I.25.303). The journey in Cervantes' novels could be seen as wayfaring in relation to desire, chance, necessity, and effective action.

Improvisation

Effective action usually means improvised action in Cervantes' novels. Nearly all of Cervantes' characters major and minor are performers without set scripts, improvisers of varying skills and pathways of action. Much of the value of their traveling resides precisely in their performance. Obvious as this may seem, it has received little recognition. This may be a symptom of the devaluation

of improvised conduct in most serious pursuits of Western arts and letters —
in classical music from at least the mid-nineteenth to mid-twentieth centuries
if not the present, for example. One need only think of Bergson's view of
Don Quixote, one of the most amazing improvisers in literature, as a laughable automaton distracted in his ways (*Le Rire* 392–95), or of Franz Liszt's
deep remorse in later life for what he called his "sacrilegious violations" in
the performance of Beethoven's works,[35] or of the demotion of performance
to mere transience as opposed to the eternal, or of ideologies of artistic perfection and the monumentalization of texts, to appreciate how alien a notion
improvisation has been in certain practices. But the novel has typically allowed for improvisation both as an artistic practice and as a genre giving greater
or lesser autonomy to characters; the theater has plenty of it too, of course,
not so much in actors' performance as in characters' performance when the
latter is irreducible to "plot function."

What is improvisation, then? What sorts of improvisation may be identified in Cervantes' novels, and how useful is this notion toward an understanding of Cervantes' travelers? As far as I'm aware, literary criticism has
scarcely dealt with this issue as such though it is touched upon indirectly in
much textual analysis. For reasons readily apparent, certain branches of musi-
cology have expressed strongest interest in improvisation. What I'd like to do
here in the briefest way, wary of some of the pitfalls, is extract out of specifically musical contexts a few principles which may have a bearing on the notion of improvisation in general and Cervantes' travelers in particular.

Broadly speaking, improvisation could be defined as unique, spontaneous
action developed with reference to codes of practice and oriented by definite
circumstances and prior sequences within a field of uncharted possibilities.
Codes of practice include preestablished procedures of action, conventions,
constraints, expectations, precedents, and types of knowledge informing action in given circumstances. Improvisation simultaneously reproduces and
revitalizes whatever practice it operates within. Practices differ widely, of course,
in how much variation, reorganization, and creativity they allow or encour-
age, and the possibilities of improvisation range accordingly. Knowledge and
savoir-faire with regard to practices are essential to improvisation. But to improvise, one needs much more than this: the ability (1) to anticipate by at-
tending to the logic of sequence, gauging the possible consequences and acting accordingly, and (2) to know how and when either to transgress limits
and come back within them or, alternatively, to find unprecedented sequences
within the limits. Timing is crucial, as dictated by rapidly changing circumstances, some of these brought upon by the improvisation itself. Hence improvisers by no means yield to the unforeseen, but they do venture into it
to the extent that they risk error, loss of control, or failure by disposing them-

selves to an attitude of laisser-aller. All of this together heightens the possibilities of imaginative, inspired action. Not surprisingly, musicians — especially jazz musicians — tend to speak of improvisation in terms of movement without planned courses, of deviations from established pathways, or of travel through uncertain terrain; they themselves are the travelers or the vehicles (e.g., Balliett 45, 105, 249; Priestley 46, 52; Davis 70, 81, 99, 101, 220, 225, 243; and all of Sudnow; cf. Lortat-Jacob 43–45, 68; Chernoff 58).

Characters in *Don Quixote* improvise primarily but by no means exclusively in the chivalric mode. The books of chivalry and related ballads and stories provide a wealth of knowledge and models with reference to which Don Quixote conducts himself. But it is important not to see his "imitation" as repetition of the same, even if he often sees it as such, for two reasons. First, inscribed within knight-errantry, and particularly within its ideology of adventure, is an imperative of improvisatory conduct. Without forsaking their principles, knights-errant must seek out and deal with challenges, risk themselves in the face of the unknown, and act to bring about an outcome deemed favorable. As though recognizing its own inadequacy or incompleteness, knight-errantry institutionalizes improvisation with respect to whatever the world might give forth. Second, the circumstances in which Don Quixote finds himself, no matter how he assimilates them to the templates of his models, are radically different from those of his heroes and hence demand that he act as much in accordance with them as with what he takes them to be. Because he doesn't move within a purely chivalric world but within a hybridized world with various codes of practice, the life situations he encounters oblige him to maneuver in unforeseen ways. Finding no precedents in chivalric practice at one point, he remarks: "But perhaps the chivalry and enchantments of our day follow a different course [*camino*] from that of those in days gone by" (I.47.557). Rather than reproducing his models, he produces something else.

Nearly all of Don Quixote's speeches and reveries as well as his adventures are impelled by an internal dynamic of improvisation which leads him either into untraveled variations or into flights of fantasy beyond the limits of traditional knight-errantry. Part of the *admiración* of those around him no doubt derives from his amazing ability to invent ex tempore with reference to preestablished procedures and to keep inventing as he goes along. It should be remembered that *discreto* and *discreción*, words applied to him and many other Cervantine characters, frequently referred to talent as well as judgment (Riquer 376). Similarly, as Stephen Gilman points out, the word *ingenio*, as in the title *El ingenioso hidalgo Don Quixote de la Mancha*, was regarded as one of two phases of the creative process: "*Ingenio* engenders or generates (*engendra*), while *invención*, governed by the understanding (*entendimiento*), slowly and conscientiously gives artistic form and coherence to whatever was engendered" (101).

Many other characters in the novel also improvise in the chivalric mode, but they do so from outside of it and generally without much risk (the first innkeeper, Dorotea as Micomicona, Sancho in El Toboso, the duke's household, Sansón, the priest and barber, etc.). This isn't just a matter of devising some deception beforehand and carrying it off according to plan, but also of inventing as they go along, as the cases of Dorotea and Sancho illustrate so well. Without Dorotea's knowledge of the style of damsels in distress through her readings, and without Sancho's squirely apprenticeship under Don Quixote, neither character would be able to pull it off.

The nomadic shepherds in *La Galatea* often have nothing better to do than improvise poetically on different themes: improvisation may well be the major pastoral activity after love. Improvisation enables them to exercise their talent, cause *admiración,* and express their individuality. Toward the end of the novel there is a long series of impromptu songs about love as well as a series of made-up riddles in verse. Proceeding within strict limits of versification and value, the shepherds exhibit the almost impossible fluidity of a Lope de Vega as their fellows emanate amazement.

The *Novelas ejemplares* and the *Persiles* are full of characters — mostly travelers — who live or perform by their wits in an ambience of uncertainty and hence partake of improvisation to one degree or another.[36] The mental motion of *discurso* and *discurrir* often comes into play in such situations. In *La ilustre fregona* one of the lead characters improvises with his guitar at an inn, composing verses on the spot as he introduces the dancers and directs their movements. A comment by the narrator could be adapted to almost any of Cervantes' improvisers: "as his wits [*ingenio*] were quick, effortless, and pleasing, with a wonderful outpouring [*corriente*] he began to sing impromptu [*de improviso*] as follows" (106). Quick-wittedness, personal style, and the ability to "engender" an improvisatory flow all figure into this statement.

Preciosa in *La gitanilla* and the glass licentiate in *El licenciado Vidriera,* both of them ambulant characters, are the outstanding improvisers of the *Novelas ejemplares,* so much so that whatever else these novels are about, they are *about* improvisation. The first half of *La gitanilla* focuses mainly on the astounding improvisatory talents of Preciosa, who amazes all with her *discreción* and virtuosity (74, 98). Even the narrator at one point doesn't know whether she's making up verses *de improviso* or whether she knew them from before (121), but he has already shown her to be capable not only of this but of improvising her way brilliantly out of tight spots (97–98). She is the performer's performer, excelling so much in the gypsy arts that the gypsies themselves wonder at her. The old woman posing as her grandmother admits that

Preciosa knows more than she has taught her, and sees her as uncannily bedeviled (*espiritada*) (83, 87). Here we have two characteristics of "high" improvisation: the ability to act beyond and above the boundaries of received knowledge, and the sensation of the source of empowerment as coming from without. For his part, Vidriera, in the bulk of the novel about him, wanders the streets answering whatever questions people might bring him. Even the university people are amazed that he should be able to "respond to every question with propriety and wit [con propiedad y agudeza]" (57). His is a very open kind of improvisation, with only the limits of his madness to contain him, but his previous travels and education enter significantly into his unpredictable responses.

Improvisation in Cervantes' novels is not simply "whatever comes out [lo que saliere]," in the words of a painter who doesn't know what he's doing (*DQ* II.3.63). Nor is it merely reactive behavior. Characters governed by their codes of practice engage in it little if at all. Improvisation involves a purposive exercise of talent in ways without exact precedent, and without the certainty of a prearranged outcome. Both recognition and surprise normally form part of others' response to it. Generating many passages in the novels, improvised action dovetails well with the journey, which deterritorializes characters into less defined arenas where improvisation can and often must thrive. When travelers set off *a la ventura* they predispose themselves to improvising. Travel is more closely related to invention than even Idisore of Seville might suspect when he remarks: "what is *invenire* (to invent) but to come (*venire*) to what one is looking for" (822). As we'll see in the final chapter, Cervantes' inventive novelizing is infused with many of the principles of improvisation discussed here. I suspect moreover that Cervantes' improvisatory writing methods showed the way for a great many other novelists from his time to the present.

Adventure

Traveling involves a successive "taking place." Here and there within its ongoing process events are construed as self-contained units distinguishable from a before and an after. This happens when certain factors come into play in such a way as to predominate over others, setting off a series of actions and reactions until they are either played out or interrupted by new factors. In the broadest sense these units are *sucesos* (events, happenings), a frequently used term evoking temporal succession both within and between them. In all the long novels and most of the short ones, characters narrate the *sucesos* they've gone through. The verb *suceder* often introduces a *suceso* or turn of events within it. Without *sucesos* there would be little or nothing to tell about in these types of novels. One indication of their importance in the larger perspective of travel novels is the appearance of either equivalents or categories of *sucesos* (e.g., adventures, fortunes, misfortunes, *faictz, trabajos, industrias,* etc.) in the full titles of novels commonly referred to by the bare names of the protagonists: *Pantagruel, Lazarillo de Tormes, Persiles y Sigismunda, Estebanillo González, Moll Flanders, Joseph Andrews, Huckleberry Finn,* and so on. Also striking is the insistent use of the word *aventura* or *adventure* in the chapter headings of such novels as *Don Quixote* and *Tom Jones.*

Aventuras are obviously a kind of *sucesos,* one which spans an enormous range of heterogeneous experience. Other categories besides the generic *sucesos* or its synonym *acontecimientos* include *desventuras* (misfortunes) and *trabajos* (trials), both terms implying moods and dynamics distinct from *aventuras.* Unlike any of Cervantes' other novels, *Don Quixote* is full of adventures as such, as evident, for example, in the title of II.58: "Of adventures that poured on Don Quixote so thick and fast that they trod upon each other's heels [no se daban vagar unas a otras]." Rarely does the word *aventura* appear in the other novels, though the verb *aventurarse* does come up now and again. Yet the following statement late in the *Persiles* may authorize a more comprehensive notion of adventure in the novels: "Here our travelers [*pasajeros*] experienced one of the strangest adventures [*aventuras*] of all those related in the course [*discurso*] of this book" (402). Here we find out that a large number of events which have gone under different names or no name at all are actually adventures whether or not the characters designate them as such. All that seems to matter is that *somebody* designate them as *aventuras* even if they're otherwise called *trabajos.* Similarly, the term *desventura* isn't necessarily opposed to *aventura,* as evident for instance in a reference to Don Quixote's *desventuradas aventuras,* "luckless adventures" (II.18.177; cf. I.18.216): there's plenty of *ventura* (meaning luck, good or bad) in both these terms.

The unattested etymology of "adventure" points to *adventura* in colloquial Latin. This would be the future participle of *advenire,* meaning "come" or "arrive"; *adventura* would denote "a thing about to happen to anyone" according to the *Oxford English Dictionary* (1971) — a rather unhelpful etymology, apparently, since it offers no leads as to what that implied thing (*res*) might be or how it comes to happen or to whom, but it does hint at some crucial aspects of adventure all the same. First, the choice of the verb *advenire* would suggest that adventure, rather than emerging out of present circumstances, comes from elsewhere; and since it comes to someone, it is liable to be met and confronted. Second, unlike the etymology of "event," that of "adventure" places one's point of view not after the fact but just before it in anticipation of an imminent occurrence.[37]

Anyone wanting to experience adventures might do better than sit at home and wait for them to arrive, for although they may take place anywhere, the likelihood of their occurrence is very unevenly distributed. If they "arrive" in some sense, they are usually met or sought out. Adventurousness implies doing something out of the ordinary or participating in an unusual experience, thereby exposing oneself to unstable situations filled with novelty and suspense — and sometimes risk. The unexpected is the norm in certain kinds of novels including the chivalric romances and *Don Quixote,* whose protagonists exemplify Heraclitus' maxim "If you do not expect the unexpected you will not discover it" (*Early* 113), but with the added imperative of seeking out the unexpected. Any social order, inasmuch as it effectively controls and regulates life, could be seen as a guard against certain types of adventure. Hence adventures are most likely to be met outside the bounds of the social order and, more generally, in any encounter with the unfamiliar, but are also found in the vulnerable spots of society (consider the case of Don Juan Tenorio) as well as in anarchic enclaves and spheres of anonymity. In short, the probabilities of adventure depend on the extraordinariness, novelty, uncertainty, and hazard there might be in any given place, activity, or situation. For this reason errancy could be characterized as perpetual adventurousness. Don Quixote has a keen sense as to where adventures might occur: "And, talking about this last adventure they followed the road to the pass of Lápice where, Don Quixote said, they could not fail to find many and diverse adventures, as it was a much traveled place [lugar muy pasajero]" (I.8.130). This is a no-man's-land with many travelers passing through it. Similarly, his anxiety to leave the tranquil home of Diego de Miranda is impelled by his desire to look for adventures "with which he was told that land abounded" (II.18.176): the territory itself contains adventures for him, including the cave of Montesinos, which is reserved for him alone (II.22.208, II.23.212). The first innkeeper has had his adventures in the seedy parts of Seville; however, when companions beg Don Quixote to go with them to Seville, "for being just the place to find adventures, for in every street and round every corner more can be met with than anywhere else" (I.14.189), Don Quixote turns them down; these aren't his sort of adventures, since a knight-errant is neither a policeman nor a *polis*-man.

Contact between strangers and locals brings about numerous adventures in Cervantes' novels. It is Don Quixote's peculiarity as a stranger that prompts the duke's household to contrive adventures: he is as much an adventure for them as their inventions are adventures for him, though in radically different modes. Doña Rodríguez and her daughter present him with an authentic adventure when they appeal to Don Quixote as a stranger capable of intervening in their affairs and setting things right (II.52–56). Georg Simmel analyzes this phenomenon insightfully in terms of proximity and distance in his essay "The Stranger," where he remarks that the stranger "often receives the most surprising revelations and confidences, at times reminiscent of a confessional, about matters which are kept hidden from everybody with whom one is close. Objectivity is by no means nonparticipation . . ." (145). This statement identifies a principle central to the interaction of much of the *Persiles* and *La señora Cornelia.* In the latter, it is the continued mediation of two strangers, Spanish nobles, which turns a potentially dishonorable love affair between Italians of high nobility into a happy marriage. The recognition of their stranger's role is signaled at the very climax of the novel, when the duke, baby in arms and Cornelia at his feet, inopportunely abandons the room to summon the Spaniards, and only then does he return to embrace Cornelia and give vent to his feelings (273). The action of the novel is one enormous adventure for the Spaniards.

In his two-volume study of the ideology of adventure, Michael Nerlich outlines six features of "adventure-ideology, adventure-mentality as well as adventure-practice" from medieval times to the present: (1) acceptance of all forms of change; (2) acceptance of the unknown; (3) acceptance of "blindness with regard to the unknown" and of all kinds of risks; (4) acceptance of chance; (5) recognition of the other, personal and cultural; and (6) "elaboration of 'search systems,' calculation of chances, minimizing of risks, elaboration of insurances, and so on" (1:xxi). All of these points are correct and significant. At the same time, the emphasis on passivity is striking: the first four points specify *acceptance,* and the fifth *recognition,* while only the last hints at any sort of active encounter with adventures, with terms like "elaboration." This is surprising in view of Nerlich's insistence on the active nature of adventure. He critiques Bakhtin, wrongly I think, for not recognizing that adventures as of medieval times are actively sought out rather than passively undergone. The chivalric adventure, says Nerlich, is "an event that the knight must seek out and *endure*" (1:4–5; my emphasis); once a knight has actively sought one out, it would seem, he must passively endure it. But Amadís, Orlando, Lancelot, and Don Quixote don't simply endure their adventures; they are motivated to act, often in improvisatory ways. There's little struggle or drama in acceptance or recognition as such, and little chance of success in mere endurance. I don't mean to detract here from the importance of Nerlich's work as a history of adventure ideology in the West as of the epoch when adventure was first glorified, elevated to the meaning of life.

The future participle in the derivation of "adventure" accords with its chance elements as well as with its improvisatory nature not only as something unforeseen but also as something which requires a certain modality of action. The interaction of at least two independent "variables" or agents, at least one of which is an adventurer, in an unregulated and uncontrolled environment produces a situation where control may be unequally shared but is nonetheless not monopolized by anyone or anything. An adventure engages all of one's attention and wits, and requires one not only to keep with the flow of events but also to anticipate what's about to happen, to think at least a few moments ahead so as to know what to do when those moments arrive. When an adventure begins there's often no turning back regardless of how high or low the stakes may be, but instead a necessary follow-through to some kind of resolution or dissolution, or success or failure, as the case may be.

In retrospect, adventures change aspect, turning into memorable events. Perhaps they attain their full value only in narrative or memory. Gone are the sensations of excitement, expectancy, and the like, but not the impressions that these have made. Adventures tend to constitute much of what's deemed memorable or tellable in certain kinds of journeys, including those in Cervantes' novels. They adapt themselves to the language and sequence of narrative and reveal a special affinity to memory, being among those events which survive intact when other happenings lapse into oblivion or mingle indistinctly. Their position within journeys more than resembles the places (*topoi, loci*) along an itinerary used in the art of memory, and their internal sequences reproduce an analogous scheme. Adventureless hours and miles of journeys often contract into little more than transitions between memorable occurrences while adventures expand out of proportion to approximate the journey in its entirety. The psychic energy and impressionability which run high in adventure are charged with their own momentum and momentousness, i.e., consequence and significance, maintaining their coherence long after the fact. As James Feibleman puts it, "The importance of events in any life is more directly proportionate to their intensity than to their extensity" (Tuan 184).

Simmel, in his essay titled "The Adventure," aptly refers to the adventure as "the exclave of life, the 'torn-off' whose beginning and end have no connection with the somehow unified stream of existence" (196). In Cervantes' episodic novels, however, adventures and other unexpected *sucesos* are by no means isolated from the rest of experience; rather, they constitute a good share of significant experience and put their stamp on it. In his book on Cervantes, Stephen Gilman makes much of the well-known distinction in German between *Erlebnis*, experience as a particular happening or event, and *Erfahrung*, experience in a more cumulative sense. The richness of these terms in their associations with living and traveling, respectively, and their correspondence to *sucesos* and the cumulative traveling, are striking. Drawing from Simmel's essay on adventure, Gilman outlines a series of oppositions corresponding to *Erlebnis* and *Erfahrung*, including "adventure versus experience, shallow skimming versus profound perusal, romance versus novel, escape versus self-discovery, 'dropping out' versus 'life as a whole' . . ." (26). I'll refrain from commenting on most of these. Particularly bothersome and misleading, however, is the way adventure is pitted against experience. Although Gilman expands upon these oppositions, he shows an awareness of the problem: "I hasten to confess that adventure is a variety of experience and that every experience, perceived and remembered as set apart from others, has an element of adventure" (27–28). This statement, it seems to me, would have served as a more useful starting point for his discussion, attuned as it is to the relationships between adventure and experience in Cervantes' novels. *Erfahrung* consists of accumulated *Erlebnisse,* and the journey in retrospect consists largely of the accumulated experience of *sucesos.* Moreover, whether or not characters go in search of adventure, their journeys are always *a la ventura,* come what may.

When someone takes no part whatsoever in an adventure, the event obviously can't amount to an adventure for that person. And by the same token, there's no stray adventure that doesn't "belong" to someone. There are nonetheless varying degrees of participation: one needn't be in the thick of some fray or intrigue to be having an adventure. Imagine an adventure involving an interaction between two people, observed by a third—let it be, for example, Don Juan wooing a lady as a servant of one or the other looks on, or Don Quixote confronting someone as Sancho watches. The event may bear the characteristics of adventure for any or all of them, but would be a different adventure for each participant depending on the relationship among (1) perceptions as to what's happening, (2) the extraordinary character accorded to it, (3) psychic involvement in it, and (4) the possibilities of improvisatory action. Any encounter with something or someone out of the ordinary contains the possibility of becoming a unilateral, bilateral, or multilateral adventure, or separate adventures derived from a single event. The experience of every island in the *Persiles* could be considered an adventure for the travelers, just as every insular world happened upon by the Rabelaisian voyagers constitutes an adventure for them. Lemuel Guilliver refers to the approaching of the island of Laputa overhead as an "adventure" in the now obsolete sense of fortuitous happening (cf. *DQ* I.23.281). Nevertheless it does mark the beginning of an adventure for him which ends with his departure. Some of Don Quixote's adventures consist of little more than chance encounters without decisive action, such as the adventure of the three images, in which nothing happens besides the unveiling of the images of three saintly knights and Don Quixote's commentary on them; this, says Sancho, is the sweetest adventure that "has happened [*sucedido*] to us in the whole course [*discurso*] of our journey [*peregrinación*]" (II.58.473). As long as there are contact and inter-vention as well as an appropriation of the experience, it's not essential that anything else happen.

Some adventures can simply happen to almost anyone who comes across them, especially when they are already "made" or already there to be had. The author of the Laputa episode might have to be Swift but the adventurer needn't be Gulliver since any sea explorer could meet with a similar fate that would start up an adventure and partially condition its unfolding. This is not quite the case in the *Persiles* because the insular worlds which the travelers chance upon are in certain ways designed for them, as we'll see; yet once they arrive at the continent, most of their *sucesos* are ready-made adventures which could have happened to anyone. Some characters, including Don Quixote, are potentially ambulant adventures for whoever crosses paths with them. How adventures turn out, however, always depends on who happens to experience them. Yet even when intervention is at a minimum and objective conditions are nearly identical for different travelers, the adventures themselves are likely to betray a personal style and signature in the ways they are carried out.

Other adventures are far from ready-made. In such cases only the raw ingredients of adventure present themselves, and these have to be concocted by someone into an adventure. A good share of travel fiction, including much of *Don Quixote,* recounts the making of adventure out of incidental circumstances that might simply pass by or develop into other kinds of experience. Together with such factors as desire and ideology (as the case may be), "personality" intervenes decisively in this process. Nietzsche's aphorism "Terrible experiences pose the riddle whether the person who has them is not terrible" (*Beyond* no. 89), could be generalized: people have kinds of adventures corresponding to who they are and what they want. *Pícaros* have picaresque adventures, knights-errant have chivalric ones, lovers have amorous ones, pilgrims have peregrine ones. A given chance encounter could conceivably produce any one of these types of adventures, and others too, according to who happens upon it.

Probably the most sustained adventure in all of the novels is Loaysa's attempted seduction of Leonora in *El celoso extremeño*. Out of idleness, this "arrow" (*virote*) invents and executes the adventure, though in the later version of the novel he ultimately fails in his objectives. The initial elements are familiar: a reportedly beautiful young woman is jealously guarded by an old husband in a fortified house, "all of which inflamed his desire to see if it would be possible, by force or cunning, to storm such a well-guarded fortress" (107). The military imagery, combined with references to the adventure as a "difficult feat [*hazaña*]" and a "strange, unprecedented *suceso*" (107, 134), recalls above all the language of chivalric adventure. Without using the word as such,

Loaysa defines the undertaking as an adventure. The intensity of his desire derives mainly from the magnitude of the challenge. He begins his journey from the outside to the inside in disguise and proceeds to employ ingenious stratagems designed to awaken appetites in the human obstacles he encounters, exploiting his talents and youth while at the same time paying close attention to practical details. As things unfold he displays the utmost improvisatory skill in turning them to his advantage, mainly through his ability to psych out the inmates, all to the purpose of gaining access to Leonora and winning her over, though he recognizes the role played by luck in the path toward fulfillment of his desires (114). This is an adventure not only for him but for the women, as may be inferred both from their behavior and from the *dueña*'s words to Loaysa: "if it seems to you that much is being asked of you, consider that much is being ventured [*se aventura*]" (123).

So much as been written on the adventures of Cervantes' prime adventurer, Don Quixote, that any extended commentary risks redundancy. Let me point briefly to a few analyses of quixotic adventure. In the history of adventure ideology, Nerlich locates Don Quixote as an unsuccessful throwback to the days before the *hidalgo* class lost its knightly function (1:20–40). Gonzalo Torrente Ballester, viewing Don Quixote as a clearheaded actor and artist, focuses on numerous adventures to determine what relationships there are between reality and invention on the part of Don Quixote. The most important of these are (1) that Don Quixote sees something which actually fits in well with his knightly behavior and recognizes it as such without having to modify it; (2) that when appearances are all he and Sancho have to go on, he assimilates them to his fantasy without modifying them as such; and (3) that when manifest realities don't serve his purposes, he transforms them by means of metaphoric substitution (104–8). These sorts of distinctions are crucial in determining how Don Quixote defines an encounter as an adventure. Howard Mancing lists ten "elements" he regards as characteristic of quixotic adventures, thereby sketching out a typical sequence within an adventure (e.g., "Reality is stated in the narration," "Don Quixote willfully transforms reality," "Sancho Panza points out the reality of the situation," and so on [46–47]).

The "adventure with a dead body" (I.19) provides an interesting and fairly typical example worth looking into. Hungry and battered by previous misadventures (*desventuras*), Don Quixote and Sancho happen to be riding along a deserted stretch of highway when the night closes in on them. The preconditions are thus favorable for adventure as the protagonists traverse a zone of no-man's-land or any-man's-land uncontrolled by institutional order and highly susceptible to irruptions of extraordinary occurrence, be it natural, human, or supernatural. In the space of a few lines the narrator twice more insists on the darkness as though intimating an ambience fraught with the possibility of things coming out from anywhere and a state of mind in which the alert senses and apprehensive imagination supply the want of visibility. The protagonists' hunger is also touched on again as a further adumbration of psychic state.

The narrator then announces the adventure before the characters are aware of it: "an adventure happened to them [*les sucedió*] which, without any artifice whatsoever, truly looked like one" (I.19.229). Here as elsewhere in the novel there's a playfulness about the dubious authenticity of quixotic adventures. The occasion for the adventure comes upon them out of the dark as something unforeseen, a freakish coincidence wrought by chance. In the distance they see a large number of approaching lights which look like moving stars.[38] The strange nocturnal vision makes Don Quixote's hair stand on end, but his fear and apprehension, unlike Sancho's, prompt him to muster up some courage. His ideology of knight-errantry after all goads him to seek out extraordinary situations and match his determination to the most hazardous undertakings without respect for limits or limitations. He accordingly defines this situation as a formidable adventure that will demand the utmost from him, and the moment he does so the happening becomes an adventure because it is defined as such and will be acted upon as such. If the choice were left to Sancho the phantom lights would undoubtedly be allowed to pass by in the hopes that confrontation might be avoided. Don Quixote joins his fate to a fortuitous occurrence which he imagines even more strange than it appears to be. As usual his adventurizing of the previously undefined is precipitate, cutting off the inductive process of inquiry with a trenchant deduction formulated on the basis of bookish assumptions. Being versed in these matters, he's able to recognize an adventure when he sees one. Although this one will inevitably belong to the chivalric mode, there's no telling as yet what kind of chivalric adventure it will be. For this he needs a closer look.

Expectancy and anxiety intensify as the adventure approaches. The lights come forth as flaming torches held by a group of riders in surplices (*encamisados*); a litter in black follows, and behind it another group of riders dressed in mourning. The evidence is sufficient for Don Quixote to imagine that this is one of the adventures out of his books. This implies that the adventure as he comes to picture it conforms not only to the general style of his books but to a precise paradigm (and indeed it is a parody on the author's part of an episode from *Palmerín de Inglaterra* [I.76]). The narrator specifies in Don Quixote's archaic language: "He imagined that the litter was a bier carrying some dead or badly wounded knight, and that the task of avenging him was reserved for himself" (I.19.230–31). Don Quixote makes three suppositions here: first, that the occupant of the litter is a wounded or dead knight; second, that this presupposes a wrong that must be avenged; and third, that of all people he alone should be the one to set things right. The suppositions and their sequence are logical from the point of view of his knight-errantry. And who are the torchbearers? Though they turn out to be priests, Don Quixote later says he took them for "the very devils in hell" just as they all thought he was a devil from hell coming to get the dead body: the circumstances allow for mutual diabolization. Carroll Johnson comments that religious processions of this sort were such a familiar sight that to infernalize them, as Cervantes does through his character, "is a scandalous proposition in the repressive environment of 1600, possible only to someone nurtured on Erasmus and his distaste for processions, someone with more than a little courage, who could furthermore put the responsibility for the scandal onto a poor psychotic who doesn't know what's what anyway" (*Quest* 13). Johnson notes that a similar episode takes place in broad daylight later (I.52).

By construing the situation as he does, Don Quixote interlocks his destiny with that of a passing corpse, forging a link between the imagined past actions of other men elsewhere and his own here and now. A fatalistic causality transforms fortuitous happenings into necessary ones: since the adventure has come to him it must have been meant for him, and his first task is to locate his own protagonism within it. This he invents in the taking of vengeance that seems incumbent upon him and no other as a duty corresponding to his knighthood. The adventure takes on significance first of all because of its extraordinary and risky character in relation to Don Quixote, but also because of his central participation in it. Though there may be as little to gain from it as from a "crossroads adventure" (I.10.147), the stakes appear to be extremely high in terms of personal danger. All his courage and strength are poised for the challenge, which is one of self-mastery, self-exertion, and of a decisive intervention in the workings of the world. Furthermore, the adventure's significance derives from the precise way it fits in with Don Quixote's adopted values and worldview and with his eutopian concept of knight-errantry, since his prime task isn't merely to disrupt the peace but to right an imagined wrong. He has now formulated the adventure out of self-deception and is ready to carry it out according to the terms in which he has fabricated it. The improvisation has already begun.

Without more ado he stations himself in the middle of the road and addresses the oncoming riders. This interaction provides the only chance there is of dispelling the adventure or at least changing it into another. He does demand to know all the right information—who they are, what they have in the litter, etc.—and leaves it open to them to confirm or contradict his suppositions, but he does so in characteristically archaic language and belligerent terms (supposed wrongs, vengeance, challenge), so that it's no surprise when one of the *encamisados* says they're in a hurry.[39] The adventure isn't mutual. Piqued at this reply, Don Quixote catches the bridle of the fellow's mule and repeats his demands under the threat of doing battle with them all. This is the critical point determining whether the adventure will take place or not, for although a single informative statement could undo it, as happens in the aborted adventure of "Las Cortes de la Muerte" (II.11), misconceptions are rampant enough on both sides for it to break loose.

Confrontation shifts irreversibly into open conflict when the frightened mule rears up and throws its rider, whereupon a servant abuses Don Quixote who in turn attacks one of the mourners and thrashes everyone left and right until the field is deserted. What stands out in the triggering of the chain reaction from the time Don Quixote unwittingly provokes the mule till he unlashes his fury is a character trait of this particular mule — its skittishness ("Era la mula asombradiza . . ." [I.19.231]). Of all the things the beast might do, it happens to rise up on its hind legs; the rider happens to fall off; a servant chances to be there, and happens to intervene on impulse in such a way as to provoke the knight-errant. In this and many other adventures, contingencies and accidents erupt in a decisive way, and the more precarious a situation is the more likely they are to do so precisely because things are tense and out of control. Rather than trying to reverse the course of chance unprecedented in his books, Don Quixote plunges into it, taking the offensive as his adversaries flee as best they can. Humorous details already signal for the reader a comic dénouement: Rocinante seems to have grown wings, the unarmed *encamisados* resemble festive masks in the torchlight, and the mourners, immobilized in their garments, helplessly receive Don Quixote's blows. But for Don Quixote victory doesn't mean an end to the adventure.

The *encamisado* who fell off the mule remains pinned under it. Threatened by Don Quixote's lance, he explains that he and his clerical companions were escorting from one city to another the body of a gentleman who died of a pestilent fever. The devils Don Quixote imagined thus turn out to be timid human beings, and the perpetrator of the gentleman's death none other than God, against whom vengeance seems impracticable. Such knowledge brings the adventure to an abrupt end and in retrospect reorients it radically for Don Quixote. The adventure he has imagined becomes false (although justifiable for him as an obligation against what seemed to be "something evil and from the other world" [I.19.233]), yet an adventure has taken place all the same, one that has been carried out under misconceptions. For all his delusions he has no less undergone the experience of an adventure and no less emerged as its victor. Here he doesn't compensate for his internal enchantment (as he often does) by alleging the workings of external enchantment. For the *encamisado,* who complains of a broken leg, the incident has been

a definite misadventure (*desventura*), as he tells Don Quixote (I.19.233). Sancho, who has watched most of it with admiration and satisfaction, declares
this to have been the most successful adventure his master has yet undertaken,
and finds even more reason to rejoice on account of the food he has unloaded
from the bags of a mule. Hence for all concerned, the shape the adventure
takes is conditioned by the part they play in or outside it and takes on a new
aspect with the perception of every turn of the action.

Many other adventures in the novel are comparable to this one because
they too are initiated by Don Quixote according to notions derived from his
readings, and they likewise fall short of his expectations all too often. If the
adventure of the cave of Montesinos lives up to his expectations this is due
to the absence of externally imposed restraints on his fantasies. As Torrente
Ballester points out, "in the *Quixote,* the parody is carried out by stripping
the imitated narrative elements of their extraordinary condition and con-
straining them to something offered as real and credible" (19). At the same
time, Don Quixote is quite right in asserting that things that happen to him
are of an extraordinary nature, though for the wrong reasons since he projects this extraordinariness on them when he needs to. Some adventures actually happen to him without his needing to transform them, as already indicated, especially when he encounters marginalized personages in the midst
of their own adventures. These include Ginés de Pasamonte (as galley slave
and later as puppeteer), the deranged Cardenio and his associates, pastoral
lovers, ambulant actors, the bandit Roque Guinart, and others. His participation in these adventures ranges from peripheral to decisive. That such adventures occur at all is a result of his traveling *a la ventura* in an aimless errantry
after the style of his fictitious predecessors. Finally there are the adventures
that other characters, knowing his madness, frame for him by reproducing
the conditions of chivalric adventures. For Don Quixote these three types of
adventures — found, invented, and framed — collapse into the first category because of his unawareness of the goings-on of the other two.[40]

In Cervantes' novels, adventures are experiences *en route.* They exemplify
the root meaning of *per* in exp*er*ience, which denotes "to try, risk," and which
produced words including *fear, peril, pirate, empiric, experiment,* and *ex-
pert.* Cumulative adventure and other *sucesos* as well as uneventful stretches
in between put traveling characters constantly to the test, engage desire in
unforeseen ways, and result in an ongoing e-ducation in life's journey. Through
this, characters become other than what they were. Travel intensifies the experience of what was previously unfamiliar and extraordinary, exposing characters to the workings of chance, and obliges them to improvise their way
along: in their journeys they venture themselves.

Cervantine Worlds

The universe therefore is not wide enough for the range of human speculation and intellect. Our thoughts often travel beyond the boundaries of our surroundings.

Longinus

Chronotopes

Whether alienated from their milieu or communal with it, Cervantes' traveling characters traverse and inhabit heterogeneous time-spaces which, far from merely providing a setting, often generate the narrative's development by determining the types of characters, the conditions of action, the modality of significance, and so on. It was Mikhail Bakhtin who appropriated the term "chronotope" for literary analysis, assigning to it a highly active role in the very production of literature (*Dialogic* 84–258). For him, the chronotope defines genre, and along with it literary language, meaning, human images, and the conditions of process and event. The chronotope, he writes, "functioning as the primary means for materializing time in space, emerges as a center for concretizing representation, as a force giving body to the entire novel" (250). Rather than offering any satisfying definition, he insightfully demonstrates in his book-length essay how numerous chronotopes work in different narrative genres.

Still, the profusion of diverse sorts of chronotopes undoubtedly poses problems for orderly minds. Consider the following examples of chronotopes perhaps unfairly abstracted from Bakhtin's text: adventure-time (the ancient Greek romance); adventure-everyday-time (Apuleius and Petronius); the life course of one seeking true knowledge (Plato, on Socrates); the public square (ancient encomiastic works); the Roman patrician family (Roman memoirs); a miraculous world in adventure-time (the chivalric romance); historicized simultaneity (Dante); human life (Rabelais); the love idyll (the pastoral); the road (the picaresque, *Don Quixote,* Grimmelshausen, Fielding, *Wilhelm Meister,* and much else from the ancients to the moderns); parlors and salons (Stendhal and Balzac); the provincial town (*Madame Bovary*); biographical time (Tolstoy); the singer and his audience (ancient epic); and many more, including the fool's world, "meeting," mystery-time, carnival-time, the threshold, as well as the chronotopes of writers and readers in their encounters with texts. Clearly these are of different orders, some within the narrative, others outside, variously stressing time, place, mode of experience, worldview, communicative situation, narrative perspective, and the like. Some govern the narrative as a whole while others provide a conditioning ambience for characters to move into and out of. Some coexist easily with others or allow passage into others, some confront others, and some exclude others. One might wonder after all this whether there really "is" such a thing as a chronotope, and if so, what applicability it could have as a concept.

With the chronotope, Bakhtin takes an enormous leap beyond the usual notions of literary space and time. Not only does he guard the integrity of time-space but he also insists on the chronotope's generativeness in terms of all that takes place within it. Claiming some licence, I take "chronotope" in the fullest sense to be any spatiotemporal field or analogue charged with its own principles, conditions, ways of thought, and so on, which to a greater or lesser extent control, define, rarefy, authorize, capacitate, and infuse with value all modes of being and interactions within it. Naturally not all of this need apply in any particular chronotope — and there are also great variations concerning the degree to which a chronotope dictates the modalities of experience within it. Besides, it should be understood from the outset that chronotopes aren't always ready-made givens. In the case of "the road," it obviously matters *who* travels that road, and *who else,* and where, why, how, and so on; all these factors together will define the specificity of the chronotope at any textual moment. And yet no matter who travels, the experience of journeys by road (before modern transport, say) has its identifiable logic of motion and deterritorialization, its own forms of encounter, its heightened contact between different strata of society, its forked choices and deviations, its opportunities and vulnerabilities, its typical exposure to dangers and hardships, its own relations to chance. Hence "the road" emerges as a chronotope which, though combinable with many others, organizes experience quite differently from the others mentioned — apart from those which behave largely as subtypes of it, such as adventure-time.

Seen from this perspective, "the road" together with other chronotopes involving travel reveals deep affinities as well as cleavages between genres of narrative across the entire spectrum; wherever it does appear, it operates like a rhizome within the workings of narrative. I need hardly stress how radically different modes of travel produce their own chronotopes in both lived experience and fictive literature, as is the case with maritime travel both as practiced in Cervantes' time and as represented in so many of his novels. One exceptional chronotopic study in this regard is Wolfgang Schivelbusch's *The Railway Journey: The Industrialization of Time and Space in the Nineteenth Century,* in which he demonstrates how train travel opened up its own modes of experiencing time and space, its unique social interactions, its peculiar desires and fears, excesses and deficiencies, and how all of this worked its way into discourse and gave rise to new types of narrative. Despite important differences among them, travel genres share much that is fundamentally alien or marginal to other types of literature. Once writers have their characters travel or not travel, much has already been decided.

Rather than viewing chronotopes as internally homogenous time-space zones, I regard them as varied in "topography" and intensity, but bounded by limits beyond which they no longer pertain. At some moments in a text more than one chronotope may coincide harmoniously or conflictively, and at others, none may be discernible — or only a passage from one to another. This would mean that any textual moment is somehow characterizable in chronotopic terms, albeit negatively or plurally at times. Hence it's not enough merely to identify a chronotope without paying attention to how and how much it exerts itself in specific circumstances. To inquire about chronotopes is to probe into the conditions and possibilities of being in some time-place. An awareness of chronotopes is crucial for an understanding of novelistic modes of discourse, focusing critical attention on the vital circumstances in which characters act, think, speak, and write.

The chronotope of "the road" — or land travel — undoubtedly pervades throughout *Don Quixote.* In so far as a causal-generative agency may be attributed to it, "the road" displaces the protagonists from their village, conditions and makes possible most of what the travelers experience en route, including their discourse, and provides access to other chronotopes which in themselves are autonomous of travel as such. From the outset the chronotope of habitual village life suddenly becomes small and irrelevant as the expansive chronotope of the chivalric world takes power over Don Quixote's imagination and seduces him into setting forth on the road to embody its ideals. Don Quixote's two-world condition has already been discussed elsewhere. Let me add here that, like the devils who "carry hell with them," Don Quixote is himself a mobile chronotope who brings about an interplay of worlds wherever he goes. Unlike Amadís, he is often radically at odds with the world in which he moves, estranging and assimilating it as he goes. The roads and byways he travels belong simultaneously to two largely coinciding but incongruous renditions of the world, as do many of the characters, places, and objects encountered along the way. Some of these two-worldly places exert their own chronotopic influence on the course of events, including the village, the locus amoenus, the inn/castle, the wilderness (the labyrinthine Sierra Morena), the household of the duke and duchess, and the city (Barcelona). In the various pastoral settings, in contrast, there prevails a chronotope quite different from either the "ordinary" world or the "chivalric" one but equally familiar to the knight-errant from his readings; Don Quixote by and large suspends his knight-errantry in such ambiences to become a participant intruder. Two unique chronotopes, the cave of Montesinos and the Insula Barataria, warrant special attention under the rubric of "worlds."

Other Cervantine characters, alone or in groups, also alter their alien surroundings to one degree or another by precipitating chronotopic interplay. Such is the effect of erudite madness in the licenciate Vidriera, who at every turn undermines popular conceptions about many aspects of the familiar world. For their part, the exotic Gypsies in *La gitanilla* disturb the rhythms of sedentary life wherever they go, as already shown. Something of this is perceptible at times in the travelers of the *Persiles,* who disrupt events in such places as the Isla Bárbara, Policarpo's island, Lisbon, and Rome, although their foreignness as such is rarely played up. As always, traveling makes all of this possible.

As a privileged subcategory of the chronotope of the land journey, the inn provides an ever-changing stage of action where the most diverse travelers come together unexpectedly and interact with each other or with innkeepers and their personnel before going their separate ways. In Cervantes' novels, the inn is a place where the designs of novelistic necessity appear in the guise of chance, a place where many dramas resolve themselves, and where narrative thickens into a node of multiple strands. Inns/castles provide the locus of action or narrative for no fewer than twenty-one of the fifty-two chapters of Part I of the *Quixote,* beginning with Don Quixote's unceremonious dubbing into knighthood—administered by an innkeeper—after he spends the first night of his initial sally at an inn. Many of the novel's meetings, adventures, colorful episodes, and narratives are made possible by the brief sojourns at inns. It is at an inn, I might add, that Don Quixote learns about the apocryphal narrative of *Don Quixote.* Much the same applies to the function of inns and similar establishments in the *Persiles, Rinconete y Cortadillo, La ilustre fregona, Las dos doncellas, La española inglesa,* and *El casamiento engañoso.*

Sea travel likewise constitutes an enormously important chronotope in Cervantes' novels, including the entire first half of the *Persiles* and some passages of the second, much of *El amante liberal* and *La española inglesa,* and episodes of *Don Quixote* (the captive's tale and events in the harbor of Barcelona) and *La Galatea* (the tale of Timbrio and Silerio). The marked differences between the first two books of the *Persiles* and the last two, so often commented on by critics,[1] may be largely attributed to a change of chronotope from the sea to the land, as reflected in this passage: "Auristela was very happy to see the hour approaching when she would set foot on dry land [*tierra firme*] and no longer have to wander from port to port and from island to island, subject to the sea's inconstancy and the changeable will of the winds" (278).[2] Another of the narrator's telling statements hints at what might be the main representational domain of "the sea": "the threat of a heavy squall began to make the sailors uneasy, for the sea is a symbol of the inconstancy of our lives, neither one promising safety or stability for any length of time" (253).[3] Perhaps "the sea"—or maritime travel—brings out the instability of human life more insistently than does any other chronotope.

The "sea's inconstancy": the expression invokes above all the anarchic, inhuman powers of the elements and the dangers they represent for seafarers. But as all of these texts show, the changeability of "the sea" is almost unlimited. In addition to natural perils of many kinds (storms, shipwrecks, sea monsters, freezing, etc.), "the sea" produces the conditions for lawlessness, "barbarism," piracy, mutiny, international hostility; in short, it is an uncontrolled arena where desire and power can exert themselves without regulating institutions, and thus where personalities expand to fill the vacuum. Together with coastlines and harbors, the unpossessable sea is the principal scene where religio-imperial struggles are waged—struggles in which many of Cervantes' characters are caught up, as Cervantes himself was. Multiplying sorrows and joys, maritime travel separates and reunites lovers, friends, and families in the most unexpected ways. Capture, escape, release, abandonment, enrichment, and impoverishment abound in the adventure-time of the sea voyage, as do opportunities for self-assertion and improvisation. Ships contain provisional floating communities where diverse dramas arise and unfold, and where characters often tell their unique life stories. When ships meet, two such communities interact. The sea voyage provides access to other worlds embodying the uncanny, the remarkable, the strange, and/or the marvelous. Finally, the ways in which the actual technology, space, and time of maritime travel are experienced give rise to a unique range of thought and sensation as well as a wide range of analogues and metaphors in relation to forms of human experience which of themselves have nothing to do with sea voyages.

As may be gathered from discussion elsewhere, extraordinary travel also generates its own chronotope(s). This is not to say that general perceptions of time and space as such are necessarily any different in this type of journey; rather, movement scarcely has any limitations, the sensation of travel is highly surreal and charged with adventure, and the kinds of experience to be had are of an equally extraordinary nature. Hence extraordinary travel permits entry into realms of experience inaccessible to ordinary travel.

The various chronotopes of travel take on immense significance in Cervantes' novels. In *Don Quixote, Persiles and Sigismunda,* and most of the *Novelas ejemplares* there is hardly an episode that doesn't either belong to or develop out of some such chronotope. I turn now to a particular genre of chronotopes: worlds.

Worlds

Seldom in Cervantine criticism has there been any reflective acknowledgment or discussion of a quite extraordinary aspect of Cervantes' novelistic writings: the tendency of the narrative and its traveling protagonists to be drawn into world-like vortices.[4] I have in mind such phenomena as the islands of the *Persiles,* the cave of Montesinos and the Insula Barataria in the *Quixote,* the Gypsies in *La gitanilla,* Monipodio's seamy community in *Rinconete and Cortadillo,* the enclosed "feminine" community in *El celoso extremeño,* the pastoral in *La Galatea* and *Don Quixote,* the Christian cosmos of earth, heaven, and hell, Christian versus Muslim spheres of influence, the New World versus the Old, and various others. These are chronotopes accessible by travel but not constituted by travel as such. Diverse as they are, they display certain common characteristics.

Whether stationary or mobile, worlds constitute place, and hence can't be reduced to ideology, though they can hardly exist without ideology. The place of a world is inhabited, having its distinctive social organization, discursive modes, cultural practice, modus vivendi, economy, politics, natural conditions, and so forth: it has a corresponding "time" characterized by definite modalities of experience and thought. It is somehow bounded, autonomous, and qualitatively different from what surrounds it. This enclosure of a peculiar system is what distinguishes worlds from other types of chronotopes such as the road, the sea, the village or city, the salon, and so on.

The notion of other worlds is by no means unfamiliar to Spanish writers of the sixteenth and seventeenth centuries. Despite the oft-noted dearth during this period of "utopian" works resembling those of More, Campanella, and Francis Bacon, a lengthy catalogue could be assembled of other sorts of worlds. These include the New World as such and the many worlds within it, spiritual worlds opened up from practices ranging from mysticism to sorcery, Christian afterworlds, eutopian projections of a better world, worlds inherited from Roman and Greek antiquity (afterworlds, the Golden Age, the many exotic places described by Herodotus and his successors), worlds of the Orient, Muslim worlds from Al-Andalus to the Ottoman Empire, the kingdom of Prester John, fabulous worlds visited by knights-errant, and so on. One or another of these may find its way into the works of any particular writer, and may be highly developed in special cases such as Teresa de Avila's *Las moradas.* For the most part, however, texts of this period overwhelmingly produce renditions of what we may call "this world" (the world in which the writers themselves lived, or fictional worlds modeled more or less directly on it) as opposed to other worlds.

Strongly focused as it is on "this world," Cervantes' novelistic enterprise is nonetheless unique in its proliferation of other worlds both within and outside of "this" one. Far more than any other Spanish writer of his time, Cervantes manifests in his writings and especially his novels a tendency to isolate and enter into autonomous systems radically different from "this world." Unlike the static descriptions one often finds in representations of other worlds in European literature of the so-called Renaissance and Baroque, Cervantes' narratives show not only how such systems are supposed to function but also how they're disturbed from either within or without. Far from content to be an ethnographer of the existent or nonexistent, Cervantes brings out the dynamics of contact between such worlds and his travelers. Psychological motivation, drama, and internal history pervade these penetrable, alterable worlds. As opposed to the timeless worlds of many other writers, *Cervantine worlds have the principles of becoming and dissolution inscribed in them.* Some of them come into being or go out of being before our very eyes. Autonomous and isolated as most of these worlds are, a good share of their dynamism issues from their incompleteness, from the interaction between them and other worlds, especially "this" one.

The term *mundo,* used as it sometimes is in the relativizing sense of "a world" rather than the totalizing sense of "the world," betrays a conceptualization of the universe as made up of various worlds. There is the geographical division between the *mundo antiguo,* of which Europe is a part, and the American *mundo nuevo* (*LV* 51). There is the onto-eschatological division between this world and infernal ones (e.g., hell, the cave of Montesinos), purgatory, and paradise (e.g., *Gal* 75, 177, 290, 366; *DQ* I.18.216, I.25.310, I.27.330, I.43.523, I.44.533, I.47.557, II.22.210, II.23.220, II.31.280, II.70. 565; *CP* 316; *PS* 191, 261, 277, 342, 395, 397, 459, 461, 463).[5] There is occasionally a less clear-cut temporal division between the way the world was and now is or between the way it is and could be (e.g., *Gal* 477; *DQ* I.10.152). Furthermore, there is the astrologico-astronomical distinction between the world and other bodies in space, as when Sancho Panza after his supposed visit to the Pleiades positions himself outside the world (*la tierra*) to describe

it as no larger than a mustard seed. Finally, there is the coloquial particulariz-
ing of world as in the expression "por esos mundos adelante," or "por ese
mundo adelante" (*PS* 334, *IF* 139). These schemes, especially the eschatological one, are internalized within the self in utterances such as the following:
"There [*Allá*] in your soul a paradise / was discovered"; "you are her heaven
and her earth"; "a fury and a hell of jealousy occupied my soul. . . ."[6]

The same kind of thinking converts both external and internal space into
labyrinths: the sea, the wilderness (Sierra Morena), thoughts, desires, discourse,
amorous relationships, and other situations of dilemma or chaos are all explicitly characterized at one moment or another as a *laberinto* (*Gal* 247; *DQ*
I.48.573; *AL* 140, 173; *DD* 106, 204, 249, 392, 462, 463, 586; *CP* 329;
PS 156, 268), sometimes with direct reference to the Cretan model. A labyrinth is as much a world as any of the other spaces called worlds. Hence to
call something a labyrinth is to make a world out of it, to think of it in terms
of a world. This is the sort of transformation that takes place so often in
Cervantes' novels and even directs the development of some of them.

There is nothing particularly world-like about an inn, for instance; more
open than closed, it serves as a resting and meeting place for all who pass
by. But when Don Quixote not only conceives of Juan Palomeque's inn as
a castle — enclosed, fortified, magnified, permanent, noble, chivalric, person-
ally hospitable — but also calls this castle a paradise (*paraíso*), the inn becomes,
for that moment at least, a world. "For here," he says to the judge who has
arrived with a beautiful daughter, "you will find stars and suns to accompany
the heaven you have brought with you; here you will find arms at their zenith
and beauty at its utmost" (I.42.515). Don Quixote thus transposes the human
collectivity gathered at the inn into a celestial realm, one that takes on the
harmony and perfection of the heavens but seems too large for even the firma-
ment to hold. For him, an order entirely different from the ordinary prevails
within the confines of the inn/castle. The notion of "paradise" here may be
only a passing metaphor, an instance of Don Quixote's more general conversion of domains of the world into other worlds. But this conversion in turn
is paradigmatic in Cervantes' novelistic practice of the tendency to isolate
autonomous systems, to identify or invent worlds. So it happens, as will be
shown ahead, that such unworld-like phenomena as a cave, a village, a house,
a valley, a confraternity, a community, and so on can assume the attributes
of a world. Among other things, the idea of "enclosure" in the etymology
of "paradise" comes to mind.

Why there are so few references to the New World in Cervantes' novels
is likely to remain an enigma. Certainly not for lack of interest, given Cervantes' repeated attempts to go there. The many years spent in the New World
by two important Cervantine characters, Felipo de Carrizales and Ortel Banedre

(*CEx* 99–101; *PS* 320),[7] merit only a few lines of narrative, enough to bring these characters back to Europe: it would appear that America as a locus of narrative is off limits. The fact is, however, that Cervantes' novels present a human universe of many worlds displaying a corresponding multiworld consciousness, a rethinking of human issues fleshed out in realms outside the familiar. Even if all of these worlds are ultimately informed by "this world" in the sense that they may be seen either as distorted projections or as equally distorted negations/inversions of it, the distancing of issues in alien contexts facilitates a more freehanded and hypothetical treatment because these contexts themselves are deliberately designed to articulate the questions foregrounded. Both Torquato Tasso in his *Discorsi del poema eroico* (1594) and Alonso López Pinciano in his *Filosofía antigua poética* (1596) were well aware of the possibilities offered by having characters travel in remote or unknown countries (Vilanova 116–29). The modalities of "this world" interfere much less elsewhere than they do in "this world." The representation of other worlds sets in motion an implicit analogic interplay between what goes on there and "here" but is never reducible to "this world."

In view of the overwhelming importance of the notion of plural worlds with regard to the works of countless writers (Lucian, Dante, Ariosto, Rabelais, Swift, Voltaire, Kafka, Borges, to mention a few), critical attention to this phenomenon has been surprisingly scant. The term "world" often surfaces and is readily understood, of course, but rarely does it have any importance in the understanding of literature. "Utopian" criticism has undoubtedly been responsible in part for the obscuring of worlds, concentrating as it does on ideologies of the desirable and undesirable and limiting its attention to worlds that embody such ideologies—"utopias" and "dystopias"—while ignoring the many fictional worlds that don't fit these molds; it thus shifts attention away from worlds as such and the kind of thinking that goes into their making.[8] Another of many factors in the obscuring of worlds, I might add, has been the insistence on Cervantes' proverbial realism and its corollaries such as verisimilitude.

More attention has been given to these phenomena in the philosophy of fields other than literary studies. In his *Principles of Psychology,* William James distinguishes numerous orders of realities, or "sub-universes," which induce, in Alfred Schutz's words, "The world of sense or physical things (as the paramount reality), the world of science, the world of ideal relations, the world of 'idols of the tribe,' the various supernatural worlds of mythology and religion, the various worlds of individual opinion, the worlds of sheer madness and vagary" (207). Schutz, a social phenomenologist, adopts James's scheme but discards the term "sub-universes" for "*finite provinces of meaning* upon each of which we may bestow the accent of reality." He explains:

"We speak of provinces of *meaning* and not of sub-universes because it is the meaning of our experiences and not the ontological structure of the objects which constitutes reality" (230). For him, as with James, the world of daily life is the master world, which he understands narrowly as the "world of working" (218); other worlds are derivative. Every world has the following characteristics among others: "a peculiar cognitive style," consistent experiences within a finite province of meaning, a "specific tension of consciousness" (e.g., wakefulness or dream), "a specific form of self experience, a specific form of sociality, and a specific time perspective" (230–33). Schutz's main example of the world of phantasms—a diverse category including play, fiction, jokes, fairy tales, dreams, etc.—is Don Quixote's confrontation with the giants/windmills, in which the knight places the accent of reality on what he imagines. Schutz's notion of world coincides with that implicit in Julio Cortázar's ingenious title, *Vuelta por el día en ochenta mundos* (*Around the Day in Eighty Worlds*): as Schutz's own title indicates, he is really talking about "multiple realities," that is, differential versions of *the* world. This is extremely important, but shouldn't be confused with the notion of a plurality of autonomous worlds each with its own space. Schutz downplays actual space and place, opting for spatialized "provinces of meaning." He deals with "world" in terms of *chronos* but not *topos*.

More recently, Thomas Pavel in his *Fictional Worlds* draws from Leibniz's concept of "possible worlds" and subsequent developments of this idea in analytic philosophy. "Possible worlds," he writes, "can be understood as abstract collections of states of affairs, distinct from the statements describing those states. . . . In Alvin Plantinga's view, a possible world defines 'a way things could have been . . . a possible state of affairs of some kind'" (50). This definition, which conceives of worlds or "salient structures" in rather static terms, raises a host of questions, not least of all whether a "state of affairs" is anything more than a convenient falsification of things in process. And if a state of affairs today gives way as it must to a slightly different state of affairs tomorrow (cf. 44), the two states constitute different worlds rather than different moments of a world. It follows that a world has no time, no duration. This reduces "world" to a mere synchrony devoid of what I take to be the radical chronotopic differentiation that marks a world from what is outside it. Nonetheless, Pavel advances useful notions about worlds. He refers to the ontological asymmetry that often obtains between worlds such that one may be accessible from another but not vice versa, as is the case of "the really real world" as opposed to a make-believe one. This allows a distinction between what he calls "primary and secondary universes within dual structures, the former constituting the foundation upon which the latter is built"

(44, 57). Pavel aptly cites Borges' "Library of Babel" (*Prosa* 1:455–62) as a prime example, and explains: "Positing a universe organized differently from the one we happen to inhabit, Borges' text sketches a detailed secondary ontology containing objects, properties, relations. We understand the secondary ontology by virtue of the primary: "galleries," "ventilation shafts," "railings," "hexagonal," "low," which are terms transported, as it were, from the nonfictional universe. In a gesture of politeness, we are also offered the key to the relation between the two ontologies: the secondary one is modeled as a library" (58). Though he doesn't identify any particular worlds in Cervantes' novels, Pavel regards *Don Quixote* itself as a paradigm of salient fictional worlds, and views Don Quixote as one of a rare breed of "ontological founders" who suffer from ontological stress and reject their inherited world to pursue their own world project (60–64, 110, 138, 142). The coexistence of the landscapes of different worlds produces ontological fusion, or what I have called a two-world condition.

My discussion of specific Cervantine worlds will be oriented by the following sorts of questions: What constitutes their "worldness"? What do they share with other worlds and how are they unique? How are they dynamized in terms of both their functioning and their mutability? How do they become events? How do they orient and articulate desire? What relationships emerge between travel and worlds? What sorts of relations do particular worlds have with "this" world? What accounts for these worlds?[9]

Any classification of worlds in Cervantes' novels is bound to run into the kinds of absurdities so poignantly exposed in a classification of animals which Borges attributes to a Chinese encyclopedia:[10] owing to necessarily inconsistent criteria, there will be overlappings, significant omissions, juxtapositions of different ontologies — and some categories will be excessively multiple or singular. Nonetheless, for heuristic purposes I've grouped worlds into the following categories: (1) remote islands; (2) unique communities; (3) Muslim spheres; (4) pastoral enclaves; and (5) quixotic worlds. Each of these reveals a fairly distinct world-making logic and method. I begin with remote islands because they can readily be seen as the most "utopian" in the etymological sense (nowhere worlds presented as somewhere out there), and proceed through communities to Muslim spheres because the notion of social world will already have been developed with regard to the remote islands. At the same time I recognize that the categories, such as they are, could be presented in a different order. Categories 1, 2, and 5 correspond to the *Persiles,* the *Novelas ejemplares,* and *Don Quixote,* respectively, each text or ensemble of texts having its own modes of generating worlds. Categories 3 and 4 crosscut all of these texts as well as the *Galatea,* though very unevenly.

Remote islands

The Dream Island

In the second book of the *Persiles* (241–45), Periandro tells ecstatically of an unknown island he came to in his travels. Like Homer's Phaiakia and Lucian's Isle of the Blest, it is an island of lush idyllic nature made for the pleasure of the five senses. Abundant fruits are always in season: "there everything was spring, everything early summer, everything late summer without its discomforts, everything a pleasant and unbelievably exquisite autumn" (241). The sand, streams, grass, and fruits are all gems. Out of an opening in the rock, he goes on, comes a carriage in the form of a broken ship drawn by lascivious apes and ridden by a beautiful woman carrying a banner with the word "Sensuality," all to the accompaniment of female musicians. Sensuality tells him that his enmity toward her will cost him his pleasure if not his life. She and her companions pass on, carrying off a number of Periandro's sailors. Another group of women follows, headed by Chastity in the guise of Periandro's "sister" Auristela; she is flanked by two attendant maidens, Self-Control and Modesty, one of whom says they won't abandon Auristela till she finishes her trials and pilgrimage in Rome. Periandro's rapture breaks the spell of his own dream.

The topos of the locus amoenus, a form of eutopia, echoes innumerable passages both in Cervantes' novels and in literature going back to classical times. As a remote island, this place is naturally bounded, self-contained, far removed from the known world—the most typical setting for utopias up through the eighteenth century, where the imaginary nowhere-existing-as-such is posited as existing in an accessible elsewhere. The Dream Island, perhaps the most sumptuous natural eutopia in Cervantes' novels though scarcely developed in social terms, is the only world acknowledged by its teller as a fiction. It is a world made for him and by him according to the egocentrism of dream logic, having no existence independent of him: its natural aspects are designed for his senses, as is Sensuality herself, and its masque-like pageant would have no meaning without reference to him, an outsider. As such it is an allegory of desire articulating Periandro's amorous relationship with his "sister"; opposing open sensuality to deferred and channeled desire dictated by moral principles and self-control, the island reveals his erotic-incestuous inclinations as much as it edifies him in the legitimacy of his pursuit of desire.

At the same time, despite Periandro's transgressions of verisimilitude which other characters are quick to pick up on, the Dream Island is imaginable within the universe of septentrional islands, following directly upon an episode with a sea monster: it is *one more* island belonging to the series of septentrional islands[11] visited by Periandro and his companions, apparently as accessible by maritime travel as any other. Yet it is accessible, as it turns out, only by dream or the telling of a dream. Hence within the fiction of the novel, the island is at first presented as ontologically parallel to other islands, and then revealed as a secondary world, an impertinent though well-told "digression." From outside the fiction, the island is a tertiary world accessible from—and similar to the worlds of—a secondary universe. This interior duplication exposes the ontology of the secondary worlds, bringing into relief their character as representation and showing them to be "made" for the travelers who find themselves so surprised in them. By the same token, these travelers could be seen as "made" for the worlds they visit.

The Barbarous Island

From the startling beginning in medias res to the closing chapters, it would be hard for any reader of the *Persiles* to miss the symbolic progression from barbarity to sanctity, embodied by the Barbarous Island and Rome, respectively.[12] Like Homer's Phaiakia, the Barbarous Island is self-sufficient in terms of "all that's needed for human life" (62). Naturally speaking, then, this island is a self-contained eutopia for the inhabitants, whose indigenous economy appears to be based on hunting, gathering, and animal husbandry, with the use of stone implements rather than metal ones, and skins rather than cloth. Yet social relations are characterized by volatile anarchy, male force, mass behavior, slavery, human sacrifice, cannibalism, superstition, self-destructiveness, and all else opposed to contemporary notions of civil society and Christianity. Auristela's handmaid Taurisa explains the dynamic which now impels the barbarians:

> The island is inhabited by barbarians, a savage and cruel people who hold as a certain and inviolable truth (being persuaded either by the Devil or by an ancient sorcerer they consider the wisest of men) that from among them a king will come forth who will conquer and win a great part of the world. They don't know who this king is that they await, but, in order to find out, the sorcerer gave them the following order: they must sacrifice all the men who come to their island, grind the hearts of each of them into powder, and give these powders in a drink to the most important barbarians of the island with express orders that he who should drink the powders without making a face or showing any sign that it tasted bad would be proclaimed their king. However, it wouldn't be this king who'd conquer the world, but his son. The sorcerer also commanded them to bring to the island all the maidens they could buy or steal and hand the most beautiful one over to the barbarian whose heroic succession would have been determined by drinking the powders. (57)

These are quintessential barbarians. So much so, that no matter what kinds of sources one might point to as informing Cervantes' conception of the island — and details such as the hearts of sacrificed men are suggestive — there is something very transparent about the portrayal precisely in its negation of socio-politico-religious ideals. The barbarians are "there" as represented, and accordingly act out a real drama within the narrative, and at the same time they unwittingly function as ideological articulations as though this were their sole raison d'être. What might happen if there were virtually no controls — ethical, religious, institutional, political, etc. — on masculine desire for women and power, and if such desire were actively incited? The Barbarous Island seems to emerge as an answer to this question: the barbarians are a kind of Freudian primal horde which self-destructs before crossing over into totems and taboos, and which almost ludicrously illuminates some aspects of the "dark side" of civilization.

The natural cruelty and savagery of the barbarians have been dynamized by delusions of power rooted in diabolic sorcery. Without the prophecy this island would presumably rely on its self-sufficiency and enact itself repetitively within its natural confines. The sorcerer's injunction has created needs which can be fulfilled only from the outside: maidens to marry and men to sacrifice. This in turn has generated widespread piracy and commerce in the entire region, where the objects of value are human victims, especially nubile women. The barbarians are now oriented toward a sequence of future goals, ultimately toward possession by conquest of other worlds within their universe. Desire has turned outward and looks for its impossible fulfillment beyond the horizon. Autochthonous barbarian virtues such as valor and cruelty, demonstrated by whoever can *stomach* cannibalism, are to be eugenically mated with exogenous feminine beauty in order to produce the future conqueror.

The novel's protagonists are drawn into the clutches of the barbarians through piracy and trade. Saved from the barbarians by a storm as he's being brought from the nearby Prison Island, Periandro enters the island stunningly decked out as a young woman with whom the barbarians are so taken that they demand an immediate sacrificial victim. Just then Auristela happens to be brought to shore dressed in male garb and is on the verge of being sacrificed when her handmaid declares her to be a woman. A chain reaction follows. The archbarbarian Bradamiro, who "scorned all laws," claims Periandro as his in defiance of the untested prophecy. An arrow from the chief kills him, a kinsman of his stabs the chief to death, and chaos breaks out as barbarians attack each other indiscriminately "with hands and daggers, son showing no respect for father, or brother for brother" (68). A group of barbarians sets fire to the chief's forest, and soon nearly the entire island is ablaze, leaving few survivors apart from the foreigners who manage to escape. Hence the gender confusions and desires put into play by the unsettling presence of Periandro and Auristela result in the annihilation of the whole community of barbarians. It is the outsiders who provide the spark for the lawlessness of the barbarians to flare up upon themselves. Ritual degenerates into dispute, which gives way to strife according to alliances, which in turn break down into patricide and fratricide, until all is up in smoke.

The Barbarous Island presents us with a world of men who communicate with each other with arrows, daggers, claws, and fire when ritual and speech break down. No indigenous women have appeared as such until now; if there are women around the dwellings, as there must be, the narrative is silent about them. The only women to actually appear besides the feminized Periandro and Auristela are likewise outsiders, both of them pressed into service as interpreters: they are Transila, a captive maiden who acts as a go-between in the transaction involving Periandro, and Auristela's elderly handmaid Cloelia, who strangely enough acts as a female "guardian" of the prison. Foreign women are the communicators between the barbarous world and the outside, and the barbarians depend on them for this. In a novel where linguistic barriers are obviously everywhere but are usually glossed over—we don't even know what language the *Persiles* (as *historia*) is supposed to be translated from— the one place where people don't understand each other is this island. Women are trans-lated, and they are the translators between men who can't communicate with each other except through warfare and trade of which women are the objects. Some remarkable gender games are going on in this episode including the transvestism of the protagonists.

The one barbarous woman who does appear after the escape is Ricla, the wife for some fifteen years of the Spaniard Antonio who has been living in hiding ever since he came ashore. His tale of their first encounters portrays her as innocent in her sensuality, as innately generous and nurturing. Unlike the male barbarians, she shows the best of what natural life can offer. She and Antonio have taught each other their languages. More important, he has baptized and instructed her in his language in the "law" of Christianity, thereby raising her out of her native barbarity. (The pattern is familiar if one thinks of the various daughters of Muslims in Cervantes' novels and plays who forsake their family, culture, and religion to adopt Christianity.) At the same time he impregnates her, as she recounts after reciting a version of the Creed: "I, simple and compassionate, turned my rustic soul over to him, and he, with Heaven's grace, has returned it to me wise and Christian. I surrendered my body to him . . . and this surrender resulted in my giving him the two children you see here who add to the number of those who praise the true God."[13] The asymmetries of giving and receiving are patent. Ricla represents the redeemability of the barbarians, which is possible only through the feminine side. There is more than a hint that for her part she has naturalized Antonio, "the Spanish barbarian," whose violent response to affronts to his honor at home and at sea drove him ultimately to the Barbarous Island. Whereas he has elevated her out of her barbarity by instructing her in the "law," his life with her has taken the barbarity out of his civilized past. [14]

Policarpo's Island

Nearly a quarter of the *Persiles* either focuses on Policarpo's Island as such or finds a setting there for Periandro's narrative about his adventures else-where. What initially sets this island apart from all the others is its character as a political eutopia. A sea captain from there explains that the people unani-mously choose the best and most virtuous man as king, a post held for life as long as the king doesn't fall into vice. Hence men compete with each other in virtue in the hopes of becoming king. The captain spells out the far-reaching social consequences of this practice:

> Thanks to this, soaring ambition's wings are clipped, greed is grounded, and although hypocrisy is everywhere at work, in the long run its mask falls off and it fails to win the prize. As a result the people live in peace, justice triumphs and mercy gleams, and the petitions of the poor are handled with dispatch while those of the rich are not dispatched one bit better because of their wealth. The scale of justice is not tipped by bribes nor by the flesh and blood of kinship, and all business dealings proceed reasonably according to the rules. Finally, it's a kingdom where everyone lives free from the threat of insolence and where each person enjoys what is his. [15]

It might be better not to question how all of this is supposed to follow from a single electoral principle, or even how this principle can be so blissfully free of trouble. Nonetheless, the idea of choosing the ruler by common consent on the basis of merit rather than having leadership pass from father to son has widespread implications for Cervantes' Spain. On Policarpo's Island, the system is designed to control nonvirtuous desires, and it can survive even when the king succumbs to vice because he's replaceable. This in effect is what happens.

The democratic, meritocratic monarchy seems to have worked well in iso-lation. The arrival of the seafaring party, however, turns the royal palace into a labyrinth of jealousy, desire, and intrigue: "Everyone desired, but no one's desires were fulfilled. . . ."[16] The seventy-year-old King Policarpo hankers after the seventeen-year-old Auristela, who is also desired in one way or another by Periandro, Arnaldo, and Clodio; the king's daughter Sinforosa swoons for

Periandro, and consults with none other than a jealous Auristela; Rutilio is infatuated with the king's other daughter, Policarpa; the Moorish sorceress Cenotia lusts for the younger Antonio, and plots with Policarpo once the youth rebuffs her advances.

At the core of the intervening group, then, are Auristela and Periandro, whose pose as sister and brother doesn't convince everyone. Curiously, in the ways they consort with each other, the lover and sibling relationships between them undergo a mutual contagion. Moreover, if the king and his daughter were to marry the protagonists, the sibling relationships would undergo some intergenerational entanglements reminiscent of Oedipus' family, though without incest as such: Periandro would be Auristela's brother and stepson-in-law, and he would be Policarpo's brother-in-law and son-in-law, while Auristela would be her own sister-in-law's stepmother, and so on. Both Policarpo and Auristela ponder the potential confusions (180, 193). Something here is amiss, namely, the aging Policarpo's inappropriate love/lust for Auristela, and this is the ultimate cause of his undoing. What the royal family lacks is a wife and mother. When the sea captain first describes the island and its royal family, he says that the two daughters "had no mother, for when she died they no longer needed her apart from her companionship since their virtues and agreeable manner were their own governesses, setting a marvelous example for the whole kingdom."[17] She may have been necessary after all, since the kingdom, or at least the king, is destabilized by her absence and Auristela's presence. This is a world that lacks its principal mother/wife — for whom virtues are no substitute.[18] Policarpo in fact reflects on his virtuous life between the death of his wife and the arrival of the guests (117), leaving no doubt that the longtime void is now being filled by an uncontrollable desire for Auristela.

Policarpo's design on Auristela is one of several highly improper erotic relations on his island—"improper" according to obvious ethical judgments within the text. Clotaldo and Rutilio, like others before them, set their sights on women far superior to them in every sense, including that of "birth." And Cenotia's craving for the younger Antonio and subsequent vengeance pits a lascivious older Moorish enchantress against an incorruptible young Spanish Christian barbarian. She offers him whatever he wants in wealth and pleasure, if only he'll make her his slave: this in itself is a promised eutopia, but not his kind of eutopia. Other desires are proper but unrequited, such as those of Sinforosa and Arnaldo. The only relationship which is both proper and requited, that of the protagonists, falls prey to jealousy. Besides providing a locus for the narrative of Periandro's adventures, the royal palace, then, constitutes a microcosm in which so many plots of erotic desire develop according to their own logic: it is a walled-in microcosm of amorous pursuit which, unlike pastoral worlds, admits marked differences of age and class and incites more improper lust and criminal intention than the pastoral can tolerate. This community disintegrates when Policarpo has his own palace set on fire and the visitors escape to the harbor. Although much that goes on in the palace has nothing to do with the surrounding political eutopia of the island, the king is put to the test and fails. The people depose Policarpo and hang Cenotia, and the system which discourages but can't preclude corruption survives intact.

Without the foreigners, nothing might have "happened" on Policarpo's Island: their presence fills the place with so much desirability as to tumble the king himself, as Policarpo confesses to Sinforosa (179). Although Periandro proved his athletic prowess to the wonderment of all on a previous visit, it is much more his and Auristela's presence than their actions which destabilizes people around them — as was the case on the Barbarous Island. It is also highly significant that the travelers don't simply arrive at or leave either one of these islands: to put it succinctly with symbolic echoes, the characters enter by birth from the grave, and exit by escape from fire. That is, just as Periandro is reborn from the "grave" as he comes out of a cave on the Prison Island (and the imagery is overwhelming), so Auristela and various others, in a different "birth" (*parto*), are "fished" as living dead out of an overturned boat and brought ashore to Policarpo's Island (51, 164); and in both places the protagonists escape from a fire which the self-destructive inhabitants have lit. It might not be farfetched in this symbolic novel to associate the fire not only with desire (the identification is explicit) but also with infernal powers which the travelers elude.

The Island of the Hermits and Soldino's sanctuary

The last island the travelers visit before arrival on the mainland is that of the hermits (253–74). The symbolism of a saintly, ascetic life reverberates in the lighthouse the hermits keep, the hilltop where they live, and the benevolent though by no means lush nature which sustains them. Because of numerous similarities between this island and Soldino's sanctuary in southern France (392–98), which is insular in its landlocked enclosure and remote in its limited accessibility, both places will be discussed together. The island having only two inhabitants, Renato and Eusebia, and the sanctuary only one, the venerable Soldino, in what sense can these places be considered "worlds"? Soldino takes the travelers into a forest to his hermitage where a cave-like stairway leads deep into the earth and opens up into an expansive, paradisiacal valley which, he assures his guests, is neither subterranean nor enchanted: "Here, fleeing from war I found peace. The hunger I felt *in that world up there [en ese mundo de allá arriba], if you can call it that,* found satisfaction here. Here, instead of the princes and monarchs who rule in *the world* and whom I served, I've found these silent trees. . . . Here I have no lady rejecting me, no servant serving me badly. *Here I'm lord of myself;* here I have my spirit in the palm of my hand, and from here I send my thoughts and my wishes [*deseos*] to heaven."[19] The absolute here/there distinctions, where "there" is "that world up there," leave no doubt that "here" must be a world too, "this world down here." Yet Soldino also refers to "the world," in contradistinction to which "here" would be simply "not (in) the world." Distanced from the vexing world of politics and society, Soldino's place of solitude obviously reproduces the age-old tradition of the *beatus ille;* this is its primary function, its raison d'être, together with its compatible purpose as a transitional domain between earthly and heavenly realms. The visitors certainly sense that they're in a radically different space and saturated by it owing not only to the paradisiacal enclosure, the beatific solitude, and so forth, but also to Soldino's epistemological access to the present and future of their own lives and of the world outside: "It seemed to them that they were surrounded by predictions and up to their souls in judicial astrology . . ." (398).

Like Renato and Eusebia, Soldino embodies the complex ideals of the ascetic/hermit.[20] A woman describes him as "this snowy mountain, this white marble statue you see moving before you" (393). Snow and carved stone likewise characterize Renato and Eusebia, whose chaste but passionate love in France froze into a sexless marriage on the island: "We gave each other our hands in lawful marriage, we buried fire in snow, and in peace and in love, like two mobile statues, we've lived in this place for almost ten years. . . ."[21] In both cases, the characters have *no desires* apart from spiritual ones.[22] Entirely independent in the valley he has appropriated, Soldino is master of himself, an "island" in need of no one and of nothing apart from what his natural enclave provides him with. Resonating with classical and Christian literary antecedents, the Island of the Hermits and Soldino's refuge match natural abundance with *desirelessness.*

It would seem that this desirelessness evinces a rejection of "this world," especially in its corruption and vice. Yet all three hermits are strongly concerned with events in "this world," of which they are all natives. Nowhere in this novel is more said about the political history of the times than on the hermits' island, where Renato's brother brings news from the world, and on Soldino's refuge, where the stargazing sage spends most of his time peering into the present and future of the world outside so as to predict what for Cervantes' contemporaries is the past. For Renato and Eusebia in particular, the center of their existence is still France, and they return once the circumstances which caused their exile no longer pertain. There are compelling reasons why they do so. By the same token they willingly abandon not only the abundance but also the desirelessness of life on the island.

Both places are significant stopping points for the protagonists on their pilgrimage to Rome, who observe and admire rather than intervene. In a sense the island and refuge are *for* them: Soldino invites these travelers into his cave because it is to their benefit ("porque les conviene" [394]). Apart from this, there is nothing that really happens in these special spaces, nothing to narrate because there is no dynamism, no desire. Periandro says in effect that although he might seek a life of solitude if he were old, the desires of youth preclude this kind of life (265). As the hermits prepare to disinhabit the island, Rutilio, in a sudden welling up of contrition over past desires, resolves to stay there and adopt a hermit's existence so as to end his life well. Without this continued ascetic presence on the island, the utopia would dissolve from sheer abandonment.[23]

The places discussed so far in the *Persiles* are by no means the only ones that might qualify as worlds, though they are by and large the most developed. Other such worlds or worlds manqué include: the Snowy Island, a desolate, uninhabited place in the middle of nowhere where two young men die together with the woman they're fighting over in a mortal duel (140–48); Transila's Island, where men practice the barbarous custom of the *jus primae noctis,* though Transila courageously escapes (111–17); an Island of Wolves, one of which tells Antonio in Spanish to leave if he doesn't want to be torn to pieces (77); the island of a displaced "pastoral" community similar to those of *Don Quixote,* though the mode of livelihood is fishing (208–17, 221–23); the house of God in Feliciana de la Voz's song—a heavenly utopia which stands for Christianity itself and evokes images of the earthly paradise as well as Solomon's temple (309–11); Lisbon, which is associated with the "promised land" and described in highly eutopian terms as a wonder city (277–83); Rome, "the heaven of the earth" (192), where the travelers consummate their pilgrimage in a conglomerate of earthly heaven and hell (426–75); and finally, the remotest islands of all, Tile and Frislanda, where Periandro and Auristela come from and will return to (465–69). In varying degrees and ways, these and other places are endowed with their own highly distinctive space, enclosure, and modus operandi. The narrative emphasis normally falls not so much on the systems of these places as on how characters either react to them or stir up activity within them. Apart from the European cities, the "worlds" are ideated on a limited number of principles, often with a positive or negative ethical value which is then revealed through harmony or conflict.

Communities

To move "backward" from the *Persiles*—particularly the first half—to the *Novelas ejemplares* is to switch from a remote sphere of insular worlds, each naturally and humanly bounded, to "this world" in its complexity of nations, cultures, and ideologies. There is always a sense of "the world" all around, a single and inescapable world system regardless of the distinct powers, languages, religions, cultural practices, and so on that mark one place off from another. The characters of the *Novelas* travel by sea and land around the Mediterranean realms and as far as northern Europe and America, all of which constitutes a vast unity defined by political geography. Yet even in such an interconnected scheme of things, there exist autonomous communities having complex relations with the surrounding world of which the community members are acutely aware. The communities to be discussed here are the household of Monipodio in *Rinconete y Cortadillo,* the household of Carrizales in *El celoso extremeño,* the Gypsies in *La gitanilla,* and the witches in the *Coloquio de los perros.*

The house of Monipodio

Shortly after entering Seville by way of the "Aduana" or customs gate of Seville, Pedro del Rincón and Diego Cortado are astounded to discover that they aren't allowed to practice their trade of thievery freely. A boy asks them how come they haven't been to Mr. Monipodio's customshouse (*aduana*): "If you don't pay [duty on thefts]," he tells them, "at least you register with Mr. Monipodio, who is the father, master, and protector of thieves" (*RC* 206). From the very beginning, then, Monipodio's mafia acts as an autonomous entity with territorial claims more or less coextensive with those of the city of Seville. This criminal underworld forms an integral part of Seville, as Cortado acknowledges when he says that since "every land has its customs [*uso*], let us observe those of this land" (206).

The community of thieves is made up of young and old, women and men, all of whom have their talents and tasks. Not only do they work for the community, but they mostly live together in the house of Monipodio and develop fully communal relationships among themselves—there are amorous quarrels, rivalries, and so on. The diverse terms applied to Monipodio's community give a composite picture of what sort of entity it is. Heading the list are *cofradía* as well as *confraternidad, hermandad,* and *congregación* (208, 211, 213, 216, 227, 238), all of which call to mind the kinds of relationships and functions of legitimate confraternities formed around such units as work guilds and connected with the church and the local cult (Sancho Panza was once a member of one [*DQ* I.21.264]). As in other confraternities, members aren't born into the community but rather are accepted and initiated into it, and normally spend a year as novices—though Rinconete and Cortadillo are exempted from this. Sometimes referred to as the "father" of the community, Monipodio is also the godfather of his *ahijados* or godchildren (207).

Focalizing through the protagonists, the narrator refers to the group by two other expressions (240): "blessed community" (*bendita comunidad*) and "infamous academy" (*infame academia*). The first plays ironically with the devoutness of these thieves who donate part of their spoils to the church, go to mass, worship the Virgin, pray for the souls of their dead, and believe they serve God in their work; and *comunidad* brings out the oneness of the group. The second, in addition to evoking a school of learning and emphasizing its notoriety, calls attention to the importance of textuality in Monipodio's world, beginning with the agenda (*libro de memoria*) of crimes to be committed.

Under Monipodio's aegis, however, the paradigm of the community or confraternity is too confining for this clan of thieves. Monipodio himself wields the authority and powers of a chief who directs the operation, admits new members into the group, settles disputes with the language and gestures of a high judge, acts as a master of ceremonies, receives outsiders at regular hours, negotiates with corrupt officials, and so on. His imposing physical presence no doubt reinforces the respect he commands. Moreover, a description of his monstrosity ends by declaring that "he looked the most rustic and disproportionate barbarian in the world."[24] What place could a rustic barbarian— doubly "other" for being nonurban and uncivilized—have in Spain's largest and most cosmopolitan city? Perhaps he exemplifies the most "barbarous" aspect of the city, its criminals, and is thus cast as a quasi-alien chief with a domain of his own.

The household of Monipodio has its own dialect marked by the rogues' slang (*germanía*) of Seville and the constant spawning of malapropisms; on the one hand, then, there is a privileged insiders' lingo, and on the other there is a botching of the language common to both inside and outside. Thus language too constitutes an essential part of Monipodio's world.[25] Rather than representing the negation of the larger society, this inner- or underworld *replicates* and *deforms* the surrounding world in its language, hierarchy, system of justice, programming of activities, division of labor, territorial claims, interpersonal relations, code of honor, religiosity, ritual, and flair for celebration. In this sense Monipodio's world functions as a distorted microcosm of the surrounding world.

Certain allowances have to be made for the conditions of illegality, of course. Identities, normally construed by occupation, place of origin, and parentage, need to be concealed here (212); names need to be adapted to the style and anonymity of the secret society, as in "Rinconete" and "Cortadillo." Furthermore, the continuity of the mafia is always in jeopardy. Although things have been calm in the four years of Monipodio's rule with only sixty-two members sent to the galleys and four to the gallows (aptly dubbed *finibusterrae*—the ends of the earth, and of life's journey), a visit by the wrong officials could bring about disaster for the community once and for all. A false alarm in fact sends everyone but the protagonists into a panic: this is a very jittery world whose existence is fraught with the possibility of its own dissolution. Even more unstable than the community as a whole are the individual fates of the members, who are in constant danger of being snatched up by the hand of justice.

The new presence of Rincón and Cortado has little effect on the community as such. As critics have pointed out, they turn into observers once they enter the group; through their observations the monopolistic world of Monipodio exposes itself.[26] As amused onlookers, they learn from Monipodio's infamous academy but transcend it from the start. For them, thievery is an art rather than a job, language a supple instrument rather than an index of inferiority, and their friendship forged with mock ritual at the beginning of the novel transcends the bonding of the group so that they can easily disengage from it and move on in a few months' time.

The house of Carrizales

Carrizales' house in *El celoso extremeño* takes on the attributes of a very different world. Carrizales on his deathbed sums up for Leonora's parents all he has done for her: "I tried to guard this jewel whom I chose and whom you gave me, with the greatest caution of which I was capable. I built up the walls of this house, I took the lights from the windows which looked on to the street, I doubled the locks on the doors, I put up a revolving door like a monastery, I banned from it for good and all everything which bore the shadow or name of a man, I gave her servants and slave girls to wait on her, I did not deny them or her anything they cared to ask of me, I made her my equal. . . ."[27] The jealous and zealous Carrizales takes possession of Leonora, confines her movements within a fortified space, and sets up for her what he hopes to be a feminine eutopia. A little world materializes and dissolves in this novel.

The making of this world depends, first, on the almost absolute isolation of all the inhabitants from the surrounding world, and second, on the peculiar rarefaction of life within it. As far as enclosure is concerned, here too various metaphorical or comparative terms have the effect of transforming the household into entities of greater magnitude. "Never was monastery more enclosed, nor nuns more withdrawn, nor golden apples more strictly guarded."[28] Life in this house is *more* isolated, more *conventual,* than life in a convent, and it is likewise collective, communal. In the allusion to the apples, which refers to the garden of the Hesperides where golden apples were guarded by a dragon, Carrizales would correspond to the dragon (just as he is compared to Argos a few lines above), and Leonora, not to the Hesperides but to the apples themselves; by extension, the invader Loaysa would correspond to none other than Herakles. The comparison exoticizes and gives a mythical dimension to this domestic time-space, associating it with an eutopian orchard.

For the would-be seducer Loaysa on the outside, Carrizales' house is a well-guarded fortress (*fortaleza*) necessitating a heroic exploit (*hazaña*) in order to penetrate it. For all the women inside, it becomes a place of enclosure and privation, a prison of sorts. But during the first year, there is a self-sufficiency about it, especially since Leonora feels no lack: as discussed elsewhere, "Her thoughts did not stray beyond the walls of her house, nor did she desire anything but what her husband wanted" (106). Domestic life is her raison d'être, or maison d'être. Her will is contained and contented within her husband's for the time being; the entire novel, in fact, has to do with the ultimate failure to enclose the will within other wills, let alone walls and locks.

Even the idea of a fortress becomes small for the household when the dueña, Marialonso, on behalf of the women requires Loaysa to swear obedience before entering their quarters: ". . . it would not be right that in exchange for listening to two or three or four songs, we should lose all this virginity that's shut up here. . . . So, my dear sir, before you come into our *realm* [*reino*], you must swear a very solemn oath that you will do nothing but what we command" (my emphasis).[29] Surmising that their command is his wish, Loaysa slyly acquiesces. The ambivalent demand and oath, whose language in its serious aspect derives from social spheres outside domesticity, constitute an impromptu rite sanctioning Loaysa's passage across the threshold into the almost sacrosanct feminine "realm."

For Carrizales, the world outside is threateningly masculine. The buffer zone between the street door and the women's quarters is neutered with a eunuch guard. And the inner space is feminine, populated by white and black female slaves, maids, a governess, and Leonora herself. There are no male animals, no male images, only females. Unlike, say, the society of Amazons, this is of course a *man-made* feminine world, one based not on any feminine design or desire but rather on the restricted movement and sexual control of women, tempered as this may be by Carrizales' material generosity.

This feminine space may be understood as the superimposition of three paradigms: an infantile paradise, a *ḥarīm* and a convent. Consider the first of these: Leonora undergoes sex with innocent indifference, plays with her subordinate companions as *equals,* enjoys the sweetmeats Carrizales brings, and even regresses in her confinement to "making dolls and other girlish things" (105), much to the satisfaction of her husband, who acts as the grandfatherly benefactor for the whole community. Adding to the paradisiacal image is the orchard and the allusion to the orchard of the Hesperides. Second, as the *serrallo* (seraglio [120]) so suggestively insinuates, Carrizales' exclusive possession of the master key to a house filled with so many women and his barring male entry into this sacrosanct space bear more than a little resemblance to practices within harems. The Arabic word *harīm* accentuates precisely the *prohibition* cast over the women of the family and their *inviolable* living space. The presence of female slaves and a eunuch, though not uncommon in affluent life of Seville, adds a touch of "Muslim" mystique to the scene. If Carrizales engages in sex only with Leonora, he nonetheless controls the sexuality of the other women by confinement and de facto possession of them. Call it a monogamized harem with one wife surrounded by virgins. It's worth noting here that, as of a certain moment, the women start to make their domain really theirs by reappropriating their own desires and setting up their own clandestine order. Third, the resemblance of the household to a monastery is twice brought out explicitly, and Loaysa refers to the women as living in *clausura* (cloistered [118]). The inviolable feminine space of the household follows this paradigm as much as it does the harem paradigm, and the notion of a community of virgins is of course much more proper to a convent. And the only nonvirgin, Leonora, actually joins a *monasterio* at the end of the novel to form part of a community of brides of Christ. Could the convent be Christ's "harem," with a few shades of filial paradise as well?[30]

The domestic world lives in happiness and stability until "the cunning disturber of the human race" chooses Loaysa as his agent of disruption. As discussed elsewhere, a good share of the novel focuses on how Loaysa awakens desires in order to gain access to the otherwise impregnable fortress. The very challenge of breaking into the exclusive, forbidden space undoubtedly prompts him to undertake the adventure. If the world inside is a *harīm* of sorts, Loaysa may be considered a *harāmī,* literally a thief, but also—being based on the same radicals as *harīm* is—an intruder who violates the sacrosanct, the honored, the taboo, the feminine. Since Carrizales makes little if any distinction between his possessions and his wife, not to mention the slaves and servants, it's not hard to make the shift from the *harāmī* as thief to the *harāmī* as violator of the *harīm.* There are certainly traces of quick-witted sacrilege in Loaysa's oath of obedience ("by this sign of the cross, which I kiss with my unclean mouth" [119]). Once Loaysa is inside, the community becomes as jittery about its potential collapse as Monipodio's clan does (126). The infiltration of an outsider into this inner sanctum and into the arms of the wife herself induces the death of the master and leads to the dissolution of the man-made feminine world. A house which enclosed almost a kingdom now shrinks to the size of a cocoon: "I was like the silkworm, making the house in which I was to die."[31]

Otherworldly Gypsies

Together with the so-called Moriscos, the Gypsies both within and outside the *La gitanilla* are about as "foreign" an ethnic group as one can find in Cervantes' Spain. They share virtually nothing with sedentary society. Cervantes wrote the novel against a background of mounting controversy concerning the "Gypsy question," a burning issue ever since the Catholic monarchs' decree in 1499 which enjoined the Gypsies either to settle down and work like everyone else, or face expulsion. A hundred years of polemics produced a variety of proposed solutions to the Gypsy problem, including several forms of assimilation, means of preventing procreation, denial of their ethnic identity, expulsion, restriction of their movement, incarceration, forced labor, and genocide. Attitudes toward the Gypsies followed class and occupational lines, the nobles being more disposed to tolerate and admire the Gypsies than the clergy or the urban population (Leblon, *Les Gitans d'Espagne* 17–53; cf. Cervantes' play *Pedro de Urdemalas* 1698ff.). One of the most bigoted, the theologian Sancho de Moncada, wrote in his discourse to Philip III in 1619 that the Gypsies were pernicious to Spain because they were enemies of the state, idle vagabonds, prostitutes, thieves (of children too), practitioners of occult arts, heretics (or "gentiles," idolaters, atheists), and speakers of an esoteric language called "Gerigonza" (Luna 45–48). Around the same time, Salazar de Mendoza wrote that the Gypsies were even more dangerous to Christianity than the Moriscos, since they venerated the body more than the soul. Bernard Leblon documents how the host society's exhaustive ignorance of Gypsy life — after nearly two centuries of coexistence — led to representations of the Gypsies as lawless, incestuous, promiscuous, ungodly, and even cannibalistic. Generally more sympathetic though not always better informed were the numerous representations of the Gypsies in the arts, especially the theater (Leblon, *Les Gitans d'Espagne* 48). Even Cervantes' knowledge of them is questionable, judging by both the canine view of them in the *Coloquio de los perros* and the much more favorable if still ambivalent portrayal of them in *La gitanilla*.[32] But regardless of how well he knew or liked them, his literary Gypsies are a world unto themselves, one which guards its autonomy and integrity and yet specializes in exploiting for its own survival and benefit the aesthetic, ethical, and conceptual boundaries of the larger world system in which it finds itself.

Many of the "world"-defining features of the Gypsy community have been taken up in a previous section. Others resemble those of worlds already discussed, and needn't be dwelt on here. In brief, the Gypsies of the novel form a tight community with its own kinds of social relations, "laws," "ceremonies," ideological orientations, autonomy over internal affairs, codes of behavior, together with an ethos of overriding *alegría* in the best and worst of circumstances. Closed as they are, the Gypsies gladly initiate the enamored Andrés Caballero as a novice in a community into which members are normally born, not admitted; "ceremonies of Andrés' *entry* to being a Gypsy" are carried out (100; my emphasis).

The old Gypsy's remarkable speech to Andrés about their way of life betrays at least three currents of thought: social eutopianism, the *beatus ille,* and a reinforcement of cultural stereotypes (100–103).[33] There is first, with the handing over of Preciosa to Andrés, an explanation of the conjugal system which sets the pattern for the entire network of internal relations. Since each man possesses his own woman and solicits no other, Gypsy men manage to maintain friendship among themselves free of jealousy. Hence, "while there is much incest, there is no adultery"; deviating women are severely chastised by the men. The old man stresses that whereas nearly all else is communally owned, women are private property. Preciosa responds that the "law" of her will is stronger than the laws of these "legislators," and she sets stiff conditions for Andrés to have her; she furthermore repudiates the "barbarous and insolent licence" with which these men punish their women or cast off old ones at will (104). This portrait, when contrasted with that of Cervantes' moralist contemporaries, shows the Gypsies possessing laws and following them so scrupulously that the men at least can live a harmonious life. The old Gypsy in effect admits the charges of incest, but renders them trivial, while categorically denying charges of promiscuity. This is an eutopian system that works well. As in Monipodio's nest of outlaws, the members consider their community a *cofradía* or *confraternidad,* but here the notion of brotherhood is blood-based and exceptionally binding. Preciosa corrects the "barbarous" abuse of male prerogatives not by provoking male authority but by asserting her own will as supreme.

Second, the speech eloquently portrays Gypsy life as free and carefree, without envy or greed, without either fear of losing honor or desire to augment it, without political or hierarchical concerns. The Gypsies live in sync with nature: they are the modern incarnation of Horace's *beatus ille,* of the Golden Age, of the happy life. The close parallels with these literary paradigms suggest that the old Gypsy's discourse has been put into his mouth and passed off as authentically Gypsy. Nonetheless, the fact that the Gypsies speak—or are made to speak—and that their life is described from within their *aduar,* is very significant even when others such as the narrator ventriloquize through

them. Berganza's hostile portrait of them in the *Coloquio* allows them no
room to speak or present themselves. His conclusion: "they are bad people,"
and incorrigible (347–49).

Third, the old Gypsy reinforces the usual preconceptions about them, especially concerning thievery. He makes it clear that this is the basis of the
community's economy and the pivotal point of relations between the Gypsies
and sedentary society, and he takes pride in the Gypsies' skill in this art. He
thus confirms the narrator's opening statement in the novel, that Gypsies "seem
to have been born into the world for the sole purpose of being thieves" (61).
Once again, highly unlikely words are being put into his mouth. Despite the
many references to theft in the novel, however, not even this aspect is unam-
biguous: the community, says Andrés later on, is no pack of thieves but a
refuge from the whole world (112); and in a finale with biblical resonance,
a sedentary girl enamored of Andrés frames him for theft, and publicly admits it at the end.

Though the community disperses in a moment of crisis and loses both
Preciosa and Andrés to the sedentary world where they came from, there's
no doubt that it will regroup itself. Cohesion and continuity are as integral
to the errant Gypsy community as the uncertainty of their life circumstances.
For her part, Preciosa will take some of the best of Gypsyness to her new
home even if she won't have the latitude to mobilize it to the same degree
as before.

Witches' Sabbaths

As with the Gypsies in *La gitanilla,* the episode of the witch in the *Coloquio
de los perros* can be read against a backdrop of historical sources which, as
modern historians have taken pains to demonstrate, by no means prove the
existence of a demonic witch cult. It happens that la Camacha, who has turned
the progeny of her fellow sorceress la Montiela into puppies, corresponds to
a sorceress (if not two sorceresses known as las Camachas) reconciled by the
Inquisition twenty years before Cervantes spent a winter in the same village
of Montilla (Huerga 453–61); oral tradition no doubt enhanced her reputation during these years. In the novel, it is the witch la Cañizares who reveals
her practices to the canine traveler Berganza, who listens and watches as she
goes into a cold trance. She draws a sharp distinction between sorcery and
witchcraft: whereas sorcery is an occult art and body of knowledge resulting
in spells, subversions of the moral order, natural disasters, metamorphoses,
and the like, witchcraft is much more of a pleasure-giving vice fixated on the
witches' Sabbath. As Julio Caro Baroja defines them, the first is a solitary
art while the second is a communal practice, a cult (126). If sorcery trans-

forms the world into another through its powers, witchcraft creates a world of its own through its community. Yet since la Camacha, la Montiela, and la Cañizares have practiced both sorcery and witchcraft, the distinction refers to different spheres of activity rather than different categories of people.

La Cañizares tells of how she and other witches anoint themselves, assume the form of winged creatures, and fly to where the devil as a he-goat receives them in their human form (342): "We go to see him a long way away from here, in a big field, where a great number of us gather, men and women witches [*brujos y brujas*], and there he gives us wretched food to eat, and other things happen there that for the sake of truth and of God and of my soul I dare not tell, so filthy and disgusting are they. . . ."[34] This is the witches' Sabbath (Sabbat), the *aquelarre* (from the Basque *akerr,* "he-goat," and *larra,* "meadow" [Caro Baroja 234]); la Cañizares calls it *convite* and *jira,* both terms denoting "feast," one stressing the invitational nature of it, the other the country setting. Her account shares with the testimonies of the accused the image of large numbers of witches feasting together, dancing, and having an orgy with the devil.

Yet there are important differences between the official versions and her description. Trial records (problematic as they are) give details about celebrating the Black Mass on special days, kissing the devil's arse, drinking his urine, eating the corpses of babies and hanged men, having one form of sex or another with the devil or many devils, and much more—all carried out with a certain amount of ceremony revering the prohibited (Caro Baroja 123–48, 211–61, Flores Arroyuelo 85–138, Henningsen 69–94). Sources point to witches as forming a sect in opposition to the church, a sort of devil's clan in which female witches are much more representative than male ones. The ritual aspect of the witches' Sabbath is almost completely absent in la Cañizares' account, which stresses instead the collective indulgence of vice which does little if any harm to others. Significantly, apart from a single reference to male witches (*brujos*), la Cañizares always refers to witches in the feminine plural, most typically by the pronoun *nosotras.*

This episode tells of two integrally related communities, one consisting of la Cañizares and her fellow sorceresses/witches living together in Montilla, and the other of the ecstatic assemblies of witches. Both constitute almost exclusively feminine domains.[35] Even the devil's apparently dominant role in the Sabbath could be reduced to that of enabling the witches to fulfill their own fantasies. Of the two communities, it is primarily the *aquelarre* that reveals otherworldly characteristics. The radically altered states, experiences, behavior, and relations in the Satanic realm constitute a separate world set in an otherwise uninhabited space. To enter the Sabbath world, la Cañizares and other witches utter a diabolic invocation while anointing themselves with unguents powerful enough to deprive the senses of this world and open up another order. And equally important, witches *travel* to the *convite*—in fantasy or reality, as the case may be—and they travel far, to a valley in the Pyrenees for instance (*CP* 340). The many separate journeys bring together a community which realizes itself in all manner of indulgence and recedes again into the surrounding world. Secretive and consciously hypocritical, la Cañizares leads such a double life, confessing herself unable to give up the "sin" of her source of pleasure even when she knows her ecstasy may not always be authentic. She and her colleagues live in two worlds, traveling back and forth between them. Since only insiders have access to the world of the Sabbath community, only they can tell about it as experience: there's no such thing as going there without believing and belonging. Berganza's contact with the world of the witches is necessarily indirect. Yet he is suspected by the villagers of being a demon—they in effect demonize him—and hightails it away to other worlds, those of the Gypsies and the "Moriscos."

While Cervantes' novels attest to a fascination with the alternative possibilities of world-like communities, they also call into question the very feasibility of such communities as permanent entities. The one group that seems most able to cope with disruption and to regroup after disbanding is that of the Gypsies, a traveling community that makes an art of improvisatory living. The Gypsies are internally united by every sort of relationship characterizing sedentary society except for ties to a particular place; in fact their nonattachment to place, together with their highly oppositional relationship to the sedentary in nearly every aspect of life, strongly reinforces their cohesion as a group. Countercommunities such as the house of thieves or the witch cult are forever threatened by the law. Other communities including insular ones reveal elemental flaws presaging dissolution, which is sometimes precipitated by travelers and intruders. Several of these communities are unable to withstand the disruptive effects of contact with the outside in the form of travelers. By contrast, the bonds forged between travelers are often stronger than those of the communal worlds they pass through. There is often more permanence in shared transience—in the special relationships that this fosters —than in territorialized communality.

Turks, "Moors," "Moriscos"

Although the bulk of *Don Quixote* is supposed to be authored by a "Moor" and translated by a " Morisco," the Moorishness of Cide Hamete Benengeli doesn't evoke another world so much as it introduces a wonderful game of estrangement which serves the novel's profoundly playful fictionalizing. But there are important worlds associated with Turks, "Moors," and "Moriscos." Not only as characters but as members of separate worlds, Muslims and/or "Moriscos" figure prominently in the three long novels as well as three of the shorter ones (*AL, EI, CP*), not to mention various plays. The following remarks acknowledge and reflect upon the importance of this rich and diverse issue so reminiscent of Cervantes' years of war and captivity, of the major imperial struggle of his time, and of the ethnic composition of Spain before the expulsion.

Part II of *Don Quixote* begins with a discussion of the Turkish menace which, it was feared, might descend on the peninsula with the blessing of the Morisco population. Don Quixote's idea of having half a dozen knights-errant take care of the invading hordes adds a ludicrous touch to the sixteenth-century confrontation between two empires, and more generally, between two worlds divided along politico-religious lines. In Cervantes' novels, piracy and warfare in the Mediterranean coerce captives into the domain of the Ottoman Empire. The only ways out are escape and ransom. It needs to be stressed that tales of the Muslim world are told by *captives*, or by narrators who sympathize with them, and thus their "observations" and inventions are highly loaded to start with. Cervantes' scarcely mediated hostility toward the Turks, manifest right through to the *Persiles*, is harshest in *La Galatea* where Turkish corsairs and a general are characterized as heathen dogs, barbarians, cutthroats, rapists, desecrators of churches, and much else (170–71, 358–63). Not that Christians are exempted from similar acts of cruelty in the longer novels. What comes across from first novel to last, however, is that the Ottoman Empire breeds an innately *alien* kind of people with almost unintelligible languages and an abhorrent religion. Classified as Turks, Moors, and renegades, the men (especially the Turks) tend to be treacherous, power-seeking, and lascivious without ethical constraints or finesse, the only really humanized Muslim man being Zoraida's father in *Don Quixote*. The exotic women, confirming the polarization of foreign women in Cervantes' novels, are either shamelessly libidinous or predisposed toward Christianity. The Ottoman world provides the ambience for such tales as *El amante liberal* and the captive's story in *Don Quixote*.

Like Ricla from the Barbarous Island, Zoraida from Algiers (*DQ* I.37–42) is an ideological creation situated in the conflict between sociocultural systems. The historical figure after which she's modeled married first the future sultan of Morocco and then, after his death, the future king of Algiers, who was a Valencian renegade no less. Cervantes gives her back her virginity, estranges her from her own world and the men in it, and has her embrace Christianity and a Spanish captive she hardly knows. So much for verisimilitude. Regardless of how one views the relationship between history and novel here, it's amazing she acquiesces to her author's fraudulent design. The pathos-filled separation of father and daughter at sea dramatizes Zoraida's choosing one religion over another even though she has a world to lose by doing so. Her defection signals one world's superiority over another, a coup for Christianity and a loss for the "Moors." This is not to deny a deeply problematic treatment of her defection.[36] Once again, however, a woman proves the religious redeemability of her own kind even if the men are hopeless cases. As the former captive puts it, "Moorish she is in body and dress, but in her soul she's a very good Christian, for she has the greatest desire to become one."[37]

Similar to the Jewish *conversos,* the *moriscos* (or nominally Christian descendants of the "Moors" in Spain) were an outgrowth of the Spanish caste system based on religious filiation. Far more than the *conversos,* however, they were perceived as remaining a caste in Cervantes' time. Berganza refers to them as a *casta* in his scathing account of their character and customs (*CP* 349–50). The *moriscos* form a separate world in Spain to the extent that they are viewed as a caste, an extensive ethnic-religious community. In one breath, the Christian dog says it's hard to find a true Christian among them *and* they hoard all the money that comes into their hands, condemning it to life imprisonment in their coffers rather than spending it. Their draining of the country's lifeblood is compounded by another problem: they *breed* uncontrollably like the descendants of Jacob. What's more, they rob "us" blind and get rich selling back to us what's "ours." Cipión applauds the expulsion order and concludes: "Spain is rearing and harboring in its bosom as many vipers as Moriscos."[38]

Américo Castro (*Pensamiento* 292–307) dismisses this and a similar diatribe in the *Persiles* (353–56) as mere repetitions of vulgar prejudice having little to do with Cervantes' truer sentiments which, he argues, come out most clearly in the authorial sympathy for the plight of the *morisco* Ricote and his family after the expulsion order (*DQ* II.54, 63–65). For Castro, the issue is Cervantes' tolerance, and he cites three passages in which characters unequivocally praise the religious tolerance of places as distant as Algeria, England, and Germany, respectively; read against such affirmations, intolerant utterances resonate with irony and satire and indict Spain. Francisco Márquez Villanueva, in his exhaustive study of the *moriscos* in Cervantes' novels (229–335), argues similarly that all three passages reveal sympathy for the *moriscos* and criticism of the proponents of expulsion. In the case of the *Quixote* and the *Persiles,* he says, Cervantes undermines the principal tenet of the expulsion which denies the existence of truly loyal, Christian *moriscos:* Márquez Villanueva furthermore disqualifies the fanatically anti-*morisco* Jarife as a judge of his own people. As for Berganza's malicious ethnographic account, the *moriscos'* faults—apart from their immunity to Christianity—amount to little more than envied virtues such as frugality, industriousness, and fertility (285–304). So far, so good: both Castro and Márquez Villanueva enrich the reading of these passages and warn against face-value interpretation of them.

What they fail to appreciate, however, is the world of difference between assimilated and unassimilated *moriscos,* and the divergent ideological roles assigned to women and men. Denying that Christianity has anything to do with the sympathy toward Ricote's family, Castro cites Ricote's statement: "la Ricota, my daughter, and Francisca Ricota, my wife, are Catholic Christians; and though I am not much of one myself"—Castro's quote stops here but the passage continues—"still there is more Christian than Moor in me, and I always pray to God to open the eyes of my understanding and make me know how to serve Him."[39] The fact is that Ricote's Christianity is undeniable and crucial: he no longer belongs to the caste of his forebears. His daughter has assimilated religiously, culturally, socially, and linguistically to the larger Christian world: "I had a Christian mother and a wise and Christian father too. I sucked the Catholic faith with my mother's milk. I was brought up with good principles, and neither in my language nor in my customs, I think, did I show any sign of being Moorish."[40] Many other details of her story indicate an estrangement from everything Muslim, Moorish, Arab, African, and an espousal of things Christian and Spanish. Once again it's the women, mother and daughter, who take the lead in abandoning their heritage and assimilating to the Spanish Christian world. Intermarriage is favorably looked upon, provided the woman, not the man, comes from "outside." But there's no sympathy for unassimilated *moriscos* in Cervantes' novels.

The *Persiles* shows the same polarization among *moriscas* as is evident among women of the Turkish empire. On the one hand the secretly Christian *morisca* Rafala warns the traveling company that her father intends to be their "executioner" that night by collaborating with a fleet of marauding corsairs. Here we have another manipulated split between father and daughter (353–59). On the other hand there is the lascivious Cenotia from Granada, the most developed sorceress in Cervantes' novels, who fled the Spanish Inquisition and ends up hanged on Policarpo's Island (200–252). The association between sorcery and *moriscos* surfaces spontaneously given the highly sophisticated tradition in Muslim Spain of folk medicines, occult arts, and the like, as well as the ways that the Islamic and the diabolic merged in popular consciousness among the Christians. The historical Camacha, according to the records, learned much of her art from an "unbaptized Moor" (*moro sin baptizar*) and a *mora* in Granada (Huerga 458–59). The woman enamored of Tomás in *El licenciado Vidriera* consults a *morisca* for an aphrodisiac which has the effect of poisoning him into his glassy madness (52). I suspect that *moras* and *moriscas* practicing the occult were seen as occupying the hidden recesses of Moorishness. Thus whereas the virtuous Rafala rejects the world of her caste, including her own father, Cenotia has come out of its deepest shadows and taken that world with her even into the Septentrion.

Pastoral enclaves

The pastoral has been widely recognized as having world-like characteristics. A subheading of Forcione's more or less sums it up: "The Garden Paradise as an Expression of World Order: The *Galatea*" (*Aristotle* 212). In the wake of many other studies, Elias Rivers' discussion of the pastoral as a chronotope ("Pastoral" 12–14) articulates the peculiar time-space within this genre. Given the consensus among Cervantistas with regard to this issue, my commentary will be brief.

There are *various* unique pastoral ambiences in Cervantes' novels, none of which quite fits the pattern set by Virgil, Sannazaro, Garcilaso, Montemayor, and others, although *La Galatea* comes close.[41] Whenever characters enter one or another of these places, the time-space changes entirely: the kinds of experiences, personages, modes of expression, activities, economy, social relations, and so on have little or no relation to the world outside. And the prose sweetens up, adopts a measured rhythm, and harmonizes both with itself and with the world it tells about. In the last book of *La Galatea* the pastoral world provides access to a secondary world, the Valley of the Cypresses (also called the Sacred Valley), where the shepherds go to honor the grave of the dead shepherd Meliso. What makes this place world-like is its double enclosure and the divine-like atmosphere inhabited by the gods and the solemn semi-presence of the dead. Four hills enclose the valley, and an even barrier of cypresses walls off the inner space. The muse Calliope appears within a flame rising from the grave and sings of those gifted souls who will some day be buried there (403–60). With its Neoplatonic principles, its natural symmetries and harmonies, this is perhaps Cervantes' most static world, a "Renaissance utopia" in the conventional sense.

The pastoral enclaves in *Don Quixote* and the *Persiles* are far more dynamic. In the *Quixote* I'm referring, of course, to Don Quixote's Golden Age speech, the episode of Marcela and Grisóstomo, the story of Leandra, Camacho's wedding, the feigned Arcadia, and Don Quixote's pastoral aspirations (I.11–14, 51, II.20–21, 58, 67); and in the *Persiles,* to the island of fishermen and the rustic dances near Toledo (208–23, 327–30). In barely twenty lines, Don Quixote enumerates all the basic ingredients of the pastoral setting when he contemplates becoming a shepherd named Quixotiz—a process in its essentials not too different from switching worlds to become a knight-errant

(II.67.548). It's curious in this regard that Don Quixote traces the origin of knight-errantry to the need to protect damsels, who in the pastoral Golden Age used to roam about scantily dressed without fear (I.11.155–57).

When Berganza strays into the hands of a band of shepherds in the *Coloquio de los perros,* he's amazed that they don't behave like the literary shepherds he has heard about. In this satirical critique of the genre, Cervantes has taken the worldness out of the pastoral: these coarse and brutal shepherds belong to the *same* world as the butchers, the slaves, the constable, the soldiers, and many others. The world of young, beautiful, gentle people harmonizing with a benevolent nature and having nothing better to do than sing of love or solitude could hardly be more distant.

Quixotic Worlds

Don Quixote boundlessly "worlds forth" in his three sallies until defeat, disillusionment, and the nearness of death reorient him exclusively to the world he once lived in as Alonso Quijano. Not only through his selective transmutation of everyone else's world into his chivalric world, but also through the playful prompting of his world on the part of other characters in both parts of the novel, *the* world assumes a radical duality through differential versions of it. Not that these are of equal ontological status: the world of Don Quixote is secondary with reference to the primary world of Alonso Quijano. Yet both of these admit a plurality of "worlds" within the world—in fact, they admit the *same* worlds except that not all of the chivalric worlds are judged authentic according to the generally accepted scheme of things. Both situate the earth within the Ptolemaic system. Hell and heaven belong comfortably to both, as do pastoral enclaves, the Muslim world, and the many worlds portrayed by geographers from Herodotus onward. At one point, for instance, Don Quixote and Sancho are mysteriously taunted as troglodytes, barbarians, cannibals, Scythians, and Polyphemuses (II.68.556).[42] If Sancho humorously mistakes them all for something else, his equally bewildered master certainly knows where these otherworldly creatures come from. But beyond this, Don Quixote's chivalric world grants full status to the many fictional worlds spawned by the authors and readers of (or listeners to) books of chivalry. The kingdoms of Micomicón and Candaya, as well as the fabulous palace visited by the Knight of the Lake, are among the more important of these in the novel (I.29, II.37–41, I.50).

The cave of Montesinos

Of all the Cervantine worlds, that of the cave of Montesinos has been most explicitly treated as "a world" apart from the world (II.22–24). Analyses by Augustin Redondo, Helena Percas, Alban Forcione, E. C. Riley, Edwin Williamson, Juan Bautista Avalle-Arce, Gonzalo Torrente Ballester, and many others have spelled this out so clearly that the briefest of commentary will suffice here. If Don Quixote denies that the cave is an *infierno,* as the "cousin" and Sancho have called it, he is denying not its worldness but only the hellish associations of the term (II.22.210). Yet his subterranean sojourn turns from an Elysian dream into more of a Hades-like nightmare than he'd like to admit. More neutrally, Sancho later refers to the cave as "the other world" (*el otro mundo* [II.23.220]), while conversely Montesinos down below speaks of the world above as "the world of the living" (*el mundo de los vivos* [II.23.216]). Everything from his ceremonious entry to his unceremonious exit endows the cave with world-like features.

Echoes of every other underworld known in literature up to that time resonate in the cave of Montesinos, faintly or distinctly as the case may be. Like so many other literary figures, Don Quixote descends into a realm where centuries of the living dead selectedly coexist to while away some or all of the rest of eternity. As he experiences it, the cave of Montesinos opens into an autonomous space holding many renowned personages ranging from Guinevere to Dulcinea in the suspense of an enchanted limbo between life and death. Transformed almost beyond recognition and showing varying degrees of vitality, the cave's inhabitants entertain the hope of being released once again into the world of the living. Enchantment is the prevailing principle: the people are enchanted without knowing why, the experience of time is enchanted such that three days and nights seem to revolve in the space of an hour, the experience of space is enchanted such that with a closing and opening of the eyes a rocky hollow opens up into an expanse of meadows with a sumptuous palace in their midst. Above all, of course, it is the dreamer who is "enchanted" by a madness that prompts him to fantasize an enchanted chivalric world.

While Don Quixote at the beginning of the novel found writing and traveling to be mutually exclusive, his two propensities now converge as he both authors the episode (by invention and narration) and protagonizes it, presenting an enchanted world of which he himself figures as a potential disenchanter. Or to follow it in sequence, he descends into the cave as an adventurer, falls asleep, and, like Periandro in the Dream Island, imagines that the journey continues from where it left off. As traveler he discovers a subterranean world of the kind that chivalric legends and texts have led him to expect there; as author he unwittingly invents his encounter with that world, though he is afterward plagued with doubt about the authenticity of what happens.[43] As traveler he has access to the underworld by going to its mouth and venturing into it; as author only he has access, since that world is a child or stepchild of his brain. His isolation from things and people of the world above enable him to conjure up the subterranean world with little outside intervention of the sort that so often contradicts and frustrates him, although his own recent experience in the world above does infiltrate into the cave toward the end of the narrative. Down below, Montesinos reaffirms Don Quixote's statement that the undertaking of this adventure was reserved for him alone (II.23.212, II.22.208). Not just the adventure, we might add, but the world he enters was reserved for him alone, because it's of his own making. Unlike Kafka's man from the country who (in that unsettling parable in *The Trial*) comes to wait at the door of the Law and grows old before discovering too late that the door was intended for him alone, Don Quixote recognizes what's his and intrepidly ventures into it.

The cave is mainly an ailing world of the past. In an odd mixture of tradition and experience Don Quixote brings an imaginary past, represented by Montesinos, Durandarte, Belerma, Lancelot, and the rest, into a likewise imaginary present, represented by himself and Dulcinea; he thus assumes a continuum between them and merges them in the same time and place. Nowhere else does he meet the "past" so directly face to face in order to interact and commune with a world of his own making less foreign to him than the uncomprehending one above. The characters below recognize him for what he "is" and Dulcinea for what she "is," and they verify chivalric legends told in the world above. The enchanted world admits him and receives him with the hospitality due an honored guest, and to some extent by its very "existence" justifies his identity, his self-appointed mission, as well as the texts and beliefs upon which his almost dead order of knighthood is founded. In the cycle of mutual belief and sanctioning, he in turn can testify to the reality of a world he has concretized in his imagination because he has been there. All of this is edifying despite the ill health, deformation, and unhappiness of the inhabitants of that otherwise *locus amoenus:* it is so gratifying and at the same time moving that Don Quixote can afterward speak of his having been taken from the most delectable life ever known to man (II.22.210). Less edifying is Dulcinea's misshapen presence among the enchanted, by now fully internalized by Don Quixote according to the way Sancho set up the initial situation of her enchantment (II.10); this remains problematic and unresolved since the dream world offers no means for her disenchantment. Also disquieting is the implicit parallelism between Don Quixote and Dulcinea, on the one hand, and on the other the moribund Durandarte and his lady Belerma who holds her shriveled heart in her hands. The latter couple being the central figures of the cave's world, the chivalric past and present are drawn together by analogy.

Two systems of value are discernible in his narrative, one proper to Don Quixote's neochivalric wordlview and the other to "this world" or more specifically to parodic degradation, what Bakhtin calls the "material bodily principle" and "grotesque realism" (*Rabelais* 19). As Don Quixote speaks and is written through, his story abounds in the most hilarious details showing the intrusion of one world into another, much to his dismay. Although coming out of his mouth, the language of parody doesn't emanate from the logic of character unless a case can be made for it as revealing the absurdities of an unedited dream. Whether disjunctive or not with regard to character, the language of the story is double, and even when Don Quixote returns as the sole witness the world below is as much a double world as the one above.

Just as Merlin, according to the story, enchanted the cave's world into existence, a breaking of that spell would disenchant it out of existence. But the enchanted, accustomed to watching their own hair and nails grow like those of the dead, aren't holding their breath. In addition to the wonderfully hybrid nature of the cave world, what dynamizes this otherwise static world where people neither eat nor defecate is the prophesied coming of Don Quixote, for whom and because of whom this underworld exists in the first place. At the same time this subterranean sojourn brings about a very significant reorientation in the traveler himself.

Sancho's *ínsula*

Sancho, too, appropriates a world for himself, a landlocked island, and gives it his unmistakable personal stamp at the same time as that world transforms him. The birth of his desire for an *ínsula* coincides with his birth as a character. In the very first paragraph about Sancho, before he's even given a name, mention is made of Don Quixote's promises to him particularly of an *ínsula*, illusory promises which lead to no less than his abandoning home, wife, and children. Squire and knight later calculate the length of Sancho's salary as of the day in which the promise of an *ínsula* was made (II.28.259). His first words are a reminder to Don Quixote not to forget the promise, to which his master replies that he intends to do more for his squire than other knights-errant ever did for theirs, possibly finding a kingdom for him to rule, but in no event is he to lower his expectations so far as to content himself with a lesser position than *adelantado,* a provincial governor (during the "Reconquest"). Though confident of his ability to govern, Sancho nonetheless entertains some doubt as to how his wife would fare as queen (I.7.127–28).

As noted elsewhere, the *ínsula* begins as a potential chivalric world modeled on the practice among knights-errant, especially Amadís, of rewarding their squires with a place to govern: "I am guided solely by the example of the great Amadis of Gaul, who made his squire Count of Firm Isle [*Insula Firme*]" (I.50.587). At first the *ínsula* is no more than an idea which Don Quixote has "impregnated" in Sancho's head, according to the barber: "It was an ill moment when you were seduced [*os empreñastes*] by his promises, and an evil hour when that island you so desire found its way into your brain" (I.47.563; cf. II.52.438). If Sancho has little concept of what an *insula* might be (a Latinism for *isla* much in vogue in the books of chivalry),[44] he understands it as an insulated territory whose ruler holds a title of high nobility and governs free of outside interference. This is what initially constitutes its worldness. The eventual whereabouts, size, and other specifics of his *insula* are of little consequence to him. Though for him it is a world realizable within his experience, it is in reality a utopia in the true sense, an imaginary world located in no place except the mind.

Ostensive motives for his wanting an *insula* may change from one passage to the next (among others, wealth, prestige, power, curiosity), but vague as it is, the idea circumscribes his primary desires to such an extent that he imagines he would be a happy governor having nothing more to desire (I.50.587). Sancho soon learns that in order for him to obtain an *insula* his master has to come out victorious from not just any adventure but one specific to *insulas*.[45] The *insula* functions as a leitmotiv throughout much of the novel as Don Quixote fails to deliver—and can hardly be blamed for doing so given the scarcity of *insulas* to be had in the arid terrain he travels. Finally, owing to the duke's maliciously playful largesse, it materializes unexpectedly as the Insula Barataria, and Sancho assumes the governorship of his "republic."

The episode of the Insula Barataria has lent itself superbly to analyses of its political "utopianism," its folkloric sources and archetypes, its theatricality, and its carnivalesque development. All of this comes into play in the short-lived world. Once the duke offers Sancho a noninsular island within his own dominions, the *insula* takes on definite characteristics as does Sancho's role within it. He would still be governor but answerable to his benefactor. The *insula* itself is fixed somewhere in the near vicinity. When Sancho expresses concern that it might no longer be there for him if he delays several years in his journey on the wooden horse Clavileño, the duke assures him that it has such deep roots in the earth that it can neither move nor be moved from where it is ("no es movible ni fugitiva" [II.41.345–46]). Soon afterward the duke gives a clearer image of the *insula* by describing it as round and well proportioned, fertile and abundant. Believing himself to have come down from the sky on horseback from where he has seen the world as tiny as a mustard seed and men no larger than hazelnuts, Sancho sees no greatness or dignity in ruling over something so low and insignificant, and says he would prefer a small part of the heavens to the greatest *insula* in the world—something the duke can't offer him (II.42.355).

The place he's taken to is like any other, a village called Baratario with over a thousand inhabitants. There's nothing world-like about it. But for him it's an *insula* in his sense of the term with a definite existence and location. He is led to believe that there's nothing new or unique about his governorship, and that there are other *insulas* of a similar sort within the dukedom. Above all, the *insula* means for him an opportunity to rule over a "republic" (II.49.406) and rule well, for which purpose Don Quixote has tutored him after the traditional manner of the education of princes while taking Sancho's idiosyncracies into account.

All of this is of course a setup devised and brought about by the duke and his household. It is they who convert an ordinary place into an *insula,* which really is insular in a figurative sense, a noplace superimposed on a chosen place and enacted there but not specific to that pláce or any other for that matter. They are experts in turning ordinary places into extraordinary ones, but only here do they devise a world as such. In the *insula* the dramatic principles of festive play predominate in the context of a supposed government. Augustin Redondo has demonstrated with a wealth of detail the episode's profoundly carnivalesque nature.[46] As he would be the first to acknowledge, there is much more to the *insula* than carnival, but it is this more than anything else that marks Barataria off from its environs and makes for its worldness. Sancho is received with pomp and "ridiculous ceremonies" and is told that according to an ancient custom he is to respond to questions and enigmas put to him so that his subjects can get a feel for their new ruler. With his arrival Baratario has turned into the Insula Barataria, a jocose world that lasts for a week or so and dissolves with his departure because the republic depends on him and could only be his.

The narration as *historia* participates fully in recreating and conveying the merriment of Barataria, initiating the mock government with a mock invocation to the sun, "the perpetual discoverer of the antipodes" no less (II.45.375). At every turn the text colludes with the duke and his subordinates in framing a world, but it also participates in a larger joke at their expense and to Sancho's credit, that of the *burlador burlado* (II.49.406). Contrary to their expectations, Sancho is more than equal to the task. Though his words and actions are mixed with shrewdness and simplicity ("con asomos discretos y tontos" [II.51.425]) according to the *tonto/listo* model (Molho 274–77), the shrewdness of illiterate Sancho holds sway to the amazement of all. It is the possibility of character change that the organizers of the *insula* have overlooked. As a "new Solomon" with charming touches of rusticism, Sancho solves all the folkloric riddles put to him as court cases, somewhat tolerates curbs on his appetites, refuses the title of "don," dispenses justice and clemency as fitting, keeps public order, cleans the republic of its drones and drifters, regulates trade and the value of commodities, pronounces aphorisms of political sagacity, and institutes reforms that become a *written* legacy in the

village long after it ceases to be an *insula*. Critics have pointed out the political significance of the *insula* within the novel, and within Cervantes' Spain,
in terms of power relations and modes of governance. Sancho turns this utopia
into an eutopia.

The *insula* is Sancho's *adventure* par excellence. It's what he's been looking for and expecting all this time, and now demands the most nimble improvisation on his part to be carried off right. He accepts the duke's offer
in the spirit of adventure: "Well now, let the isle come; . . . and it's not out
of greed that I want to leave my poor shacks and rise to greater things, but
from my desire to find out what it tastes like to be a governor."[47] The Insula
Barataria is a *world in the making*. The duke and his accomplices are the
immediate "authors" of this world: they set up the *insula,* direct its situations,
improvise half the "script" and allow Sancho to improvise the rest according
to the role they've led him to believe he has; in his impromptu role he steals
the stage. (I use these terms advisedly according to the theatricality of the
insula and the emphasis placed throughout on writing and illiteracy.) The
ideologies of errancy and sedentariness with regard to Sancho's *insula* have
been pointed out elsewhere; I should stress here that journey imagery infiltrates into his sedentary governance and highlights its improvisatory character. Don Quixote urges Sancho to let the author Cato be his "polestar and
guide to direct you [*que te encamine*] and bring you to a safe port, out of
this stormy sea on which you are about to set sail" (II.42.357). God is also
said to guide (*guiar, encaminar*) him in his judgments (II.43.365, II.45.379).
Sancho has to "make his way" according to the difficult and ever-changing
circumstances in which he finds himself. How he does so determines the shape
of the Insula Barataria: there is no "always already," nothing already established, but rather a constant going and making of a new world.

Although the inhabitants receive Sancho as the "perpetual governor of the
Insula Barataria" (II.45.376), the *insula* itself lasts only four, seven, eight,
or ten days (the count varies): the *insula* is an *event* with its own gestation,
birth, and death, as though it were a human life. Sancho resolves to observe
Don Quixote's advice and "thereby to bring the pregnancy of his government
to a good birth" (II.43.360), in the words of the narrator. And Sancho's government is coextensive with the life of the *insula* because the latter would
be nothing without it. The final prank in the form of a nocturnal attack provokes Sancho to abandon the sedentary life of the *insula*. He seems to have
some awareness of the setup by now: "these tricks aren't to be played twice"
(II.53.445). Sancho was born into the governorship and has now died, coming back to life as his former self: "let me go and seek my past life, and rise
again from this present death. I was not born to be a governor. . . . Tell the
duke that naked I was born and naked I am now; I neither lose nor gain.

I mean that I came into this government without a farthing, and I leave it without one. . . ."[48] The deathly end of Sancho's government prompts Cide Hamete Benengeli to meditate gravely on the transitoriness and irreversibility of human life, which runs swiftly to its end: "our author says this owing to the swiftness with which Sancho's government ended, was consumed, was undone, vanished into shadow and smoke."[49] (The asyndetic sequence here recalls the death imagery in Góngora's famous *carpe diem* sonnet, "Mientras por competir con tu cabello.") The melancholy and awareness of death are overwhelming in the chapters beginning with Sancho's saturnine departure and including his live burial in the depths of the earth. His encounter with Ricote is a meeting of exiles forced out of worlds that were theirs.

The *ínsula* has come a long way from beginning to end. Culled out of chivalric language and at first conceived according to the supposed tradition of knights giving newly won territories and titles to their squires, it has passed as a quixotic promise to Sancho, who in turn has appropriated it as the prime motive of his peregrination without knowing what it is but having changing notions about what it might be. The duke and his subordinates have taken all of this into account and cleverly combined it with other notions ranging from the republic to festive play so as to realize an *ínsula* in the shoreless vicinity. Sancho is unaware of his participating in a make-believe world. This is due to deception, of course, but more specifically to the fact that Barataria is designed for him, cut to the shape of his dreams, and he makes it much more his own than was expected; yet it undercuts his desires by systematically frustrating them. The island is his and not his, familiar and foreign to him. Whereas previously he carried his potential world with him, he now leaves it behind definitively, though he takes away with him a desire to rule and be obeyed (II.63.521).

There's hardly a major character in Cervantes' novels who doesn't get caught up in one world or another, and some go into and out of many: these worlds are an essential part of the traveling in the novels, and travelers in turn very often affect them in decisive ways and are profoundly affected by them. Except for a few places like Soldino's sanctuary and Renato's island, Cervantine worlds are highly dynamic, subject to change and even dissolution. Entering any one of these worlds means in-vading an entirely different time-space with its distinctive way of being, modes of thought and behavior, system of value, relations to nature, social forms, and so on. Cervantes goes very far indeed in exploiting both the reality and the possibility of a plurality of worlds within "this world." In doing so, he novelistically explores questions of vital, primordial concern irreducible to mere literary conventions or topoi of the marvellous. Such exploration might not have been possible at all had he kept his characters within "this world."

The notion of "world"—in the plural sense derived from *the* world—enables a diverse group of *chronotopic* phenomena to be seen as having certain fundamental principles in common without losing their uniqueness. It is precisely the definition of "world" as a type of chronotope which distinguishes the term as used here from other notions of multiple worlds. Unlike terms such as "utopia," "dystopia," "garden paradise," "community," "island," "pastoral," and so on, "world" comprehends all of the isolated, autonomous, heterogeneous time-spaces in the novels, and lets them be considered together, comparatively, rather than separately as curiosities of the imagination. As such I take it to be a key category of thought and a proliferating function in Cervantes' literary production, perhaps the most basic unit after "character" (also in the plural sense), allowing insight into the workings of the novelizing process itself.

Narrative Passages

Pasos de un peregrino son errante
cuantos me dictó versos dulce Musa
en soledad confusa,
perdidos unos, otros inspirados.
Luis de Góngora, *Soledades*

I only wrote that, thinking it would be a pity to cross the Shirakawa Barrier without writing something.

Basho

Anxious to get on, I just scribbled it down, as if my sandals were already in motion.

Basho

El libro de Cambios. The Wandering and the Book: Deambularvagabundeaban por Londres leyendo de corrido el libro de sus vidas más o menos imaginarias. O merodeaban ciegamente, al azar de su parodisea, en busca de aventuras. Su grafomanomadismo mano a mano les hacía errar erre que erre. Eme que eme. Vivir lo escrito y escribir lo revivido era uno de los trabajos parafrasisifosos de su insensatolondrado novelón de bellaquerías. Escrivivir, lo llamaban, sin caer en la cuenta de que se desviían en el empeño.

Julián Ríos

In view of the overwhelming importance of the journey in the long narrative fiction of Western Europe from the fifteenth to the eighteenth century, I intend to explore here questions concerning the conversion of journey experience into discourse and conversely the proliferation of journeys by means of narrative. These two processes are simultaneous in journey fiction, the second occurring in the guise—and as though by the modus operandi—of the first. In all journey literature, whether fictional or not, the narrative necessarily

198

assumes characteristics of the journey it recounts, participating in what it tells about, tracing the routes of the travelers, conveying something of their experiences and the diverse spaces in which they move, and sometimes explicitly characterizing itself in terms of the journey it narrates.

Recounting and Inventing Journeys

As Don Quixote sets out on his first sally, he anticipates a chronicling of his *peregrina historia* even if he wrongly guesses the genre and style (I.2.82). He, like Sancho and many other characters, shows an obsessive awareness that his traveling will be rendered into narrative. The most widely used term for "journey" in Cervantes' novels is *peregrinación,* which, like the Latin *peregrinatio* (from *pereger,* "one who is away from the land," which in turn derives from *per,* "through," and *ager,* "field"), includes the pilgrimage but broadly covers all travel to faraway places. While the adjective *peregrino/a* often means rare, strange, extraordinary, it resonates with connotations pertaining to the travel of *peregrinos* from which its rarity derives. Hence it's no happenstance that the narratives of so many narrators and characters, including all of the *Persiles,* are referred to as a *peregrina historia,* not only because of their extraordinariness but also because they are tales of *peregrinaciones* (e.g., *DQ* I.41.513, I.47.564; *PS* 248, 253, 274, 419). When the happenings to be narrated are peregrine (*DQ* I.42.514; *CEn* 282; *PS* 88, 110), they oblige the teller to recount them, and they transfer their peregrine character to the tale itself. The telling and the told, including the protagonists, are bound together in analogous itineraries. The twists and turns as well as the interruptions and resumptions of Periandro's tale replicate in their own ways the traveling he narrates, as one character implies: "What roundabout ways [*rodeos*] and farfetched connections you've used to tie your wandering story [*peregrina historia*] together, Periandro!" (248). Sancho's amusing reference to the *escrituras andantes,* "errant writings," of the books of chivalry reflects the same kind of transfer from the narrated to the narrative (I.47.557).

A curious episode toward the end of *Persiles y Sigismunda* exploits all the senses of *peregrino/a* and reflects the status of the entire narrative as a *historia peregrina* (415–19). Dressed from Lisbon onward as pilgrims (*peregrinamente peregrinos* [279]), Periandro and Auristela together with their companions meet an ingenious pilgrim who has the unusual and novel (*peregrina y nueva*) idea of composing a book of aphorisms gathered from other pilgrims with their own signatures.[1] These are the alms he asks for. The book is to be entitled *Flor de aforismos peregrinos,* though the narrator says he might well call it *Historia peregrina sacada de diversos autores,* a title which describes the *Persiles* as a whole not only because the book is a *peregrina historia* but also because it is composed to a considerable degree of the life stories of its traveling characters. Several of the aphorisms distortedly condense the lives of their authors in a single sentence: this is an aphoristic displacement of Cervantes' novel of travel, composed en route in the form of personalized alms from pilgrims to a pilgrim.

The very fact that a story recounts a journey integrally af-fects and in-fects the narrative, bringing about an inevitable transference from subject matter to medium. If the journey heightens the possibilities of chance encounters, of diverse and "superfluous" happenings, of relatively disconnected series of events and digressions, the narrative of travel necessarily takes this into its account no matter how it may subjugate the journey to its own logic and purposes. The authorial figure of the *Persiles* reflects on this issue in a major statement on travel narrative, the narratability of events, and the differences between history and novel:

> Long journeys [*peregrinaciones*] always bring with them diverse events, and since diversity consists of different things [*cosas*], the situations [*casos*] will necessarily be different.
>
> This history is a case in point, for the threads of events get cut off, leaving us unsure as to where it will be best to tie them back together. Not everything that happens makes for good telling, and there are things one could let pass untold without diminishing the story; there are acts that precisely because of their greatness ought to be passed over in silence, and others so insignificant they shouldn't be mentioned. The outstanding thing about history is that anything written in it is made palatable by the taste of truth it brings with it. Fiction [*la fábula*] doesn't have that advantage, and its action must be prepared with such accuracy and good taste, and with such verisimilitude, so that in spite of the lie, which generates some dissonance in the mind, it forms a true harmony.
>
> Taking advantage of this truth, then, I go on to relate that continuing their journey, the handsome band of pilgrims came to a place . . . whose name I don't recall. . . .[2]

According to what it can say and deems worth saying, travel narrative as history silences certain *casos* of lived experience, *passing* over them or letting them *pass* by, but incorporates the diversity and discontinuity of the remaining subject matter to become diverse and discontinuous itself. Its working materials are the very *casos* and threads abstracted from the journey into passages of narrative. Because its events supposedly happened, "history" enjoys considerable licence to narrate whatever *casos* and threads are available to it, whereas fiction in essence has to justify its narrative by its own criteria in a void of historical truth. Cervantes' complacent historian of course exercises illusory licence, unaware that he and his history are figments of imagination edited according to the criteria of fiction.

The journey's diversity tends to consist largely of a series of encounters, potentially as wide-ranging as the vast and open chronotopes of travel allow. Travel accounts convert the journey's course into discourse, disproportionately focusing on novel and extraordinary experience. The tendency toward heterogeneity in journey experience is matched by the potential for inclusivity in extensive narrative, which accepts the serial nature of disparate events and tracks its travelers through diverse encounters. And each time an encounter is left behind, the narrative thins out to allow for new and unexpected happenings. Rather than developing any unity of action, narrative converts the adventures and other remarkable experience of the journey into a succession of "episodes," a word which adds a couple of prefixes to *hodos,* "road," "pathway": journey narrative already has the road inscribed in its episodic itinerary. This makes it difficult for journey narrative to achieve the complexity of intrigue and sustained intensity realizable in narratives whose action unfolds mainly in one place, as is the case in some of Cervantes' shorter narratives such as *El curioso impertinente* and *El celoso extremeño,* not to mention works ranging from the *Iliad* to most of the great nineteenth-century European novels. This by no means precludes the profound character development and the many sorts of cumulative momentum especially evident in *Don Quixote,* and to a lesser degree in *El coloquio de los perros* and *Persiles y Sigismunda,* whose sequences both depend on and transcend the specific succession of happenings. Yet these novels are episodic, periodically thickening and thinning out and thereby making possible all the diversity that comes their way. How else would practically all of Spain figure into the *Quixote* and the *Coloquio,* or much of Europe into the *Persiles?* How else could they adopt such a radical strance vis-à-vis everything aleatory, marginalized, improvisatory, *un*necessary, digressive?

Diversity is only one of many properties of the journey appropriated by narrative. Elsewhere I've discussed at length how the language referring to narrative in Cervantes' novels primarily adopts travel imagery, to the extent that the narrative's routes and movements are at times confused with those of the journey it recounts. Owing both to the processive nature and referential capacity of narrative discourse, the analogy runs deep. We've seen, for instance, how the main verbs characterizing the narrative process coincide with the primary verbs of motion used to narrate journeys, while narrative borrows its space, routes, and movements from experiential analogues. Travel narrative enacts its own "movements" while telling about a journey. As an autonomous discursive process, it "moves" along its own pathway *at the same*

time as its travelers are made to move along theirs, but it also "moves" *with*
them and *after* them by tracking and reviving the journey it tells about. The
sensation of accompaniment recalls Stendhal's image of the novel as a "un
miroir qu'on promène le long d'un chemin,"[3] where the writer invades the
time-space of the characters and moves along with them while reflecting their
movements. By reviving a past journey, travel narrative reenacts a *corso* as
a *ricorso,* to adapt Vico's terms.

That both narrative and the journey proceed "together" obviously doesn't
mean that the telling corresponds to the experience narrated in terms of pace,
selection, or sequencing—and I hardly need to insist on this given the attention it has received on the part of narratology from the Russian formalists
onward. Time and again narrators declare that days or months passed by
without there being anything to tell about. Even Don Quixote and Sancho
Panza, about whom almost everything seems tellable, can go for up to six
days without anything noteworthy happening to them (II.60.491). Sometimes
periods of years are relegated to a single sentence, while a few brief moments
may extend over considerable reading time. However, Cervantes' constant attention to pace—as when Cipión warns Berganza that "at the rate you're going, you won't even get to the middle of your story" (*CP* 304; cf. *PS* 234,
244–45)—never allows the narrative to drag to the extent that Sterne so playfully does when he devotes five chapters to Walter Shandy and Uncle Toby
descending a staircase (*Tristram Shandy* IV.9–13). Narrative elision occasionally reaches the point of absurdity, as when Periandro says: "For two months
we sailed without anything of note happening, although we cleared the seas
of rubbish in the form of more than sixty corsair ships and, since they were
corsairs, appropriated their stolen goods . . ." (*PS* 245; cf. 149). Citation
uniquely matches characters' words with textual words, regardless of how fast
or slow characters speak or readers read. Yet Cervantes' narrative generally
avails itself of narrative's ability to economize on verbiage and thereby ab-
breviate narrative time relative to the time of events told. The absurdity of
making narrative time match the time of repetitive events narrated is brought
out to some extent in Sancho's story of the goatherd who has his goats cross
the river, and is illustrated more vividly by an analogous story told in
Avellaneda's "false" second part of *Don Quixote* where Sancho interrupts his
narrative on the pretext that he has to wait a couple of years for a countless
number of geese to cross a river one by one on a narrow bridge (22.207–10).

As far as order is concerned, clearly every narrative text has a unique sequencing of its story's events, concentrating and starting where it will and
including forward and backward displacements as well as digression within
its own rather linear discourse. Although Berganza in the *Coloquio,* for instance, insists on telling events in the order in which they occurred, his strat-

egy breaks down in the episode of the witch, whose present focuses on his own possible origins and future metamorphosis. At the other extreme is the narrative of the *Persiles,* which begins in medias res and reaches retrospectively further and further into the past as the journey progresses until the story's initial events are revealed in the final pages. Narrative can't avoid running a course autonomous of the journey's.

Most commonly, narrative elides journey experience which is allegedly "not worth" telling, and includes what "deserves" telling (e.g., "things happened to them, so many, so important, and so novel that they deserve to be written down and read" [*DQ* II.10.113]; "nothing worth recording [digna de ponerse en escritura] happened to him [*DQ* II.60.491]; "Some other things happened to them on the way to Barcelona, but none important enough to deserve writing [que merezcan escritura]" [*PS* 360]; "they walked for many days without anything happening to them worth telling" [*PS* 400]). If narrative suppressions often leave one guessing as to the criteria for leaving unmentioned things out, narrative inclusions indicate much about what "deserves" to be told. The entire dynamics of narrating *for* others largely conditions this process, of course, whereas traveling is rarely done for others in the same sense. Novels such as *Don Quixote,* the *Coloquio,* and the *Persiles* are rich in audience response adumbrating how people or dogs would like narratives to proceed — or even how they would like narrative to *alter* the experience it tells about (e.g., *DQ* II.3.61). Despite occasional tedium and other negative responses, Cervantine characters place an extremely high value on narrative as a creative performance that gives pleasure and satisfies the inexhaustible desire to know the real or ficticious *sucesos* of others. At the very least, narrative needs to be intelligible and engaging, and to bring this about it has to move at a good pace along interesting pathways without straying too far into the extraneous, the farfetched, the incoherent, the unsayable, or the unvalued.

Journey narratives operate in large part as a function of the memorable, in terms not only of what is remembered and re-membered from the dismembered travels, but also of what narrators desire others to consider and remember. While first-person narrators and "historians" may at times express the limits of their memory or knowledge, they generally remember or know far more than they tell. The dog Berganza says that "ever since I was strong enough to gnaw a bone I've had the desire to speak, to say many things which were stored up for so long in my memory that they were going moldy or getting forgotten. However, now that I see myself so unexpectedly endowed with this divine gift of speech, I intend to enjoy it and take advantage of it as much as I can, making haste to say everything I can remember, even if it's all jumbled up and confused, because I don't know when this blessing, which I consider to be on loan, will be revoked" (301). Berganza recognizes that discourse activates memories otherwise left to decay in storage. But his initial intention of saying whatever comes to mind even if it comes out confused soon gives way to sequencing more appropriate to the modalities of discourse and of memory alike. Reflecting on his knowledge and memory, he not only marvels at what he says but is astonished at what he doesn't say (310). His discrete experiences, *Erlebnisse,* have turned into cumulative experience, *Erfahrungen,* which constitute the vital itinerary retraveled by discourse. As we've seen, the dogs are well aware of the analogies between Berganza's travels and his narrative of it. For his part, Campuzano, who has listened with his memory unoccupied, claims to have transcribed verbatim the dogs' colloquy and particularly Berganza's travels (*CEn* 294), which have already been converted into discourse: transcription means citation following the discursive sequences of memory.

As I've stressed elsewhere, the ancients initiated the art of memory with the discovery that memory works extremely well by making associations with places and moving along the routes connecting them; *any* discursive sequence could be remembered by reference to a given itinerary. Effective as this artificial art may have been, memory recollects much more vividly still when its associations with places and routes aren't arbitrary but engraved in the very experience of places and routes. Unlike the itineraries of the art of memory, the places of the journey are novel and unfamiliar, and the routes are entirely outside the routine. I for one tend to remember the sequences of travel experience far more lucidly than those of equally remarkable experience that occurred within a routinized, sedentary span. What's more, travel facilitates the successive linking in memory of the most disparate experience, which again points to the intimate affinities between the journey and memory. For Berganza, telling his life story means discursively retracing and activating the memory of a life en route, with a focus on the exceptional, the memorable.

Practically any adventure is by its extraordinary nature prime material for narrative, having become a *facinus memorabile,* a memorable action; in many journey narratives such as the novels of chivalry, the itinerary serves primarily as transition between adventures and other *sucesos.* Memory and "history" favor the survival of experience thought or felt to be novel, strange, curious, striking, painful, gratifying, amusing, and so on, recollecting images and sequences of such experience and subjecting them to processes of discursive alchemy. But some of this may not be readily adaptable to narrative. As Tristram Shandy observes, the offerings of remembered experience don't necessarily correspond to the narrator's necessities or abilities: "There is nothing more pleasing to a traveller—or more terrible to travel-writers— than a large rich plain . . ." (VII.42). Nor do such offerings necessarily correspond to the narrator's strategies of communication or to the specific narra-

tive logic already in process. Some experience may be regarded as intrinsi-
cally memorable or significant and yet be thought for one reason or another
to be inappropriate to the tale. Sometimes, as a special case of this, journey
experience generates more than one narrative, with the result that any attempt
to tell it all would mean veering way off the discursive track of the narrative
in process (*Gal* 364; *EI* 281; *CP* 354; *PS* 320). Conversely, other experience
may be considered scarcely worth living and nonetheless figure importantly
in the telling, or it may acquire significance only in retrospect—in narrative,
for instance.

Notwithstanding the autonomy of narrative with regard to the journey,
the telling aligns itself with what it tells and thereby mobilizes two simultaneous and parallel processes. Journey narrative tends to both direct and sympathize with the ongoing travels, varying its rhythms, moods, and attitudes
accordingly, as Longinus so eloquently shows. At the same time, the journey
prompts its own telling, sometimes to a fault as when the main narrator of
the *Persiles* gets so involved in the theme of jealousy, we're told, that he ne-
glects his task as *historiador* (158), and is so affected by the apparent death
of the characters in an overturned ship that the events themselves dictate his
narration: "In conclusion, the overturning of the ship and the certainty of
death for those in it put the preceding words into the pen of the author of
this great and sad history, as well as those to be heard in the next chapter"
(161). The editor of the manuscript adds that the overturning of the ship "overturned" his judgment as well, involving him so much in the *sucesos* as to in-
capacitate him with respect to the dual process he's supposed to be steering.
Despite the ironies here, a narrator's involvement with the events and personages of his or her story is desirable and inevitable. Perhaps the most extreme case of this is the warning at the end of *Don Quixote* that Cide Hamete's
pen will give to anyone who should profane it by attempting a sequel: "For
me alone was Don Quixote born, and I for him. It was his to act, mine to
write; we two together make but one" (II.74.593). The slippage of first-person
singular adjectives from feminine (*sola*) to masculine (*satisfecho y ufano*)
evinces the synecdochal relationship between the pen and Cide Hamete. Narrator and protagonist are co-gnates, born together and for each other, living
parallel lives engaged in parallel activities, the pen being the sacralized symbol of their unity.

The togetherness of narrative and the journey is an effect of narrative itself
by way of its ability to coordinate the time of telling and the time of what's
told. But narrative everywhere acknowledges its posteriority and the corresponding differences between past experience and present narrative, not least
of all in its use of past tenses. Radically different circumstances reflect qualitative differences, as Periandro recognizes: "If it's true, and it is, that it's very

sweet to tell of the storm in present tranquility, and of the dangers of past war in present peace, and of the sufferings of illness in times of health, then it will be sweet for me to tell of my trials in this time of rest" (*PS* 254; cf. 261). Relatively calm and disengaged, narrative turns turmoil, danger, and suffering into sources of pleasure—almost as if painful experience occurred only in order to be told. As a former reader and present maker of history, Don Quixote knows that a good share of the value of his deeds lies with the telling, even if this process is mysterious and beyond his control. Sancho voices concern precisely that Don Quixote's adventures in deserted places without witnesses will remain in perpetual silence: his deeds will be in vain if no one tells them, and even Sancho's modest actions will go unrecorded. While at other times Don Quixote expresses ambivalence about the wise enchanter who he supposes has written and continues to record his actions as they transpire, he trusts here in the transmission of fame to set the stage for his triumphant entry at some court (I.21.258). Although narrative is not an end in itself for him, since he takes part in a cult of fame which will bring him power and *eros,* there is a strong sense that his knight-errantry is undertaken *for* future narrative, without which it would remain deficient and unfulfilled.

Perhaps no one has formulated more outlandishly than Homer the notion that the purposes of human action lie not in the vital circumstances of the people involved but rather in the value such action might have as raw material for future narrative, as Nietzsche comments:

> Is there anything more audacious, uncanny or unbelievable shining down on the destiny of man like a winter sun than that idea we find in Homer:
>> then did the gods make resolve and ordain unto men
>> *destruction, that in after times too there might be matter for song.*
> Thus we suffer and perish so that the poets shall not lack *material*—and this according to the decree of the gods of Homer, who seem to be very much concerned about the pleasures of coming generations but very indifferent to us, the men of the present. (*Human* 260)

Subordinate to the intentions of narrative, people experience things in order to be represented later as doing so. It's quite understandable that narrators might have such a bias since one of their tasks is to make sense of past experience, to endow it with intelligibility and value within the context of the present undertaking. Tellable experience seems to be made for the telling. It's also understandable that the actors themselves should shift some of the significance of their experience to narrative since the latter is a principal means by which the past can be revived. But for the gods, the makers of human destiny as though it were concurrent narrative, to adopt this view is entirely inexcusable.[4]

The Arabic radicals *ḥdth* superbly illustrate the integral relationship between experience and telling. Verb form I (*ḥadatha*) means to happen, take place, occur as new, while verb form II (*ḥaddatha*) means to tell, relate, talk to someone about something. Other verb forms (III, IV, V, VI, X) bring out a range of related meanings, including discuss, produce, originate, create, provoke, renew, and invent. The adjective *ḥadīth* means new, recent, novel, modern. Corresponding nouns include *ḥadath* (novelty, innovation, event, incident), *ḥadīth* (conversation, talk, account, tale, narrative, as well as the enormously important prophetic traditions relating deeds and utterances of the Prophet),[5] and *ḥāditha* (event, theatrical plot, incident, episode). The causative relationship between the first two verb forms, whereby form II normally denotes *making* form I *happen,* condenses the relationship of event and narrative: to tell is to make something occur, to renew it—even to invent or create it, because this too is to make it happen.[6] Happenings and narrative discourse issue from the very same radicals and presuppose each other throughout. Journey experience and the narration of it in the peregrine histories of Cervantes also issue from the same radicals, as the Arab historian Cide Hamete must have known.

In fiction, apparent *facta* are of course nothing more than *ficta:* there is no journey experience as such, no memory or verbalization of it. The causative force of *ḥaddatha* is intensified in fiction, as narrative "makes happen" things which never happened. Discourse makes the journey's course rather than remaking it. Fictive experience is de facto meant exclusively for narrative because it is made by and for narrative. Whatever autonomy characters might acquire in relation to their authors derives nonetheless from their being internal agents of discourse. Although the fatalism of Diderot's Jacques is more than suspect as a philosophy, it could hardly be more appropriate to the ontological status of his own world in which everything that happens really is "écrit là-haut." The writer in *Jacques le Fataliste,* in contrast, isn't bound by the same fatalism since the fate of his characters and to some extent that of his "reader" are subject to his whims: "So you see, reader, that I'm well on my way [*chemin*] and it's entirely within my power to make you wait a year, or two, or three for the story of Jacques's loves, by separating him from his master and making each of them run whatever hazards I liked. What is there to prevent me from marrying off the master and having him cuckolded? Or embarking Jacques for the Indies?" (36–37). What remains unthought and unwritten during the writing process (*chemin*) is as yet indeterminate, including the characters' destinies.

Writers (or narrators) *travel* their characters: "travel" becomes a transitive verb whose object is the traveler. In the same vein, Tristram speaks of moving his characters about: "whilst Obadiah has been going those said miles and back, I have *brought* my uncle Toby from Namur, quite across all Flanders,

into England: — . . . and have since *travelled* him and Corporate Trim in
a chariot and four, a journey of near two hundred miles down into York-
shire . . ." (II.8; my emphasis).[7] The ways God is said to move people along
certain pathways provide perhaps the closest equivalent of such transitive traveling in Cervantes' novels, but narrators too exercise the powers of transitivity over their characters even when they're recounting actual events, as Periandro advises Ortel Banedre: "Tell us, sir, whatever you'd like, adding whatever
little details you may want. . . . Therefore, sir, continue your story, tell about
Alonso and Martina, kick your Luisa, marry her off or don't, and let her be
free and easy as a falcon, for the key isn't in an easy delivery but in the events."[8]
The transitive licence in effect extends to the transient protagonist of the tale,
Ortel himself. In a very different mode, Kafka's Sancho too travels part of
himself, "diverting" his demon from himself and calling him Don Quixote,
who in turn performs mad exploits and does no harm to anyone. "A free man,
Sancho Panza philosophically followed Don Quixote on his crusades, perhaps
out of a sense of responsibility, and thus enjoyed a great and profitable entertainment to the end of his days" (quoted in Benjamin 139). Hence Sancho
converts his own demon into errant entertainment. Don Quixote could just
as easily be Cide Hamete's or Cervantes' demon — both of whom travel their
knight-errant — or one of the demons tormenting Cervantes' Spain.

A great deal, including genre, rides on *who* is traveled *where.* Cervantes
travels all the major types of characters developed by the literature of his time,
including the shepherd(ess), the knight-errant, the pícaro, and the *peregrino/a
de amor* (Vilanova 98–151), all of which have the kinds of experience corresponding to who they are and move about in chronotopes appropriate to
them — except for Don Quixote, who nonetheless creates around himself the
chivalric chronotope from which he's so radically displaced. Yet, as we've seen,
Cervantes' catalogue of travelers is so much more varied than the established
types that the categories break down. If certain types of people are more likely
to travel than others, nearly anyone can turn traveler in his novels — with the
possible exceptions of mothers *as* mothers, and young children. All of his
travelers give idiosyncratic shape and significance to what happens "to" them,
and the chronotopes they move in generate potentially unlimited series of
sucesos, which in turn provide episodes for narrative. The shifting relationships between character and chronotope as portrayed through the narrative
contrive the ideological coordinates and largely set the mood and tone. It would
be redundant to demonstrate this since nearly everything said about travelers
and chronotopes in previous chapters bears this out provided the ficticity of
characters and chronotopes is fully taken into account.

The episodic sequence without necessary consequence gives enormous lee-
way for the invention of travels because the episodes as presented generally

don't need to happen. Odysseus needs to get home to recover his wife and kingdom, but he could have met with any other adventures along the way. Similarly, Don Quixote needs to get back home, it seems, to recover his wits, but his experiences en route, though mainly in line with the chivalric mode, could have been quite different from the ones we know even if certain motifs have to work themselves out somehow. Persiles and Sigismunda must get from the fringes to the center of the world, and they must constantly prove their mettle, but the *sucesos* of their journey could also have materialized in other ways. For some characters there's neither an imperative return nor a destination; for others there's a resettling in exile. Displaced lovers obviously need to find each other and resolve their desires, but everything else that happens tends to do so with little necessity or plot function to constrain it. This leaves space for the aleatory, the whimsical, the extraneous, the inconsequential, the gratuitous, all of which releases the inventor of travels to one degree or another from prescriptive plotting and at the same time disengages the travelers from whatever functions they might have. Episodic narrative has any number of routes open to it because it enjoys the luxury of ridding itself of previous situations and characters. It simply leaves them behind.

Many of the qualities hailed as the distinguishing features of the novel and of prose, including their processive character, open-endedness, errancy, plasticity, diversity of content, freedom from "formal" constraints, and so on, pertain more to journey fiction than to any other sort of narrative practiced before *Finnegans Wake*. Echoing Bakhtin's concept of the novel (e.g., *Dialogic* 7–39), for instance, Kittay and Godzich speak of prose as "supremely indifferent to categories of wholeness and autonomy," as having "no ultimate shape that [it] needs to achieve," as enabling the subject to see itself in flux and as flux, as abandoning the "Parmenidean belief in the equation of language and being," and has having the capacity to "give us the world" (205–9). Cervantes' *Coloquio de los perros,* to name only one of his journey narratives, exemplifies all of these characteristics.

If many fictional journeys coincide neatly with one generic mode or another, the journey in some ways is prior to genre, which it determines as it proceeds. Hence the predicament of the poet who has more than enough material to write a play about Periandro and Auristela and knows the mode of their *sucesos* but not the outcome; he is unable to assign any definitive genre to the play because their "lives were still running" (285). Their life's journeys are generically open, and their travels full of travails keep the main narrative moving while the narrative keeps the travelers on their feet. This affords a clue to the enormous success of journey narrative: the journey keeps narrative going, and vice versa. In Cervantes' time, the journey is the primary means of doing so, and Cervantes runs the journey for all it's worth.

Improvisatory Writing

Characterizing Cervantes' novelistic writing as improvisatory obviously presents certain problems. "Improvisatory writing" almost sounds like a *contradictio in adjecto*. Unlike the musician, actor, or speaker who improvises without a script in performance time, the novelist writes a text in "composition time" and can alter what's already written, take his or her time, meditate and write impulsively, and stop and resume more or less at will. Moreover, if the term "improvisation" were adapted to convey inventiveness and experimentalism, any artistic experimenter would be an improviser ipso facto. Whereas Beethoven, known to be an accomplished improviser as performer, painstakingly reworked his pieces as composer, Schubert often composed to the flow of his pen without revisions (Düring 35). Cervantes is known to have both reworked his texts and composed *a vuelapluma,* and, as nearly all his readers have recognized along with Cervantes himself, his inventiveness within and outside established models manifests itself supremely throughout the novels, though more so in some than in others. What is improvisatory writing? Borges' Pierre Menard comes close to identifying it with reference to none other than Cervantes: "My affable precursor did not refuse the collaboration of fate; he went along composing his immortal work a little *à la diable,* swept along by inertias of language and invention. I have contracted the mysterious duty of reconstructing literally his spontaneous work" (*Prosa* 1:430; trans. Anthony Bonner). Besides "*à la diable,*" the key expressions to be kept in mind are "collaboration of fate," "he went along composing [iba componiendo]," "swept along by inertias of language and invention," and "spontaneous."

Another brief incursion into improvisatory music will allow improvisatory writing to come into relief. When discussing improvisatory action in Chapter 3, I defined improvisation provisionally as "unique, spontaneous action developed with reference to codes of practice and oriented by definite circumstances and prior sequences within a field of uncharted possibilities." Improvisers attend to timing and the logic of sequence, anticipate the consequences of possible courses of action, and act on the move according to shifting circumstances. Not surprisingly, musicians tend to describe improvisation in terms of uncharted movement.

Most musical improvisation presupposes definite modalities of melodic, rhythmic, and harmonic sequencing, as well as procedures of interaction between instruments, which allow one degree or another of variation, unique expressiveness, and transgressiveness. The musicologist Jean Düring describes improvisation as "the spontaneous appearance during the course of a performance of elements possessing a certain degree of unforeseeability as well as limits of their own, both of these defined at the core of the musical system in question" (Lortat-Jacob 68). Such "elements," I would add, appear through *procedural* activity on the part of the musicians who are able to exploit for expressive purposes the variability and limits of the sort of music they're playing. Improvisation plays recognition (familiar sequences, repetition) and surprise (the unforeseen, unprecedented, spontaneous) against each other and depends on both to bring about the effects it strives for. A sympathetic audience expects not only to recognize the music but also to be surprised by it. Francesco Giannattasio observes that musical improvisation could be considered "a sonorous realization of the dialectic between *reproduce* and *renew* (or between *revive* and *revitalize,* or yet between the Latin *tradere* and *tradire*) and may have as an extreme consequence the creation and stabilization of new utterances, models and forms. In this sense, it always implies a dynamic intention" (Lortat-Jacob 69). There's much more than just music going on during an improvisatory performance.

Improvisation initiates a special dynamic between musicians and audience that conditions the ways of playing and listening, taking into account the fact that the performance is not only interpretive but also compositional. This shifts value away from fidelity, perfection, order, and unity toward spontaneity, risk, inspiration, imagination, and movement. Except perhaps in free jazz, unconstrained improvisation is often viewed as superficial, uncreative, and excessively disruptive (Chernoff 58–60, 112; Düring 37). John Chernoff, for example, documents at length how important constraints are in West African drumming, what their particular features are, and how they allow for improvisation. Every genre and style of music at a given time and place evinces its own constraints and its possibilities, if any, for improvisation. Paul Valéry expresses it this way: "l'art naît de contraintes, vit de lutte et meurt de liberté" (Düring 38).

Among the musical genres and styles that not only allow for improvisation but require it are the various kinds of *modal* music, which tend to make few demands on musicians in terms of harmonic sequences and thereby allow for improvisatory exploration within a given mode, scale, or melody type. I have in mind such types of music as the Indian *rāga,* the Arab *maqām,* medieval liturgical chants, Renaissance music employing modes, and the modal jazz of Miles Davis, John Coltrane, and Charles Mingus.[9] "What I had learned about the modal form," says Miles Davis, "is that when you play this way, go in this direction, you can go on forever. You don't have to worry about changes and shit like that. You can do more with the musical line" (225). Düring comments that modal music often brings about "a state in which the performer is submerged, as though possessed by the essence of the mode (*maqām, dastgāh, rāga*) or of the rhythmic cycle, which dictates its own internal law without the artist's having the impression of participating in this enactment through his/her own will: the artist's own performance becomes unforeseeable to him/her, and this could constitute the summum of improvisation. This impression is undoubtedly related to the idea, current in various traditions, that music comes from an external source which the performer does no more than capture" (43–44). Modal music is capable of inducing inspired psychic states in which the musician's body seems to become the music's instrument as the music itself takes on its own unpredictable impetus. Impelled by its own *laisser-aller,* it can "go on forever." As we'll see, literature has rough equivalents to modal music.

Improvisation depends on the psychic disposition of the performers, who have to be willing to take calculated risks, abandon familiar terrain, deviate from set patterns even when they have a score in front of them, use a language appropriate to the ever-shifting moment, enter into affective modes and change with them, and give style to their performance. Improvisers know how to exploit the interesting possibilities of errors, as Bartok once did so startlingly on the piano when the percussionist made a mistake; for them, errors are entryways into deviation, pathways into improvisatory errancy. They make it their business to anticipate where they're going and to know how to deal with whatever might happen—this is when they thrive most. Miles Davis says he always told his sidemen "to play what they *know* and then play *above that.* Because then anything can happen, and that's where great art and music happens" (220; his emphasis). Improvisers can try to bring on inspiration but have no control over whether it actually happens. John Coltrane, for instance, says he sometimes feels as though he's just playing notes: "When I become aware of it in the middle of a solo, I'll try to build things to the point where this inspiration is happening again, where things are spontaneous and not contrived. If it reaches that point again, I feel it can continue, it's alive again. But if it doesn't happen, I'll just quit, bow out" (Priestley 47). For him as for so many jazz musicians, the search for new pathways of expression marks out his artistic quest in which performances are places along the way: "I'm still primarily looking into certain sounds, certain scales. Not that I'm sure of what I'm looking for, except that it'll be something that hasn't been played before. . . . And in the process of looking, continual looking, the result in any given performance can be long or short. I never know. It's always one thing leading into another. It keeps evolving, and sometimes it's longer than I actually thought it was while I was playing" (Priestley 52).

As already noted, the most obvious difference between a composer and an improvising performer is that they carry out their activities in disparate sorts of time. If this difference affecting the very nature of each activity resists any breakdown, the distinction between composer and improviser nonetheless admits blurrings and gradations. Everything said thus far about improvisation could serve to question the methods, genres, psychic disposition, and so on, of composition as activity. Although the finished work of a composer may offer little indication as to how it was made, it does reveal something of its constraints and possibilities for variation and novelty as well as the value placed on qualities associated with improvisation, and this, together with whatever might be known about a composer's methods and dispositions, can afford glimpses into how improvisatory the composition might be. There's obviously room for differentiation between composers who write what comes to mind more or less as it does so and those who continually revise their writings. And as Philip Alperson observes, composers often improvise as they compose by trying out different sequences — on the piano, say — or imagining how they might sound (19). Irrespective of how spontaneously they write, composers show varying degrees of experimentalism, unpredictability, *laisser-aller,* and inspiration in what they write. By the same token, improvisers are composers to a varying extent: their "improvisations" may be made up on the spot, or borrowed from other musicians, or previously rehearsed and varied on many occasions such that the piece results in a multiply revised composition. The pieces themselves reveal a greater or lesser capacity or willingness to explore and exploit their improvisatory possibilities.

Hence, although spontaneity is an essential factor, improvisation often involves much more than on-the-spot composition in a performative act. It needn't be carried out in performance time at all. Nor does the presence of one or another sort of script prevent it from occurring (Gil Evans and Miles Davis, for instance, had to tell classically trained musicians "*not* to play exactly like it was on the score" [Davis 243]). Nor is improvisation always a hard-to-sustain act of limited scope generated by a few ideas or whims (as improvisatory music and theater are often thought to be). Nor need it contravene established modes of playing. Nor does it preclude some degree of premeditation, foresight, direction, rehearsal, repetition, borrowing, rethinking, reworking, concerted effort, and so on. Such considerations may make it harder to distinguish what is from what isn't improvisation. But they also allow improvisation to be rethought as a procedural activity operative in a range of artistic/intellectual undertakings.

It should be recalled that when musicians speak of improvisation, they most often do so in terms of movement and traveling (within the Rabelaisian paradigm of "les chemins cheminent"): the improvisers themselves are travelers along the routes their medium opens up to them, or they're conveyed by the music, or the music moves of its own doing. Improvisation involves movements along uncharted routes, excursions or incursions into spaces which materialize with the traveling. Improvisers may have some idea of where they're going and what to expect without knowing exactly what they're getting into or how one thing will lead to another, and if they know what they're doing they'll be able to make imaginative use of their knowledge and pro-ficiency in the makeshift circumstances through which they move.

When writing as activity proceeds with these sorts of kinetics and dynam-ics, it too is improvisatory. Italo Calvino's remark that "from the beginning *Orlando furioso* announces itself as the poem of movement, or rather an-nounces the particular kind of movement that will run through it from begin-ning to end, a movement in broken lines, a zigzag movement"—not only the spatial wanderings of the travelers but also "the errant movement of Ariosto's poetry" (quoted in Hart 34)—could apply equally well to Cervantes' prose, not to mention a great many other journey narratives. The *laisser-aller* of so many of Cervantes' characters, their attitude of "come what may," their col-laboration with fate, their wandering *a la ventura,* their passage from one incident to another, and so forth, are no doubt shared by Cervantes in his modus scribendi of many peregrine tales. Cervantes' "friend" in the prologue to *Don Quixote* Part I aptly refers to Cervantes' writing in the progressive subjunctive ("lo que fuere escribiendo" [57]): this is the tense and mood of improvisatory writing as it anticipates the indeterminacy that lies ahead. In retrospect this process is characterized by an imperfect progressive; to cite Pierre Menard once again, "he went along composing [iba componiendo] his immortal work a little *à la diable,* swept along by inertias of language and invention."

A critical awareness of improvisation in speech and writing goes back at least as far as Plato's *Ion.* Quintilian writes an exhilarating passage on it (X.7), referring to it as "ex tempore dicendi facultas" (the ability to speak ex tem-pore) and *temporis munera* (gifts of the moment), and valuing it as the *max-imus fructus* or crown of the study of rhetoric (Norton 85–87; Ménager 101). Writers including Castiglione and Rabelais develop the notion too. In his es-say "Du Parler prompt ou tardif," Montaigne draws upon the classical tradi-tion of discursive improvisation, but unlike Quintilian he dissociates it from the exercise of memory in rhetoric. For him, "le parler prompt" (which he extends to writing as well, especially his own) occurs as a release from the dead weight of memory. Responding to the moment, it is inspirational, be-yond one's forces or premeditated design, a gift of fortune, as though coming from without in the form of impelling movement and agitation. Montaigne's essay on travel ("De la vanité" [III.9]) both exemplifies his notion of inspired improvisation and explicitly develops it, as may be appreciated in the epi-graph to the first chapter of this book.

I scarcely need to reiterate that from his first novel to his last Cervantes characterizes both narrative and writing in terms of movement and travel. As early as the prologue to *La Galatea,* he speaks of how the vernacular opens up a "fertile and spacious expanse through which [writers] can run freely" (58); some writers are able to travel through this open space in relative safety, others less sure of themselves venture forth (*se aventuran*) despite the hazards. With obvious authorial approval, the canon in *Don Quixote* similarly finds one good thing in the novels of chivalry despite their all-round foolishness, formal monstrousness, and preposterous journeys: "that they offered a good intellect a chance to display itself, for they provided a broad and spacious field through which the pen could run without let or hindrance, describing shipwrecks, tempests, encounters and battles," bringing out the best qualities of their protagonists, "now depicting a tragic and lamentable incident, now a joyful and unexpected event," and generally allowing for diversity. He goes on: "Because the *unfettered writing* [*escritura desatada*] of these books enables the author to show his talent for the epic, the lyric, the tragic, and the comic" (I.47.566–67; my emphasis). Torrente Ballester makes much of the expression *escritura desatada,* stressing freedom from constraint, free play, and inventiveness, and pointing out that this one good quality of the parodied genre is shared by the parody (21–22). *Escritura desatada* means writing unbound and thus capable of movement. Mobile writing allows the writer to move in any desired direction, to follow hunches and intuitions, to direct discourse spontaneously without preconceived plans — and be carried along by the discourse. This recalls Montaigne's errant writing in the *Essays:* "I head for change, undiscerningly and tumultuously. My style and my mind go roving in the same way" (III.9.973). Similarly, Scarron in *Le Roman comique* says he writes his book "like those who put the bridle on the neck of their horses and let them go as they will" (I.12.111).

Unlike Torrente Ballester, I don't understand *escritura desatada* to imply total artistic freedom "without limits" (21). There are multiple constraints at every moment of Cervantes' novels, some of which were defined at the time as problems about verisimilitude and the marvellous, unity and variety, historical and poetical truth, and the like, as we've come to know all too well. Add to this constraints of style, language, decorum, ethics, chronotope, genre, character, the unsayable, the prohibited, the "true," and every other sort imaginable, taking into account anticipated expectations of readers and the manipulation of their sensibility, and the writer is still left with an expanse of possible courses for discourse. No matter how Cervantes deals with such constraints at given instants in his novels, many of them are not so much limits barring movement as principles guiding and orienting movement. Verisimilitude, for instance, may be seen less as a set of restrictions than as a range of means for making the writing effective and convincing within the fiction. According to the canon, the many desirable effects of fictive writing are unattainable for a writer "who flees from verisimilitude and imitation" (I.47.565).

Improvisatory writing tests its constraints/strategies, plays with them, transgresses them at times, looks for novelty within them, depends on them, and times its sequences in interesting ways with reference to them. This enables it to function with relatively free-ranging mobility.

To use Umberto Eco's terms, Cervantes' novels belong not only to the category of "open works" but more specifically to a subcategory of it, "works in movement," which "display an intrinsic mobility, a kaleidoscopic capacity to suggest themselves in constantly renewed aspects to the consumer" (12, 15).[10] While these novels by no means suppress altogether the notion of causation (consequence), they often suspend it to allow for seriality (sequence). Most of what happens in them is *unnecessary,* including their discursive movements from one passage to another. Perhaps Pierre Menard was unwittingly right in asserting that *Don Quixote* itself was a contingent, unnecessary book (Borges 1:430).

When improvisatory writing takes the journey as its subject, a profoundly sympathetic double process is set in motion, each activity impelling the other in its wandering, exploration, spontaneous impulses, risk, diversity, and inexhaustibility. The potentially endless series of novel encounters, places, and moods of the journey incites fictional travel writing to proliferate in potentially endless variation and experimentation. The journey may have its imperative of destination or return, but in the meantime it can "go on forever," in-venting (i.e., coming upon) any number of episodes and playing them out one after another. The episodic principle, evident throughout the *Quixote,* and *Coloquio,* and the *Persiles* in particular, is essential to this sort of experimental writing. Mutatis mutandis, fictional travel writing is a literary counterpart to modal music, capable of modulating from one style or mood or theme to another and ready to play into the unknown.

Focusing primarily on *Don Quixote,* much insightful criticism has been written about Cervantes' specific strategies of invention, the decisions he must have made, his desire to experiment, the orientation of his invention, etc. To cite only a few of these studies, R. M. Flores in an important article on *Don Quixote* Part I shows on the basis of internal and bibliographical evidence how Cervantes made up his novel as he went along, exploiting new possibilities as they emerged, developing his story far beyond the original scheme, interpolating material extraneous to the main story, rearranging episodes already written, and constantly reorienting his narrative. Inspired in part by Flores' analysis, Stephen Gilman reflects further on how Cervantes had no preconceived plan of composition, and how "the narrative passes through phases that correspond to the artistic decisions Cervantes made in the course of writing," resulting in a "new mode of fiction writing" (200). He also devotes many pages to the notion of invention and Cervantes' "well-meditated choice of Daedalus over Orpheus" (86, 72–102); the episodic principle is a key to Cervantes' inventiveness. Gonzalo Torrente Ballester illustrates the chain reactions of inventive play in *Don Quixote* as the author invents Alonso Quijano who invents Don Quixote who invents Dulcinea (76–77); he also emphasizes the irrelevance of perfection as an aesthetic value in the making of the novel (154). John Weiger closes *The Substance of Cervantes* with thoughts concerning Cervantes' desire to experiment radically in virtually all of his novels (233–34), and Edwin Williamson likewise comments on Cervantes' experimentalism and innovation (78, 228). For his part, Francisco Ayala observes that the distinguishing creative feature of Cervantes' novelistic enterprise is that "it constitutes a scrutiny of human life in search of its immanent sense instead of referring it to a pattern already given from outside" (79). The conclusions of all of these critics support the notion of Cervantes as an improvisatory writer always ready to experiment by generating novel sequences and letting his characters improvise their way along, and Ayala's remark in particular argues that this experimentalism, far more than an idle pastime, was inductively oriented toward finding sense in experience. Let me stress once again that it is the journey more than anything else that allows all of this to happen.

Even if Cervantes, as Mary Gaylord Randel puts it, "did not wholly embrace the brave new world of his own making" ("Cervantes' Portrait" 87), and even if he misjudged the impact his various novels would have, he repeatedly lets his readers know that he's well aware of the novelty of his inventions. In the *Viaje del Parnaso* Mercury tells him it wasn't in vain that Apollo endowed him with the "superhuman instinct / of a rare inventor. . . . Pass through, oh rare inventor, press ahead / with your subtle designs, and help / Apollo, for your assistance matters much to him" (1.217–18, 223– 25). In the prologue to the *Novelas ejemplares* too he refers to himself as one who "dares to go out with so many inventions into the world's plaza," and declares that he is the first to write *novelas* in the Spanish language (50–52). An introductory poem dedicated to him, adulatory as it is, contends that Daedalus' *ingenio* in designing the labyrinth pales in comparison to that of Cervantes in the twelve labyrinthine *novelas* (55). These and other passages reveal Cervantes as a writer with dynamic, deterritorializing intentions who prizes invention as his primary quality and is disposed to take the risks necessary to follow his inclinations.

If Cicero could claim in *De inventione poetica* that *inventio,* the orator's art of discovering convincing arguments, was the most important of the five divisions of rhetoric and could hence be learned through the discipline, Cervantes' more modern sort of invention eludes the precepts of books or formal instruction. Bruce Wardropper points out in this regard: "A kind of learning went on in Cervantes' mind in Algiers which could not have been obtained from a university. A *letrado* could never have written his books. Only an autodidact, an *ingenio lego* with genius, was capable of that accomplishment. But the fees paid to the school of hard knocks were high." Citing Ruth El Saffar, he strongly suspects that the apparent encomium of the Jesuit schoolmasters in the *Coloquio* is a veiled attack, and he observes that many Cervantine characters, both female and male, endowed with one or another sort of intelligence, "have sharpened their wits on 'el uso,' the way of the world. The self-education of these characters easily outdoes the booklearning of *bachilleres* and *licenciados*" ("Education" 190–92). The fact that nearly all of these characters learn the way of the world while traveling suggests that Cervantes, like Gracián a half century later, espoused what Antonio Vilanova calls the "cult of experience as human education"—a cult practiced primarily by travel (114, 150, 155). Even more than the migrant surgeon who was his father, Cervantes led an exceptionally itinerant life, the experience of which leaves palpable traces throughout the inventions of his "meandertales" (to use a pun in *Finnegans Wake* picked up by Carlos Fuentes [107]). The mirror that Cervantes as writer "promène le long d'un chemin" has a prismatic edge to it, often reflecting displaced fragments of his own previous travels. And the very last self-image he shows, in the prologue to the *Persiles,* is one of himself en route. In an epitaph published with the *Persiles* he is the "peregrino Cervantes" (43)—and although he like everyone else "made his journey" of life, the epithet is peculiarly apt in his case.

Borges concludes *El hacedor* with an enigma on the relationship between world, art, and artist: "A man undertakes the task of drawing the world. Through the years he populates a space with images of provinces, kingdoms, mountains, bays, ships, islands, fish, rooms, instruments, stars, horses, and people. Shortly before dying, he discovers that that patient labyrinth of lines traced the image of his face."[11] The relationships here are primarily genitive: the image *of* the world turns out to be the image *of* the face; hence world and face somehow correspond through the common image although the world as such may be inaccessible. Since an artist with a different face would produce a correspondingly different image of the world, there is also a generative relationship whereby the image of the face is unwittingly projected onto and constitutive of the image of the world. Even allowing for intertextuality, Cervantes' writings could be seen as analogous to a drawing of the world, a mappa mundi or series of them, projected from his own "face," except that the world mediated by experience has also shaped his "face." The status of the world is uncertain except as representation, map, writing. World and "face" have a common image perhaps because a person, especially as experienced traveler and writer, is conceivable as multiple place. When told that his travel narrative full of misfortunes is tiring out his listeners, Periandro responds cryptically: "Sir Arnaldo, I am made like this thing called place, which is where all things fit and nothing is out of place, and in me all misfortunes take place, although since I've found my sister Auristela I consider them fortunate, for no evil that ends without ending one's life is an evil."[12] Periandro is a mobile place consisting of a composite of places and routes; like Cervantes, he is a partial microcosm of the universe he experiences and narrates in his own image, including places not on the map.[13]

Cervantes' novels are concerned not with place as such, but with places. Where does he write from? Michel de Certeau's reflections on writing and place merit some thought: "Writing is born from and deals with the acknowledged doubt of an explicit division, in sum, of the impossibility of one's own place. It articulates an act that is constantly a beginning: the subject is *never authorized* by a place, it could never install itself in an inalterable *cogito,* it remains a stranger to itself and forever deprived of an ontological ground" (quoted in Deleuze and Guattari, *Kafka* ix). I would prefer to qualify these statements by arguing that even if they are tenable as general assertions about writing, they apply more to some types of writing than to others. To borrow terms from Deleuze and Guattari, writing can and most often does territorialize or reterritorialize the subject in some kind of "here" which lends authority to it, in some kind of place with established ideological orientations, in some kind of knowledge and system of power. Writing can also deterritorialize the subject, language, modes of writing, meaning, etc., to some "elsewhere" and bring about a continual displacement.

The case of Cervantes could be seen both ways, neither of which excludes the other. On the one hand, no matter how "liberal" his attitudes on personal, social, political, and religious issues (as evident in his writings) may have been for his time, they nonetheless appear to be inscribed within the acceptable possibilities of Counter-Reformation Spain. So much has been written on the values he attaches to such qualities as chastity and religiosity, to institutions such as marriage, to Catholicism versus Protestantism and Christianity versus Islam and paganism, to the *patria,* that no more needs to be said here.

On the other hand, his writing continually moves on the peripheries, on the outside, in the in-between and marginalized enclaves, in variant modes of life and thought. Furthermore, his novels in particular evade a reproduction of established genres and character types, and reveal characteristics strongly marked by improvisation. Cervantes' characters "become animal," mobile, finding their own uncharted ways through the worlds of the novels, and he takes his errant prose with them. In this sense Cervantes practices nomadic writing unauthorized by place or by an "inalterable *cogito,*" as Certeau puts it, "a stranger to itself and forever deprived of an ontological ground." Whether or not he affirms values consecrated by place-centered institutions, whether or not God and Truth are in the inaccessible background, the restlessness of desire drives it away from place, which betrays vacuousness and no longer suffices, into unpredictable intensities of experience. The majority of Cervantes' novelistic protagonists, as well as Pedro de Urdemalas in the play bearing his name, are in one sense or another artists who live by their wits, some of them truly homeless and nearly all of them displaced and mobile. Forcione calls attention in Cervantes' works to "the association of the artist with exile, distant lands, wandering, criminality" (*Christian* 161): this is where the novelist's interests move, and this is where he writes his novels from at the same time as he writes them from within a sedentary existence.

Walter Benjamin speaks of two tribes of storytellers, one home based and the other itinerant, each having its own resources of knowledge and experience. These two prototypes, he adds, coexist and interact with each other and can be fused in the same storyteller who has returned home after long travels, thus bringing together the lore of the distant and the lore of the past (84–85). For my present purposes I would substitute the terms "knowledge and experience" for "lore" and insist that locally based storytelling involves much more than some kind of transmission of the past. Given these revisions, Cervantes exemplifies a complex fusion of the itinerant and the lococentric in their breadth and depth: he is a traveler who returns home but keeps moving about in his life and writings, never quite at home and never entirely cut off from home, a kind of *xenos* (which meant a stranger from another Greek city, not a foreigner [Détienne 9]), or to borrow Lope de Vega's contradictory title, a "peregrino en su patria." In so far as he and his writings are nomadic, they modestly anticipate Nietzsche's ideal of "spiritual nomadism" for unfettered, free-ranging spirits (*Human* 263),[14] a notion appropriated by several modern thinkers, most notably Deleuze; and more to the point, they recall Georg Lukács' vision of the novel as the "the form of transcendental homelessness" (Benjamin 99) as well as one of Bakhtin's key ideas in "Discourse in the Novel": "The novel begins by presuming a verbal and semantic decentering of the ideological world, a certain linguistic *homelessness* of literary consciousness, which no longer possesses a sacrosanct and unitary linguistic medium for containing ideological thought" (*Dialogic* 367; my emphasis).

Reading Cervantes' novels involves enacting their diverse mobility and participating in their homelessness. As happens with all reading, readers become absentminded, schizo-phrenic, simulating a presence in more than one place. The locus of reading (usually sedentary), the locus of writing (usually assumed sedentary), and the locus of discourse (usually mobile) are three such places, for a start. Ortega celebrates the novel as possessing a "power which multiplies our existence, which frees us and pluralizes us, which enriches us with generous transmigration!" (Gilman 2). More nonchalantly, Nietzsche speaks of reading in a similar vein but with more emphasis on motion: "In my case, every kind of reading belongs among my recreations—hence among the things that liberate me from myself, that allow me to walk about in strange sciences and souls—that I no longer take seriously" (*Ecce Homo* 698). Reading necessarily draws us away from ego-centered sedentariness. Narratives of travel intensify this sensation of mobility elsewhere. Cervantes' journey narratives exploit the possibilities of kinesis of the full, enabling us to escape beyond escapism as we travel with travelers and their transient desires, traverse worlds familiar and strange, accompany narrators as they make their way composing *à la diable*, and move with the currents of discursive passages.

Notes

Bibliography

Index

Notes

Preface

1. In an insightful article, Mary Gaylord Randel also associates Cervantes and his image of the artist with Vulcan, the crippled god enamored of Beauty ("Cervantes' Portrait" 99–102).

2. If the original identification of Mercury with Hermes in Roman mythology was rather forced, the Mercury of Cervantes' long poem obviously has the attributes of the Greek Hermes, more in line with the Mercury of Ovid's *Metamorphoses,* for instance.

3. *Don Quixote,* trans. John Ormsby, ed. and rev. Joseph R. Jones and Kenneth Douglas (New York: W. W. Norton, 1981); *The Adventures of Don Quixote,* trans. J. M. Cohen (Harmondsworth, Middlesex: Penguin, 1950); *The Trials of Persiles and Sigismunda: A Northern Story,* trans. Cecilia Richmond Weller and Clark A. Colahan (Berkeley: U California P, 1989); and *Exemplary Stories,* trans. C. A. Jones (Harmondsworth, Middlesex: Penguin, 1972).

4. I have modified Hollingdale's translation, which comes out rather stilted.

Chapter 1. Motion in Language, Language in Motion

1. *Discurso* and its verb form, *discurrir,* are treated in much more detail in the next chapter.

2. "Como están nuestras almas en continuo movimiento, y no pueden parar ni sosegar sino en su centro, que es Dios . . ." (275).

3. *Laws* 896a. For the full discussion of motion relating the soul's movement to divinity, see sections 889–99.

In Chapter 2 I take up the Cervantine passages referring to the continual movement of the soul.

4. E.g., Genette, Todorov. I deal with this in my article on citation in Cervantes' *Casamiento/Coloquio* and Islamic *ḥadīth.*

5. *The Will to Power* 280 (section 517). See also sections 510–22. Nietzsche's critique reaches back to early Greek philosophy in his *Philosophy in the Tragic Age of the Greeks.*

6. Isidore 278–79. My translation. "Usus litterarum repertus propter memoriam rerum. Nam ne oblivione fugiant, litteris alligantur."

7. Charles Peirce, who argues for the eventfulness of discourse, would in all likelihood go along with this (Sheriff 100).

8. It should be noted that the Greek *stasis* conveys, in addition to static meanings, the notions of struggle, strife.

9. "By second-order entities we shall mean events, processes, states-of-affairs, etc., which are located in time and which, in English, are said to occur or take place, rather than to exist; and by third-order entities we shall mean such abstract entities as propositions, which are outside space and time" (Lyons 443).

10. James Liu analyzes the etymology of the Chinese word for poetry in similar terms: "the whole composite phonogram . . . for *shih* ('poetry') is seen to consist of *yen* ('word') plus *ssu* ('attendant') or *chih* ('go/stop'), with etymological associations with 'foot.' The late Ch'en Shih-hsiang suggested that the 'syno-antonym' (a word he coined) *chih,* meaning both 'to go' and 'to stop,' here refers to dancing and rhythm" (67–68).

11. Mark Johnson and George Lakoff plot out some of this cluster of time/movement metaphors as used in colloquial English (42–44).

12. Chapter 25 in the Garnier edition of Pierre Jourda. In some editions, including that of Jacques Boulenger and Lucien Scheler (Paris: Gallimard, 1955), this episode figures in chapter 26.

The authorship of the postumously published Fifth Book has long been in doubt. This and some other episodes appear to me to be authentically Rabelaisian, unlike others which are clearly not, but the authorship question is of scant importance here.

13. Blanchot refers skeptically to this etymology, perhaps with good reason (112). It immediately becomes clear, however, that for him *rhuthmos* implies some kind of back-and-forth repetition, "the welling up and sinking back of what flows," and not the flowing itself. This is precisely the notion of rhythm that Meschonnic argues against.

14. For a range of further examples, see Vico 35 (citing Horace), Liu 67–69, Nietzsche, *Gay Science* 43 (referring to Homer).

15. The plural of *locus* interestingly differs: places are usually neuter *loca,* while passages and topoi retain the masculine gender as *loci.*

16. In a similar vein, Maurice Blanchot—citing Heidegger's "house of Being"—speaks of "the dangerous leaning toward the sanctification of language" (110). The following quotations will suggest some of the ways in which this highly complex and controversial issue is articulated (I cite them at length so as to deflect possible skepticism and hostility away from my seemingly irreverent statement.)

"Some time ago I called language, clumsily enough, the house of Being. If man by virtue of his language dwells within the claim and call of Being, then we Europeans presumably dwell in an entirely different house than Eastasian man" (Heidegger, *On the Way* 5).

"No thing is where the word is lacking. We could go further and propose this statement: something *is* only where the appropriate and therefore competent word names a thing as being, and so establishes the given being as a being. Does this mean, also, that there is being only where the appropriate is speaking? Where does the word derive its appropriateness? The poet says nothing about it. But the content of the closing line does after all include the statement: The being of anything that is resides in the word. Therefore this statement holds true: Language is the house of Being" (Heidegger, *On the Way* 63, commenting on a poem of Stefan Georg; see also 87, 140).

"The word is *logos.* It speaks simultaneously as the name for Being and for Saying" (Heidegger, *On the Way* 80).

"But we can only conjecture why it is that, nonetheless, the being of language no-where brings itself to word as the language of being. There is some evidence that the essential nature of language flatly refuses to express itself in words—in the language, that is, in which we make statements about language. If language everywhere with-holds its nature in this sense, then such withholding is in the very nature of language. Thus language not only holds back when we speak it in the accustomed ways, but this its holding back is determined by the fact that language holds back its own origin and so denies its being to our usual notions. . . . the being of language puts itself into language nonetheless, in its own most appropriate manner" (Heidegger, *On the Way* 81; see also 121).

"the word first bestows presence, that is, Being in which things appear as beings" (Heidegger, *On the Way* 146).

"The word begins to shine as the gathering which first brings what presences to its presence.

"The oldest word for the rule of the word thus thought, for Saying, is *logos:* Saying which, in showing, lets beings appear in their 'it is.'

"The same word, however, the word for Saying, is also the word for *Being,* that is, for the presencing of beings. Saying and Being, word and thing, belong to each other in a veiled way . . ." (Heidegger, *On the Way* 155).

"It is the world of words that creates the world of things . . . by giving its concrete being to their essence, and its ubiquity to what has always been" (Lacan, *Écrits* 65).

"Lacan calls this pre-linguistic, pre-Oedipal stage the realm of the 'Imaginary.' . . . Since repression is neither experienced nor acknowledged, there is, according to Lacan, no unconscious at this stage. . . . The absence of a gap for the child between a con-cept and its application is a proof of the concept's inadequacy; the ego-concept has never been tested in use. The gap appears with the initiation of the child into the order of language, what Lacan calls the 'Symbolic Order'" (Wright 108–9).

"The unconscious is that which, by speaking, determines the subject as being" (Lacan, quoted in Wright 110).

"Lacan sees an identity between language-forms and the response to repression: the dictum 'the unconscious is structured like a language' is more than an analogy, for the unconscious is born to be no more than its linguistic birthmarks. The fact that every word indicates the absence of what it stands for intensifies the frustration of this child of language, the unconscious, since the absence of satisfaction has now to be accepted. Language imposes a chain of words along which the ego must move while the unconscious remains in search of the object it has lost" (Wright 111).

"the nature of things being the nature of words. . . . In the 'Agency of the Letter in the Unconscious' (1957) Lacan said that the whole structure of language is to be found in the unconscious, the elemental unit of meaning being the letter: 'By "letter" I designate that material support that concrete discourse borrows from language'" (Ragland-Sullivan 282; see also 236).

"By linking psychoanalysis to symbol, signifier, and metaphor and demonstrating that dreams and psychotic language are both decipherable when viewed as pictures of linguistic situations, Lacan has shown the system of language to be a defense against unconscious knowledge. Similarly, language attests to the presence of an unconscious order in being that leaves no human action outside its field" (Ragland-Sullivan 178–79).

"Having discovered that the unconscious 'thinks' by words and [linguistic] sounds and is structured by the same kinds of laws as is concrete language and that these phenomena affect normal language use, Lacan proposed that elusive signifieds — unconscious truths — give themselves up to incessant individual variations by clustering around certain words, sounds, or themes" (Ragland-Sullivan 220; see also 97, 143, 150, 160, 170–72, 182).

17. Cf. Nietzsche's early essay *Philosophy in the Tragic Age of the Greeks*, in a refutation of Parmenides: "if thinking in concepts, on the part of reason, is real, then the many and motion must partake of reality also, for reasoned thinking is mobile. It moves from concept to concept. It is mobile, in other words, within a plurality of realities. Against this, no objection can be made; it is quite impossible to designate thinking as a rigid persistence, as an externally unmoved thinking-in-and-on-itself on the part of a unity" (88).

18. Following Kerenyi, he observes "the difference in usage between *theates,* the ordinary word for spectator, and the word *theoros,* which refers to a more solemn and greater spectacle at a distant place or city and to which one must travel to participate. [Kerenyi] also notes that the daughters of Oceanus, who come as onlookers from a distance to view the suffering of Prometheus, are called *theoroi* whereas a spectator viewing a religious celebration in his hometown simply is referred to by the ordinary designation *theates*" (Jager 236–37).

19. I've discussed this in "El movimiento en la obra de Antonio Machado: Paradojas eleáticas."

Chapter 2. The Language of Movement in Cervantes' Novels

1. Other definitions in the *Diccionario de autoridades* include "facultad racional con que se infieren unas cosas de otras, sacándolas por consecuencias de sus principios"; "espacio que corre o pasa de un tiempo a otro, o de una cosa a otra." Joan Corominas and José A. Pascual, in the *Diccionario crítico y etimológico castellano e hispánico,* note some instances of *discurrir* and *discurso* in fifteenth-century Castilian texts; they cite Juan de Valdés, and add that the terms were already common in the second half of the sixteenth century, and "frequent since *Don Quixote.*" The *Oxford English Dictionary* (1933), in the seven meanings indicated for *discourse,* includes "Onward course; procession or succession of time, events, actions, etc.; = Course" (examples given 1540– 1612) and "Narration; a narrative, tale, account" (examples 1572–1647). Sources in Italian, French, and Portuguese show a similar range of meanings.

The following passage from a *loa* of Juana Inés de la Cruz, spoken by none other than an allegorical figure named "El Discurso," echoes a number of the meanings of *discurso* developed in this section:

> Yo me sigo, del concurso,
> pues si a buena luz lo siento,
> por fuerza al Entendimiento

> ha de seguir el Discurso;
> y así mi incesable curso
> ofrezco a su discernir,
> pues llegándolo a advertir
> todo, y todo a comprehender,
> a un perspicaz entender,
> sigue un sutil discurrir.
>
> (237–38)

2. E.g., "penuria de discurso" = "poverty of resource"; "cuando hubo hecho este discurso" = "when he had made up this speech"; "en el discurso de su vida" = "in the course of their lives"; "sin hacer más discursos" = "without further discussion"; "discurriendo a todas partes" = "galloped all over the place"; "por buen discurso, bien se puede entender" = "it's reasonable to suppose"; "tu buen discurso" = "your excellent intelligence"; "hombre de flacos discursos" = "a fool"; "sin tener otro discurso ni intento" = "My only wish and purpose"; "discurre con bonísimas razones" = "he speaks very rationally"; "juicios sin discurso y temerarios" = "unreasoning and rash minds"; "sin hacer discurso ni advertir al manifiesto peligro" = "regardless of all fear and danger" (trans. J. M. Cohen).

3. "Esta filosofía cortesana, el curso de tu vida en un discurso, te presento hoy, letor juizioso" (62).

4. "Se ha turbado el curso de mi buena vida, y finalmente, he caído desde la cumbre de mi presunción discreta hasta el abismo bajo de no sé qué deseos" (*PS* 179).

I should add that occasionally the word *curso* denotes rapid and violent movement of the mind, analogous to a gusting of wind or rushing of water, as in Damón's poem, "El vano imaginar de nuestra mente, / de mil contrarios vientos arrojada / acá y allá con *curso pressuroso* . . . " (*Gal* 288); or in the case of Periandro's agitated soul, "llena de mil imaginaciones y sospechas, *discurriendo con velocísimo curso del entendimiento* lo que podía suceder, si acaso Auristela entre aquellos bárbaros se hallase . . ." (*PS* 59).

5. "Viene a ser mayor este milagro en que no solamente hablamos, sino en que hablamos con discurso, como si fuéramos capaces de razón, estando tan sin ella que la diferencia que hay del animal bruto al hombre es ser el hombre animal racional, y el bruto, irracional" (299).

6. "Ahora digo que no ha sido sabio el autor de mi historia, sino algún ignorante hablador, que a tiento y sin algún discurso se puso a escribirla, salga lo que saliere . . ." (II.3.63).

In the *Persiles,* Periandro opts for expressing his thoughts in writing rather than in speech, as he believes that with more prudent *discurso* he can put his soul in his pen rather than in his tongue (186); when he comes face to face with Auristela, however, he forgets all the written *discursos* (191).

7. "Lo mismo acontece en las razones que concibe el entendimiento de un lastimado amante, que acudiendo tal vez todas juntas a la lengua, las unas a las otras impiden, y no sabe el discurso con cuáles se dé primero a entender su imaginación" (460).

Note that *pensamientos* (thoughts) has the same relation to *discurso* in the following phrase as *razones* often has: "yo volveré a mejor discurso mis pensamientos" (I will turn my thoughts to better *discurso* [*DQ* 273]).

8. E.g., "si se ponen de por medio deseos amorosos, suelen errarse los discursos que, al parecer, van más acertados" (*PS* 219); "entre estos discursos e imaginaciones se mezclaban los celos" (*PS* 426); "Con grandísimo silencio estuvo escuchando Periandro a Auristela, y en un breve instante formó en su imaginación millares de discursos, que todos venieron a parar en el peor que para él pudiera ser, porque imaginó que Auristela le aborrecía" (*PS* 460). Examples of errant/erroneous *discurso:* "Grandes eran los discursos que don Quijote hacía sobre la respuesta de la encantada cabeza, sin que ninguno dellos diese en el embuste" (*DQ* II.63.521); "En todos nuestros discursos dimos muy lejos de la verdad del caso" (*DQ* I.40.487).

9. Thought and imagination both accompany and transport the characters they belong to in many instances (e.g., *Gal* 103, 398; *AL* 138; *DQ* I.23.280, I.28.355, II.60.491; *PS* 437).

10. E.g., "y yo, ciego del enojo y turbado con el deseo de la venganza, sin hacer algún prudente discurso, me embarqué en este navío y los seguí" (*PS* 232); "Y sin hacer más discursos, echó mano a su espada y arremetió a los gallegos" (*DQ* I.15.191); "volvíme a mi posada, vendí a mi huésped la cabalgadura, y cerrando todos mis discursos en el puño, volví al río y al barco" (Ortel Banedre telling of his decision to go to "Oriente," *PS* 320); cf. also *DQ* I.27.342, I.33.406, I.46.550.

11. The same appears to be the case with the much rarer verb *escurrir,* which applies both to the movement of discourse and to spatiotemporal motion—e.g., *DQ* I.26.324, II.52.434.

12. E.g., *Gal* 351, 358; *DQ* I.18.223, II.14.135, II.34.310, II.45.375.

There is also in *discurrir* a special sense of spreading or disseminating in different directions at once that goes beyond the limits of *discurso:* a sensation like burning ice diffuses in the veins, happiness spreads among people, gossip and fame disseminate (*Gal* 111; *PS* 308; *Git* 62; *DQ* II.2.56).

13. Usage in the *Persiles,* for example, suggests something of the range of meaning: 59, 174, 284, 435, 443, 471.

14. "Sigue tu cuento, Sancho, y del camino que hemos de seguir déjame a mí el cuidado" (I.20.242).

15. "Por vida vuestra, hijo, que volváis presto de Tembleque, y que, sin enterrar al hidalgo, si no queréis hacer más exequias, acabéis vuestro cuento" (II.31.280).

16. "Seguid vuestra historia línea recta, y no os metáis en las curvas o transversales" (II.26.242).

17. Metaphors of discursive traveling are very diversely developed in some of Cervantes' "successors" including Fielding (e.g., *Joseph Andrews* II.1.99–100; *Tom Jones* II.1.87–88, XI.9.545–46, XII.13.598, XVIII.1.813), and Sterne (e.g., *Tristram Shandy* I.6.41, I.14.64–65, I.22.94, II.11.127, IV.20.296–97, IV.33.444, VI.1.397, VII.19.480, VII.28.492).

18. "Basta, Berganza; vuelve a tu senda y camina" (2:309). "Sigue tu historia y no te desvíes del camino carretero con impertinentes digresiones; y así, por larga que sea, la acabarás presto" (321). "Bien se me trasluce, Berganza, el largo campo que se te descubría para dilatar tu plática, y soy de parecer que la dejes para cuento particular" (354).

19. In addition to what has been said about *discurso,* diverse movements are also associated with the agitation of tongues, voices, and pens in Cervantes' novels.

In reply to Don Quixote's statement that primary impulses ("primeros movimientos") are not within one's control, Sancho says: "en mí la gana de hablar siempre es primero movimiento, y no puedo dejar de decir, por una vez siquiera, lo que me viene a la lengua" (*DQ* I.30.379). Not only in the loquacious Sancho but in numerous other characters is the urge to speak a "first movement," a movement of words coming to tongues and setting them in motion with voice. Cervantes' last novel opens with shouts ("voices") out of the "mouth" of a dungeon: "Voces daba el bárbaro Corsicurbo a la estrecha boca de una profunda mazmorra" (*PS* 51).

Throughout Cervantes' novels, tongues are "moved" by pain, love, laughter, reason, by feelings, intentions, and inclinations of all sorts. Most tongues move in place without going anywhere, while language actually does the traveling. Nonetheless some tongues, including Sancho's and the slanderer Clodio's, nearly always roam freely: the imagery of loose or untied tongues and of tying or reining them in implies that tongues behave like dogs or horses (e.g., *DQ* I.22.273, II.13.134, II.31.277; *PS* 118; *DD* 205; *SC* 274). Tongues move along, trip, flee from telling certain things, carry gossip, etc. Some tongues struggle to free themselves from silence. Others travel routes such as the road to the public square (making public what should remain private) or look for paths they can travel to articulate what they want to say (e.g., *PS* 157; *Gal* 452; *Git* 114).

The mouth and tongue occupy the threshold through which language passes on its way from inside to outside. The key verb *salir,* "to go out" or "come out," appears almost invariably in such lingual boundary crossings. Sancho says: "sé más refranes que un libro, y viénenseme tantos juntos a la boca cuando hablo, que riñen, por salir, unos con otros; pero la lengua va arrojando los primeros que encuentra, aunque no vengan a mano" (*DQ* II.43.362; cf. *Gal* 208, 232, 257; *PS* 119, 166, 170, 181, 221; *DQ* II.31.277). The mouth serves as a charged place of transit between the concealed inner space of the self where discourse originates and the outer space of the social domain where discourse becomes autonomous and visible, as it were (*PS* 135–36). The tongue takes words, *discursos,* proverbs, truths, thoughts, etc., as they come to it from one inner source or another and casts them into full view of others.

Yet the visual imagery pertaining to oral discourse seems to end here, superseded by the imagery of voice and hearing. With variations, the stock phrase used is "llegar a los oídos (de alguien)"—to arrive at or come to (someone's) ears—which is what words, news, names, voices, sighs, and whispers do, passing through the air (e.g., *Gal* 411, 419, *PS* 142, 294, 344, 376, *DQ* I.13.177, I.27.329, II.33.298). Having "arrived," voices often "lead" people to their source.

Orality also predominates in the imagery of fame, which carries discourse far and wide. Cervantes' representations of fame are highly conventional: one passage refers to "talkative fame with quick steps and swift wings" (*Gal* 416), another, to the fleet running of fame from one pole to the other (*Gal* 449), others, to the way that discourse passes "from tongue to tongue and from people to people" (*DQ* I.14.180; cf. *PS* 327; *CP* 334), or from generation to generation. The general image is one of discourse traveling outward, either in successive transmissive waves relayed by tongues and human populations or borne by an almost incorporeal fame. News travels in similar ways (e.g., *Git* 133; *FS* 86, 89; *DD* 160), but often with more definite itineraries.

Writing, too, occurs with movement—in the first instance, the movement of the pen, which easily shifts into metaphorical movement since the *pluma* (feather, pen; cf. Latin *penna*), the instrument of writing, lends itself to flights of the spirit. As primary instrument of writing, the pen comes to resemble the primary instrument of speech: "the pen is the soul's tongue," as Don Quixote admirably expresses it ("la pluma es lengua del alma" [II.16.157]); pens presumably take on some of the mobility of tongues (*PS* 118; *DQ* I.47.566; cf. Augustine, *Confessions* XI.2, "lingua calami," "my pen's tongue"). Calliope and Apollo both "move the pen" of writers they inspire (*Gal* 422, 452; cf. *IF* 198). The generic openness of *Don Quixote* provides vast space for the pen to run in—a movement which is brought to a definitive end when Cide Hamete pronounces the narrative done and hangs up his quill for it to remain perpetually immobile (*DQ* II.74.592; cf. *Gal* 343).

20. "Pero dejémosle aquí, que no faltará quien le socorra, o si no, sufra y calle el que se atreve a más de a lo que sus fuerzas le prometen, y volvámonos atrás cincuenta pasos, a ver qué fue lo que don Luis respondió al oidor, que le dejamos aparte, preguntándole la causa de su venida a pie y de tan vil traje vestido" (I.44.537). Cf., among other examples in *Don Quixote* alone, I.9.139, I.25.318, I.26.321, I.38.469, II.13.34, II.14.145, II.44.368, II.44.375, II.54.447.

21. "Sería meterme en un laberinto donde no me fuese posible salir cuando quisiese" (329).

22. Consider, for example, the following dialogue between the priest and Dorotea (as the princess Micomicona), which not only brings "proseguir adelante" into relationship with the discursive movement of "esto lleva camino," but also produces an ambiguity in which "proseguir adelante" could refer as much to Micomicona's journey as to her story.

—Y esto *lleva camino*—dijo el cura—, y *prosiga* vuestra majestad *adelante*.
—No hay que *proseguir*—respondió Dorotea—, sino que, finalmente, mi suerte ha sido tan buena en hallar al señor don Quijote. . . . (*DQ* I.30.375)

23. "Esténme vuestras mercedes atentos, y vayan conmigo" (II.1.44).

24. Even the Muse Calliope, the inspirational guide through discursive heights, finds herself at a loss for verbal ways to eulogize a certain writer: "¿Qué modos, qué caminos o qué vías / de alabar buscaré . . . ?" When she turns to venerating another obscure genius, her tongue finds no adequate ways (*caminos*) at all, no matter how it tries: "Que no podrá la ruda lengua mía, / por más caminos que aquí tiente y prueve, / hallar alguno assí qual le desseo / para loar lo que en ti siento y veo" (*Gal* 451, 452). In this case there is no *inventio,* or "coming upon," of rhetorical paths leading to desired ends, and no new ones are made or invented for the occasion.

25. Typical expressions include "ir a parar" and "tirar al blanco." To cite a few variants: one character realizes she's digressed from her narrative course ("Pero ¿dónde me divierto?"); another speaks of having perhaps "walked/gone too far" ("andado demasiada"), i.e., exaggerated, in some part of her story (*DQ* II.38.334, I.30.376). Don Quixote's impromptu speeches are sometimes called preambles, which seem to

be preliminary to nothing and therefore more like verbal excursions—or "walks out in front," as the etymology would have it.

Both Sancho and Periandro speak of the safe-conduct (*salvoconducto*) granted by their audiences for them to say what they will, as though by speaking they were traveling in hostile territory.

And one further example from among many: after telling a long stretch of his travels, Periandro takes leave of his companions, as though they were fellow travelers at the end of a day's journey, or *journée;* he needs to rest for the night so as to have the strength to "enter into" the narration of his subsequent exploits. Here telling is traveling of sorts—or travail, *trabajo,* a key word that figures in the full title of the novel.

26. "Y venid al punto sin rodeos ni callejuelas" (*DQ* II.47.394). Here as elsewhere I've kept the original imagery in the translation in order to make a point.

27. *Paradiso* II.1–20 (cf. *Purgatorio* I.1–6). In the last canto of *Orlando Furioso,* the poet sails into harbor after a long and perilous journey and is welcomed by a fanfare, roaring crowds, nobles, and friends. Rabelais' Alcofrybas uses the metaphor when excusing himself from going any further into an abstruse discussion on symbolism: "Mais plus oultre ne fera voile mon equif entre ces gouffres et guez mal plaisans: je retourne faire scale au port dont suis yssu. Bien ay je espoir d'en escripre quelque jours plus amplement" (I.9.42).

28. A fuller exposition would lead into an array of variations and tangential remarks, and would deal with passages such as the dedication and prologue of *La Galatea,* which are alive with metaphors of movement that seem to get out of hand in all their comings and goings.

29. Referring to an oral prophecy, for instance, la Cañizares tells the dog Berganza: "Your mother took it down in writing and in memory, and I fixed it in mine" ("Tomólo tu madre por escrito y de memoria, y yo lo fijé en la mía" [*CP* 339]).

Books, narratives, histories, and the like also do their own sort of moving about apart from the discursive movement that takes place within them. Perhaps the key verb in this regard is *andar* (here: "go"): narratives go about in print, they go about lost without getting into print, etc. (e.g., *NE* 1:50, 52; *DQ* II.2.57, II.3.60, II.8.94). Much of this movement is disseminative as literary works go to people and present themselves, or pass from one person to another. In the very first introductory poem of *Don Quixote,* the legendary Urganda advises the book to approach good readers and not to end up among idiots. And in the dedication to Part II of the novel, Cervantes writes to the count of Lemos that Don Quixote, previously "waiting with his boots ready spurred to go and kiss your Excellency's hands," is now "on the way, and if he arrives I think I shall have done your Excellency some service; for much pressure has been put on me from countless directions to purge the disgust and nausea caused by another Don Quixote who has been running about the world masquerading as the second part." Thus the book has taken the form of its traveling protagonist, just as the "inauthentic" second part by another author runs about as a false Don Quixote. There are numerous other instances of personified, and hence mobilized, books, above all in the many satirical references to certain kinds of books as condemned bodies, as excommunicated heretics fit to be burned or "banished from the Christian Republic like worthless people" (*DQ* I.5–6, I.47.566).

30. "Disparó la flecha con tan buen tino y con tanta furia, que en un instante llegó a la boca de Bradamiro, y se la cerró quitándole el movimiento de la lengua y sacándole el alma con que dejó admirados, atónitos y suspensos a cuantos allí estaban" (*PS* 68).

31. "No se te mueran . . . las palabras en la boca . . . los males comunicados, si no alcanzan sanidad, alcanzan alivio. Si tu pasión es amorosa, como lo imagino, sin duda bien sé que eres de carne, aunque pareces de alabastro, y bien sé que nuestras almas están siempre en continuo movimiento. . . . Mujer soy como tú; mis deseos tengo, y hasta ahora por honra del alma no me han salido a la boca, que bien pudiera, como señales de la calentura; pero al fin habrán de romper por inconvenientes y por imposibles, y siquiera en mi testamento, procuraré que se sepa la causa de mi muerte" (170).

32. E.g., "and without being able to go ahead [*pasar adelante*], she fainted and fell into Isabela's arms" (*EI* 264; cf. *AL* 164; *DQ* I.25.300).

33. E.g., *Lysis* 221d–222a; *Philebus* 35a–b; *Symposium* 200a–201b; *Republic* 437, 585a–b.

34. See, for example, Anne Carson's insightful book *Eros the Bittersweet* 10, 16, 18, 20–33, 65, 67, 76. Carson also discusses desire in more dynamic terms, particularly with reference to movement (13, 17, 19, 28, 48, 49, 57, 66).

35. Ruth El Saffar, Carroll B. Johnson, Louis Combet, and various others have dealt insightfully with desiring characters. I should stress that this section deals primarily with how narrators and characters speak about desire. The ways in which characters experience desire, especially in relation to their journeys, is explored in Chapter 3.

36. "Verdad es que amor es padre del desseo, y entre otras difiniciones que del amor se dan, ésta es una: amor es aquella primera mutación que sentimos hazer en nuestra mente, por el apetito que nos conmueve y nos tira a sí, y nos deleita y aplaze; y aquel placer engendra movimiento en el ánimo, el qual movimiento se llama desseo; y en resolución, desseo es movimiento del apetito acerca de lo que se ama, y un querer de aquello que se possee, y el objecto suyo, es el bien . . ." (308).

By way of contrast, Juan Huarte de San Juan, in his *Examen de ingenios para las ciencias* (1575), describes the physiological movements of desire in general and (male) sexual desire in particular: "Estos son los espíritus vitales y sangre arterial, los cuales *andan vagando por todo el cuerpo* y están siempre asidos a la imaginación y siguen su contemplación. El oficio de esta sustancia espiritual es despertar las potencias del hombre y darles fuerza y vigor para que puedan obrar. Conócese claramente ser éste su uso considerando los *movimientos* de la imaginativa y lo que sucede después en la obra. . . . Si el hombre está contemplando en alguna mujer hermosa, o está dando y tomando con la imaginación en el acto venéreo, luego *acuden* estos espíritus vitales a los miembros genitales y los levantan para la obra" (96–97; emphasis mine).

37. In his edition of Garcilaso de la Vega's *Obras completas,* Elias Rivers discusses the importance in medieval and Renaissance erotology of the "spirits" passing from the eyes of the beloved to those of the lover, as in Garcilaso's sonnet 8: "De aquella vista pura y excellente / salen espirtus bivos y encendidos, / y siendo por mis ojos re-

cebidos, / me passan hasta donde el mal se siente" (86–89). Desire is in motion here.

38. Consider the psycho-physiology of desire as movement in a very different context, Sappho's fragment 31 (quoted in Carson 12–13):

> —oh it
> puts the heart in my chest on wings
> for when I look at you, a moment, then no speaking
> is left in me
>
> no: tongue breaks, and thin
> fire is racing under skin
> and in eyes no sight and drumming
> fills ears
>
> and cold sweat holds me and shaking
> grips me all. . . .

39. Besides its widespread use in Plato's dialogues, see Foucault's discussion of the term: "Nature intended . . . that the performance of the act be associated with a pleasure, and it was this pleasure that gave rise to *epithumia,* to desire, in a *movement that was naturally directed* toward what 'gives pleasure,' according to a principle that Aristotle cites: desire is always 'desire for the agreeable thing.'. . . It is true— Plato always comes back to the idea—that for the Greeks there could not be desire without privation, without the want of the thing desired and without a certain amount of suffering mixed in; but the appetite, Plato explains in the *Philebus,* can be aroused only by the representation, the image or the memory of the thing that gives pleasure; . . . it is the soul and only the soul that can, through memory, *make present* the thing that is to be desired and thereby arouse the *epithumia*" (*History of Sexuality* 2:43; emphasis mine).

40. "Este primer movimiento—amor o desseo, como llamarlo quisieres—" (310).

41. In Cervantes' play *Pedro de Urdemalas,* Pedro echoes this passage as he reflects on his own life of changes, though desire doesn't seem to be the protagonist here, and if God is the principal agent no mention is made of God as center:

> ¡Válgame Dios qué de trajes
> he mudado, y qué de oficios,
> qué de varios ejercicios,
> qué de exquisitos lenguajes!
> Y agora, como estudiante,
> de la reina voy huyendo,
> cien mil azares temiendo
> desta suerte inconstante.
> Pero yo ¿por qué me cuento
> que llevo mudable palma?
> *Si ha de estar siempre nuestra alma*
> *en contino movimiento,*
> Dios me arroje ya a las partes
> donde más fuere servido.
> (2676–89; my emphasis)

42. "Pero viendo el hazedor y criador nuestro que es propria naturaleza del ánima nuestra estar contino en perpetuo *movimiento y desseo* . . ." (310–11; my emphasis).

43. "Es el desseo principio y origen de do todas nuestras passiones proceden, como qualquier arroyo de su fuente" (298).

44. "El amor . . . unas veces vuela y otras anda; con éste corre, y con aquél va despacio; . . . en un mesmo punto comienza la carrera de sus deseos, y en aquel mesmo punto la acaba y concluye . . ." (I.34.424).

45. "Pero, puesto caso que corran igualmente las hermosuras, no por eso han de correr iguales los deseos . . . que si todas las bellezas enamorasen y rindiesen, sería un andar las voluntades confusas y descaminadas, sin saber en cuál habían de parar; porque, siendo infinitos los sujetos hermosos, infinitos habían de ser los deseos" (I.14.186). As usual, I have preserved the language of movement even though a better translation might suppress it.

46. In a typical poem in *La Galatea,* fear pursues, disdain catches up, hope and delight flee from desire, while a lack of deserving approaches together with an excess of misery, and so on (260).

47. E.g., "Do my desires seem to be off course to you?" (*PS* 460).

48. "Todas las vezes que el desseo de alguna cosa se enciende en nuestros coraço-nes, luego nos mueve a seguirla y a buscarla, y buscándola y siguiéndola, a mil de-sordenados fines nos conduce. Este desseo es aquel que incita al hermano a procurar de la amada hermana los abominables abrazos . . ." (*Gal* 298).

49. "Y así, con estos tan agradables pensamientos, llevado del estraño gusto que en ellos sentía, se dio priesa a poner en efeto lo que deseaba" (*DQ* I.1.75).

50. There are numerous variations on this theme: people send desires elsewhere, they put them on track or on routes, they pull them along behind, they bring them out into the public square, they move other people's desires, etc.

51. E.g., "no la ofenderás en fingir palabras que se encaminan a *conseguir* buenos deseos' (*PS* 193); "que las esperanzas propincuas de *alcanzar* el bien que se desea, fatigan mucho más que las remotas y apartadas" (*PS* 235); "Quisiera buenamente *lograr* sus deseos a pie llano, sin rodeos ni intervenciones" (*PS* 249); "Estaba tan ciego el mísero y anciano cadí, que si otros mil disparates le dijeran, como fueran encami-nados a *cumplir* sus esperanzas, todos los creyera, cuanto más que le pareció que todo lo que le decían llevaba buen camino y prometía buen suceso" (*AL* 175).

52. His companion Erastro continues the song by wishing Galatea would return the soul and heart she has "stolen" from him (*Gal* 75–76; cf. *Gal* 68–69, 82, 276, 346; *DD* 228).

53. "Yo no sé cómo en tan pequeño espacio de tiempo me transformé en otro ser del que tenía, porque yo ya no vivía en mí, sino en Artidoro—que ansí se llama la mitad de mi alma que ando buscando—: doquiera que bolvía los ojos me parecía ver su figura . . ." (*Gal* 113–14; cf. *Gal* 115; *Git* 123).

54. For instance, one character's amorous behavior toward another is likened to the pursuit of the hunt—chasing after rabbits (*Git* 103–4).

55. "[La voluntad], atropellando inconvenientes, desatinadamente se arroja tras su deseo, y pensando dar con la gloria de sus ojos, da con el infierno de sus pesa-dumbres. Si alcanza lo que desea, mengua el deseo con la posesión de la cosa de-seada" (85).

56. The narrator of *La española inglesa* illustrates this last point when referring

to Ricaredo's anticipated "taking possession" of Isabela (the terms are very explicit) in marriage: "The day finally arrived, not when Ricaredo would put an end to his desires but rather when he would find new qualities in Isabela that might move him to love [*querer*] her more . . ." Perhaps the motion of the Latin *quaerere* (to seek) can still be sensed here in the verb *querer*.

57. I might add that despite the wide-ranging versatility of these metaphors, and despite the fact that they can at times work in conjunction with economic metaphors, each sort of language reveals some of the limitations of the other, expressing the diverse experience of desiring in radically different terms. A key difference is that whereas economic metaphors emphasize possession as the goal of desire, metaphors of movement tend to recast possession as arrival: moving desirers don't really possess anything.

58. Consider the following sample passages by and about Lacan concerning the relations between desire and lack:

"[I have] produced the only conceivable idea of the object, that of the object as cause of desire, of that which is lacking" (Lacan, *Four* ix).

"the *objet a* is most evanescent in its function of symbolizing the central lack of desire" (Lacan, *Four* 105).

"It is in so far as [the child's] desire is beyond or falls short of what [the mother] says, of what she hints at, of what she brings out as meaning, it is in so far as his desire is unknown, it is in this point of lack, that the desire of the subject is constituted" (Lacan, *Four* 218–19).

"But in all these postures, Desire — as a structural lack in the subject — defines the trajectory of pleasure and freedom in their relation to power and law" (Ragland-Sullivan 303).

"In such a context Desire derived from lack (*manque-à-être* or want-of-being) elicits Desire as exchange" (Ragland-Sullivan 40).

"what man approaches in the sexual act is not so much the woman's body as the cause of his Desire (lack). As the *objet a* of Desire . . . he puts her in the place of the dark face of his own unconscious being. And he identifies her with the unconscious, the unknown, and truth — what Lacan tellingly terms the face of God. In this sense, man finds fulfillment through woman precisely because of a lack that he consciously denies" (Ragland-Sullivan 292).

"Lacan can claim, therefore, that the structure of self or ontology comes from Real gaps (wants) in being, which desire causes (in the form of various *objets a*) and for which Desire compensates in expressing itself in language" (Ragland-Sullivan 172).

59. In his highly acute and synthetic article on the Spanish "Baroque," Wardropper outlines useful criteria, both stylistic and ideological, for distinguishing the "Renaissance" from the "Baroque." While such criteria are readily applicable to a number of writers of the period, the case of Cervantes is much more ambiguous.

I should add that I reserve the right to modify my opinion on the "Baroque" in the future.

60. In *Genesis* 47.8–9, Joseph speaks of the years of his life as days of a journey, as the Vulgate renders it: "Quot sunt dies annorum vitae tuae? Respondit: Dies peregrinationis meae centum triginta annorum sunt, parvi et mali, et non pervenerunt

usque ad dies patrum meorum quibus peregrinati sunt." Antonio Vilanova documents other biblical passages referring to the journey of life (103–4).

61. This echoes numerous passages including one from Cristóbal Suárez de Figueroa's *El pasajero* (1617): "Nuestra vida es todo peregrinación, y lo confirman todas las cosas del mundo, cuyo ser por instantes vuela." Suárez de Figueroa reflects further: "Sin duda es de corazón humilde y plebeyo asistir de continuo en su casa y estar en todo tiempo como clavado en su propia tierra. Generoso y casi divino el que, imitando a los árabes, se goza con ello en su movimiento. Del sabio se dice peregrina con utilidad en cualquier parte donde reside; esto es, investigando, observando, y deprendiendo. En fin, la dificultad consiste en emprender; que emprendido, todo es fácil" (Vilanova 154–55).

62. Gracián 188, 785, 288, 634, 296. "Dime, ¿no caminas cada hora y cada instante sobre el hilo de tu vida . . . ?" (765).

63. For an allegorical reading of the *Persiles,* see Alban Forcione, *Cervantes' Christian Romance* 29–63.

64. "Quiere hacer uno un viaje largo, y si es prudente, antes de ponerse en camino busca alguna compañía segura y apacible con quien acompañarse: pues ¿por qué no hará lo mesmo el que ha de caminar toda la vida, hasta el paradero de la muerte, y más si la compañía le ha de acompañar en la cama, en la mesa y en todas partes, como es la de la mujer con su marido?" (II.19.180).

65. "Y aunque la noche volaba con sus ligeras y negras alas, le parecía a Rodolfo que iba y caminaba no con alas, sino con muletas: tan grande era el deseo de verse a solas con su querida esposa" (*FS* 95). There is an almost identical passage in *La española inglesa* (265).

66. A rather literal translation, with apologies: "I'll not ask you to come sweet, savory, / since you won't find a road, path, or way / to bring me back to the being I have lost. / Auspicious hours for anyone else! / That sweet one of the mortal cross-over, / only that of my death I ask you for" (*Gal* 344).

67. "¿Adónde me lleva la fuerza incontrastable de mis hados? ¿Qué camino es el mío o qué salida espero tener del intrincable laberinto donde me hallo? . . . ¿Qué fin ha de tener esta no sabida peregrinación mía? . . . ay de mí una y mil veces, que tan a rienda suelta me dejé llevar de mis deseos" (*DD* 204).

Chapter 3. Travelers

1. This is what happens in the 1613 version; adultery prevails in the earlier version.

2. Here I would like to single out Antonio Vilanova's impressive essay "El peregrino andante en el *Persiles* de Cervantes," written a half century ago, and Juergen Hahn's study, *The Origins of the Baroque Concept of* Peregrinatio. Vilanova traces the evolution of the *peregrino* in sixteenth- and seventeenth-century Spanish prose, sketching out some of the coordinates between character type, world, and genre. The article provides insight into conceptions of and attitudes toward travel as evident in the literature of the time. With a wealth of documentation, Hahn develops further the wide-ranging notions of *peregrinatio* in relation to real and fictional travelers, and proceeds to concentrate on the *peregrinatio amoris* and *peregrinatio vitae*.

Works giving explicit recognition to the importance of the journey in Cervantes' novels, especially *Don Quixote* and the *Persiles,* include Américo Castro's "La estructura del *Quijote*," Alban K. Forcione's books on the *Persiles* and the *Novelas ejemplares,* Carroll B. Johnson's *Madness and Lust,* Ruth El Saffar's "Sex and the Single Hidalgo: Reflections on Eros in *Don Quixote*," and Sybil Dümchen's "The Function of Madness in *El licenciado Vidriera.*"

3. "Si je craingnois de mourir en autre lieu que celuy de ma naissance, si je pensois mourir moins à mon aise esloingné des miens, à peine sortiroy-je hors de France; je ne sortirois pas sans effroy hors de ma parroisse. Je sens la mort qui me pince continuellement la gorge ou les reins. Mais je suis autrement faict: elle m'est une partout. Si toutesfois j'avois à choisir, ce seroit, ce croy-je, plustost à cheval que dans un lict, hors de ma maison et esloigné des miens" (III.9.956).

Here and elsewhere I've consulted and usually modified the translation of Charles Cotton, W. Hazlitt and Blanchard Bates (New York: Random House, 1949) as well as that of George B. Ives (Cambridge: Harvard UP, 1925).

4. "Que m'en chaut-il! Je ne l'entreprens ny pour en revenir, ny pour le parfaire; j'entreprens seulement de me branler, pendant que le branle me plaist. Et me proumeine pour me proumener. Ceux qui courent un benefice ou un lievre ne courent pas; ceux là courent qui courent aux barres, et pour exercer leur course" (III.9.955).

5. I originally found these anecdotes in Jonathan Smith's *Map Is Not Territory* (102), where they are preceded by interesting commentary not unrelated to my own theme.

6. Eric Leed notes that "St. Augustine (fourth century), St. Bernard (tenth century), and St. Thomas Aquinas (thirteenth century) had all regarded *curiositas* as a venial sin, as 'lust of the eye,' a desire 'not for fleshly enjoyment but for gaining personal experience through the flesh'" (179).

Comparable attitudes, often epistemologically rather than ethically focused, may be found in the most diverse religious texts including the *Tao te Ching* ascribed to Lao Tzu:

> Without stirring abroad
> One can know the whole world;
> Without looking out of the window
> One can see the way of heaven.
> The further one goes
> The less one knows.
> Therefore the sage knows without having to stir. . . .
>
> (108)

7. See also, for example, the studies of Benito Brancaforte, Louis Combet (401–28), Francisco Márquez Villanueva ("Locura"), and Edwin Williamson (91–99).

8. With the titles *The World of Don Quixote* and *Los dos mundos del* Quijote: *Realidad y ficción,* both Richard Predmore and Guillermo Barriga have written books nominally about Don Quixote's world or worlds. Neither book actually develops the notion of world, although Predmore's has valuable insights on illusion, enchantment, reality, and related topics. For Predmore, the two contrasting worlds are simply "the given world of Cervantes' day and the created world of books" (2; cf. 97). Rather similarly, for Barriga (3–4), the two clashing worlds of the novel are those of fiction

(understood largely as archaic, medieval), and reality (understood as modern, conventional, belonging to Cervantes and the majority of characters in *Don Quixote*).

With the idea of "two-world condition" I am proposing a different notion of world, of the relationship between worlds, and of the makeup of specific worlds within the *Quixote*. See Chapter 4, "Cervantine Worlds."

9. "Se había dado a aquel honroso oficio, andando por diversas partes del mundo, buscando sus aventuras [en varios lugares] donde había ejercitado la ligereza de sus pies, sutileza de sus manos, haciendo muchos tuertos, recuestando muchas viudas, deshaciendo algunas doncellas y engañando a algunos pupilos, y, finalmente, dándose a conocer por cuantas audiencias y tribunales hay casi en toda España" (I.3.88–89).

10. "El buen gobernador, la pierna quebrada, y en casa" (II.34.307). Sancho has adapted a proverb in which the honorable maiden (or honorable wife) is to stay at home. See proverbs below.

11. The matter doesn't quite end here, since Sancho later whimsically states that he'd like to be a count, and Don Quixote accordingly promises him a kingdom or county in the future, thus reestablishing the initial pattern (II.65.538).

12. "Es doctrina de Theologos, que solo el vagar, sin otra información, es vehemente sospecha de delito capital" (Luna 49; George Borrow's 1843 translation in *The Zincali* 1:175).

13. Cervantes' play *Pedro de Urdemalas* offers a number of parallels to *La gitanilla.* Belica is thought to have been stolen by the Gypsies when she was a baby (although it turns out she was handed over to them), and she is reinstated at the very highest level of society. Unlike the exuberant Preciosa, Belica is a sulking character whose obsessive dream of royalty comes true; there's nothing of the Gypsy in her. Pedro de Urdemalas, in contrast, is a protean, homeless character who, abandoned as a baby, serves a long list of masters, travels to America and back, becomes an adept in all manner of picaresque endeavors and, among other metamorphoses, turns Gypsy for a short while.

14. For analyses of female characters, see, among other studies, Ruth El Saffar's *Beyond Fiction,* Diana de Armas Wilson's "Cervantes' Last Romance: Deflating the Myth of Female Sacrifice," Debra D. Andrist's "Male Versus Female Friendship in *Don Quijote,*" as well as Combet's typology (41–100).

15. Or heptagon, if the libidinous Halima is included.

16. Diana de Armas Wilson insightfully connects transvestism, and generally the splitting and fusion of sexual difference, with the trope of syneciosis whereby "a contrary is joined to its opposite or two different things are conjoined closely" ("Splitting" 44); she also cites references associating transvestism with homosexuality (47).

17. I am adapting this extremely suggestive notion from John Chernoff's *African Rhythm and African Sensibility,* where it refers to the complex effect of two or more percussionists drumming "conflicting rhythmic patterns and accents" in autonomous time signatures (46). The adaptation loses the term's musical specificity, but is meant to fill a terminological void concerning what I see as an integral and usually ignored aspect of experience.

18. "Y viendo que ya el sol apressurava su carrera para entrarse por las puertas de occidente, no quisieron detenerse allí más, por llegar a la aldea antes que las sombras de la noche" (331).

19. "Bien tomaron por partido los que escuchando a Elicio y a Erastro ivan que más el camino se alargara, para gustar más del agradable canto de los enamorados pastores. Pero el cerrar de la noche, y el llegar a la aldea, hizo que dél cessassen . . ." (335).

20. "Era tanto el desseo que el enamorado Timbrio y las dos hermosas hermanas Nísida y Blanca llevavan de llegar a la hermita de Silerio, que la ligereza de los passos no era possible que a la de la voluntad llegasse" (337).

21. "No pudo ni quiso el pressuroso Timbrio aguardar a que más adelante el pastor Lauso a su canto passasse, porque . . . hizo muestras de adelantarse, y assí todos le siguieron . . ." (339).

22. "En lo que se detuvo Lauso en dezir estos versos y en alabar la singular hermosura . . . de su pastora, a él y a Damón se les aligeró la pesadumbre del camino y se les passó el tiempo sin ser sentido, hasta que llegaron junto de la hermita . . ." (343).

23. John Weiger aptly observes a quasi-cinematographic technique in the narration of *La Galatea* (128).

24. "Yendo, pues, caminando nuestro flamante aventurero, iba hablando consigo mesmo y diciendo: '¿Quién duda sino que en los venideros tiempos, cuando salga a luz la verdadera historia de mis famosos hechos, que el sabio que los escribiere no ponga, cuando llegue a contar esta mi primera salida tan de mañana, desta manera: "Apenas había el rubicundo Apolo tendido por la faz de la ancha y espaciosa tierra las doradas hebras de sus hermosos cabellos, y apenas los pequeños y pintados pajarillos con sus arpadas lenguas habían saludado con dulce y meliflua armonía la venida de la rosada aurora, que, dejando la blanda cama del celoso marido, por las puertas y balcones del manchego horizonte a los mortales se mostraba, cuando el famoso caballero don Quijote de la Mancha, dejando las ociosas plumas, subió sobre su famoso caballo Rocinante, y comenzó a caminar por el antiguo y conocido campo de Montiel"'" (I.2.80; cf. *Gal* 216).

25. "Y en tanto que él iba de aquella manera menudeando tragos, no se le acordaba de ninguna promesa que su amo le hubiese hecho, ni tenía por ningún trabajo, sino por mucho descanso, andar buscando las aventuras, por peligrosas que fuesen" (I.8.132).

26. "Sonó una trompeta, soltaron la cuerda y arrojáronse al vuelo los cinco; pero aún no habrían dado veinte pasos, cuando con más de seis se les aventajó el recién venido, y a los treinta ya los llevaba de ventaja más de quince; finalmente se los dejó a poco más de la mitad del camino, como si fuesen estatuas inmóviles, con admiración de todos los circunstantes, especialmente de Sinforosa, que le seguía con la vista, así corriendo como estando quedo, porque la belleza y agilidad del mozo era bastante para llevar tras sí las voluntades, no sólo los ojos de cuantos le miraban. Noté yo esto, porque tenía los míos atentos a mirar a Policarpa, objeto dulce de mis deseos, y de camino, miraba los movimientos de Sinforosa" (152–53).

27. Stephen Gilman, referring to *Don Quixote,* notes in passing "the extent to which a narrative structure based on continuity and interruption involves a corollary attention to gait—creeping forward . . . charging and hanging back . . . leaping . . . plodding . . . —and to posture—riding high, knocked down, slumped over, sitting up in bed" (62).

28. "Porque éste es estilo de los libros de las historias caballerescas y de los encantadores que en ellas se entremeten y platican: cuando algún caballero está puesto en algún trabajo, que no puede ser librado dél sino por la mano de otro caballero, puesto que estén distantes el uno del otro dos o tres mil leguas, y aun más, o le arrebatan en una nube o le deparan un barco donde se entre, y en menos de un abrir y cerrar de ojos le llevan, o por los aires, o por la mar, donde quieren y adonde es menester su ayuda" (II.29.262).

29. Instances of "psychic" travel abound in many other texts as well, including the following two, which call to mind the adventure of the enchanted boat. In *Estebanillo González,* the picaresque protagonist and a postilion accompanying him suppose, under the displacing and disorienting spell of Bacchus, that they have traveled more than two hundred posts, only to be shown as they become sober the nearby church tower of the place they departed from (chap. 10 [2:429–30]). Tristram Shandy also comments on a duplicity of experience in his own travels: "When the precipitancy of a man's wishes hurries on his ideas ninety times faster than the vehicle he rides in—woe be to truth! and woe be to the vehicle and its tackling . . ." (Sterne VII.viii).

30. The expression calls to mind not only the cases mentioned here, but also mystic transports such as those of Sor María de Agreda, who, a quarter century after the publication of Cervantes' last novels, convinced many including her great admirer Philip IV that she had spiritually traveled to New Spain and carried on missionary work there without ever having left her district.

31. Observe that in the paradox presented to governor Sancho, all those who pass over a bridge have to take an oath about *where they are going* and what for, and anyone caught lying is to be hanged on the gallows. When one man says he's going to be hanged, the enforcers of the law are caught in an irresolvable bind. Even had he given a straight answer, true or false, how could he be disproven?

32. Though Dante's etymology of *romeo* may be wrong, as Leo Spitzer has shown, what matters here is that there was a linguistic distinction between types of pilgrims according to their destination.

33. In any event, much criticism has touched on these questions in one way or another; among others, see Fu 20–56.

34. Nietzsche broadens this phenomenon into an interesting aphorism: "During the journey we commonly forget its goal. Almost every profession is chosen and commenced as a means to an end but continued as an end in itself. Forgetting our objectives is the most frequent of all acts of stupidity" (*Human* 360).

35. The entry on "improvisation" in *The New Grove Dictionary of Music and Musicians* tellingly states: "In the Germanic tradition the balance had always been weighted more strongly in favour of the composer, the performer being treated with considerable mistrust in regard to ornamentation. In Beethoven this tradition produced a figure of such forcefulness and individuality that a creative collaboration in which the performer added something of his own to the composer's conception became increasingly unthinkable, and the performer was made to feel that his highest calling—going beyond the traditional good taste to an almost spiritual mission—was to subject himself to the composer's will as the means by which his masterpieces were communicated to the world" (Sadie 9:49). The article also documents how such great im-

provising performers as Bach and Mozart understandably left little or no space in their published compositions for improvisation on the part of other performers, e.g., the Salieris of this world.

36. The play *Pedro de Urdemalas* is also remarkable for the improvisation of its protagonist, as are several of the *entremeses* including *El retablo de las maravillas* and *La cueva de Salamanca*.

37. Michael Nerlich dismisses the etymology and the distinction from event because of the unattested origin, and he quickly shifts to adventure as "a special event that takes one by surprise" (1:3, 5). Had he followed through with the etymological implications he might have dealt with adventure differently, more in accord with the ways characters experience it, as we'll see.

38. Torrente Ballester singles out this adventure to illustrate the second category of relations between reality and invention mentioned above, that of assimilating appearances to his fantasy without modifying them.

39. Reflecting on Don Quixote's militancy, Torrente Ballester stresses that Don Quixote leaves home armed with the intention of engaging in combat, and has to invent his adversaries (91).

40. Curiously, a case could be made that the second category dominates in Don Quixote's second sally, the third dominates in the third sally, and there is an instance of the first (the adventure of Andrés) in the first brief sally, though all the categories are evident in all three journeys.

Chapter 4. Cervantine Worlds

1. See Avalle-Arce's introduction to his edition of the *Persiles* 13–21. Undoubtedly the evolution of Cervantes' novelistic writing enters into these differences if, as evidence suggests, Books I and II were written considerably earlier than Books III and IV. My point here is that criticism has shown little awareness of the generative faculty of chronotopes. See also Forcione, *Cervantes' Christian Romance* 11, 46–47, and Diana de Armas Wilson, "Splitting the Difference" 35–37.

2. "Contentísima estaba Auristela de ver que se le acercaba la hora de poner pie en tierra firme, sin andar de puerto en puerto y de isla en isla, sujeta a la inconstancia del mar y a la movible voluntad de los vientos. . . ."

3. "El recelo de alguna gran borrasca comenzó a turbar a los marineros: que la inconstancia de nuestras vidas y la del mar simbolizan en no prometer seguridad ni firmeza alguna largo tiempo."

4. As far as I am aware, only Antonio Vilanova in "El peregrino andante en el *Persiles* de Cervantes" and Alban Forcione in *Cervantes, Aristotle, and the* Persiles (212–45) have taken the question seriously. Vilanova focuses primarily·on character types (the *peregrino andante*, the *pícaro*, the knight-errant, etc.) and their relations to corresponding worlds. Under the heading of the marvellous, Forcione discusses numerous instances of the "garden paradise" in the three long novels, dealing with them in terms not of genre, chronotope, or ideology but of the theoretical literary debates in which Cervantes was supposedly engaged (questions of verisimilitude, *admiratio*, harmony, order, unity, variety, and so on). Forcione's repeated assertions that

the purpose of the paradisiacal gardens is "exclusively literary" place these garden-worlds in an unnecessarily narrow framework, it seems to me, which nonetheless doesn't keep him from making interesting observations.

Torrente Ballester also refers to literary worlds but doesn't develop the idea beyond the principle of congruency between character and fictional world (113–14). In fact his denial of the authenticity of Don Quixote's world detracts from the notion of plural worlds and reinforces *the* world in which Alonso Quijano acts out his knightly roles.

Despite the presence of "world" or "mundo" in the titles of various critical works on Cervantes, none of these looks into the question of worlds as such.

5. Not all of the passages cited actually use the word *mundo*. But the notion of *mundo* is implied in terms such as *suelo* and *tierra,* when used in opposition to such words as *cielo* or *infierno,* and ubiquitous terms such as the latter always imply a multiworld system of which the world is one of several worlds.

6. "Allá en el alma tuya un paraíso / fue descubierto" (*Gal* 200); "tú eres su cielo y su tierra, el blanco de sus deseos" (*DQ* I.33.416); "me ocupó el alma una furia y un infierno de celos" (*EI* 143; cf. *PS* 188; *Git* 85).

7. In the play *Pedro de Urdemalas,* Pedro's narrative of his journey to America receives similar treatment.

8. See my article "Mapping Utopias" for a critique and reconceptualization of "utopia." My starting point is More's coinage of the term as "no place"; by extension, utopia would mean an imaginary world regardless of whether it's good or bad or neither. The term utopia has much greater potential as a literary concept and mode of thought than as a label for places characterized by the naturally, socially, ethically, or politically desirable, which I call "eutopias" (good places), following More's playfully profound terminology. Eutopias are a major class of utopias, but sometimes actually materialize and therefore fall outside the range of utopias.

The most important study of "utopian" thought in Cervantes' novels, Antonio Maravall's *Utopía y contrautopía en el* Quijote, falls into the category of traditional "utopian" criticism, though much can be learned from it.

9. An observation by Tuan interestingly stresses the correlations between human beings and their world(s): "the single term 'world' contains and conjoins man and his environment, for its etymological root '*wer*' means man" (34).

10. "On those remote pages it is written that animals are divided into (a) those that belong to the emperor, (b) embalmed ones, (c) those that are trained, (d) suckling pigs, (e) mermaids, (f) fabulous ones, (g) stray dogs, (h) those that are included in this classification, (i) those that tremble as if they were mad, (j) innumerable ones, (k) those drawn with a very fine camel's-hair brush, (l) others, (m) those that have just broken a flower vase, (n) those that resemble flies from a distance" (Borges, "El lenguaje analítico de John Wilkins," *Prosa* 2:223). Translation by Ruth L. C. Simms.

11. Cervantes was familiar with Olaf Magnusson's map included in his *History of the Northern Peoples* (Rome, 1555). One indication of the remoteness of these places, the sense of a distant "there" as opposed to here, is the narrator's interjection: "—for in those parts the sea ebbs and flows just as in ours—" (62).

12. George Mariscal, for instance, convincingly argues that the *Persiles* ought to

be read as "one more text in a vast series of writings that worked to represent the barbarian (*lo bárbaro*)" (96).

13. "Yo, simple y compasiva, le entregué un alma rústica, y él—merced a los cielos—me la ha vuelto discreta y cristiana. Entreguéle mi cuerpo . . . y deste entrego resultó haberle dado dos hijos, como los que aquí veis, que acrecientan el número de los que alaban al Dios verdadero" (82).

14. The potential or actual barbarity of "civilized" people is never far from the surface in the *Persiles*. Murder, rape, vengeance, enslavement, poisoning, magic spells, theft, and so on, whether intended or actually carried out, motivate many of the characters in the novel. Even Prince Arnaldo, who awaits events offshore, plays the game of selling slaves to the barbarians, and Periandro is at first much concerned about whether he took sexual advantage of Auristela while she was in his power.

15. "Con esto se cortan las alas a la ambición, se atierra la codicia, y aunque la hipocresía suele andar lista, a largo andar se le cae la máscara y queda sin el alcanzado premio; con esto los pueblos viven quietos, campea la justicia y resplandece la misericordia, despáchanse con brevedad los memoriales de los pobres, y los que dan los ricos, no por serlo son mejor despachados; no agobian la vara de la justicia las dádivas, ni la carne y sangre de los parentescos: todas las negociaciones guardan sus puntos y andan en sus quicios, finalmente reino es donde se vive sin temor de los insolentes y donde cada uno goza lo que es suyo" (150).

16. "Todos deseaban, pero a ninguno se le cumplían sus deseos . . ." (176). The statement refers not only to erotic desire, which clearly dominates in the place, but also to the desire of Mauricio, Antonio padre, and Rutilio to return home.

17. "No tenían madre, que no les hizo falta, cuando murió, sino en la compañía: que sus virtudes y agradables costumbres eran ayas de sí mismas, dando maravilloso ejemplo a todo el reino" (150).

18. There is more than a little mystery in the scarcity of women as mothers in Cervantes' novels. Ruth El Saffar's interesting essay "Sex and the Single Hidalgo: Reflections on Eros in *Don Quixote*" hypothesizes on the importance of maternity in Cervantes' works without dealing as such with the absence and scarcity of mothers.

19. My emphasis. "Aquí, huyendo de la guerra, hallé la paz; la hambre que en ese mundo de allá arriba, si así se puede decir, tenía, halló aquí a la hartura; aquí, en lugar de los príncipes y monarcas que mandan en el mundo, a quien yo servía, he hallado a estos árboles mudos . . . aquí no veo dama que me desdeñe, ni criado que mal me sirva; aquí soy yo señor de mí mismo; aquí tengo mi alma en mi palma, y aquí por vía recta encamino mis pensamientos y mis deseos al cielo" (395).

20. Forcione discusses this in *Cervantes' Christian Romance* 100–101.

21. "Dímonos las manos de legítimos esposos, enterramos el fuego en la nieve, y en paz y en amor, como dos estatuas movibles, ha que vivimos en este lugar casi diez años . . ." (264).

22. The arrival of Renato's brother, and the prospect of being reintegrated into French society as a consequence of his news, evidently alters the balance of desire.

23. This must happen, in fact, since Rutilio reappears later in the novel.

24. "Él representaba el más rústico y disforme bárbaro del mundo" (211; my translation). The terms are strikingly reminiscent of the description of the barbarian Mileno

in Antonio de Guevara's *Relox de príncipes*. Both Mileno and Monipodio have deep-set eyes (*hundidos*), thick beards, a phenomenal growth of hair on the chest, swarthy skin. Both are referred to as "rustic" and "barbarian." A precursor of the noble savage, Mileno represents a fascinating mixture of wild man, barbarian, rustic eutopian, and various other types including colonial reformist (Hutchinson, "Genealogy").

In her article on *Rinconete y Cortadillo,* Dian Fox comments insightfully on the social satire brought about by a perversion of utopian ideals.

25. Harry Sieber notes as much in his introduction to the *novela:* "La entrada en el mundo de Monipodio es una entrada lingüística" (27).

26. The dog Berganza takes on a similar role when he enters the household of Monipodio in the *Coloquio de los perros* (329–30).

27. "Quise guardar esta joya, que yo escogí y vosotros me disteis, con el mayor recato que me fue posible. Alcé las murallas desta casa, quité la vista a las ventanas de la calle, doblé las cerraduras de las puertas, púsele torno, como a monasterio; desterré perpetuamente della todo aquello que sombra o nombre de varón tuviese. Dile criadas y esclavas que la sirviesen; ni le negué a ellas ni a ella cuanto quisieron pedirme; hícela mi igual . . . (132–33).

28. "No se vio monasterio tan cerrado, ni monjas más recogidas, ni manzanas de oro tan guardadas" (106).

29. "No sería razón que a trueco de oír dos, o tres, o cuatro cantares nos pusiésemos a perder tanta virginidad como aquí se encierra. . . . Así es que, señor de mi corazón, vuesa merced nos ha de hacer primero que entre en nuestro reino un muy solene juramento de que no ha de hacer más de lo que nosotras le ordenaremos" (123).

30. All the motifs mentioned here with regard to the infantile paradise, the harem, and of course the convent can be found in one form or another in the writings of Spanish nuns of the sixteenth and seventeenth centuries, published as *Untold Sisters* by Electa Arenal and Stacey Schlau.

31. "Yo fui el que, como el gusano de seda, me fabriqué la casa donde muriese" (133).

32. Leblon insinuates that *La gitanilla* may have germinated out of a family affair: the amorous liaison between the future duke of Infantado, Diego de Mendoza, and the Gypsy María Cabrera resulted in the birth of Don Martín, future archdeacon of Guadalajara and seducer of Cervantes' aunt, who gave birth to Cervantes' cousin Martina (*Les Gitans d'Espagne* 24).

33. In the play *Pedro de Urdemalas,* the "count" of the Gypsies, Maldonado, gives a similar version of Gypsy life and values. Like other Gypsies in theatrical works of the time, he speaks with a heavy lisp.

34. "Vamos a verle muy lejos de aquí, a un gran campo, donde nos juntamos infinidad de gente, brujos y brujas, y allí nos da de comer desabridamente, y pasan otras cosas que en verdad y en Dios y en mi ánima que no me atrevo a contarlas, según son sucias y asquerosas . . ." (339).

35. This and other arguments concerning Cervantine witchcraft are developed in my forthcoming article in *Cervantes* (1992), "Las brujas de Cervantes y la noción de comunidad femenina."

36. In his valuable study of the episode, Francisco Márquez Villanueva (92–145)

cautions against viewing this story as religiously edifying. Much of his argument hinges on his portrayal of Zoraida as egotistical, cold, and calculating with few if any redeeming qualities. This, it seems to me, is a one-sided view of her. Also, by insisting on her literariness and by bringing out folkloric antecedents, Márquez Villanueva allows himself to dismiss Cervantes' falsification of historical personages and sequences of events as almost irrelevant. This strategy focuses analysis on character and interpersonal relationships (Zoraida and the captive, Zoraida and her father), and obscures what it means to belong to one world or another.

37. "Mora es en traje y en el cuerpo; pero en el alma muy grande cristiana, porque tiene grandísimos deseos de serlo" (*DQ* I.37.463).

38. "España cría y tiene en su seno tantas víboras como moriscos" (350).

39. "La Ricota mi hija y Francisca Ricota mi mujer son católicas cristianas, y aunque yo no lo soy tanto, todavía tengo más de cristiano que de moro, y ruego siempre a Dios me abra los ojos del entendimiento y me dé a conocer cómo le tengo de servir" (II.54.452).

40. "Tuve una madre cristiana y un padre discreto y cristiano, ni más ni menos; mamé la fe católica en la leche; criéme con buenas costumbres; ni en la lengua ni en ellas jamás, a mi parecer, di señal de ser morisca" (II.63.527).

41. For discussion on this, see, inter alia, Castro (156–90); Avalle-Arce (Introd. to *La Galatea*); Forcione (*Aristotle* 212–24); Poggioli; El Saffar (*Beyond Fiction* 5–7); Rivers ("Pastoral"); Stagg; Lowe; and M. G. Randel.

42. A similar sequence in Cervantes' interlude, *El rufián viudo,* leaves no doubt that the cannibals are associated with America: "Fuera yo un Polifemo, un antropófago, / un troglodita, un bárbaro Zoílo, / un caimán, un caribe, un come-vivos" (*Entremeses* 83).

43. Arguing against Salvador de Madariaga and Gonzalo Torrente Ballester, who claim that Don Quixote's tale of the cave is a conscious fiction, E. C. Riley makes a convincing case for the dream logic of the episode ("Metamorphosis" 111–19).

44. As far as I know, Sancho always uses the term *insula* except on one occasion where he uses the familiar *isla,* as does his interlocutor Sansón Carrasco (II.3.62). For that matter, the land-based Sancho may well have no concept of what an *isla* is. However that may be, he never does discover what an *insula* is, since even after his departure from the Insula Barataria, Ricote fails to convince him that *insulas* are only to be found in the sea, not on *tierra firme* (II.54.453). His wife for her part has no idea what he's talking about when he refers to *insulas.* Interestingly, she later tells Sancho to go off and be "a government or *ínsulo*" ("idos a ser gobierno o ínsulo" [II.5.76; cf. "sin ínsulos ni ínsulas," I.26.324]).

45. When Sancho begs his master for an *insula* after the victory against the Basque, Don Quixote replies: "Observe, brother Sancho, that this adventure and others like it are adventures not of *insulas* but of crossroads, from which nothing is to be gained but a broken head and the loss of an ear. Be patient, for adventures will occur whereby I shall be able to make you not only governor, but something greater still" (I.10.147).

46. Redondo analyzes the carnivalesque associations with, among other things,

the name "Barataria," the symbolism of the dress and the animal Sancho rides, the types of spectacle and trials, the birth and death imagery, the roles played by those who participate actively in the joke, the name of the doctor who persecutes Sancho, and the expulsion reminiscent of the battle between Carnival and Lent ("Tradición carnavalesca" 51–70).

47. "'Ahora bien', respondió Sancho, 'venga esa ínsula; . . . y esto no es por codicia que yo tenga de salir de mis casillas ni de levantarme a mayores, sino por el deseo que tengo de probar a qué sabe el ser gobernador" (II.42.356).

48. "Dejadme que vaya a buscar la vida pasada, para que me resucite de esta muerte presente. Yo no nací para ser gobernador. . . . digan al duque mi señor que, desnudo nací, desnudo me hallo: ni pierdo ni gano; quiero decir, que sin blanca entré en este gobierno, y sin ella salgo" (II.53.444–45; cf. II.5.74).

49. "Aquí nuestro autor lo dice por la presteza con que se acabó, se consumió, se deshizo, se fue como en sombra y humo el gobierno de Sancho" (II.53.440).

Chapter 5. Narrative Passages

1. For a fuller discussion of this episode, see Mary Gaylord Randel, "Ending and Meaning in Cervantes' *Persiles y Sigismunda*" 154–56, and Diana de Armas Wilson, "Cervantes' Last Romance" 110–11.

Given Cervantes' own lifelong labors first in the service of Mars and later in that of Apollo and Mercury, the pilgrim's astrological influences and life trajectory are significant: "Sobre la mitad de mi alma predomina Marte, y sobre la otra mitad Mercurio y Apolo. Algunos años me he dado al ejercicio de la guerra, y los más maduros, en el de las letras. En los de la guerra he alcanzado algún buen nombre, y por los de las letras he sido algún tanto estimado. Algunos libros he impreso, de los ignorantes non condenados por malos, ni de los discretos han dejado de ser tenidos por buenos. Y como la necesidad, según se dice, es maestra de avivar los ingenios . . ." (416).

2. "Las *peregrinaciones largas* siempre traen consigo diversos acontecimientos, y como la diversidad se compone de cosas diferentes, es forzoso que los casos lo sean.

"Bien nos lo muestra esta historia, cuyos acontecimientos nos cortan su hilo, poniéndonos en duda dónde será bien anudarle; porque no todas las cosas que suceden son buenas para contadas, y podrán pasar sin serlo y sin quedar menoscabada la historia: acciones hay que, por grandes, deben de callarse, y otras que, por bajas, no deben decirse; puesto que es excelencia de la historia, que cualquiera cosa que en ella se escribía puede pasar al sabor de la verdad que trae consigo; lo que no tiene la fábula, a quien conviene guisar sus acciones con tanta puntualidad y gusto, y con tanta verisimilitud, que a despecho y pesar de la mentira, que hace disonancia en el entendimiento, forme una verdadera armonía.

"Aprochándome, pues, desta verdad, digo que el hermoso escuadrón de los peregrinos, prosiguiendo su viaje, llegó a un lugar, no muy pequeño ni muy grande, de cuyo nombre no me acuerdo . . ." (342–43).

3. I am grateful to Lorin Uffenbeck for the following citations from Stendhal's *Oeuvres complètes* 1:288 and 2:224 — *Le Rouge et le noir* I.13 and II.19 — (the attribution to Saint-Réal turns out to be apocryphal):

Un roman: c'est un miroir qu'on promène le long d'un chemin.
SAINT-RÉAL.

Eh, Monsieur, un roman est un miroir qui se promène sur une grande route. Tantôt il reflète à vos yeux l'azur des cieux, tantôt la fange des bourbiers de la route. Et l'homme qui porte le miroir dans sa hotte sera pour vous accusé d'être immoral! Son miroir montre la fange, et vous accusez le miroir! Accusez bien plutôt le grand chemin où est le bourbier, et plus encore l'inspecteur des routes qui laisse l'eau croupir et le bourbier se former.

4. The terrible *telos* of experience here recalls Mallarmé's famous statement "Tout le monde existe pour aboutir à un livre."

5. For a study of the transmission of *ḥadīth*, see my article, "Counterfeit Chains of Discourse: A Comparison of Citation in Cervantes' *Casamiento/Coloquio* and in Islamic *Ḥadīth*.

6. Other very suggestive Arabic terms relating experience or movement and discourse include the verb *sāfara* (to travel), with related nouns *safra* (journey), *sifr* (book, especially one of the scriptures), and *safīr* (mediator, ambassador); *qaṣṣa*, whose basic idea is to cut, but in the expression *qaṣṣa atharahu* means to follow someone's tracks (or follow a trace, or pursue the course of the tradition), and in form VIII means to tell, narrate — the derivative nouns figure among the most important terms for denoting narrative, tale, storyteller, novelist; and words derived from the root *nql,* a very basic set of radicals for describing not only movement but also verbal transmission, translation, passages of discourse, and so on.

7. The transitivity of traveling here recalls Nietzsche's phrase "sie werden eigentlich *gereist*" (*Human* 271).

8. "Contad, señor, lo que quisiéredes y con las menudencias que quisiéredes. . . . Así que, señor seguid vuestra historia, contad de Alonso y de Martina, acocead a vuestro gusto a Luisa, casalda o no la caséis, séase ella libre y desenvuelta como un cernícalo, que el toque no está en sus desenvolturas, sino en sus sucesos" (322–23).

9. Under "mode," *The New Harvard Dictionary of Music* (ed. Don Michael Randel) states that "no single concept usefully embraces all that has been meant by the term throughout the history of Western music as well as all that is meant by the terms associated with non-Western music that have at one time or another been translated as mode." Referring to scale, melody, and emotion, it goes on to say that "in some non-Western art musics . . . such concepts may explicitly underlie a largely improvisatory practice. The latter may include the *maqām* and *dastgāh* of musics of the Near and Middle East and the *rāga* of South Asia. In jazz, the term mode has been applied to scales other than the major or minor scale that may serve as the basis for sometimes extended improvisation over a simple harmony, as in some music by Miles Davis." (Other discussions of modal music include Sadie 12:376–450 and Kernfeld 1:561 and 2:116–17).

10. Though Eco seems to associate the open work almost exclusively with the twentieth century, and though he clings to the notion of structure with reference to both thought processes and the temporal arts even as he critiques Lévi-Strauss (12, 24, 217–21), his inquiry into a poetics of the open work is highly relevant to such works in general, regardless of where and when they were produced. Curiously, his point of departure is none other than experimental music.

11. My translation. "Un hombre se propone la tarea de dibujar el mundo. A lo largo de los años puebla un espacio con imágenes de provincias, de reinos, de montañas, de bahías, de naves, de islas, de peces, de habitaciones, de instrumentos, de astros, de caballos y de personas. Poco antes de morir, descubre que ese paciente laberinto de líneas trazó la imagen de su cara" (155–56).

12. "Yo, señor Arnaldo, soy hecho como esto que se llama lugar, que es donde todas las cosas caben, y no hay ninguna fuera del lugar, y en mí le tienen todas las que son desgraciadas, aunque, por haber hallado a mi hermana Auristela, las juzgo por dichosas; que el mal que se acaba sin acabar la vida, no lo es" (227).

13. I take this expression from the narrator in La gitanilla, who says that "hunger sometimes impels the imagination to things that aren't on the map" (63).

14. This notion is a leitmotiv throughout his writings. Here are a few sample passages:

"Not settled. — . . . This is the life of modern men: they are in everything too thorough to be settled" (Human 366).

"We who are homeless. —We children of the future, how could we be at home in this today? We feel disfavor for all ideals that might lead one to feel at home even in this fragile, broken time of transition" (Gay Science no. 377).

"The settled and the free. — . . . the mother of Odysseus died of grief and of longing for her child! One person moves restlessly from place to place, and the heart of another who is settled and tender breaks as a consequence: so it has always been! Sorrow breaks the heart of those to whom it happens that he whom they love best deserts their faith — this is part of the tragedy which free spirits produce and of which they are sometimes aware! Then they too have at some time or other to go down to the dead like Odysseus to assuage their grief and soothe their tenderness" (Daybreak no. 562).

"From all mountains I look out for fatherlands and motherlands. But home I found nowhere; a fugitive am I in all cities and a departure at all gates. . . . Thus I now love only my children's land, yet undiscovered, in the farthest sea: for this I bid my sails search and search" (Zarathustra 233).

Bibliography

Adams, Percy. *Travel Literature and the Evolution of the Novel.* Lexington: UP Kentucky, 1983.

Akhundov, Murad D. *Conceptions of Space and Time: Sources, Evolution, Directions.* Trans. Charles Rougle. Cambridge, Mass.: MIT Press, 1986.

Alperson, Philip. "On Musical Improvisation." *Journal of Aesthetics and Art Criticism* 43 (1984): 17–29.

Alzieu, Pierre; Robert Jammes; and Yvan Lissorgues, eds. *Floresta de poesías eróticas del siglo de oro.* Toulouse: Université de Toulouse, 1975.

Anderson, John M. *The Grammar of Case: Towards a Localistic Theory.* Cambridge: Cambridge UP, 1971.

Andrist, Debra D. "Male Versus Female Friendship in *Don Quijote.*" *Cervantes* 3 (1983): 149–59.

Arac, Jonathan. "Lyric Poetry and the Bounds of New Criticism." In *Lyric Poetry beyond New Criticism,* ed. Chaviva Hošek and Patricia Parker. Ithaca, N.Y.: Cornell UP, 1985. 345–55.

Arenal, Electa, and Stacey Schlau. *Untold Sisters: Hispanic Nuns in Their Own Works.* Albuquerque: U New Mexico P, 1989.

Ariosto, Ludovico. *Orlando Furioso.* Trans. Guido Waldman. New York: Oxford UP, 1974.

Aristotle. *The Basic Works of Aristotle.* Ed. Richard McKeon. New York: Random House, 1941.

Augustine. *Confessions.* Trans. Rex Warner. New York: Mentor, 1963.

Avalle-Arce, Juan Bautista. *Nuevos deslindes cervantinos.* Barcelona: Ariel, 1975.

Avellaneda, Alonso Fernández de. *El ingenioso hidalgo don Quijote de la Mancha.* Ed. Agustín del Saz. Barcelona: Juventud, 1980.

Ayala, Francisco. *Cervantes y Quevedo.* Barcelona: Seix Barral, 1974.

Bakhtin, Mikhail M. *The Dialogic Imagination: Four Essays.* Trans. Caryl Emerson and Michael Holquist. Ed. Michael Holquist. Austin: U Texas P, 1981.

Bakhtin, Mikhail M. *Rabelais and His World.* Trans. Hélène Iswolsky. Boston: Massachusetts Institute of Technology, 1968.

Bakhtin, Mikhail M. *Speech Genres and Other Late Essays.* Trans. Vern W. McGee. Ed. Caryl Emerson and Michael Holquist. Austin: U Texas P, 1986.

Bakhtin, Mikhail M., and P. N. Medvedev. *The Formal Method in Literary Scholarship: A Critical Introduction to Sociological Poetics.* Trans. Albert J. Wehrle. Cambridge, Mass.: Harvard UP, 1985.

Balliett, Whitney. *Improvising: Sixteen Jazz Musicians and Their Art.* New York: Oxford UP, 1977.

Ballmer, Thomas T., ed. *Linguistic Dynamics: Discourses, Procedures and Evolution.* New York: Walter de Gruyter, 1985.

Barriga Casalini, Guillermo. *Los dos mundos del* Quijote: *Realidad y ficción.* Madrid: José Porrúa Turanzas, 1983.

Basho, Matsuo. *The Narrow Road through the Provinces (Oku no Hosomichi). Japanese Poetic Diaries.* Trans. and ed. Earl Miner. Berkeley: U California P, 1969. 157–97.

Benjamin, Walter. *Illuminations: Essays and Reflections.* Trans. Harry Zohn. Ed Hannah Arendt. New York: Schocken Books, 1968.

Benveniste, Emile. *Indo-European Language and Society.* Trans. Elizabeth Palmer. London: Faber and Faber, 1973.

Bergson, Henri. *Creative Evolution.* Trans. Arthur Mitchell. New York: Henry Holt, 1907.

Bergson, Henri. *Le Rire. Oeuvres.* Paris: Presses Universitaires de France, 1970. 383–485.

Blanchot, Maurice. *The Writing of the Disaster.* Trans. Ann Smock. Lincoln: U Nebraska P, 1986.

Bloom, Harold, ed. *The Art of the Critic: Literary Theory and Criticism from the Greeks to the Present.* 7 vols. New York: Chelsea House, 1985.

Bloom, Harold, ed. *Cervantes: Modern Critical Views.* New York: Chelsea House, 1987.

Bordwell, David. *Narration in the Fiction Film.* Madison: U Wisconsin P, 1985.

Borges, Jorge Luis. *El Hacedor.* Madrid: Alianza, 1972.

Borges, Jorge Luis. *Prosa completa.* 2 vols. Barcelona: Bruguera, 1980.

Bowman, Leonard J., ed. Itinerarium: *The Idea of Journey.* Salzburg: Institut für Anglistik und Amerikanistik, 1983.

Brancaforte, Benito. "El diálogo de Cervantes con la locura." In *Homenaje a José Antonio Maravall,* ed. María Carmen Iglesias, Carlos Moya, and Luis Rodríguez Zúñiga. Madrid: Centro de Investigaciones Sociológicas, 1985. 329–42.

Braudel, Fernand. *The Mediterranean and the Mediterranean World in the Age of Philip II.* Trans. Siân Reynolds. 2 vols. New York: Harper & Row, 1976.

Butor, Michel. "Travel and Writing." *Mosaic* 8 (1974): 1–16.

Campbell, Mary B. *The Witness and the Other World: Exotic European Travel Writing, 400–1600.* Ithaca, N.Y.: Cornell UP, 1988.

Canavaggio, Jean. *Cervantès.* Paris: Mazarine, 1986.

Caro Baroja, Julio. *Las brujas y su mundo.* Madrid: Revista de Occidente, 1961.

Carson, Anne. *Eros the Bittersweet.* Princeton: Princeton UP, 1986.

Castro, Américo. "La estructura del *Quijote.*" *Hacia Cervantes.* Madrid: Taurus, 1967. 308–17.

Castro, Américo. *El pensamiento de Cervantes.* 1925. Madrid: Editorial Crítica, 1987.

Certeau, Michel de. *Heterologies: Discourse on the Other.* Trans. Brian Massumi. Minneapolis: U Minnesota P, 1986.

Cervantes Saavedra, Miguel de. *El cerco de Numancia.* Ed. Robert Marrast. Madrid: Cátedra, 1984.

Cervantes Saavedra, Miguel de. *Don Quijote de la Mancha*. Ed. Luis Andrés Murillo. 5th ed. 3 vols. Madrid: Castalia, 1987. (*DQ*)

Cervantes Saavedra, Miguel de. *Entremeses*. Ed. Eugenio Asensio. Madrid: Castalia, 1970.

Cervantes Saavedra, Miguel de. *La Galatea*. Ed. Juan Bautista Avalle-Arce. Madrid: Espasa-Calpe, 1987. (*Gal*)

Cervantes Saavedra, Miguel de. *Novelas ejemplares*. Ed. Harry Sieber. 2 vols. Madrid: Cátedra, 1981. (*NE*) Abbreviations and page numbers of the *novelas* are the following:

La gitanilla	*Git*	1:59–134
El amante liberal	*AL*	1:135–88
Rinconete y Cortadillo	*RC*	1:189–240
La española inglesa	*EI*	1:241–83
El licenciado Vidriera	*LV*	2:41–74
La fuerza de la sangre	*FS*	2:75–95
El celoso extremeño	*CEx*	2:98–135
La ilustre fregona	*IF*	2:137–98
Las dos doncellas	*DD*	2:199–237
La señora Cornelia	*SC*	2:239–77
El casamiento engañoso	*CEn*	2:279–95
El coloquio de los perros	*CP*	2:297–359

Cervantes Saavedra, Miguel de. *Las semanas del jardín*. Ed. Daniel Eisenberg. Salamanca: Diputación de Salamanca, 1988 [1989]. (*SJ*)

Cervantes Saavedra, Miguel de. *Teatro completo*. Ed. Florencio Sevilla Arroyo and Antonio Rey Hazas. Barcelona: Planeta, 1987.

Cervantes Saavedra, Miguel de. *Los trabajos de Persiles y Sigismunda*. Ed. Juan Bautista Avalle-Arce. Madrid: Castalia, 1969. (*PS*)

Cervantes Saavedra, Miguel de. *Viaje del Parnaso*. Ed. Vicente Gaos. Vol. 1 of *Poesías completas*. Madrid: Castalia, 1973.

Chernoff, John Miller. *African Rhythm and African Sensibility: Aesthetics and Social Action in African Musical Idioms*. Chicago: U Chicago P, 1979.

Clark, Katerina, and Michael Holquist. *Mikhail Bakhtin*. Cambridge, Mass.: Harvard UP, 1984.

Combet, Louis. *Cervantès, ou les incertitudes du désir*. Lyon: Presses Universitaires de Lyon, 1980.

Criado de Val, Manuel, ed. *Cervantes: Su obra y su mundo. Actas del I Congreso Internacional sobre Cervantes*. Madrid: EDI, 1981.

Couliano, Ioan P. *Eros and Magic in the Renaissance*. Trans. Margaret Cook. Chicago: U Chicago P, 1987.

Cull, John T. "The 'Knight of the Broken Lance' and his 'Trusty Steed': On Don Quixote and Rocinante." *Cervantes* 10 (1990): 37–51.

Curtius, Ernst Robert. *European Literature and the Latin Middle Ages*. Princeton: Princeton UP, 1953.

Davis, Miles, with Quincy Troupe. *Miles: The Autobiography*. New York: Simon and Schuster, 1989.

Deleuze, Gilles. *Cinema I: The Movement-Image.* Minneapolis: U Minnesota P, 1986.

Deleuze, Gilles. "Nomad Thought." In *The New Nietzsche,* ed. David Allison. New York: Delta, 1979.

Deleuze, Gilles, and Félix Guattari. *Kafka: Toward a Minor Literature.* Trans. Dana Polan. Minneapolis: U Minnesota P, 1986.

Deleuze, Gilles, and Félix Guattari. *A Thousand Plateaus: Capitalism and Schizophrenia.* Trans. Brian Massumi. Minneapolis: U Minnesota P, 1987.

Derrida, Jacques. *Of Grammatology.* Trans. Gayatri Chakravorty Spivak. Baltimore: Johns Hopkins UP, 1976.

Derrida, Jacques. *Writing and Difference.* Trans. Alan Bass. Chicago: U Chicago P, 1978.

Détienne, Marcel. *Dionysos at Large.* Trans. Arthur Goldhammer. Cambridge, Mass.: Harvard UP, 1989.

Díaz Migoyo, Gonzalo. "La ficción cordial de *El amante liberal.*" *Nueva Revista de Filología Hispánica* 35 (1987): 129–50.

Diderot, Denis. *Jacques le fataliste et son maître.* Ed. Yvon Belaval. Paris: Gallimard, 1973.

Díez Borque, José María. *La sociedad española y los viajeros del siglo XVII.* Madrid: Sociedad General Española de Librería, 1975.

DiSalvo, Angelo J. "St. Augustine and the *Persiles* of Cervantes." Ed. Donald W. Bleznick. York, S.C.: Spanish Literature Publications, 1984. 55–64.

Duhem, Pierre. *Medieval Cosmology: Theories of Infinity, Place, Time, Void and the Plurality of Worlds.* U Chicago P, 1985.

Dümchen, Sybil. "The Function of Madness in *El licenciado Vidriera.*" In *Cervantes's Exemplary Novels and the Adventure of Writing,* ed. Michael Nerlich and Nicholas Spadaccini. Minneapolis: Prisma Institute, 1989. 99–123.

Düring, Jean. "Le Point de vue du musicien: Improvisation et communication." In Lortat-Jacob 33–44.

Early Greek Philosophy. Ed. Jonathan Barnes. London: Penguin, 1987.

Eco, Umberto. *The Open Work.* Trans. Anna Cancogni. Cambridge, Mass.: Harvard UP, 1989.

Eisenberg, Daniel. *A Study of* Don Quixote. Newark, Del.: Juan de la Cuesta, 1987.

El Saffar, Ruth. *Beyond Fiction: The Recovery of the Feminine in the Novels of Cervantes.* Berkeley: U California P, 1984.

El Saffar, Ruth. *Novel to Romance: A Study of Cervantes's* Novelas ejemplares. Baltimore: Johns Hopkins UP, 1974.

El Saffar, Ruth. "Persiles' Retort: An Alchemical Angle on the Lovers' Labors." *Cervantes* 10 (1990): 17–33.

El Saffar, Ruth. Rev. of *Cervantès ou les incertitudes du désir,* by Louis Combet. *Modern Language Notes* 97 (1982): 422–27.

El Saffar, Ruth. "Sex and the Single Hidalgo: Reflections on Eros in *Don Quixote.*" In *Studies in Honor of Elias Rivers,* ed. Bruno M. Damiani and Ruth El Saffar. Potomac, Md.: Scripta Humanistica, 1989. 76–93.

El Saffar, Ruth. "Tracking the Trickster in the Works of Cervantes." In Bloom, *Cervantes: Modern Critical Views* 151–68.

El Saffar, Ruth. "The Woman at the Border: Some Thoughts on Cervantes and Auto-biography." In *Autobiography in Early Modern Spain,* ed. Nicholas Spadaccini and Jenaro Talens. Minneapolis: Prisma Institute, 1988. 191–214.

El Saffar, Ruth, ed. *Critical Essays on Cervantes.* Boston: G. K. Hall, 1986.

Erasmus, Desiderio. *Adages.* Trans. Margaret Mann Phillips. Vol. 31 of *Collected Works of Erasmus.* Toronto: U Toronto P, 1982.

Espinel, Vicente. *Vida del escudero Marcos de Obregón.* Ed. María Soledad Carrasco Urgoiti. 2 vols. Madrid: Castalia, 1980.

Fabian, Johannes. *Power and Performance: Ethnographic Explorations through Proverbial Wisdom and Theater in Shaba, Zaire.* Madison: U Wisconsin P, 1990.

Fernández Gómez, Carlos. *Vocabulario de Cervantes.* Madrid: Real Academia Española, 1962.

Fielding, Henry. *The History of the Adventures of Joseph Andrews and of His Friend Mr. Abraham Adams.* Ed. R. F. Brissenden. Harmondsworth, Middlesex: Penguin, 1977.

Fielding, Henry. *The History of Tom Jones.* Ed. R. P. C. Mutter. Harmondsworth, Middlesex: Penguin, 1966.

Flores, R. M. "Cervantes at Work: The Writing of *Don Quixote,* Part I." *Journal of Hispanic Philology* 3 (1979): 135–60.

Flores Arroyuelo, Francisco J. *El diablo y los españoles.* Murcia: Universidad de Murcia, 1976.

Forcione, Alban K. *Cervantes and the Humanist Vision: A Study of Four* Exemplary Novels. Princeton: Princeton UP, 1982.

Forcione, Alban K. *Cervantes and the Mystery of Lawlessness: A Study of* El casamiento engañoso y El coloquio de los perros. Princeton: Princeton UP, 1984.

Forcione, Alban K. *Cervantes, Aristotle, and the* Persiles. Princeton: Princeton UP, 1970.

Forcione, Alban K. *Cervantes' Christian Romance: A Study of* Persiles y Sigismunda. Princeton: Princeton UP, 1972.

Foster, Susan Leigh. *Reading Dancing: Bodies and Subjects in Contemporary American Dance.* Berkeley: U California P, 1986.

Foucault, Michel. *The Archaeology of Knowledge and The Discourse on Language.* Trans. A. M. Sheridan Smith and Rupert Sawyer. New York: Harper & Row, 1972.

Foucault, Michel. *The History of Sexuality.* 3 vols. New York: Random House, 1985–86.

Foucault, Michel. *Les Mots et les choses.* Paris: Gallimard, 1966.

Fox, Dian. "The Critical Attitude in *Rinconete y Cortadillo.*" *Cervantes* 3 (1983): 135–47.

Fu, James S. *Mythic and Comic Aspects of the Quest:* Hsi-yu chi *as Seen through* Don Quixote *and* Huckleberry Finn. Singapore: Singapore UP, 1977.

Fuentes, Carlos. *Cervantes o la crítica de la lectura.* Mexico City: Joaquín Mortiz, 1976.

Gadamer, Hans-Georg. *The Relevance of the Beautiful and Other Essays.* Ed. Robert Bernasconi. New York: Cambridge UP, 1986.

García de la Torre, Moisés. "Realidad histórica y ficción literaria: El mundo de los caminos en Cervantes y su época." *Anales Cervantinos* 20 (1982): 113–23.

Gellrich, Jesse M. *The Idea of the Book in the Middle Ages*. Ithaca: Cornell UP, 1985.

Genette, Gérard. *Narrative Discourse: An Essay in Method*. Trans. Jane E. Lewin. Ithaca, N.Y.: Cornell UP, 1980.

Gilman, Stephen. *The Novel according to Cervantes*. Berkeley: U California P, 1989.

Girard, René. *Deceit, Desire, and the Novel: Self and Other in Literary Structure*. Trans. Yvonne Freccero. Baltimore: Johns Hopkins UP, 1965.

Gold, Ann Grodzins. *Fruitful Journeys: The Ways of Rajasthani Pilgrims*. Berkeley: U California P, 1988.

[González, Estebanillo ?] *La vida y hechos de Estebanillo González, hombre de buen humor*. Ed. Nicholas Spadaccini and Anthony N. Zahareas. 2 vols. Madrid: Castalia, 1978.

Gracián, Baltasar. *El criticón*. Ed. Santos Alonso. Madrid: Ediciones Cátedra, 1980.

Guevara, Antonio de. *"El villano del Danubio" y otros fragmentos*. Ed. Américo Castro. Princeton, N.J.: Princeton UP, 1945.

Hahn, Juergen. *The Origins of the Baroque Concept of* Peregrinatio. Chapel Hill: U North Carolina P, 1973.

Haley, George. "The Narrator in *Don Quixote:* Maese Pedro's Puppet Show." *Modern Language Notes* 81 (1966): 145–65.

Harding, D. W. *Words into Rhythm: English Speech Rhythm in Verse and Prose*. New York: Cambridge UP, 1976.

Hart, Thomas R. *Cervantes and Ariosto: Renewing Fiction*. Princeton: Princeton UP, 1989.

Havelock, Eric A. *The Muse Learns to Write*. New Haven: Yale UP, 1986.

Hebreo, León [Leone Ebreo]. *The Philosophy of Love (Dialoghi d'amore)*. Trans. F. Friedenberg and Jean H. Barnes. London: Soncino, 1937.

Heidegger, Martin. *Being and Time*. Trans. John Macquarrie and Edward Robinson. London: SCM Press, 1962.

Heidegger, Martin. *Nietzsche*. Trans. David Farrell Krell. London: Routledge & Kegan Paul, 1981.

Heidegger, Martin. *On the Way to Language*. Trans. Peter D. Hertz. New York: Harper & Row, 1971.

Helms, Mary W. *Ulysses' Sail: An Ethnographic Odyssey of Power, Knowledge, and Geographical Distance*. Princeton, N.J.: Princeton UP, 1988.

Henningsen, Gustav. *The Witches' Advocate: Basque Witchcraft and the Spanish Inquisition (1609–1614)*. Reno: U Nevada P, 1980.

Hopper, Paul J. "Discourse Analysis: Grammar and Critical Theory in the 1980s." *Profession (PMLA)* (1988): 18–24.

Huarte de San Juan, Juan. *Examen de ingenios para las ciencias*. Ed. Esteban Torre. Madrid: Editora Nacional, 1976.

Huerga, Alvaro. "El proceso inquisitorial contra *la Camacha*." In Criado de Val 453–62.

Hutchinson, Steven. "Counterfeit Chains of Discourse: A Comparison of Citation in Cervantes' *Casamiento/Coloquio* and in Islamic Ḥadīth." *Cervantes* 8 (1988): 141–58.

Hutchinson, Steven. "Genealogy of Guevara's Barbarian: An Invented 'Other.'" *Civilization and Its Others: Formulations of Difference.* Ed. Mary Layoun and Jane Tylus. Forthcoming.

Hutchinson, Steven. "Mapping Utopias." *Modern Philology* 85 (1987): 170–85.

Hutchinson, Steven. "El movimiento en la obra de Antonio Machado: Paradojas eleáticas." In *Divergencias y unidad: Perspectivas sobre la Generación del '98 y Antonio Machado,* ed. John P. Gabriele. Madrid: Editorial Orígenes, 1990. 245–54.

Isidore of Seville, Saint. *Etimologías/Etymologiarum.* Ed. José Oroz Reta and Manuel-A. Marcos Casquero. 2 vols. Madrid: Biblioteca de Autores Cristianos, 1982.

Jager, Bernd. "Theorizing, Journeying, Dwelling." In *Duquesne Studies in Phenomenological Psychology,* ed. Amedeo Giorgi, Constance T. Fischer, and Edward L. Murray. 2 vols. Pittsburgh: Duquesne UP, 1975. 2:235–60.

Jakobson, Roman. "Linguistics and Poetics." In *The Structuralists: From Marx to Lévi-Strauss,* ed. Richard T. de George and Fernande M. de George. New York: Doubleday, 1972. 85–122.

Johnson, Carroll B. Don Quixote: *The Quest for Modern Fiction.* Boston: G. K. Hall, 1990.

Johnson, Carroll B. *Madness and Lust: A Psychoanalytical Approach to* Don Quixote. Berkeley: U California P, 1983.

Juana Inés de la Cruz. *Inundación castálida.* Ed. Georgina Sabat de Rivers. Madrid: Castalia, 1982.

Kamen, Henry. *Spain, 1469–1714: A Society of Conflict.* New York: Longman, 1983.

Kernfeld, Barry, ed. *The New Grove Dictionary of Jazz.* 2 vols. New York: Macmillan, 1988.

Kittay, Jeffrey, and Wlad Godzich. *The Emergence of Prose: An Essay in Prosaics.* Minneapolis: U Minnesota P, 1987.

Kolodny, Annette. *The Lay of the Land: Metaphor as Experience and History in American Life and Letters.* Chapel Hill: U North Carolina P, 1975.

Kristeller, Paul Oskar. *The Philosophy of Marsilio Ficino.* Trans. Virginia Conant. Gloucester, Mass.: Peter Smith, 1964.

Kristeva, Julia. *Revolution in Poetic Language.* Trans. Margaret Waller. New York: Columbia UP, 1984.

Kristeva, Julia. *Tales of Love.* Trans. Leon S. Roudiez. New York: Columbia UP, 1987.

Lacan, Jacques. *Écrits: A Selection.* Trans. Alan Sheridan. New York: Norton, 1977.

Lacan, Jacques. *The Four Fundamental Concepts of Psycho-Analysis.* Trans. Alan Sheridan. New York: Norton, 1977.

Lakoff, George, and Mark Johnson. *Metaphors We Live By.* Chicago: U Chicago P, 1980.

Leblon, Bernard. *Les Gitans dans la littérature espagnole.* Toulouse: Institut d'Etudes Hispaniques et Hispano-Américaines, 1982.

Leblon, Bernard. *Les Gitans d'Espagne.* Paris: Presses Universitaires de France, 1985.

Leed, Eric J. *The Mind of the Traveler: From Gilgamesh to Global Tourism.* New York: Basic Books, 1991.

León, Luis de. *Obras completas castellanas.* Ed. Félix García. 2 vols. 4th ed. Madrid: Biblioteca de Autores Cristianos, 1957.

Lévi-Strauss, Claude. "The Structural Study of Myth." In *The Structuralists: From Marx to Lévi-Strauss,* ed. Richard T. de George and Fernande M. de George. New York: Doubleday, 1972. 169–94.

Liu, James J. Y. *Chinese Theories of Literature.* Chicago: U Chicago P, 1975.

Longinus. *On the Sublime.* Trans. D. A. Russell. In Bloom, *Art of the Critic* 1:325–59.

Lortat-Jacob, Bernard, ed. *L'Improvisation dans les musiques de tradition orale.* Paris: SELAF, 1987.

Lowe, Jennifer. "The *cuestión de amor* and the Structure of Cervantes' *Galatea.*" *Bulletin of Hispanic Studies* 43 (1966): 98–109.

Lozano, Jorge; Cristina Peña-Marín; and Gonzalo Abril. *Análisis del discurso: Hacia una semiótica de la interacción.* Madrid: Cátedra, 1982.

Lucas, George R., Jr. *The Genesis of Modern Process Thought: A Historical Outline with Bibliography.* London: Scarecrow Press and the American Theological Library Association, 1983.

Luna, José-Carlos de. *Gitanos de la Bética.* Madrid: EPESA, 1951.

Lyons, John. *Semantics.* 2 vols. New York: Cambridge UP, 1977.

Madariaga, Salvador de. *Guía del lector del* Quijote: *Ensayo psicológico sobre el* Quijote. 1926. Madrid: Espasa Calpe, 1976.

Mancing, Howard. *The Chivalric World of* Don Quixote: *Style, Structure, and Narrative Technique.* Columbia: U Missouri P, 1982.

Maravall, José Antonio. *Utopía y contrautopía en el* Quijote. Santiago de Compostela: Pico Sacro, 1976.

Mariscal, George. "*Persiles* and the Remaking of Spanish Culture." *Cervantes* 10 (1990): 93–102.

Márquez Villanueva, Francisco. *Personajes y temas del* Quijote. Madrid: Taurus, 1975.

Martin, Wallace. *Recent Theories of Narrative.* Ithaca, N.Y.: Cornell UP, 1986.

Marx, Karl, and Friedrich Engels. *The Marx-Engels Reader.* 2d ed. Ed. Robert C. Tucker. New York: W. W. Norton, 1978.

McGaha, Michael D., ed. *Cervantes and the Renaissance.* Easton, Penn.: Juan de la Cuesta, 1980.

Medam, Alain. *L'Esprit au long cours: Pour une sociologie du voyage.* Paris: Anthropos, 1982.

Meltzer, Françoise. *Salome and the Dance of Writing: Portraits of Mimesis in Literature.* U Chicago P, 1987.

Ménager, Daniel. "Improvisation et mémoire dans les *Essais.*" *Bulletin de la Société des Amis de Montaigne* 7 (1985): 101–10.

Meschonnic, Henri. *Critique du rythme: Anthropologie historique du langage.* Paris: Verdier, 1982.

Miller, Georga A., and Philip N. Johnson-Laird. *Language and Perception.* London: Cambridge UP, 1976.

Moi, Toril. *Sexual/Textual Politics: Feminist Literary Theory.* New York: Routledge, 1985.

Molho, Mauricio. *Cervantes: Raíces folklóricas.* Madrid: Gredos, 1976.

Moner, Michel. *Cervantès conteur: Écrits et paroles*. Madrid: Casa de Velázquez, 1989.

Montaigne, Michel Eyquem de. *Oeuvres complètes*. Ed. Maurice Rat. Paris: Gallimard, 1962.

More, Thomas. *Utopia*. Trans. Paul Turner. Harmondsworth, Middlesex: Penguin, 1965.

Navarro González, Alberto. "Cambio de itinerario en el *Persiles* y en el *Quijote* de Cervantes." In *Essays on Narrative Fiction in the Iberian Peninsula in Honour of Frank Pierce*, ed. R. B. Tate. Valencia: Dolphin, 1982. 89–93.

Nelson, John Charles. *Renaissance Theory of Love: The Context of Giordano Bruno's Eroici furori*. New York: Columbia UP, 1958.

Nerlich, Michael. *Ideology of Adventure: Studies in Modern Consciousness, 1100–1750*. Trans. Ruth Crowley. 2 vols. Minneapolis: U Minnesota P, 1987.

Newton, Arthur Percival, ed. *Travel and Travellers of the Middle Ages*. New York: Alfred A. Knopf, 1926.

Nietzsche, Friedrich. *Basic Writings of Nietzsche*. [Includes *The Birth of Tragedy, Beyond Good and Evil, On the Genealogy of Morals, The Case of Wagner, Ecce Homo*.] Trans. and ed. Walter Kaufmann. New York: Random House, 1968.

Nietzsche, Friedrich. *Daybreak: Thoughts on the Prejudices of Morality*. Trans. R. J. Hollingdale. New York: Cambridge UP, 1982.

Nietzsche, Friedrich. *The Gay Science*. Trans. and ed. Walter Kaufmann. New York: Random House, 1974.

Nietzsche, Friedrich. *Human, All Too Human: A Book for Free Spirits*. Trans. R. J. Hollingdale. New York: Cambridge UP, 1986.

Nietzsche, Friedrich. *Philosophy in the Tragic Age of the Greeks*. Trans. Marianne Cowan. Chicago: Henry Regnery, 1962.

Nietzsche, Friedrich. *The Portable Nietzsche*. [Includes *Thus Spoke Zarathustra, Twilight of the Idols, The Antichrist*, and *Nietzsche contra Wagner*, as well as selected letters and fragments.] Trans. and ed. Walter Kaufmann. Harmondsworth, Middlesex: Penguin, 1954.

Nietzsche, Friedrich. *The Will to Power*. Trans. Walter Kaufmann and R. J. Hollingdale. Ed. Walter Kaufmann. New York: Random House, 1967.

Norton, Glyn P. "Strategies of Fluency in the French Renaissance Text: Improvisation and the Art of Writing." *Journal of Medieval and Renaissance Studies* 15 (1985): 85–99.

Ong, Walter J. *Orality and Literacy: The Technologizing of the Word*. New York: Methuen, 1982.

Ortega y Gasset, José. *Meditaciones del* Quijote. *Con comentario por Julián Marías*. 2d ed. Madrid: Revista de Occidente, 1966.

Ostransky, Leroy. *The Anatomy of Jazz*. Seattle: U Washington P, 1960.

Paiewonsky-Conde, Edgar. "Cervantes y la teoría renacentista del deseo." *Anales Cervantinos* 23 (1985): 71–81.

Parr, James A. Don Quixote: *An Analysis of Subversive Discourse*. Newark, Del.: Juan de la Cuesta, 1988.

Pavel, Thomas G. *Fictional Worlds*. Cambridge, Mass.: Harvard UP, 1986.

Percas de Ponseti, Helena. "The Cave of Montesinos: Cervantes' Art of Fiction." In *Don Quixote: The Ormsby Translation, Revised Backgrounds and Sources Criticism*, ed. Joseph R. Jones and Kenneth Douglas. New York: W. W. Norton, 1981. 979–94.

Percas de Ponseti, Helena. *Cervantes the Writer and Painter of* Don Quixote. Columbia: U Missouri P, 1988.

Percas de Ponseti, Helena. "Los consejos de don Quijote a Sancho." In McGaha 194–236.

Pérez Botero, Luis. "La concepción del mundo en las tres salidas de don Quijote." In Criado de Val 515–19.

Plato. *The Collected Dialogues of Plato Including the Letters.* Ed. Edith Hamilton and Huntington Cairns. Princeton: Princeton UP, 1961.

Plutarch. *Alexander.* Trans. Bernadotte Perrin. Vol. 7 of *Plutarch's Lives.* New York: G. P. Putnam, 1919.

Poggioli, Renato. *The Oaten Flute: Essays on Pastoral Poetry and the Pastoral Ideal.* Cambridge, Mass.: Harvard UP, 1975.

Pokorny, Julius. *Indogermanisches etymologisches Wörterbuch.* Bern: Francke, 1959.

Predmore, Richard L. *Cervantes.* New York: Dodd, Mead, 1973.

Predmore, Richard L. *The World of Don Quixote.* Cambridge, Mass.: Harvard UP, 1967.

Priestley, Brian. *John Coltrane.* London: Apollo, 1987.

Quevedo, Francisco de. *La vida del Buscón llamado don Pablos.* Ed. Domingo Ynduráin. 2d ed. Madrid: Cátedra, 1980.

Rabelais, François. *Oeuvres complètes.* Ed. Pierre Jourda. 2 vols. Paris: Garnier, 1962.

Ragland-Sullivan, Ellie. *Jacques Lacan and the Philosophy of Psychoanalysis.* Chicago: U Chicago P, 1986.

Ramaiah, C. *The Problem of Change and Identity in Indian Philosophy.* Tirupati: Sri Venkateswara UP, 1978.

Randel, Don Michael, ed. *The New Harvard Dictionary of Music.* Cambridge, Mass.: Harvard UP, 1986.

Randel, Mary Gaylord. "Cervantes' Portrait of the Artist." *Cervantes* 3 (1983): 83–102.

Randel, Mary Gaylord. "Ending and Meaning in Cervantes' *Persiles y Sigismunda.*" *Romanic Review* 74 (1983): 152–69.

Randel, Mary Gaylord. "The Language of Limits and the Limits of Language: The Crisis of Poetry in *La Galatea.*" *Modern Language Notes* 97 (1982): 254–71.

Rawson, Philip, and Legeza, Laszlo. *Tao: The Chinese Philosophy of Time and Change.* New York: Thames and Hudson, 1973.

Redondo, Augustin. "El proceso iniciático en el episodio de la cueva de Montesinos del *Quijote.*" In Criado de Val 749–60.

Redondo, Augustin. "Tradición carnavalesca y creación literaria, del personaje de Sancho Panza al episodio de la Insula Barataria en el *Quijote.*" *Bulletin Hispanique* 80 (1978): 39–70.

Reverte Coma, José Manuel. *La antropología médica y el* Quijote. 2d ed. Madrid: Fur, 1980.

Reyre, Dominique. *Dictionnaire des noms des personnages du* Don Quichotte *de Cer-*

vantès, suivi d'une analyse structurale et linguistique. Paris: Editions Hispaniques, 1980.

Ricoeur, Paul. *Interpretation Theory: Discourse and the Surplus of Meaning.* Fort Worth, Texas: Texas Christian UP, 1976.

Ricoeur, Paul. *Time and Narrative.* Trans. Kathleen McLaughlin and David Pellauer. Vol. 2. Chicago: U Chicago P, 1984.

Riley, E. C. Don Quixote. London: Allen & Unwin, 1986.

Riley, E. C. "Episodio, novela y aventura en *Don Quijote.*" *Anales Cervantinos* 5 (1955–56): 209–230.

Riley, E. C. "Metamorphosis, Myth and Dream in the Cave of Montesinos." In *Essays on Narrative Fiction in the Iberian Peninsula in Honour of Frank Pierce,* ed. R. B. Tate, Valencia: Dolphin, 1982. 105–119.

Riley, E. C. *Teoría de la novela en Cervantes.* Trans. Carlos Sahagún. Madrid: Taurus, 1981.

Ríos, Julián. *Larva: Babel de una noche de San Juan.* Madrid: Mondadori, 1988.

Riquer, Martín de, ed. *Don Quijote de la Mancha.* By Miguel de Cervantes Saavedra. Barcelona: Juventud, 1968.

Rivers, Elias L. "Pastoral, Feminism and Dialogue in Cervantes." In La Galatea *de Cervantes — cuatrocientos años después (Cervantes y lo pastoril),* ed. Juan Bautista Avalle-Arce. Newark, Del.: Juan de la Cuesta, 1985. 7–15.

Rivers, Elias L. *Quixotic Scriptures: Essays on the Textuality of Hispanic Literature.* Bloomington: Indiana UP, 1983.

Rivers, Elias L., ed. *Garcilaso de la Vega: Obras completas.* Madrid: Castalia, 1974.

Robert, Marthe. *The Old and the New: From Don Quixote to Kafka.* Trans. Carol Cosman. Berkeley: U California P, 1977.

Rosmarin, Adena. *The Power of Genre.* Minneapolis: U Minnesota P, 1985.

Ruta, María Caterina. "Zoraida: Los signos del silencio en un personaje cervantino." *Anales Cervantinos* 21 (1983): 119–33.

Sadie, Stanley, ed. *The New Grove Dictionary of Music and Musicians.* 20 vols. London: Macmillan, 1980.

Said, Edward W. *The World, the Text, and the Critic.* Cambridge, Mass.: Harvard UP, 1983.

Salih, Tayeb. *Season of Migration to the North.* London: Heinemann, 1976.

Sarduy, Severo. *Barroco.* Buenos Aires: Editorial Sudamericana, 1974.

Saussure, Ferdinand de. *Course in General Linguistics.* Trans. Wade Baskin. Ed. Charles Bally and Albert Sechehaye. New York: McGraw-Hill, 1966.

Scarron, Paul. *Le Roman comique.* Ed. Yves Giraud. Paris: Flammarion, 1981.

Schivelbusch, Wolfgang. *The Railway Journey: The Industrialization of Time and Space in the Nineteenth Century.* Berkeley: U California P, 1986.

Schutz, Alfred. "On Multiple Realities." *The Problem of Social Reality.* Vol. 1 of *Collected Papers.* Boston: Martinus Nijhoff, 1962. 207–59.

Serres, Michel. *Hermes: Literature, Science, Philosophy.* Ed. Josué V. Harari and David F. Bell. Baltimore: Johns Hopkins UP, 1982.

Sheriff, John K. *The Fate of Meaning: Charles Peirce, Structuralism, and Literature.* Princeton: Princeton UP, 1989.

Simmel, Georg. *On Individuality and Social Forms: Selected Writings.* Ed. Donald N. Levine. Chicago: U Chicago P, 1971.

Smith, Jonathan Z. *Map Is Not Territory: Studies in the History of Religions.* Leiden: E. J. Brill, 1978.

Smith, Paul Julian. *Writing in the Margin: Spanish Literature of the Golden Age.* New York: Oxford UP, 1988.

Soja, Edward W. *Postmodern Geographies: The Reassertion of Space in Critical Social Theory.* New York: Verso, 1989.

Stagg, Geoffrey L. "*Illo tempore:* Don Quixote's Discourse on the Golden Age, and Its Antecedents." In La Galatea *de Cervantes — cuatrocientos años después (Cervantes y lo pastoril),* ed. Juan Bautista Avalle-Arce. Newark, Delaware: Juan de la Cuesta, 1985. 71–90.

Steiner, George. *Martin Heidegger.* Harmondsworth, Middlesex: Penguin, 1978.

Stendhal. *Oeuvres complètes.* Ed. Victor del Litto and Ernest Abravanel. 2 vols. Geneva: Edito-Service, 1967.

Sterne, Laurence. *The Life and Opinions of Tristram Shandy, Gentleman.* Ed. Graham Petrie. Introd. A. Alvarez. Harmondsworth, Middlesex: Penguin, 1967.

Stubbs, Michael. *Discourse Analysis.* U Chicago P, 1983.

Sudnow, David. *Ways of the Hand: The Organization of Improvised Conduct.* Cambridge, Mass.: Harvard UP, 1978.

Tao te Ching. Trans. D. C. Lau. Harmondsworth, Middlesex: Penguin, 1963.

Tompkins, Jane P. "The Reader in History: The Changing Shape of Literary Response." In *Reader-Response Criticism from Formalism to Post-Structuralism,* ed. Jane P. Tompkins. Baltimore: Johns Hopkins UP, 1980. 201–32.

Torrente Ballester, Gonzalo, *El* Quijote *como juego, y otros trabajos críticos.* Barcelona: Destino, 1984.

Traugott, Elizabeth Closs. "Spatial Expressions of Tense and Temporal Sequencing: A Contribution to the Study of Semantic Fields." *Semiotica* 15 (1975): 207–30.

Tuan, Yi-Fu. *Space and Place: The Perspective of Experience.* Minneapolis: U Minneapolis P, 1977.

Vico, Giambattista. *The New Science.* Trans. and ed. Thomas Goddard Bergin and Max Harold Fisch. Ithaca, N.Y.: Cornell UP, 1970.

Vilanova, Antonio. "El peregrino andante en el *Persiles* de Cervantes." *Boletín de la Real Academia de Buenas Letras de Barcelona* 22 (1949): 97–159.

Vološinov, V. N. [and M. M. Bakhtin]. *Marxism and the Philosophy of Language.* Trans. Ladislav Matejka and I. R. Titunik. Cambridge, Mass.: Harvard UP, 1986.

Voltaire. *Romans et contes.* Ed. René Pomeau. Paris: Garnier, 1966.

Wardropper, Bruce W. "Cervantes and Education." In McGaha 178–93.

Wardropper, Bruce W. "Temas y problemas del barroco español." In *Siglos de Oro: Barroco,* ed. Bruce W. Wardropper. Vol. 3 of *Historia y crítica de la literatura española,* ed. Francisco Rico. Barcelona: Editorial Crítica, 1983. 5–48.

Weber, Max. *The Methodology of the Social Sciences.* Trans. Edward A. Shils and Henry A. Finch. New York: Macmillan, 1949.

Weiger, John G. *The Substance of Cervantes.* New York: Cambridge UP, 1985.

Williamson, Edwin. *The Half-Way House of Fiction:* Don Quixote *and the Arthurian Romance.* Oxford: Oxford UP, 1984.

Wilson, Diana de Armas. "Cervantes' Last Romance: Deflating the Myth of Female Sacrifice." *Cervantes* 3 (1983): 103–20.

Wilson, Diana de Armas. "Splitting the Difference: Dualisms in *Persiles.*" *Cervantes* 10 (1990): 35–50.

Wittgenstein, Ludwig. *Philosophische Untersuchungen / Philosophical Investigations.* Oxford: Basil Blackwell & Mott, 1958.

Wright, Elizabeth. *Psychoanalytic Criticism: Theory in Practice.* New York: Methuen, 1984.

Yates, Frances A. *The Art of Memory.* London: Routledge & Kegan Paul, 1966.

Index